Pentecostal Preacher Woman

PENTECOSTAL PREACHER WOMAN

The Faith and Feminism of Bernice Gerard

Linda M. Ambrose

UBCPress · Vancouver

© UBC Press 2024

All rights reserved. No part of this publication may be reproduced, stored in a retrieval system, or transmitted, in any form or by any means, without prior written permission of the publisher, or, in Canada, in the case of photocopying or other reprographic copying, a licence from Access Copyright, www.accesscopyright.ca.

Originally printed in Canada
Print and bound by CPI Group (UK) Ltd, Croydon, CR0 4YY

UBC Press is a Benetech Global Certified Accessible™ publisher. The epub version of this book meets stringent accessibility standards, ensuring it is available to people with diverse needs.

Library and Archives Canada Cataloguing in Publication

Title: Pentecostal preacher woman :
the faith and feminism of Bernice Gerard / Linda M. Ambrose.

Names: Ambrose, Linda McGuire, 1960- author.

Description: Includes bibliographical references and index.

Identifiers: Canadiana (print) 20240441753 | Canadiana (ebook) 20240441761 |
ISBN 9780774869164 (hardcover) | ISBN 9780774870252 (PDF) |
ISBN 9780774870269 (EPUB)

Subjects: LCSH: Gerard, Bernice. | LCSH: Pentecostal churches—British Columbia—Vancouver—Clergy—Biography. | LCSH: Women clergy—British Columbia—Vancouver—Biography. | LCSH: Clergy—British Columbia—Vancouver—Biography. | LCSH: Women city council members—British Columbia—Vancouver—Biography. | LCSH: City council members—British Columbia—Vancouver—Biography. | LCSH: Evangelists—British Columbia—Vancouver—Biography. | LCGFT: Biographies.

Classification: LCC BX8762.Z8 G473 2024 | DDC 289.9/4092—dc23

UBC Press gratefully acknowledges the financial support for our publishing program of the Government of Canada, the Canada Council for the Arts, and the British Columbia Arts Council.

This book has been published with the help of a grant from the Canadian Federation for the Humanities and Social Sciences, through the Scholarly Book Awards, using funds provided by the Social Sciences and Humanities Research Council of Canada.

UBC Press is situated on the traditional, ancestral, and unceded territory of the xʷməθkʷəy̓əm (Musqueam) people. This land has always been a place of learning for the xʷməθkʷəy̓əm, who have passed on their culture, history, and traditions for millennia, from one generation to the next.

UBC Press
The University of British Columbia
www.ubcpress.ca

For Rob

CONTENTS

List of Illustrations / ix

Acknowledgments / xi

Introduction / *3*

1 Life with the Gerards / *24*

2 Delivered by Strong Women / *37*

3 Fighting for Her Faith / *52*

4 Finding Family / *67*

5 The McColl-Gerard Trio and Professional Belonging / *82*

6 Campus Life / *108*

7 On the Radio / *134*

8 Challenging Patriarchal Authorities / *159*

9 Feminism, Footnotes, and Family / *177*

10 Public Engagement / *201*

Conclusion / *231*

Notes / *242*

Bibliography / *276*

Index / *293*

ILLUSTRATIONS

I.1 Gerard protesting public nudity / *4*

I.2 Gerard at pulpit / *9*

I.3 "Into a Mirror" Bernice Gerard "selfie," 1951 / *15*

1.1 Bernice, 1925 / *27*

1.2 Bernice (a.k.a. Peggy) and Helen Duncans / *31*

1.3 Inscription on back of photograph / *31*

2.1 Bernice, age thirteen (at time of rescue) / *39*

2.2 Bernice (with glasses), 1938 / *47*

3.1 Bernice, high school graduation picture / *57*

3.2 High school graduation certificate / *61*

3.3 Provincial Normal School diploma / *62*

4.1 Gerard's elementary class in Rossland, BC / *69*

4.2 McColl-Gerard Trio postcard / *70*

4.3 Velma and Bernice with cello / *74*

5.1 Tent meeting crowd, Scranton, Pennsylvania / *86*

5.2 Cincinnati ad for McColl-Gerard Trio / *88*

5.3 Velma and Bernice, Acapulco beach / *98*

5.4 Collapsed tent / *100*

5.5 Velma and Bernice airline flight to Costa Rica / *101*

5.6 "Orphans" / *102*

6.1 Chaplains at boardroom table / *118*

6.2 Abortion protest, Parliament Hill / *130*

7.1 Gerard in radio studio with guest / *135*

7.2 CJOR 600 portrait shot / *147*

8.1 Gerard with David Mainse / *162*

8.2 Certificate of Ordination, Assemblies of God, 1948–49 / *170*

9.1 McColl-Gerard Trio with Scranton Assembly of God sponsor / *178*

9.2 Dick, Velma, and Bernice / *188*

9.3 Bernice, Velma, and Dick Chapman at home / *192*

9.4 Velma and Bernice at pulpit / *195*

10.1 Anti-porn Queen, *Georgia Straight* cover / *202*

10.2 Gerard at *Caligula* protest / *213*

10.3 Gerard in *Vancouver Sun* editorial cartoon / *218*

C.1 Velma and Bernice in Israel / *234*

C.2 Bernice Gerard, 1974 / *239*

ACKNOWLEDGMENTS

THE STORY OF HOW THIS BOOK came to be involves many people and several years. Back in 2009 Margaret Kechnie gave me a photo of the McColl-Gerard Trio that she had saved from her childhood in the 1940s, along with a copy of Bernice Gerard's autobiography. She was persuaded that with my new-found interest in the gendered history of Canadian Pentecostal women, this biography was a project waiting to be written, and I was the one to do it. When the world suddenly screeched to a halt in March 2020 I had already been researching Gerard for several years, snatching blocks of time whenever I could, to plow through archives, immerse myself in her extraordinary life story, and craft conference papers to test my arguments. During the lockdowns, writing *Pentecostal Preacher Woman* became my primary focus as I enjoyed the privilege of a six-month sabbatical. With no obligations to teach and no option to travel, I had loads of uninterrupted writing time. Despite the countless hours I spent churning out pages in that dystopian context of physical distancing, it must be said that this book was not born in isolation, and I have many people to thank.

I used to think that writing was strictly a solitary undertaking, but in recent years I have become a "social writer," thanks in part to my writing groups both in Sudbury and online with conference friends from afar, with whom I kept finding ways to connect before, during, and after the pandemic. I am so grateful for the camaraderie and good humour of my writing friends, near and far, including Joel Belliveau, Ernst Gerhardt, Susan Glover, Kristin Hall, Alicia Hawkins, Matthew Heiti, Andrea Johnson, Sara MacDonald, Leah Payne, Dan Scott, Shelley Watson, and Nicole Yantzi. We met in cafés and restaurants,

xii — *Acknowledgments*

sometimes by Zoom, and in person whenever we could. My academic friends from the Canadian Society of Church History and the Society for Pentecostal Studies have been good company, gracious listeners, and enthusiastic publishing partners as I tested my theories and arguments in conference panels and edited collections. Michael Wilkinson, my good friend and collaborator, has been a constant encouragement, urging me to give one more paper, write one more chapter, and see this book through to the finish. All the while he kept inviting me to contribute to his ambitious projects on Canadian and global Pentecostalism, introducing me to wider academic networks, and welcoming me to join larger interdisciplinary conversations with scholars of global Pentecostalism, for which I am very grateful.

My writing life has also been enriched by several writing coaches and their important guidance. Margy Thomas, of *ScholarShape*, created a series of modules that helped me identify my audiences and hone my story-argument; using her prompts, I filled a whole journal working out exactly what I was trying to say with this book, and to whom I wanted to say it. Helen Sword, of *Helen's Word*, persuaded me that playfulness and pleasure both have a place in my writing world. And then there's Michelle Boyd, of Inkwell Academic Writing Retreats. After my "bucket-list" plan to attend her in-person writing retreat was quashed because of the pandemic, I joined the first iteration of her online writing retreat, and I was astonished when I managed to draft the eight-thousand-word introduction of this book in just one week! Afterwards, I signed up for Michelle's weekly online coaching sessions where she taught a small group of retreat alumni how to write in community, trust our processes, build writing refuges, fiercely guard precious writing time, and savour the accomplishments (small and large) that bring joy to the writing life. Michelle gave me tools to help me thrive as I munched my way through "tiny-bite writing" and got up the courage to share "good enough" drafts with peers and publishers. In the winter of 2021 I timidly sent a very rough draft of this book to Catherine Plear, a developmental editor, copyeditor, and indexer extraordinaire, who offered invaluable insights and suggestions for refining, rearranging, and rethinking my arguments. Catherine's questions and observations gave me the direction I needed at a crucial stage of the project.

Of course, before I could write any of it or ask anyone to read my drafts, there was the research phase. Historians and archivists have a symbiotic relationship, and there are so many helpful people who opened doors (and held them open) for me. Laurie Van Kleek (now retired), from the Hudson Memorial Library at Summit Pacific College in Abbotsford, gave me unlimited access to Bernice Gerard's papers, books, and memorabilia. His successor, Kimberly

Acknowledgments xiii

Brown, has been equally accommodating in the final stages of the project. Jim Craig, at the Pentecostal Assemblies of Canada Archives in Mississauga, has been steadfastly enthusiastic about all my research projects, and his knowledge of the collections he oversees is unmatched. Archivists and reference staff at the City of Vancouver Archives and the UBC Archives were helpful and efficient, both when I spent time in the Vancouver archives during the winter of 2015 and after. David Wells, general superintendent of the Pentecostal Assemblies of Canada, who is also a global leader of Pentecostalism, agreed to talk to me about Bernice because of her influence in his life and ministry career. Other leaders in the Canadian Pentecostal community also took time from their busy schedules to chat, offering stories of personal encounters with Bernice and Velma. I am especially grateful to Jim Cantelon, Brian Stiller, and Susan Wells. At Laurentian University, Patrick Beaudry, Jacob Belcher, Sarah de Blois, Alissa Droog, Nathan McCoy, Stephanie McPherson, Rosie Parent, Thomas Radder, Laura Robinson, David Scott, and Ellen Sheppard worked as my research and teaching assistants during the life of this project. It has been a privilege to share classrooms with these folks, and now to count many of them as friends.

I first pitched this book to Darcy Cullen of UBC Press in 2015. When I returned to the project a few years later, I had the good fortune to work with James MacNevin, the acquisitions editor who skilfully ushered the project through various stages of board approval, rounds of peer review, and a successful grant application, waiting patiently for my manuscript during some unforeseen delays due to my personal circumstances. Carmen Tiampo, UBC Press production and copyright specialist, lent her invaluable expertise in the final stages of the project. Meagan Dyer guided me through the production phase, while copyeditor Robyn So, proofreader Alison Strobel, and indexer Emily LeGrand caught things I had missed. Thank you all! Anonymous peer reviewers for UBC Press generously spent time with the manuscript and offered very helpful suggestions that improved this book because they engaged with my arguments to think about what Gerard's story means for the history of British Columbia, Canadian women, and Pentecostalism.

I gratefully acknowledge that this book has been published with the help of a grant from the Federation for the Humanities and Social Sciences through the Scholarly Book Awards, using funds provided by the Social Sciences and Humanities Research Council of Canada.

Parts of Chapter 9 were previously published as "Canadian Pentecostal Women in Ministry: The Case of Bernice Gerard and Feminist Ideologies" in Margaret English de Alminana and Lois E. Olena, eds., *Women in Pentecostal and Charismatic Ministry: Informing a Dialogue on Gender, Church, and Ministry* (Leiden, NL: Brill, 2017): 229–46; and as "A Messy Mix: Religion, Feminism, and Pentecostals" in *Gender & History* 34, 2 (2022): 369–83. Parts of Chapter 10 appeared in an abbreviated form in *After the Revival: Pentecostalism and the Making of a Canadian Church* by Michael Wilkinson and Linda M. Ambrose (Montreal and Kingston: McGill-Queen's University Press, 2020), 118–22.

Family means the world to me. Meredith, Chad, and Meghan, you have all my respect for who you are, all you do, and who you are becoming. And Garnet, I still can't believe you're gone; I often think about you when I think about Bernice. I am grateful for my grandkids, Jaedyn, Avah, Benjamin, Elyanah, Yarah, Jaxon, Nyah, and Judah. Our sleepovers, camping trips, crafting projects, read-aloud books, baking, and tea parties are such welcome diversions! Virtual chats from Moncton with my sister Kate, and with Elizabeth, my friend who feels like a sister, are good tonic for my soul. Sadly, during this project we said goodbye to my mom, (Hazel) Doreen and then my other mom, Rosemary. Gordon Ambrose, you are the best dad in the whole wide world! And your generous spirit and great good humour inspire me. And finally, here's to Rob, and the forty-plus years we've shared, so far! You've been at my side throughout this project and all the others: with enthusiasm you plan unforgettable shared travel and research adventures; with endless patience you resolve all those tech problems that baffle me; and with generosity you make space for me to spend all those hours writing, revising, presenting, and talking. So much talking! We've shared life's ups and downs, and as we set aside the religious certainties, it all just seems to become more wondrous. Never could I ever have wished for a better soulmate. You're still the one.

Pentecostal Preacher Woman

INTRODUCTION

WHEN BERNICE GERARD, Vancouver's flamboyant Pentecostal preacher, led a silent protest along a beach frequented by nudists in the summer of 1977, the political cartoonists had a heyday. "Barely anybody around for Gerard's march," one journalist quipped, as the media playfully and dismissively mocked this moral crusader.[1] Apparently, she had been born at the wrong time and place. "Forget the silly protest, Miss Gerard. The hole in the knee of your swimsuit is showing," chided a *Vancouver Sun* editorialist.[2] Meanwhile, Vancouver's church folks shook their heads too, wondering why she insisted on being so public and theatrical in her crusading. Wasn't she just making all evangelicals look crazy and intolerant, like ridiculous extremists who were outrageously outdated and out of touch? After all, it was the 1970s, not the 1870s, and the nude beach was in Canada's "hippest" West Coast city. But Gerard knew why she was there. And although she kept silent that day, as she had promised she would, she was persuaded it was the right thing to do no matter who disagreed. And she fully expected her actions would not be popular. But she marched anyway because in her mind, it was part of her calling.

In 2000, it was popular to make lists of significant individuals to mark the end of the new millennium and the beginning of a new century, and the *Vancouver Sun*'s religion editor published a list of his own. Consulting with scholars of religion and other authorities, Douglas Todd compiled a list of British Columbia's most influential spiritual leaders of the twentieth century. At the top of that list was none other than the Reverend Bernice Gerard.[3] And yet, beyond her own life writing, no full-length biography of Gerard exists.

FIGURE I.1 In July 1977, Bernice Gerard and her supporters famously walked along a Vancouver beach to silently protest the spread of nudism on public beaches. | Vancouver Province, *July 11, 1977, 17*. Photographer: Wayne Leidenfrost.

Pentecostal Preacher Woman tells her story, with attention to broader themes about the ways conservative religious women navigate life stages with evolving views about faith, ideas, and public engagement. Taking a woman-centred approach, I explore the complexities of Bernice Gerard's life to illustrate the pitfalls of adopting binary judgments about women of faith. While some judge her as a hero of the faith and a successful model for women in ministry, others dismiss her as a rigid and outdated public figure who was easily caricatured. The truth about Gerard and women like her is far more complicated.

The Rev. Bernice Gerard seemed to cause a stir everywhere she went: to church folks, she was so unlike other proper church ladies; to liberal-minded residents of Vancouver, and for local political cartoonists, her actions and stances were so easy to mock – such a moralistic crusader! Yet, her radio phone-in show that went live every Sunday night in Vancouver and the northern part of Washington State had a very large and diverse audience because it was so entertaining, even compelling. Gerard invited her callers to phone in and ask her anything. Literally, anything. Her discussion topics covered the gamut of sex and drugs and rock 'n' roll. She talked to callers who were experimenting with Eastern religions, including transcendental meditation, and to others who were experimenting with drugs. Callers tried to explain to the radio host why their behaviours were enjoyable or, in some cases, why they were less than fulfilling. Her answers were never dull, yet she was neither sarcastic nor rude to her callers. She listened intently, with respect and curiosity, before offering responses informed by her Pentecostal world view. Gerard patiently insisted that her callers were all seeking some spiritual experience, not simply a physical high, relief from depression, or enhanced sexual pleasures. Her recommendation to every listener was always the same: only Jesus could satisfy their deepest human desires, and only the Holy Spirit could give listeners the power to live with satisfaction and joy.

To Gerard, her listeners' appetites were spiritual in nature and she was very happy to share the good news about how to meet those needs.[4] As her personal archives reveal, when listeners wrote to tell her their most intimate secrets, she wrote back and established ongoing correspondence in order to understand more about their stories. Meanwhile Vancouverites mocked the way Alderman Gerard leveraged her political office to add weight to her moral crusading, and her own denominational leaders wondered why she would not just stick to evangelism and learn to submit to the organization's lines of authority as other women did. But Bernice Gerard had a resilience born of her life experience and an intellectual curiosity that made her a force to be reckoned with. She was very sure about what she was called to do.

The life of Bernice Gerard is a compelling story. What possessed her to walk on a nude beach and lead a silent protest that would make her the laughingstock of her city, and in the eyes of her fellow believers, a problematic sister? What gave her the confidence to think that she had answers for every caller's need? I argue that Bernice Gerard's life provides a fascinating example of how conservative religious women use a process of self-narration to manage the dissonances that inevitably arise as they interact with institutional religion, encounter the wider secular society, and make sense of their own evolving journeys of faith. To the skeptical or irreligious onlooker, women like Bernice Gerard seem hopelessly stuck in their ways, but I maintain that in their interior worlds, they are negotiating complex realities in ways that make sense to them. Such women must come to terms with a variety of obstacles including insiders to their faith tradition, for example, when the patriarchy of church subcultures inevitably collides with a woman determined to live out her personal sense of calling. At the same time, for women like Gerard, finding allies outside one's own faith group is tricky because secular feminists and other liberal-minded people can be suspicious of religion when they presuppose that religion and feminism are categorically incompatible. Moreover, during a lifetime of belief and practice, individuals like Gerard find their views inevitably evolve as their life experience grows and they face unexpected opposition, and sometimes acceptance, from both the like-minded and the critics.

I suspect that many readers (especially women) from evangelical traditions, including Pentecostals, will find Bernice Gerard intriguing because of how she navigated her life, shaped by her travels, her education, her work, and her own family history. Discontented evangelicals and former evangelicals sometimes turn to writers and bloggers like Sarah Bessey and the late Rachel Held Evans,[5] who engage with disenchanted and formerly religious individuals (sometimes called "ex-vangelicals") to help resolve the dissonance they encounter when conservative religious subcultures and evolving Canadian social mores collide. The process that has come to be called "deconstructing one's faith" typically focuses on attempts to reconcile conservative religious experience with commitment to issues including truly egalitarian church cultures, genuine reconciliation with Indigenous peoples, and effective social justice activism on issues including racism, marriage equality, and affirmation of LGBTQ+ people, among others.[6]

Bernice Gerard was not a progressive Christian, and she would not have endorsed the openly radical positions of some twenty-first-century believers/ former believers on these issues. But she would recognize the process of encountering changing social mores and having to reconcile her previous beliefs with her expanding experience. Gerard's circle of acceptance of those outside her tradition broadened and evolved as she aged. Moreover, on many issues including support for refugees, affordable housing for the poor, and compassion and acceptance for those struggling with mental illness and addictions, she was ahead of her time. Susan Wells, a Pentecostal Assemblies of Canada (PAOC) insider, married to the denomination's general superintendent, emphasized in our conversation about Gerard that on many of these issues, she had both "insight and foresight," making her "a hero of the faith" for twenty-first-century Pentecostals.[7]

Other people find Bernice Gerard's story fascinating for different reasons. In the early stages of this writing project, I spent part of one winter in the Vancouver archives. In a coffee shop conversation with someone I was meeting for the first time, he asked what brought me to Vancouver. When I told him that I was planning to write a book on a Vancouver personality, he asked me who it was. At the mention of her name, this British Columbian laughed heartily and said, "Oh my! Bernice was quite a character!" My conversation partner that day knew of Gerard from her time as a municipal politician (1977–81) and had vivid memories of the way some of her most well-known exploits (including the Wreck Beach protest) had gripped the city's attention. That unforgettable personality had clearly made a deep impression on my new friend, who had been a student at the University of British Columbia at the time. For those who lived in Vancouver during the turbulent 1970s, and for others who only know Vancouver and the West Coast by its reputation for progressive values and practices, the fact that Bernice Gerard was a Vancouverite might seem a bit surprising. But the presence of conservative Christians in British Columbia is part of the province's character.[8]

In religion and also in politics, both progressive views and conservative ones have coexisted there for a long time, as the electoral history of New Democratic and Social Credit governments demonstrate.[9] As well, there is a little Bible belt in the area around Abbotsford, BC, just a short drive from Vancouver, and it represents another characteristic of the most westerly Canadian province, namely the presence of a Christian right in this country.[10] While people often associate the province, and especially the city of Vancouver, with its more liberal West Coast vibe, the province is actually a site where conservative and progressive politics and values often collide. It is also a prime site of the growing census category in Canada of those who identify their religious affiliation as none.[11] It is not a coincidence that British Columbia is home to important studies about irreligion in Canada.[12]

Other readers who may be intrigued by this biography include Canadian Pentecostals, charismatics, and evangelical leaders who knew Gerard personally or remember her through her media ministries. Indeed, some of the leading individuals among Canadian evangelicals, the Rev. Brian Stiller (formerly head of Evangelical Fellowship of Canada and currently the global ambassador of the World Evangelical Alliance) and the Rev. David Wells (general superintendent of the PAOC and president of the Pentecostal World Fellowship) both think of Bernice Gerard as an important influence and mentor in their lives.[13] Gerard also cooperated with the late Rev. David Mainse, another of Canada's best-known Christian television personalities, who founded the Crossroads television network.[14]

I did not grow up in church, but I remember seeing Bernice Gerard on television in the late 1970s and early 1980s. My late father, who had a perfect attendance record at his Sunday school through the 1920s and 1930s, no longer attended church by the time I was a school-aged child in the mid-1960s. Like many others, our family had become casual adherents of the United Church but stopped attending church at the time of rural church closures, parish amalgamations, and incidentally, when the denomination introduced its new curriculum.[15] For entertainment, sometimes my dad would watch television evangelists and shake his head at their exploits. He referred to Bernice Gerard as "that preacher woman"; her broadcasts intrigued him for a variety of reasons, not the least of which was her deep, masculine voice. When Gerard sang, she sang baritone – a very unusual pitch for a woman.[16]

But on the continuum between the national and global evangelical leaders and members of disaffiliated families like mine, there were many people who were drawn to Bernice Gerard for a variety of reasons. To those who reminisce about her place in North American Pentecostalism and hold her memory up as an exemplar of a bold and unapologetic women in ministry, this book might reinforce that view. However, as a denomination that claims to welcome women into leadership, the PAOC also admits that its practices and reality do not match its ideals, and women like Bernice Gerard were more the exception than the rule. By the 1990s, that denomination was failing to recruit as many women to positions as pastors, evangelists, and missionaries as they had in the past. In a 1991 article titled "Next Generation of Women in Ministry Please Stand Up!" published in the *Pentecostal Testimony*, the PAOC was asking itself what had happened to diminish the number of women who became full-time ministers of the gospel.[17] It was also painting a glorified picture of the women who had risen to prominence in the past, erasing any trace of the conflicts such women had initiated, and making no mention of how challenging it was to manage characters like Gerard who seemed to have trouble submitting to regional and national leaders.

Well into the twenty-first century, very few women occupy senior ministry positions with the PAOC; according to the denomination's published membership statistics, the number of women who occupy lead pastor roles stubbornly persists around 5–6 percent.[18] The PAOC organization claims to be committed to improving that record, and gender equity is a laudable goal. However, welcoming cohorts of ordained women with the same indomitable spirit that Bernice Gerard possessed (if such women even existed!) would present a serious challenge to the patriarchal nature of the PAOC's organizational culture. Those who remember Gerard with fondness, suggesting she is a model for other women, nostalgically minimize the controversies that so often surrounded her. Gerard's story serves as a reminder that endorsing women in leadership roles within conservative Protestant denominations like the PAOC is tricky, especially when those women have strong personalities and unwavering convictions about their own authority.

Another group of readers who may be intrigued by Bernice Gerard are my academic peers, especially feminist historians, both religious and secular. This

FIGURE I.2 Bernice Gerard was a gifted public speaker whose preaching style incorporated humour, storytelling, and references to current events. | *Pentecostal Assemblies of Canada Archives.*

biography joins a growing body of literature about Pentecostalism in Canada in general, and of women in Canadian Pentecostalism specifically. Church historians who teach in confessional settings might assume that Gerard was a role model for women in ministry because her life could serve as an inspiration for younger women who sense a similar call. The way that women's history within Pentecostalism has been crafted is very inspirational indeed. Characters like Aimee Semple McPherson, who hailed from small-town rural Ontario and is perhaps the best-known Pentecostal in all of North America with her celebrity status at Angelus Temple in Los Angeles, is a case in point.[19] Another is Alice Belle Garrigus, the American who established Pentecostalism in Newfoundland, where a future premier, Joey Smallwood, grew up in her St. John's church and led his province to boast a provincially funded Pentecostal school system.[20] Such Pentecostal women are widely known and celebrated. Even for those of less well-known reputation, there is a common element in the way their stories are popularly told. For each woman, when sympathetic biographers tell their stories, there is emphasis on celebration, providential intervention, and general amazement at their levels of commitment and obedience to God. Their stories tend toward hagiography.

It is tempting to write with that tone about Bernice Gerard too, because her life was surely an extraordinary one. But a glowing rendition of her life might erase any trace of her unpopular alliances with Roman Catholic charismatics when many Protestants (including the PAOC) were still firmly opposed to that kind of ecumenism. And her fiery presence as a municipal politician and a national lobbyist when Pentecostals and evangelicals generally were divided about their entry into public life and politics makes it tricky for them to celebrate everything she did. Bernice Gerard never married, but she did have a lifelong partnership with another woman, and while their mutual affection is unmistakable, peering into their domestic arrangement raises uncomfortable questions. To tell Gerard's story while leaving these pieces out would be an overly sanitized version of events. Part of what makes Gerard so compelling as a historical figure is the degree of complexity that she embodied.

Scholarship on Canadian Pentecostalism continues to develop, but over the past fifteen years, the trend has been to consider this revivalist movement in its historical and cultural contexts, rather than leave the writing to insiders who are entirely sympathetic to the movement.[21] Some of the most important recent work on Canadian Pentecostalism has been written by Michael Wilkinson, a sociologist at Trinity Western University, in Langley, BC, and his collaborators across Canada, the United States, and globally.[22] Wilkinson and Ambrose's 2020 book, *After the Revival: Pentecostalism and the Making of a Canadian Church*, was the first volume to adopt a cultural lens that considered how one Pentecostal denomination, the Pentecostal Assemblies of Canada, rose to centre stage among evangelicals.[23] Wilkinson and Ambrose trace Pentecostalism's rise from a marginal revivalist movement that was typically caricatured as a group of "holy rollers" to its prominence in the religious scene of Canada. For example, the PAOC now dominates evangelicalism in this country. If success is measured by both its participation rates and its material assets, these Pentecostals are outpacing the United Church of Canada on both scores.

Another important development in the scholarship on Canadian Pentecostalism was the creation of an interdisciplinary online journal, *Canadian Journal of Pentecostal-Charismatic Christianity*, which ran for ten years, publishing dozens of peer-reviewed articles by established and emerging scholars.[24] The growing literature takes up a variety of topics including debates about the relationship of Canadian and American Pentecostalism, showing that in Canada the movement was polygenetic, with concurrent sites of Pentecostal "firsts," not monogenetic as some American versions of the history argue in their emphasis on tracing Pentecostalism to the Azusa Street Revival in Los Angeles. For Canadians, the story is more complicated, with influences from the United States, but also from Britain and other global sites.[25] Establishing Canada's early history in this regard has been an important development arising from the scholarship. So, too, has the evolving theology of the PAOC[26] and Canadian Pentecostalism's relationship to broader evangelicalism.[27]

What first drew me to Pentecostal studies was a gender history question about the ambivalent position of women in the movement. And here, I knew my feminist colleagues in academia would be intrigued. While women are celebrated as early founders of various Christian traditions, from New France's Roman Catholic sisters to nineteenth-century Wesleyan Methodism, they do not typically share equally in the leadership positions of the churches. This question of women's history and church history is a global one, especially for Pentecostalism. Whether one focuses on North America, Europe, Australia, Asia, or Africa, global Pentecostalism shares the common thread of women in the origin stories of Pentecostalism.[28] Varying degrees of commitment to the principle of egalitarianism between the sexes are on display in these stories, with some emphasizing that it is an essential characteristic of Pentecostalism to see men and women as equally called to serve. Other versions of the past, especially in North American cases, emphasize the men who solidified the governance structures, policies, and material assets of the movements as the churches were established. In the latter stories, women's contributions are seen as exceptional because women become more difficult to trace over time; after their marriages, their names are lost in the records when archival holdings, conforming to the social customs of the mid- and late-twentieth century, cata- logue women by their husbands' names, not their own family names. This renders their ministry careers prior to marriage invisible. Archival practices aside, the truth is that women's involvement in Pentecostal churches in North America does ring true with the so-called institutionalization thesis, which argues that women and other historically marginalized groups become side- lined in new religious movements as the movement matures and carves out respectability for itself.[29] That development often comes at the cost of women and racialized groups being sidelined and silenced.[30]

In the case of Bernice Gerard, who never married, the usual problem of losing her identity through a name change is not part of the story. Moreover, Gerard had the force of personality to continue to emphasize that she had an individual calling from God, and for her, that trumped the conformity to denominational or church mores that would have seen her take a lesser role. Given the trajectory of Gerard's own conversion and ministry story, she found the question of whether women should lead a moot point. She did engage and spar with those who disagreed with her on the roles of women in the church, but for the most part she ignored the debates and pragmatically just carried on with what she knew she was called to do.[31]

This book also joins a broader and ongoing scholarly conversation about women, religion, and feminism. Gerard revealed in her 1988 autobiography that she had been shaped by feminist writers, both Christian and secular.[32] When I discovered that she was reading Germaine Greer, for example, I knew that the ears of my feminist historian friends would perk up just as mine did! Gerard was convinced that Jesus was a feminist because of his regard for women as spiritual equals, and she also took inspiration from many strands of second-wave feminist thought about women's empowerment, especially when it came to questions about women in public ministry and church governance. At a Pentecostal women's conference where she spoke in the late 1960s, Gerard challenged her listeners not to build their personal security around their relationships with men because losing one's own personhood was a dangerous spiritual path. She warned that in the next life, women would stand before God as individuals, not as anyone's wife or mother.[33] That kind of talk seemed edgy for postwar churchwomen immersed in conservative subcultures. Given evangelicals' suspicions about feminism, and the perceived dangers they associated with it as a slippery slope toward humanism and secularism,[34] Gerard went too far for some when she kept insisting that women were equally as capable and qualified as men to lead churches.

At the same time, Gerard's antiabortion stance made it difficult for those outside the church to even consider the idea that Gerard was a feminist. While the PAOC denomination debated how to relate to women like the Rev. Bernice Gerard, the incorrigible woman pastor-turned-activist in their midst, Vancouver feminists feared the influence that this antiabortion crusader and alderman could wield. Gerard justified her actions and told herself that a prophet's life was sometimes a lonely one, and she remained true to her convictions, though they sometimes were contrary to both the church and other feminists. She saw no contradiction between her feminist principles, her Pentecostal faith, and her public service. But some of my academic friends will not be so sure; when I have presented conference papers about Gerard's feminism, skeptical colleagues remain unconvinced.

I am intrigued by religious women like Gerard who claim to be feminists yet continue to associate themselves with faith communities that minimize their authority and prescribe gendered limitations on the roles they are permitted to occupy. I am especially intrigued by Gerard's claim to be a feminist even as she worked tirelessly to oppose abortion in Vancouver during the 1970s and 1980s, a city commonly associated with its liberal stance on social questions. My purpose in this biography is neither to defend nor endorse Gerard's views but rather to assert that her life provides a useful case with which to explore larger questions about the seemingly paradoxical relationship between conservative religious women and feminism, and how the two can be reconciled.[35] Focusing on that very question, sociologist Orit Avishai points to what she calls "the feminist dilemma of religion" where "assumptions about religion's inherent incompatibility with the interests of women and gender and sexual minorities ... results in ambivalence and hostility toward *studying* religion and *learning* from religious cases."[36] Indeed, scholarship in women's and gender studies "has historically viewed religion as an obstacle to feminism's goals," and as a result, "gender scholars across disciplines ... have approached religion with ambivalence, hostility, or indifference, thereby stifling interest in religion among gender scholars and narrowing the analytical frames available for understanding religion cases."[37] The ways that religion and feminism converged in Gerard's life are fascinating, and this biography takes up that paradox.

Gerard's life story invites us to think about the possibility of secular and religious feminisms coexisting.[38] To accept that religion and feminism are not completely incompatible[39] requires gender scholars to "suspend their normative critiques of and assumptions regarding religious affiliation as a paradox to explain or a puzzle to solve and instead interrogate religion cases on their own terms – taking seriously religious subjects' desire to affiliate, focusing on their lived experiences."[40] Critics of Western feminist scholarship insist that it is time to reconsider implicit biases and assumptions that privilege progressive women to the exclusion of others. Multidisciplinary scholarship on religious women, feminism, and gender is posing new questions to redress that imbalance and this biography of Gerard joins that rich conversation.[41]

According to one theorist, "what makes conservative religions' gender regimes particularly interesting to gender scholars (beyond their empirical significance) is that they are rife with conceptual tensions."[42] Certainly, Bernice Gerard's life is rife with "conceptual tensions," and when conflicting aspects of her life collided, Gerard continually engaged in what psychology educator Elizabeth Weiss Ozorak calls "cognitive restructuring," where she reframed her experiences to explain to herself and others that what was happening to her was neither surprising nor too much to bear.[43] Gerard remained with the same Pentecostal denomination throughout her career, although she disagreed with denominational authorities on several issues. She framed that decision by saying she simply wanted to get on with the work God was calling her to do despite the naysayers. Sociologists of religion help us understand women like Gerard by interrogating "a paradox that ponders women's complicity" as they "remain in patriarchal faith systems," inviting us to think about women who "do religion" as "a mode of conduct and being, a performance of identity – not only a purposeful or strategic action."[44] In other words, women who are religious have religious reasons for doing things, and scholars must come to terms with the idea that "religion may be done in the pursuit of religious goals – in this case, the goal of becoming an authentic religious subject against an image of a secular Other."[45] Studying a Pentecostal woman like Gerard by listening to how she narrated her own life experiences means setting aside preconceived notions about religion and feminism and looking "beyond professed attitudes to how people actually lived their lives and allow for messiness."[46] As an antiabortion feminist and a Pentecostal politician, Gerard's life teemed with messy contradictions. Yet it is those very paradoxes that make Gerard so intriguing.

As I study Pentecostal women, I start from the premise that women's religiosity should be respected, and when they claim religious motives for their church and public involvement, I must listen closely to their own self-narratives, contradictions and all. This is in step with cultural theorists, anthropologists, and feminist sociologists of religion who start from the premise that religious women should be heard in their own voices when they speak about their religiosity. This woman-centred approach is a promising way to understand conservative religious women like Gerard. The idea of "self-authoring" insists we recognize that religious women do not tell their stories from a "discursive vacuum."[47] As Avishai explains, women's religious experiences and how meaning is made of them is shaped by both structural and institutional contexts. In this book I demonstrate that Gerard practised self-authoring on many topics, to make meaning from the complexities she embodied.

When Gerard invoked her own life experiences to account for her convictions, when she explained that her public activism was dictated by her calling, and when she revealed that debates about women's ordination were something she did not care to engage, she was using her own story to explain her convictions. At other times, I am convinced that her silence on some topics is significant, and even when she did not make direct links to her early experiences as deeply formative for her later protest work, I see a connection. For example, I have a hunch that the extremely conservative views she held on

FIGURE I.3 Bernice Gerard, "Into a Mirror." Gerard took this 1951 "selfie" in Mexico when she was travelling as part of the McColl-Gerard Trio. Her photography provided a record and reflection of her life experiences, and her autobiographical writing served a similar purpose. | *Summit Pacific College, Hudson Memorial Library, BX8762 Z8 M121 1951.*

moral issues, and for which she was often mocked, were tied to the sexual violence she experienced as a child, even though she remained largely silent about her own abuse for most of her public life.

What we do know about Gerard's early years, we know because she wrote two versions of her autobiography. The first one, published in 1956, *Converted in the Country: The Life Story of Bernice Gerard,* was a text written with church audiences in mind, clearly illustrating how religious identity framed the author's narrative about herself as she embraced Pentecostalism. Gerard was forthright about her purpose in that life writing. Anticipating her reader's curiosity, she closed the book asking directly, "Why do I write my story?" Her answer puts religion at the centre of her rationale: she wrote it "to influence others to give their lives to the Lord Jesus Christ."[48] Clearly religiosity was central to her identity, and because she frames her identity in terms of her beliefs, Gerard is a prime example of what scholars of life writing call "self-narration."[49] She tells her life story with rich detail about how her life and beliefs unfolded. Gerard's religious views evolved throughout her life, and her life writing is framed by the rationale she offered to herself and others for why she did what she did and how her actions were informed by her beliefs. In addition to what we know about Gerard from her own thoughts, there is a great deal of contextual evidence to situate her reflections. Taken together, her self-narration and her life experiences confirm Gerard as a fascinating case study of the ways in which conservative religious women interact with institutional religion and the broader society to make sense of the conflicting cultural mores and ideas they encounter. In short: it's complicated!

While we have the chance to "hear" Gerard's versions of her own story through the published autobiographies, we also have a rich collection of her other life writing sources. Historian Barbara Caine, in her book *Biography and History*, points out that the scope of "life writing" has broadened to include "many different kinds of life story and many different forms of writing – including sermons and eulogies, privately written sketches produced for members of a family, and fragmentary sketches of lives."[50] To piece together Gerard's story told in her own words, there is a rich archival record, including her sermons, scrapbooks, and other personal records now housed in the archives at Summit Pacific College, in Abbotsford, BC; university archives that encompass her work as a chaplain at the University of British Columbia and Simon Fraser University; municipal records held by the Vancouver City Archives that include Gerard's time as a city alderman; and numerous religious and secular print media sources including newspapers and magazines.

Gerard wrote her first autobiography when she was thirty-three years of age to tell the story of her early family life in her adoptive father's irreligious household and her conversion to Christianity.[51] That book was intended to establish not only how young Bernice (then known as "Peggy") became a believer, but how she changed her initial theological understanding from what those first itinerant preachers taught her about their exclusive view of who qualified as a "real" Christian, to embrace a broader definition of true believers. The central message of that book was the transformation she experienced after that conversion when she accepted the work of the Holy Spirit in her life and became a Pentecostal.[52] This was a crucial pivot point in her identity formation.

It is important to recognize that Gerard's first autobiography was serving a bigger purpose than merely telling her story. Throughout her childhood, Gerard was exposed to a variety of religious experiences, and when she looked back and chronicled those formative years, she emphasized her evolving spirituality and changing affiliations.[53] Later in her life Gerard garnered a reputation for being conservative and rigid in her views. While it is true that she had firm convictions on a range of social issues, her interior life of faith was actually an evolving journey. Her early life writing is a clear example of religious studies scholar Susan E. Henking's assertion that "the personal is the theological."[54] As Henking claimed, it is obvious to me that Gerard was using her personal experiences to formulate and revise her theology and I make this case throughout the book.

Gerard published her second autobiography, *Bernice Gerard: Today and for Life,* in 1988, when she was sixty-five years old.[55] While this second version of her life covered some of the same ground as the earlier book, there was obviously a lot more life experience to include in the later work. As Gerard reflected back on her own life story, she wanted to make it explicit why she had done some of the things she did and explain how her actions and her interior life aligned. In other words, her life writing helped her to make meaning from her experiences. Gerard's life writing parallels what scholars find in other religious women's autobiographies, namely that "the dialogue between selves presented therein provides us with a clear notion of self as process, both selves and intellectual products as historically and culturally located concoctions."[56] The life story that Bernice Gerard "concocted" helped her to resolve cognitive dissonances including how she came to embrace her public ministry roles in a spiritual tradition that professed equality between men and women but frequently stumbled over how to implement that conviction. Gerard proceeded with her ministry and public roles because she was convinced that God had called her to them, and when her own denomination hesitated in the 1980s over what position they would take on "the woman question," Gerard was engaged but not distracted by the renewed debate. She quipped that she was not being "belligerent" but was simply "bored" by a so-called dilemma that she had resolved in her own mind decades before.[57]

What is noteworthy about this second autobiography is how Gerard reflected on those who held different points of view on issues including abortion, morality, and the role of women in the church. A close reading of the sources suggests she actually took a more moderate stance on many issues than her critics recognized or gave her credit for. Moreover, when it came to issues of her own faith, she became much more ecumenical as time passed because experience broadened her views of other faith traditions and of human nature itself. In the second book, Gerard displayed a maturity that allowed her to delve into issues of a very personal nature including her adoption story and the conflicts she had encountered as a woman in church leadership, as a media personality, and as a politician. She had obviously reflected a lot on the joys and hardships of her life, and she also disclosed more about her affections, including the joys of finding her birth family and of sharing her life with Velma McColl Chapman. At the same time, one is struck by the fact that while her conversion was an experience locked in time that she used as a reference point to define her identity and to ground her faith, it did not dictate that her interior life was stagnant or that her mind was made up on every question. Her intellectual curiosity, rich networks of global relationships, and ecumenical efforts born of the charismatic movement had definitely broadened her mind. In step with what scholars of women's life writing observe, the way Gerard told her story continued to evolve even as she aged.[58]

Gender theory and the sociology of religion provide useful ways to think about how Gerard narrated her life story and explained the decisions she made. As a Pentecostal minister and social activist within the contexts of the church structures of her denomination and of Vancouver politics in the 1970s and 1980s, Bernice Gerard was "doing religion." The story she told herself and others about what motivated her ministry and her municipal involvement follows the line of testimony that is common among many Christian traditions. Testimony and "narratives of calling" are particularly significant for Pentecostals, and exploring them by using narrative discourse theory and literary theorists' work on women's conversion and call narratives is helpful for rethinking the life writing of conservative religious women like Gerard.[59]

With such a rich and varied collection of Gerard's life writing, we are offered rare and sustained insights into her interior world and the evolution of her thought over a lifetime of ministry work. At the same time, it must be recognized that placing Gerard's first-person accounts at the centre of this study introduces certain limitations. When she is silent on specific issues that were central to the context of her time, such as labour relations and union activity, the Canadian government's dispossession and internment of Japanese Canadians, or race relations issues more broadly, the biographer cannot presume to know what (or if) she thought about these things. The silences in the autobiographical writing also belie the religious context of Gerard's world. For example, like many evangelicals of her time, Gerard subscribed to premillennial views about eschatology and theories about the end times that were tangled up with world affairs, making her quite sympathetic to the State of Israel. She visited Israel multiple times, first as a religious tourist and later as a tour guide (with her ministry partner) for others.[60] However, it would be an oversimplification to assume that Gerard's fascination with the place was politically motivated because she did not voice uncritical support for American foreign policy or push for Canada to form closer ties with Israel. Rather, Gerard retained a sense of childlike wonder; her visits to the Holy Land meant she was walking where Jesus had walked, and the imminent second coming of Christ would involve apocalyptic battles being waged there. When she recounted her travels, Gerard seemed entranced with the way she could be transported to enjoy the geography and landscape of places she felt she already knew quite well from her lifelong study of the Bible.

Gerard wrote her autobiographies as a form of testimony, but she was also explaining to herself and her readers how she resolved the conflicting views that she encountered. She introduces her readers to the individuals and experiences that shaped her actions and beliefs, and she provides insights into the ways her faith and religiosity evolved over time. While she maintained her identity within global Pentecostal circles, she changed her views on many things over her lifetime. Her evolving self-narration provides a rich example of listening to women's own voices as they describe their spirituality, rather than trying to typecast people. How Bernice Gerard arrived at and reconciled those changing views is the focus of this book. And it's complicated!

THIS BOOK IS ORGANIZED into ten chapters. The first three chapters deal with Gerard's complicated early years. Chapter 1 reveals the instability of her life as a young child who was adopted at birth, only to be subjected to abuse and violence. Her earliest exposure to religion was not a positive one, but this gave way to a dramatic conversion experience that not only provided a way of escape but would also become the core of her individual identity. Chapter 2 begins after Gerard was delivered from the home of her adoptive father with her encounters with child welfare professionals and the foster families who were central figures during her adolescence, introducing her to a wider variety of life experiences that ran parallel with her evolving religious awareness. A bright student, Gerard's tremendous potential was identified early on by her caseworkers, and the leading provincial child welfare authority took a personal interest in her, convinced that this child could thrive if only she would embrace the opportunities her middle-class foster family in Vancouver could offer her. Chapter 3 traces Gerard's experience during secondary school, the tension between middle-class values, upward social mobility, and her attraction to Pentecostalism, a movement on the fringe of respectability at the time. With her caregivers' encouragement she trained to become a teacher but continued to resist their suggestions that she needed to tone down her teenaged religious excesses and embrace the social mores of mainstream society. Despite their best efforts, by the time she was a young adult, Bernice Gerard had firmly established her identity as a Pentecostal, complete with the persecution mentality she embraced while taking such a firm stance on her convictions.

Chapters 4 and 5 trace Gerard's first tastes of independent adult life as a professional. Out from under the constraints of the provincial child welfare system, Gerard deepened her sense of self and worked to establish her sense of belonging, both personally and professionally. When Bernice met Jean and Velma McColl, Pentecostal women who invited her into their private lives and their ministry work, she found a warm welcome as part of the McColls' extended family, took the opportunity to search for her own birth family, and as she addressed some nagging childhood issues, she developed an even deeper empathy for those who suffer on the margins of society. Her career as a teacher was short-lived, and as Chapter 5 shows, she quickly threw off one profession for another to become an international travelling evangelist. Those geographic adventures were key to Gerard's expanding life experiences, but they also solidified her identity as a Pentecostal. Through her religious networks, Gerard encountered Pentecostals around the world and joined a truly global phenomenon with its complex cultural and theological diversity. She published the story of her conversion in a book documenting her spiritual journey from irreligion to Pentecostalism. Gerard's confidence grew as she told and retold that story, settling into who she was in relation to her own family history, her new ministry partners, and the wide and expanding world of Pentecostalism. Giving one's testimony is an important ritual for Pentecostals and other evangelicals, and Gerard embraced her life writing as part of her continuous process of personal meaning making.

The next two chapters follow Gerard's return to Vancouver after the McColl-Gerard Trio disbanded. Chapter 6 opens as Gerard was left to figure out how to remake herself in a life without the travel or companionship she had so enjoyed. But Bernice was not entirely alone in this period because her close ties with Velma McColl and Velma's new husband, Dick Chapman, included sharing their Vancouver home, a place that served her well as a refuge and a ministry base. Facing a new phase of life, Gerard's intellectual curiosity and academic ability combined to compel her to enter university as a mature student. While she was studying at the University of British Columbia (UBC), both as an undergraduate and during her graduate work, Gerard regarded the campus as her mission field and after she was appointed as a university chaplain, she thought deeply about the best strategies for reaching the university community. Once again, her autobiographical work and her other life writing provide important clues for understanding Gerard's complex intellectual world. Chapter 7 focuses on Gerard as a radio host, and how she became a widely recognized media personality with her own open-line radio show. A woman radio host was not unheard of, but Gerard's ability to forge intimate ties with her listeners was remarkable, something that many people attributed to her intellect and her gender.

Central to the last three chapters of this book is gender; Gerard pushed the boundaries that usually framed the lives of Canadian Pentecostal women in ministry. While churches in this tradition were familiar with women evangelists and preachers, it was far less common for women to become full-time pastors in a denomination that claimed commitment to egalitarian principles but structured itself in patriarchal ways. Gerard stood outside the expected Pentecostal norms in a variety of ways. Chapter 8 includes two issues where Gerard was more progressive than the majority of her PAOC colleagues. First, she was an early adopter of the charismatic movement in the 1960s, joining an ecumenical cast of fellow chaplains who influenced her to expand her intellectual horizons with a growing appreciation of other faith traditions. Gerard's curiosity about what the Spirit was doing led her to openly embrace Roman Catholic charismatics, putting her at odds with many in PAOC circles. Gerard's ecumenism evolved as she responded to the religious context around her. She stood apart from many others in conservative churches on another cultural development of the 1960s and '70s: increasing equality between the sexes called for by the second-wave women's movement. Given her career as a professional Pentecostal, Gerard found it tiresome when debates (re)emerged in the 1980s about whether women should be in ministry, in part because she had already enjoyed a long and successful ministry which gave her the firm conviction that strong women were used of God. She was impatient with the rhetoric of men in the PAOC who sought to limit women's roles while claiming that when they rejected feminism in their ranks, they were resisting "worldly" cultural encroachment. Gerard disagreed.

Bernice Gerard lived a woman-centric life and Chapter 9 gives attention to some of the enigmatic aspects of Gerard's interior world and her private life. When she resisted the patriarchy within her own denomination, she reflected deeply on why she could not agree with those who put limitations on women's potential. Her feminism, she argued, was not worldly at all, but completely in step with Jesus, whom she claimed was feminist also. Gerard wrote at length about this, inviting her readers to follow her footnotes to understand how she arrived at her complicated convictions about this. The second part of Chapter 9 considers something Gerard did not write much about: her domestic arrangements and her private life with Velma. Bernice and Velma lived together for decades, including their years on the road, the decades when they co-pastored a church, and during their retirement years. Gerard shared a Vancouver home with the Chapmans throughout Velma's marriage, and the two women continued to live together after Velma's husband passed away. Thus, Bernice and Velma remained a ministry "couple" until they were separated by death. The nature of that relationship between two women with lifelong ties is intriguing and the chapter concludes with a consideration of their shared love.

Although her private life remains an enigma, Gerard's public life regularly made headlines. Chapter 10 circles back to focus on Gerard as a municipal politician and her public lobbying efforts, including the episode of the famous beach walk that opens this book. Gerard was particularly outspoken about three issues: abortion, public nudity, and standards of morality in theatre and the arts. It is this work that most Vancouverites remember her for, and for which she is caricatured as a throwback to earlier moralistic times. Yet, in the midst of all that opposition, Gerard truly felt she was doing important work to fulfill her calling as a prophet, a role she reluctantly embraced only after she was convinced that God was calling her to do it. How she arrived at that conclusion is tied to her identity as a Pentecostal, but I argue that her motivation also sprang from the lasting impact of her early childhood.

When I first began to do research on Pentecostal women in Canada, my mentor and friend Dr. Margaret Kechnie, who grew up in a Pentecostal church in southwestern Ontario, gifted me a copy of Gerard's autobiography and told me that Bernice Gerard was someone I should write about. When Margaret was a small child in the 1940s, the McColl-Gerard Trio visited her church in Windsor, Ontario, and Margaret still had a postcard/photograph as a souvenir of the occasion. I had the luxury of a sabbatical in 2015 and by that time, I had already begun to present scholarly papers about Pentecostal women and the puzzle of how gender was at work in that movement. Some academic feminists were baffled by the connection I was making between Gerard and feminism, and they were not the only ones. In January 2015 I went to Vancouver for archival research about Gerard, and I met some friends. My dinner companions confirmed that Gerard's story, with all its flair and contradictions, needed to be told. Catherine, a freelance editor, knew some Catholics in Northern Ontario who had joined the charismatic movement in the 1970s, and she wondered if Gerard's story might shed some light on a phenomenon that intrigued her. And Scott, a Vancouver-based artist who had been a UBC student when Gerard was a chaplain there, was still amused by the media's caricatures of

Gerard from her time at Vancouver City Hall.

Perhaps the reader identifies with churchgoers like little Margaret, who squirmed in her pew enduring those long but lively Pentecostal meetings, or with Catherine, who grew up Catholic but was left wondering what was unfolding as she watched some of her family members embrace the charismatic movement that was central to Gerard's religiosity in the 1960s and 1970s. Like my fellow academics, some readers will squirm at the suggestion that an antiabortionist like Gerard could ever be considered a feminist. Still others, like Scott the Vancouverite, will be amused by the antics of a prudish preacher's protest on a nude beach. Whether readers knew Bernice Gerard personally, indirectly, or not at all, I predict they will be surprised by the complexity of her biography, a story tracing her path from child welfare case to travelling evangelist, from campus chaplain to moral crusader, and from unlikely feminist to lifelong partner of another woman. This book offers insight into the case of a conservative religious woman and the factors that shaped her identity and public life. At first Bernice Gerard appears to be a reductionist thinker holding to simplistic notions of right and wrong, but I argue that she was a complicated character whose rich inner life informed her evolving faith.

Chapter 1

LIFE WITH THE GERARDS

"CHILDHOOD MEMORIES – what do they bring me? Even now a sense of fear and dread."[1] That is how Bernice Gerard described the lingering effects of her earliest years, before she became a ward of the state under the care of the provincial Child Welfare Department.

The drama of Gerard's early years is multilayered because she was adopted at birth, only to find herself in a dangerous home situation where she said "the good things are overclouded by recollections of an abusive, alcoholic foster [adoptive] Father and dreadful drunken brawls that filled my heart with terror."[2] Her adoptive mother had died shortly after she brought baby "Peggy"[3] home, and the little girl was left in the care of Leo Gerard, together with his sons, who made their living as fishermen on the Fraser River. While it seemed obvious to neighbours and extended family members that this was hardly a suitable or safe situation for a little girl, Peggy Gerard only left that dangerous home after she reported her father's abuse to a trusted adult, and steps were taken to get her out of the place that was causing her such dread, fear, and terror. During these formative years, Gerard's earliest religious experiences helped her cope with the continuing upheavals that she faced, providing her a sense of security and creating touchstones she would return to throughout her life. Indeed, from a very tender age, Gerard's religion was central to her identity formation.

Reflecting on Gerard's life story, one is struck by the truth of the idea "that adults are only children grown up and that children are adults in germ."[4] A lot of traumatic things happened *to* Gerard in her early years that were beyond her control, but at the same time it is clear that she did exercise some agency and demonstrate surprising levels of resilience. Childhood and youth experiences shaped Gerard profoundly and provide insight into her later life. Peggy Gerard was a youngster who had lost two mothers before the age of three, and, until age thirteen, she lived under the control of a father known for his violent outbursts and binge drinking. Late in life, she revealed that the trauma she experienced in the Gerard home never left her. But there were positive influencers from her early years too. In her extended family and in the schoolhouse she attended, she caught glimpses of women in professional roles as nuns, teachers, and preachers, sparking her imagination about possibilities for her future self if only she could escape the grim reality of her family situation.

Scholarship that focuses on the social construction of childhood begins from the premise that "children do become adults and the kinds of adults they are likely to become are shaped by the kinds of childhoods they are experiencing today."[5] As she negotiated her childhood and youth, Gerard was both "being" a child and "becoming" an adult; the adult Bernice was the child grown, and the child Bernice was that adult in germ. Without question the most central aspect of Gerard's evolving sense of self was tied to her religious experiences. Designated as British Columbia's most significant spiritual figure of the twentieth century, her inclination for all things religious can be traced through her evolution from an irreligious child with no church connection, to a young convert with inflexible fundamentalist views about who qualified as a "real" believer, to an enthusiastic Pentecostal/charismatic with an open mind toward the inclusive ways of the Holy Spirit and a profound compassion for society's outcasts.

This chapter traces Gerard's early childhood and preteen years, relying on her autobiographies as key sources to provide access to her interior world. Gerard's life writing is framed by her religion as she moved from her first and only childhood visit to a church when she attended the funeral of her aunt, a Roman Catholic nun, to a significant early teenage conversion experience. Later on, her exposure to a variety of Christian denominations and her young adult professional training broadened her life experience, but it also put her in conflict with liberal-minded guardians and middle-class caregivers. It is important to resist the impulse to view Gerard's faith story simply as a timeless trope of Christian testimony with the familiar plot moving from preconversion through conversion and consecration. The trauma of Gerard's early years stayed with her despite the more positive episodes that followed. The time she spent in the Gerard household marked her for life.

It is rare for historians to have access to published sources of childhood memories told in the first person, especially if those accounts focus on difficult situations. While journalistic impressions, such as those offered by Canadian essayist Robert Thomas Allen in his 1977 book *My Childhood and Yours: Happy Memories of Growing Up,* may stir nostalgic feelings about an idyllic past, the experience of being a carefree child was completely different from what Gerard went through during the first thirteen years of her life. Recent historiography on childhood has made great strides to trouble the notion that children in Canadian history lived in some utopic state of naiveté. Sanitized and romantic views of children's experiences fail to account for the experiences of youngsters who were vulnerable and at risk because of their disadvantaged social realities. To correct that oversight recent scholarship in the history of childhood[6] sets out to "explicitly consider the construction and impact of vulnerability within the context of adoption history."[7] Doing so provides an important antidote to nostalgic, overly romanticized depictions of childhood. Bernice Gerard was one such vulnerable child whose case record must have comprised a very thick file.

Gerard's 1956 autobiography begins with this dramatic statement: "My first loss was irretrievable – I lost my Mother."[8] The mother she refers to here was the woman who gave birth to her. But in a tragic twist of fate, in fact, Gerard lost two mothers before the age of three: her birth mother and the woman who adopted her at birth but died a few years later. Gerard knew very little about her birth mother and the truth about her birth family would only surface much later in her life. Her adoptive mother was Annie (Edwards) Gerard. Annie was a Stó:lō woman, married to a French Canadian fisherman, Leo Gerard, with whom she had three sons.[9] In late 1923, Annie had become ill and was sent to New Westminster for treatment at the Royal Columbian Hospital. The nature of her illness is not clear, but one surmises that it must have been a gynecological or obstetrical complication, perhaps a miscarriage or stillbirth, because she was being treated in the same part of the hospital where babies were delivered. Before she was discharged from care, Annie learned that there was a newborn baby in the hospital without a mother and she inquired about taking that baby home with her. The arrangements were made, and she returned to Leo Gerard with Baby Peggy in her arms. What no one could have predicted was that in less than three years, Annie Gerard would die, leaving the child without a mother for the second time in her short life.[10] Annie, who is buried in the Langley Prairie Cemetery, is remembered as a skilled commercial fisher. Bernice recalled that at her mother's funeral, a neighbour held the little girl's hand, telling her to "say goodbye because you will never see your mother

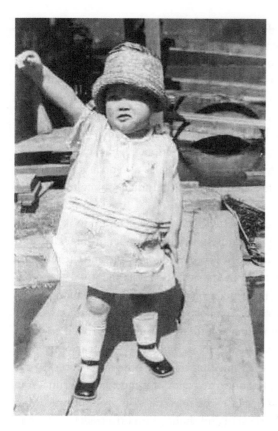

FIGURE 1.1 Pictured here at approximately two years of age, Bernice was called "Peggy" by her adoptive parents, Leo and Annie Gerard. | *Summit Pacific College, Hudson Memorial Library, uncatalogued.*

again." Gerard remembered thinking that "she would have been a good mother to me, had she lived."[11]

After his wife's death, Leo Gerard scrambled to make arrangements for the little girl's care, sometimes relying on extended family members and sometimes on the hospitality of neighbours.[12] Such arrangements were typical of the precarious kinds of child care that bereaved families employed in the first decades of the twentieth century.[13] One of Bernice Gerard's favourite caregivers was Annie's mother, Grandma Edwards. Annie's parents, Josephine and Patrick Edwards, were "among the first students at the Roman Catholic Indian Mission School."[14] The institution in question was St. Mary's Indian Residential School in Mission, BC, notorious for the abuses that children suffered there while they were entrusted to the care of the oblates.[15] In spite of her schooling, Josephine Edwards maintained her language and cultural pride, and Gerard had happy memories of observing her grandmother's Indigenous knowledge in action. "Grandma had knowledge about which fungi were mushrooms and which were toadstools, what greens growing wild could be eaten, and what medicine could be found in the wilds."[16] Visits from extended family members and a wonderful sense of community were other happy memories. "At the Edwards' place a good part of living was the pleasure of watching so many people come and go. Besides Grandma's sons and daughters and grandchildren, there were regular visitors from Harrison Lake and Chemainus. In the berry season pickers and helpers ate in a common dining room. It felt good to be on the receiving end of so much playful affection."[17] Those happy childhood memories may explain why fifty years later, as a Vancouver alderman Gerard was inclined to vote in favour of creating an Indigenous cultural centre in Vancouver.[18]

By the time she was old enough to attend school, Leo Gerard took the little girl back into his home; sharing that household with her older brothers, Gerard recalls that she grew up as a tomboy. She loved outdoor living, and she recounts that "there were good and pleasant memories of course: the joy of catching brook trout in a nearby stream, the expeditions to the marsh on cranberry hunts and the devotion of my own Cocker Spaniel puppy."[19] The Gerard boys were masters of many skills central to their mother's culture that proved essential for their rural life on the river. The Stó:lō are known as "river people," and Annie's sons passed their knowledge along to their little sister too. "In the years before I turned thirteen, I had learned a lot of things: how to run a trap line – that was worth learning because one muskrat skin brought one dollar and a quarter; how to make a sling shot and shoot a bird off a tree; how to load and fire a rifle or a shotgun. Oh yes, not to neglect mechanical skills, the boys taught me how to run the gas boat. They also taught me how to paddle the canoe noiselessly, Indian style."[20] Those all-important skills for life on the river were constantly being reinforced, and Gerard remembers the sobering reality, when she was twelve years old, of two young girls who drowned in the Fraser River right in front of her family home.[21] Peggy Gerard was an athletic child and she enjoyed rough play with her brothers and other boys at school. "Softball was my first love, but the boys considered me a fair football player also. When spring came and the girls played with jacks, I changed my social circle and played football with the boys."[22]

But despite her love of sport, nature, and outdoor adventures, all was not well for young Peggy. When her father and brothers went out to fish at night, she remembers being left all alone. "The wail of a distant train blowing at a country crossing makes me think of nights alone in the big, empty house on the river," she recalled as a young adult. "The Canadian National Railway tracks were fifty yards from our back door. When the train was still two miles

[3 km] away, the house would begin to shake and every window in it would rattle. When the engineer blew the whistle for the crossing, every one of the dogs would howl." She recounted that "countless times I pleaded with my foster [adoptive] father to take me on the boat with him rather than leave me in the big house alone." On those occasions when Leo Gerard granted that request, the little girl escaped the fear of being alone, accompanying him as "through the night he would travel up and down the mist-laden river, casting his net again and again. Curled up in a blanket on the open deck over the fish box, lay the sleeping form of his adopted child."[23]

As scary as it was for a small child to be left alone overnight, the nights when Leo Gerard was at home could be even worse. He was especially scary when he was drunk. In her own words, Gerard described nights filled with terror when "my drunken and abusive adoptive father was stumbling and pawing about."[24] His clumsy advances were sometimes directed at his live-in housekeepers, who were drinking companions and victims of his abuse.[25] A succession of different women moved in and out of that role, joining the Gerard household as domestic workers to provide oversight for young Peggy and to keep house for the men who lived there. But when they joined Leo in his drinking binges, these women were hardly a source of stability for the little girl, because they, too, were "heavy on the bottle and none too careful of their language."[26]

Indeed, the presence of these women did not protect little Peggy from the effects of her father's carousing and sexual violence. Her life writing reveals that she, too, was one of Leo Gerard's victims. Although she does not give details about her father's "pawing about" when she wrote about this later in life it is very clear that she had been living in a constant state of fear, dreading his advances. In her second autobiography, she did provide some detail about the level of domestic violence and sexual assault she witnessed. She regarded her father's housekeepers as her "protectors," because if he was with one of them, she might be spared. "One night as I was sleeping in a double bed with her [the housekeeper], he forced himself upon her in the bed, while the two of them discussed the issue of 'What if the kid wakes up?'" She was convinced that one woman "never really consented to being his common-law wife but wanted only to be his housekeeper. But on one of their drinking days when I walked into the kitchen from school, they were busy having sex on the kitchen floor."[27]

Her father's violence toward women included an episode when young Peggy witnessed a housekeeper hiding from Leo among some bales of hay in the yard, "When he began beating her, it seemed to me I was the only one who could save her life. Terrified, I stole ... [into the house and] grasped the butt of a gun in the rack that held firearms for hunting ... The Gerards had shown me how to handle a rifle and a shotgun. In the panic of the moment, nothing was clear to me except someone had to help the woman; perhaps it was his life against hers."[28] At the last minute, the child stopped herself and instead ran from the house "screaming at the top of my voice, 'Help – please – Daddy is killing the cook!'" Although a neighbour did hear her desperate plea, they decided not to intervene because "he said later that he was afraid the quarrelers would make peace with each other and turn on him."[29] There was no loss of life that day, but decades later Gerard was still traumatized by these episodes of physical and sexual violence. Writing in 1988, when she was sixty-five years old, she revealed that horrible memories continued to plague her, confessing "the terror diminished, but the nightmares did not ever go away entirely."[30]

The physical assaults were compounded by emotional abuse. Peggy Gerard was a child who did not feel loved. When she learned that she was adopted, it only magnified her feeling that she did not belong. Traces of the harsh rejection she endured in her childhood are sprinkled throughout Gerard's personal archives. A photograph in one scrapbook depicts the youngster as a toddler with a mean-spirited inscription on the back: "This is Helen Duncans and Peggy Gerard. Both as homely as they make them" (see Figure 1.3).

This nastiness was reinforced in the school yard when Gerard asked her peers what "adopted" meant since she had never heard the word before. A playground bully gave the cruel explanation that "it means that your own Mother and Dad didn't love you; they just threw you out and let somebody else take you."[31] Her adoptive father added to her pain with his own verbal and emotional abuse. "Whenever I was bad, which unfortunately was quite often," Gerard recounts, "my [adoptive] Father would say, 'We should send you to an orphanage. You really don't belong here anyway, we just took you in.'"[32] Gerard learned the truth of her genealogy when Gerard's housekeeper tipped her off about where she could find the adoption papers. Sneaking a look at the documents, young Peggy noted two important facts: her birth mother's family name and the name of the law firm that had arranged the adoption.[33] These two details would prove very important later in her life.

Adding to the danger and alienation she felt living with Leo Gerard, young Peggy found no comfort or sense of belonging in religion either. Indeed, her earliest exposure to church rituals only served to reinforce the anxieties she associated with her father's outbursts. Although the Gerards were French Catholics, and some of her father's sisters were even serving the church as

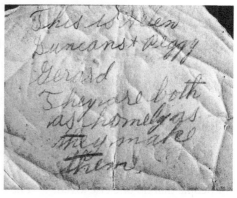

Figure 1.2 Bernice (*left*) and her childhood friend, Helen Duncans, who had also lost her mother. As a toddler, Gerard spent time with many members of her adoptive parents' extended families and neighbours, with some of her fondest memories associated with her Stó:lō grandparents, the Edwards. | *Summit Pacific College, Hudson Memorial Library. Bernice Gerard Collection, uncatalogued.*

Figure 1.3 The abusive environment where Gerard spent much of her childhood is hinted at in the inscription on the back of this photograph that reads "This is Helen Duncan and Peggy Gerard. They are both as ugly as they make them." | *Summit Pacific College, Hudson Memorial Library. Bernice Gerard Collection, uncatalogued.*

nuns in Washington State, Leo Gerard was very hostile toward the church. When the aunts visited and suggested that little Peggy might be better off in their care or placed in a convent school, Leo exploded with anger. She recalls, "He stoutly refused to give consent. The matter came up for discussion several times after the Sisters departed and he repeated again and again that if any priest set foot on his property, he would fill him full of salt. They had a way of taking buckshot out of a shotgun and filling the shell with coarse salt. I had seen stray dogs get the salt treatment. It was really just big talk but in all the noise his true sentiments on religion were expressed."[34]

It is possible that Leo Gerard only broke all his ties with the church after his wife died, or perhaps Annie was more devout than he, because Peggy's stepbrothers had at least some familiarity with Catholic rituals. When the family attended a funeral for their aunt while Peggy was a little girl, one of her brothers gruffly corrected her when she mistook the holy water for a drinking fountain.[35] Young Peggy found the ceremony of the Catholic funeral completely foreign, and she described that "the incense, the mournful chanting and the sight of my Aunt cold and still" were all too much. She felt "sick to my stomach. It was a great relief when the funeral was over."[36] Although she had pleasant memories of her aunts' kindnesses to her through their letters and small gifts, she considered herself a "religious illiterate" when it came to Catholicism; she had never seen a Bible and had to ask the teacher at her school what that strange book was. Her unfamiliarity with the church and her father's hostility toward it reinforced her feeling of not belonging within those church circles.

Given her fragile emotional state of feeling unwanted, and terrified of being left alone or subjected to Gerard's drunken assaults, it is no wonder that when two travelling evangelists came to her local schoolhouse preaching about the love of God, the young Gerard girl was intrigued. Peggy walked to those meetings with a school friend, a familiar trek the children made every day, and she described the message she heard from those women: "It was all about a Man who was so wonderful that even His enemies could find no fault in Him. He took the little children in His arms and blessed them ... He cared for people that no one else loved."[37] The prospect of such unconditional love was overwhelming to her. "Could it be that He loved me? Why nobody had ever loved me."[38] Reflecting on the instability of her childhood and the ad hoc arrangements that characterized her formative years after her adoptive mother died, Gerard revealed that by the age of thirteen, she had lived in nine different households.[39] But the one common thread that Gerard revealed about all that upheaval was this: "In none of these places had I really belonged."[40] A sense of belonging was one of the things that Gerard's new-found religion would provide to her during her tumultuous teen years and after.

It is significant that under the influence of two women evangelists Gerard had her life-changing religious conversion experience. Indeed, within days of the experience, the enthusiastic young convert had set her sights on a new career aspiration: to be a travelling preacher like the women whom she had encountered at the evangelistic meetings at her schoolhouse. At a community gathering that had turned into a "rough party" where neighbours were drinking and dancing, Gerard found herself in conversation with several other people, minding babies and small children while their parents partied. "Sitting on a large wooden barrel in a corner with a few others around me I voiced my disapproval of the celebration. To my own surprise I spoke out loudly in favor of the gospel meetings. 'When I grow up,' I said, 'I am going to give my life to God like the preacher ladies have done.' There were comments favorable and unfavorable but I stood my ground. All I had thought of for days were the gospel meetings and the possibility of a new life following Christ."[41] Gerard's conversion in an evangelistic meeting held at the local rural schoolhouse was one of the defining features of her life. She came back to that experience as a touchstone for the rest of her life, and her religious life was absolutely central to her sense of self from then on.

The women who guided her through her conversion experience presented Gerard with more than a potential career option to be emulated. They became her means of escape from Leo Gerard's abuse. The adult that young Peggy trusted with her terrible truth was one of the "preacher ladies," Frances Layden,[42] who had paired up with Clara Manary to travel as itinerant evangelists affiliated with a group called the "Two by Twos." As part of that group, Layden and Manary were preaching a separatist, fundamentalist gospel message with a very narrow view of who would qualify as a "real Christian" and be granted entrance to heaven. A late nineteenth-century offshoot of the Holiness movement, the Two by Two movement has its roots in Ireland and a complicated history of division and internal conflict. The group takes a radical position in its rejection of other Christian churches and denominations, teaching that anyone who claims to be a Christian but belongs to an organized church is an imposter. While little documentation exists about the doctrines of the Two by Twos (they prefer oral communication of their beliefs), the church rejects the doctrine of the Trinity and believes charismatic elements should be suppressed. They do emphasize the necessity of following the teachings of Jesus and of suffering for the gospel, although they reject the divinity of Christ. Meeting in small groups, they consider themselves to be a restoration of the early church and claim that they only teach what the Bible says. Believing themselves to be authentic Christians, they dress very conservatively in modest dark clothing and do not hold meetings in church buildings but rather in private homes or rented community halls, schoolhouses, and other public spaces. The idea behind this is not to become entrapped by "worldly" distractions like fashion or real estate.[43] Although the Two by Two movement is a marginal, little-known group, it continues to have a worldwide presence. When a pair of their preachers came to Gerard's schoolhouse, she found their message of God's love to be irresistible and transformative.

Her exposure to the Two by Two teachings was brief, but Gerard was fully persuaded by the message and by the women who delivered it. Later, Gerard reassessed their extreme conservatism and after she had experienced other forms of Protestant Christianity, she broadened her views. But her loyalty to the women who first preached the gospel message to her ran deep because they introduced her to things that she knew nothing about. The preachers gave her two very treasured gifts: a hymn book and a copy of the New Testament. When news of Gerard's conversion experience reached her brothers, one of them mocked her, saying that all her fun would now be over; he informed her that joining the so-called black legion (one of the nicknames for the Two by Twos) was "worse than becoming a nun."[44] Gerard was confused by her brother's assessment since she did not share his perception at all. She recounted, "I had no idea what he meant by, 'All your fun is over.'"[45] Peggy Gerard's life was hardly "fun" given the sexual and emotional abuse she constantly had to navigate. The Gerard men, father and sons, were not sympathetic to her new beliefs. "They took my hymn book and New Testament away and laughingly declared that a thirteen-year-old could not possibly know anything about religion."[46] Losing connection to the one thing that seemed to bring her some comfort and pleasure, Gerard recounts that she was desperate for a solution to all the adversity she was facing.

Reflecting back on her family taunting her, Gerard told herself "They might laugh and refer to the preachers with their black stockings and dark clothes as the black legion but I admired and respected them. To be just a little like them when I grew up seemed an ambitious goal."[47] To realize that big goal, the first step would be to escape from Leo Gerard's control over her. After her conversion, Gerard prayed that God would perform a miracle for her and provide "a way out." In the eyes of the child who had endured so much abuse, what happened next was nothing less than a direct intervention by God Himself.

Life with the Gerards   35

In desperation I cried out to God. My preacher friend would soon be leaving the district and then who would help me? It occurred to me to run away. Common sense told me they would find me somehow and bring me back. Then there would be my foster [adoptive] Father's rage to face. Troubled and fearful of the future I confided in my preacher. It was right after that God wrought a miracle on my behalf.[48]

What Gerard recounted as a miraculous act of God actually involved a great deal of human agency. Her escape was due in part to her own actions and also to the interventions of women in positions of professional responsibility. First, Gerard made the risky and courageous decision to report her father's abuse to the evangelist, Frances Layden, who wasted no time in taking action to report to the appropriate authorities what she had heard from her new child convert. Gerard described how she had gone to school as usual one morning, sharing the excitement and anticipation of the other students because report cards were being distributed that day. After a knock on the schoolhouse door, the teacher stepped out to speak with a visitor. Gerard and her classmates were curious to see who the visitor might be and after "a few minutes the teacher stepped back into the room, walked to my desk and said, 'The school nurse is here. She wants to speak to you.'" In a matter of minutes, Gerard was whisked from her schoolhouse and into a waiting car. "The school nurse had come to take me away. I did not understand what it was all about but I willingly went with her after she assured me that I would never have to go back to my [adoptive] home."[49]

Beyond the obvious relief at escaping from the abuse, leaving Leo Gerard behind was a demarcation point for Bernice because her new-found religious convictions set her apart from his rejection of all faith traditions. After her own conversion experience, she put even more distance between herself, her adoptive family's French Catholic religious heritage in general, and Leo Gerard and his irreligion in particular. Growing up in an abusive family setting, Gerard's religion provided much more than a spiritual experience. Her conversion also coincided with her deliverance from abuse.

Part of the child rescue process included a formal hearing to establish that the adoptive father "had failed to live up to his side of the adoption agreement."[50] Gerard recounted her memory of that momentous day: "I had to bear witness against him myself. At the hearing, he asked to see my privately one last time, and all he said was, 'How could you do this to me?' I never saw him again; he died some years later when I was traveling in the United States."[51] The fact that Leo Gerard's request to see his victim privately was granted seems surprising, but in the mid-1930s, the system of child protection in British

Columbia was still in its early days. The remarkable resilience that Peggy had exhibited to live through his abuse for several years, to report it, and to face her abuser one last time demonstrates her strength of character, even at such a young age.

The effect of the abuse stayed with Gerard for her whole life, despite her best efforts to pray it away and request that God heal her mind and her memories. She described in her second autobiography that the trauma surfaced repeatedly. "My sleep was all too frequently disturbed with terrifying reruns of my childhood,"[52] and night terrors continued to plague her late in life. The abuses she experienced as a little girl may help to explain why she become such a fierce opponent of liberalizing social and sexual mores and a tireless protector of the innocent during her lobbying efforts to oppose what others perceived as progressive expressions of sexuality.

Finding her own religion, especially one that was as narrow and fundamentalist as the Two by Twos, was a key pillar in Bernice Gerard's identity formation. That affiliation helped her to establish that she was not at all like the Gerards when it came to matters of faith. To a young girl escaping abuse, that demarcation mattered. While Gerard framed her deliverance from abuse as an act of God, human intervention is central to the story. Her deliverers took the form of several women who stepped in to protect her and remove her from her abuser, although Gerard would ultimately have a complicated relationship with professional social workers and other agents of British Columbia's fledgling child welfare system.

Chapter 2

DELIVERED BY STRONG WOMEN

THE ABRUPT WAY that Gerard left the schoolhouse on the morning of her rescue took a toll on her emotions. Scooped into a waiting car and driven to a Vancouver orphanage, she recalled that trip saying, "At one point on the journey I broke into tears. She [the social worker] tried to cheer me up and said that the best days of my life were in the future. I clutched the report card the teacher had given me as I left the country school. All my marks were good. My guardian said, 'Do you like school?' 'Yes,' I replied. With a smile she said, 'You are going to have the opportunity to continue in school and get all the education you can absorb.'"[1] Unlimited education held great appeal for Gerard. She was a smart and curious student, and she would continue to excel in academic settings through secondary school and beyond, eventually setting her sights on becoming a teacher. But she accomplished all that academic success despite an extraordinary amount of continuing turmoil in her personal life.

By the time Gerard concluded her education and graduated from the provincial child welfare system, she had experienced seventeen different living arrangements. In the care of the provincial child welfare authorities Gerard went from an institutional care facility to a series of foster care arrangements spanning from her junior high and secondary school years to teacher training. While many children would be defeated by all that upheaval, Bernice Gerard emerged as a highly resilient person with firm religious ideas and a penchant for speaking her mind and defending her conservative views. Entry into state care started Gerard on a path of educational opportunity and expanding social circles that broadened her self-definition as a Pentecostal with very wide international connections. Her beliefs and the networks she built provided the foundation for her public engagement as she resisted Canadian society's liberalizing social mores and trend toward secularism in the second half of the twentieth century. The seeds of who she would become had sprouted, and by the time she reached her young adult years, Bernice Gerard had established deeply held convictions that help to explain the complexity of her adult life.

Detailed accounts about these formative experiences exist because Gerard's published life writing is characterized by her well-crafted storytelling about this period. Her accounts reveal her rich interior life and demonstrate how, as a teenager and young adult, she used self-reflection to make a coherent and compelling narrative out of her complex circumstances. From these formative experiences, Gerard framed her religious identity and laid the foundations for her future ministry and public roles, culminating in the *Vancouver Sun*'s designation of her as a historically significant spiritual figure.

It is important to set Gerard's experience of state care within the larger story of British Columbia's fledgling child protection system. Professional social workers oversaw the development of coordinated services to rescue children at risk and bring them into care. Gerard's case invites us to consider important themes in the history of the welfare state, women's life writing, and the formation of religious identity. Her rescue took place at the height of the Great Depression and she left university during the Second World War. Throughout the time that Gerard interacted with provincial authorities and child welfare programs, she sometimes embraced the opportunities held out to her and sometimes resisted the constraints imposed on her.

Children in abusive settings, especially rural and remote settings like Gerard's, were particularly vulnerable because social services tended to be concentrated in more urban settings, But the fact that in the mid-1930s, four professional women (a preacher, a teacher, a school nurse, and a social worker) colluded to rescue Peggy Gerard provides evidence of a system that worked effectively on the child's behalf in her case. However, that system was not without its own prejudices. In a time period when mothers were assumed to perform most of the parenting work, the fact that Peggy Gerard was living in a household with only a father and older brothers made her particularly vulnerable in the eyes of the middle-class women who arranged her rescue. Leo Gerard's ethnicity, his deceased wife's identity as a Stó:lō woman, and the presence of those older, mixed-race stepbrothers would have magnified the danger in the minds of her middle-class rescuers. While those factors might have been enough to prompt her removal from the Gerard home, the reports of alcohol abuse and violence and especially the revelation of sexual

FIGURE 2.1 Bernice was thirteen years old when she was rescued from her adoptive father's home after she reported his abuse to a woman she trusted, Frances Layden, a travelling preacher. | *Summit Pacific College, Hudson Memorial Library, Bernice Gerard Nielson Family Scrapbook.*

abuse made the case even more urgent. Moreover, factors such as Peggy being white, aged thirteen, and academically gifted probably reinforced the urgency of removing her from the setting. In this young girl, her rescuers saw a promising individual who, given the right supports, could become a success story. If a little girl like Peggy Gerard was going to be made into a self-reliant future citizen, she needed an intervention and British Columbia's professional social workers were in place for exactly that kind of situation.

While child protection agencies have a history in Canada stretching back to the late-nineteenth century, when Peggy Gerard became a ward of the state during the 1930s, British Columbia was still in the early stages of implementing a province-wide system of child protection.[2] In 1927, amid reports of scandalous conditions for children in care and abuse of resources by those in authority, the province had invited Charlotte Whitton, the executive secretary of the Canadian Council on Child Welfare, to conduct a study of the Vancouver Children's Aid Society and recommend reforms.[3] Whitton's main advice was to recruit professional social workers to create a child protection field service and organize home placements for children who needed to be removed from their own families. According to Whitton, "If the child's own home fails him utterly, the consensus of modern opinion is that the very best substitute is another family home as nearly as possible like what his own home should have been."[4] The social workers who managed Bernice Gerard's case had definite ideas about what her new life should look like.

Isobel Harvey was British Columbia's most respected child welfare authority in this period and while she led the reorganization and expansion of child protection services in her role as superintendent of child welfare, she also gave personal oversight to Gerard's file. Harvey was a graduate of UBC, where she completed her undergraduate and master's degrees in English literature.[5] The daughter of a wealthy businessman, she enjoyed a privileged family life, evidenced by her father's membership in the Vancouver Club and the family's home addresses in some of the wealthiest neighbourhoods in the city.[6] Harvey's Scottish Presbyterian family taught her to value hard work, material success, and community involvement. As a young adult, she devoted herself to volunteer work at the Vancouver General Hospital, where she developed an interest in working on behalf of children, prompting her return to university studies in the field of social work after Whitton's survey had highlighted the need for professionally trained social workers. After graduation, Harvey joined the provincial government staff, first in the Mothers' Allowance Branch and later in the Child Welfare Division. While she was regarded as a progressive thinker at the time, many of her attitudes are troubling in hindsight. For example, from 1937 to 1944 Harvey was a member of the Eugenics Board, a group that reviewed cases and made recommendations on applying the province's Sexual Sterilization Act.[7] She was a devoted social worker, administrator, and bureaucrat who oversaw the placement of hundreds of British child evacuees from London to British Columbia during the Second World War.[8] She ended her career as a research consultant advising the government on reforms, investments, and best practices for the child welfare sector.[9] Harvey was highly regarded as a leader in social work who brought provincial child welfare out of a Victorian mindset emphasizing charity and institutional care, toward a more progressive model of foster care placing children in family settings, maintaining careful case records, and building teams of professional social workers who laboured tirelessly with the shared goal to "build self-reliant citizens for the future."[10] Harvey took a personal interest in Bernice Gerard's case, monitoring her young charge very closely with that citizenship goal in mind.

As the provincial care system expanded, a group of intrepid social workers did field service outside of Vancouver and Victoria under Isobel Harvey's supervision. The work itself presented adventures because of its unpredictability; these young, middle-class women, venturing into unfamiliar settings like outposts, logging camps, institutions of all kinds, and urban slums, had to muster their courage. Work in rural and remote communities meant driving on roads that were hardly passable and doing so in all kinds of weather. One of the women who worked in the Okanagan Valley and oversaw Gerard's file reminisced that the territory she was responsible for included "all the small mining towns up in the hills. There were no such things as winter tires and our overshoes had velvet tops! There were no finished roads."[11] But the adventure was part of the attraction of the job because "the sense of being an unusual, courageous woman who escaped the more predictable life of wife and mother is suggested in their accounts" of social work.[12] Moreover, the work varied from case to case and the women "felt hugely independent in making decisions," while they maintained a spirit of optimism that their efforts really could make a difference for vulnerable children and disadvantaged families. These unconventional experiences were precursors of the adventures Gerard would later embrace in her religious vocation.

While British Columbia's social workers were conscious of the fact that their work held the prospects of social change because the social welfare state was in a formative stage and they were on the front lines, these women held a deep commitment to reform and a confidence that government intervention through programs and personnel could transform children's lives. Gerard would come to share that conviction about being a potential changemaker based on her own experience of being rescued. Moreover, as she absorbed that shared belief it helps to explains why she would grow up to be a woman who lobbied governments and even made a foray into municipal politics herself. Like the social workers she met in her youth, she thought she could make change in people's lives.

Historians also point out that professional social workers like Harvey and her field workers in the 1930s and '40s were "women [who] also stood up for their beliefs."[13] Indeed, while standing up for your beliefs was something Gerard came to embrace, during her teen years she felt that the provincial staff members from child welfare were wielding too much control over her choices as they tried to guide her toward becoming a so-called self-reliant citizen for the future. As we shall see, there was a recurring theme to the conflicts that arose between Gerard and Harvey as their competing agendas collided: the provincial authority wanted to shape Gerard into accepting middle-class values and practices, and Gerard wanted to set herself apart as a young woman with conservative religious convictions.

Although Gerard's autobiographies highlight the conflicts she had with her guardian and some of her foster families, she did develop an affection for some of her immediate caseworkers who gained her confidence. About one, she recalled, "She kept an eye on me in my new home, worked out problems between me and my foster-home and saw to it that ... [Isobel Harvey's] wishes were carried out. Most important of all she was a friend and a counsellor. When everything went wrong with everybody else, one had the feeling that [she] had one's best interest at heart."[14] That relationship sounds almost pastoral, and it was a model of the kind of attentive listening, caring, and intervention that Gerard carried out as a pastor, chaplain, and politician later in life. Clearly, these strong women in professional roles influenced their young client in ways that were both intended and unintended.

One of the goals of the child protection workers was to provide their young clients with the advantages they would need to thrive as middle-class citizens. For Bernice Gerard and others, that meant access to education. During the 1930s access to secondary school education was not universal and was certainly not the shared experience for most rural children and youth in Canada.[15] When Gerard was whisked away from her rural schoolhouse to be placed in temporary care in Vancouver, her future was set on a different course because now she had the prospect of secondary school and even postsecondary education if she chose that path. The pleasure she had taken in attending school would have ended abruptly if she had stayed with Leo Gerard because he had made it clear that he would not allow her to continue to high school. When her driver told her she could have "all the education you can absorb," Bernice was delighted as she thought to herself, "What a wonderful promise!"[16] Education played a very important role in Gerard's life, not only because she was an excellent student, but also because she would become an educator herself, and she would return as a mature student to complete her university education that had been interrupted by the war.

Her removal from the Gerard household closed one chapter of her life and opened another one filled with new and different complexities. She recounts her foster care experiences in great detail in her autobiographical writing, framing them in religious terms. Each care location, whether temporary or more long-term, was a site where Gerard was engaging in her teenaged identity formation as she constructed her understanding of who she was and what she believed. At the age of thirteen, when she left the remote rural setting where Leo Gerard was abusing her, she was a courageous but naive survivor. Resilient but sheltered, she had a new-found faith but very little life experience.

The day Gerard was rescued from her abusive father, she was taken to the Alexandria Orphanage in Vancouver, a place that families who fell on hard times sometimes used as a temporary placement for their children until they could return to claim them.[17] Gerard's stay at the Alexandria was also quite short-lived, only until she could be placed into foster care. When she first learned where she was being taken, Gerard protested to her caseworker that she did not want to live in an orphanage. The social worker reassured her, explaining that

> I would not be at the orphanage very long, just long enough for her to find a more suitable place for me to live. It occurred to me that she might have it in mind to leave me there permanently and was just not saying so. But nothing could be done about it, and it did seem that all of this was part of the answer to my prayer.[18]

Gerard recounted that, contrary to her initial expectations, she quite enjoyed her time at the orphanage. She liked the routines, the companionship of girls her own age, and the instruction she received on matters like personal hygiene. What she did not enjoy or understand were the ways in which her peers plotted to defy the rules and act out. Gerard overheard other girls planning to sneak off to meet boyfriends or talking "wildly of getting out and going on a good drunk. How any kind of a 'drunk' could be 'good' was beyond *my* power to imagine!"[19] To Gerard, having just escaped from her alcoholic abuser, the institution provided a welcome refuge from the horror of the home life she had endured. Unlike many other accounts about the abuses of institutional life, for Gerard the Alexandria represented safety. Her experience aligns with historian Diane Purvey's challenge of the "social control" interpretation, noting that the orphanage was rarely a permanent placement and even for children placed there by their own families, "the argument that the child was sacrificed for the sake of the family is also weak because it implies a false assumption: that the child's life prior to admittance into the Home was 'perfect.'"[20] Certainly, as a victim of abuse, the home Gerard was fleeing was far from perfect and the institution provided a welcome refuge. "Many of the older ones hated the Orphanage," Gerard recounted, "but I had no resentment toward the Alexandria. It was heaven compared to what I had heard about such places."[21]

Because she had been through so much, Gerard was prone to volatile reactions to everyday situations, and she was frustrated with herself because whenever she made even a small mistake or somehow disappointed the orphanage staff, "I broke into a flood of tears and went crying off into a corner."[22] While the staff worked to understand her reactions, Gerard later wrote, "I wanted to make it right with the matron but what could I say? How could she understand that I felt all torn up by the roots. I had a strong need to belong but there was nowhere to belong. My stay at the Alexandria lasted just long enough for me to begin to enjoy some new friends at the Kitsilano Junior High. Then my guardian made arrangements for me to go to the Okanagan Valley to live."[23] Just as Isobel Harvey had promised, Gerard's stay at the Alexandria orphanage was short-lived.

Because child rescue facilities in Vancouver, including the Alexandria Orphanage, were often beyond capacity during the Great Depression, provincial authorities sought solutions for placement opportunities elsewhere. Finding foster families in the Okanagan Valley would be part of that solution. Historian Veronica Strong-Boag explains that the 1930s were difficult for the foster care system because "the Great Depression effectively eliminated poorer families from taking in unrelated children without reimbursement, and the tiny pool of middle-class applicants for foster children dwindled even further,"[24] making the challenge of placements profound. One social worker in the Okanagan Valley who managed Gerard's case file recalls that up to the late 1930s "there were very few children placed in the valley in foster homes." But that changed abruptly when "an order came through for us to place 200 children. These were not all Okanagan children but the Superintendent of Child Welfare [Isobel Harvey] dictated which children should go where and she thought the Okanagan the most desirable area so pressure was put on us to find homes."[25] To increase Vancouver's capacity for placing children, social workers in the Okanagan Valley were expected to recruit suitable families willing to take in children. This explains why Bernice Gerard left the Alexandria Orphanage and boarded a train for Summerland, British Columbia, where she would meet her new caseworker and her first foster family.

Isobel Harvey herself put Bernice Gerard on that train in Vancouver and Nancy Lott, the child protection officer for the Okanagan Valley, was waiting to meet her when the train pulled into the Summerland station a few hours later. The family who welcomed Bernice into their home was John and Emily Mott, who had four children, all younger than Bernice. Strong-Boag points out that while there was a decline in families willing to take foster children during this period, the one exception to that trend were the "more evangelical Christians"[26] whose family-centred values made them enthusiastic hosts to foster children. The Motts, a faithful Baptist family, fit that pattern. Gerard recounts that she was in a rather emotional state with the stress of leaving the Alexandria, the solo train ride, and meeting her new family. Attempting to comfort the child and help her settle in, Mrs. Mott drew her into conversation as soon as she arrived. "I sat at the kitchen table and cried. It was silly to cry but the tears kept coming just the same ... She wanted to know why I was unhappy. That was a hard question to answer because I was glad to be at their house and could not explain why I felt upset – so lost. Then she asked, 'Are you saved?'" It seems a very unusual thing to ask a crying child, yet it belies at least in part, the motive that the Motts had for their fostering work as they hoped to proselytize the children they took in. Gerard, confused by the question, replied that she was not saved, and Mrs. Mott patiently explained, "All of our family are saved ... right down to Preston [the youngest of her four children]. As young as he is, he loves Jesus too." Stuck on the semantics of her recent conversion experience, after some supplementary questions Gerard realized what she was being asked and replied in the affirmative, "Oh yes, I'm a Christian. I got converted through the schoolhouse meetings."[27] With that awkward exchange behind them, Gerard was left with a strange impression. "It struck me that there was something funny about this family," she wrote in her autobiography.[28]

But what Gerard found funny about this family was not their eagerness in sharing their beliefs or even the troubling idea that if she was truly "saved," then she would not be so tearful even under her circumstances. What was upsetting to Gerard about this new family was their belief system: she was convinced they had it all wrong. "Their regular attendance at the Baptist church was a big problem to me,"[29] she confessed. According to the Two by Twos, whose views Gerard had accepted uncritically, anyone who attended a church was not a true believer. So, when the Motts expected Gerard to attend their church with them, conflict and misunderstanding ensued.

The problem was that Gerard had heard very clearly from the Two by Twos that attending any denominational church was an error because "to my knowledge the followers of Jesus did not build churches. I did not intend to have anything to do with anybody but the true Christians."[30] For confirmation that she was taking the correct stance, Gerard corresponded with Frances Layden to lay out the problem. "These people are trying to get me to go to the Baptist church. Didn't you tell me churches are worldly and wrong? Please tell me, is it wrong for me to go to one? If you say I shouldn't go, I won't go and they can't drag me."[31] No answer was forthcoming from Gerard's first spiritual mentor because, as she learned later, Isobel Harvey had intervened, intercepting the letter and telling Layden that "if she gave any advice contrary to her wishes, she would not be permitted to correspond with me at all."[32]

With that restriction in place, Gerard was left to her own devices to reconcile what she had first learned from the Two by Twos and what she was now hearing from the Mott family as they tried to persuade her that her ideas about who qualified as a "true Christian" were far too narrow. Patiently nudging her to be a little more open-minded, the Motts' influence did cause Gerard to adjust her views. She was convinced by the fact that they were such a loving family, and also by her realization that she had some shortcomings of her own, not the least of which was the rough language she had acquired during her years with Leo Gerard. Over the course of several months, Gerard became convinced that the thing she and the Motts held in common was their belief that having "a personal knowledge of Jesus Christ as Saviour" was the key distinction. On that basis, Gerard conceded and adjusted her views to arrive at the conclusion that "heaven was still small but not as small as I first had thought. The Holiness Movement people would be there and some of the Baptists."[33] That adjustment to her belief system was the first of many as Gerard's understanding of her faith expanded in step with her life experiences. Having made peace with the Motts over who was "in" and who was "out," after just a few months of settling in with this family, her new views would be challenged further. "They were just nicely 'in,'" Gerard recorded, "when my guardian moved me to Kelowna, British Columbia."[34]

The move to Kelowna, approximately sixty-five kilometres away, meant that Gerard would be living in a larger community, with more amenities. Indeed, the reason she was transferred to a new foster family was tied to the fact that Gerard needed medical care she could not get in Summerland. She had been battling a serious skin condition, and it was arranged for her to become the patient of a doctor with a practice in Kelowna, a doctor whom Isobel Harvey knew from their student days at UBC. Gerard's new foster family was a Swedish couple, John and Evelyn Lindahl, and their two young children, Stanley and Vera.

The experience of living with the Lindahls would serve to expand Gerard's religious outlook even more than at the Motts. Of all the placements that Bernice would experience in the child welfare system (and there would be eight in total) she described her time with the Lindahls as "the happiest days of my young life."[35] She remembers John Lindahl as "a good man who loved his wife dearly, showed a lot of affection to his little daughter ... held high hopes for his son," and was "willing to get into long discussions with me."[36] The family as a whole "were very supportive, among the first really affirming people I had met."[37] Gerard described herself as eager "to learn to be a part of things," and open to all kinds of information about daily living. "Nobody had ever told me before, for example, that in setting for a tea table, the cups and saucers should be matched."[38] The Lindahls lived a life characterized by "a wholesomeness and naturalness in all they did,"[39] making nutritious food from the bounty that was close at hand in the Okanagan, and introducing Gerard to the rhythms of

FIGURE 2.2 Gerard spent her teenaged years in the care of provincial child welfare authorities and a series of foster homes. | *Summit Pacific College, Hudson Memorial Library, Bernice Gerard Nielson Family Scrapbook.*

family life and encouraging her to enjoy a variety of teenaged activities including biking, swimming, community corn boils, tobogganing, and babysitting. The Lindahls were very active in their local church and as part of their household, Bernice Gerard came to share their high levels of involvement and embrace a wide variety of experiences in the church as well. Yet despite that very positive outcome and Gerard's fond memories, the relationship got off to a shaky start.

Like the Motts, the Lindahls were very active in their local church and although Gerard had now come to accept that "real" Christians could include those beyond followers of the Two by Twos, at first she was not ready to accept what her new host family represented. The Two by Twos were active in Kelowna and she had been hoping to join their meetings and reinforce her ties with believers like the schoolhouse evangelists. But that was not to be. Gerard's first day in her new foster home was memorable because of the conversation about religion, but rather than confront her new arrival, as Mrs. Mott had done, with a question about whether or not she was "saved," Evelyn Lindahl simply announced to Gerard that the family would be attending church that evening. This seemed odd since it was a Tuesday, but having an expanded view of who might qualify as a "real" Christian, Gerard was curious.[40] However, when she learned that the Lindahls were Pentecostals, Gerard was shocked. "Perhaps I had been wrong about the Holiness Movement and some of the Baptists but there could be no mistake about these Pentecostals," she mused.[41] Even with her rather limited exposure to organized religion, Gerard recounted, "Along the way I had been warned about the Pentecostal people who were said to be, of all the heretics in the world, the most dangerous. If Hell had one place hotter than another, they would certainly be consigned to it."[42]

In the late 1930s, Pentecostals in Canada were still very much on the fringe of respectable society, perceived as a ragtag group of fanatical followers, "holy rollers," who let their emotions run away with them and whose embodied practices of spiritual expression were highly suspect. They conflicted with the state authorities during the First World War because while some claimed to be conscientious objectors, others did not, and their internal divisions led to confusion.[43] The Canadian census counted Pentecostals for the first time in 1911, when just over five hundred people identified their religion as Pentecostal. The 1931 census showed a growing trend with 26,349 Pentecostals, and more than double that number, to 57,742, reporting to be Pentecostals by 1941.[44] During Bernice Gerard's childhood no one would have predicted that almost one hundred years later Pentecostalism would enjoy a central place across the globe with a commanding presence that continues to grow exponentially, or that the Pentecostal Assemblies of Canada (PAOC) would occupy a central place on the Canadian religious landscape as the largest expression of conservative Christianity.[45]

When Gerard met the Lindahls, this Swedish immigrant family was attending Kelowna's Evangel Temple, a PAOC church, with a minister who was Italian Canadian. Given the lingering suspicion about immigration and the overt racism of the time, the multi-ethnic character of many Pentecostal groups only served to reinforce the suspicion and prejudices against them that many respectable, white, middle-class Canadians felt toward them. The Pentecostal movement had garnered a reputation for being a collection of "down and out" people whose own marginalized situation and lack of ethnic, economic, or able-bodied status had attracted them as a means of meeting their personal and psychological needs. Many other Christians, both liberal and conservative, regarded the Pentecostals as extremists with dangerous beliefs and practices tending toward heresy.

Bernice Gerard shared that judgmental view about Pentecostals. However, as she had learned from her previous placement, there was no point in arguing with Isobel Harvey, her guardian back in Vancouver, or with the social workers in the field. In Kelowna it was a young social worker named Wini Urquhart who befriended Gerard and directed that she was expected to attend church wherever her foster family attended. The inner turmoil young Bernice experienced over her own religious affiliation should not be underestimated. As a child who had taken the risk to trust an itinerant preacher woman, Gerard's personal loyalty to Frances Layden and the Two by Twos was very deep. She felt indebted to Layden for arranging her rescue and grateful to have been introduced to her faith in Jesus, and she was convinced that her future would be to follow in Layden's footsteps as a travelling preacher. But Gerard had surmised that she would need to keep her guard up because, as she understood it, when it came to Pentecostals, "not only were they in error but they had a subtle way of snaring others so that they were completely trapped before they even knew it. At once, I saw the danger of my position," Gerard reported. "I was living with Pentecostal people!"[46]

Gerard recounts this part of her life story in her published autobiographies with self-deprecating humour about her youthful arrogance and certainty, but the struggle and angst she felt as a conflicted teenager finding her way was a very serious matter for her at the time. She was hesitant to displease Layden and the ones who had witnessed her conversion and helped to arrange her rescue, yet eager to embrace the warm hospitality and sense of belonging that the Lindahls were offering. The theological dispute between groups who were convinced that overemphasis on the Holy Spirit was a heresy and Pentecostals, for whom the Holy Spirit was central, was fiercely debated among Christians. But for Gerard this conundrum was as much about divided personal loyalties as it was about competing belief systems; she felt forced to choose between her first spiritual guides and her new experience of affectionate family life.

Gerard's initial approach was to attend the Pentecostal meetings despite her prejudices, but to keep her guard up against the "heresies" she expected to hear as a means of protecting herself from subversive Pentecostal persuasion. The rituals of Pentecostal worship were unfamiliar and uncomfortable to her, and she did not understand the "moaning and groaning"[47] she observed as part of the services. But she found it difficult to be inattentive, and she was surprised to hear preaching about Christ and about the need for salvation that matched her own rigid but evolving beliefs. During a series of meetings that lasted for two weeks, she was immersed in teachings from a series about the Holy Spirit in the life of the believer and at the end of it, she came away convinced that she had been misled by those who told her the Bible had nothing to say about speaking in tongues or about baptism in the Holy Spirit. "The impression under which I had been laboring that there was not one verse in the whole Bible to support speaking in tongues as a meaningful, Biblical phenomenon was entirely wrong."[48] To her own astonishment, she conceded, "the Pentecostal people had not made it up – it was in the Bible."[49] Yet becoming persuaded by the logic of Pentecostal preaching about the Holy Spirit and having a personal Pentecostal experience were two different things, and Gerard recognized that mental ascent would not suffice. "Making up my mind that I was willing to go for all the Lord had for me, even if it meant I would be a Pentecostal, did not make me one," she realized.[50]

For many Pentecostals speaking in tongues is regarded as a first sign that Spirit baptism really has taken place. This set Gerard on a path to seek out the Pentecostal experience of being baptized in the Spirit and speaking in tongues. She describes a process of several weeks where she earnestly prayed to that end. Reflecting on that process, she writes, "Step by step I came to see that what my heart cried for was not an experience for its own sake, and not a ritual, however mysterious, but a love relationship with God."[51] In fact, Gerard was learning about the rituals of Pentecostal practices, including the practice during worship services, that believers often verbalize from their pews by shouting "Amen" or some other affirming expression to signal their agreement with preachers. In a Pentecostal meeting, the worshippers' praise could become ecstatic when the English language was blended with glossolalia, and it is common for those who were moved by the Spirit to cry, shout, or make some other emotional outburst. All of these responses are normalized as expressions of praise and of spiritual passions on display; in effect, such behaviours are Pentecostal rituals.

Having decided for herself that she wanted to identify with the Pentecostals, Gerard writes, "As a result of my decision I sought the Lord and was soon filled with the Holy Spirit, speaking the praises of God in an unknown tongue."[52] That experience was a high point in Gerard's spiritual journey, and it would become another important touchstone in her identity formation. For Gerard, this was a significant milestone on her journey to solidify her religious identity, but she still wrestled with the realization that she was making a significant shift in her beliefs and would do so at the expense of disappointing her earlier influencers.

Convinced that she had found a new truth and excited by how deeply it had impacted her, Gerard faced a very difficult task as she sat to write a letter explaining her new convictions to Frances Layden:

> Dear Frances,
>
> I'm sorry to have to write something I know will displease you but I don't know what else to do. When I first came to Kelowna I rejected the message of the Baptism of the Holy Spirit as preached by the Pentecostal people. Then I saw the truth of it in the Bible and now I have the experience myself. It may seem to you that I have been side-tracked but I want you to know that I love Christ now more than ever. I must put God first.[53]

With some trepidation, Gerard awaited a reply by return mail. While the letters she exchanged with Frances Layden were sometimes intercepted by her social workers, this time the letter reached her, and Gerard was relieved to find that the tone was "warm and affectionate, filled with tender regard and concern." Even so, Layden could not compromise on her own objections to Pentecostal beliefs, and she simply told Gerard, "I understand that these people have been in a position to influence you unduly. I will keep on praying for you that you will come back to the true way."[54]

That reply was at once both a reaffirmation of Layden's investment in Gerard and a parting of the ways. Gerard reflected on that loss, reconciling in her own mind that Layden had simply never experienced Pentecostalism first-hand and was unlikely to become more open-minded. Nevertheless, she imagined a scene in heaven where she and Layden would cross paths and her childhood preacher would react with surprise, "You here? Why I gave up all hope for you. I thought my labors were in vain."[55] But for Gerard herself, "Heaven was getting bigger all the time. It was clear to me now that the shouting Pentecostals would not be barred from that wonderful place."[56]

As a Pentecostal youth embracing her new spiritual experiences and a more expressive faith, Gerard flourished. She bonded even more deeply with the Lindahl family, who gave her a first taste of what real belonging felt like, while their church reinforced her growing identity as a Pentecostal and provided her with a sense of community and opportunities for leadership among the youth of Kelowna. No doubt her spiritual experience and her home life were two important factors in explaining why Gerard claimed that her time with the Lindahls had been the happiest part of her young life. However, that happy home life and church involvement was soon to be disrupted, plunging her back into a very trying phase where once again her religious convictions were tested and her newly established Pentecostal identity was called into question.

Chapter 3

FIGHTING FOR HER FAITH

ACCORDING TO HER autobiography, life with the Lindahls was a very happy time for Gerard, when her biggest problems were typical teenaged concerns: "Life Buoy, Lux and Ivory – I tried them all. I ate yeast cakes and drank carrot juice – still no success! I read all the advertisements on complexion care and carefully followed everybody's advice on home remedies. But in spite of constant medical care my bad skin condition failed to improve."[1] With attentive care from her caseworker, Gerard was scheduled to make a trip to Vancouver for some further medical tests and procedures to address her skin problems, including a complete medical checkup. During the Christmas break of her second year in high school, Gerard recounts the memory of a joyous Christmas celebration with the Lindahl family, and she was happily anticipating the trip to Vancouver, having discussed with her pastor and friends from the church youth group that a visit to the city might afford the opportunity to visit some other Pentecostal churches and bring back ideas to enhance the youth programming at Evangel Temple, her Kelowna church. But she had no idea that the trip to Vancouver meant her life was about to take a drastic turn because the way that Gerard had imagined the trip is not at all how it unfolded.

Instead of a quick medical visit and an enriching tour of other Pentecostal practices, Gerard found herself on an extended stay in Vancouver, never to return to her happy life as part of the Lindahl household. There were two reasons for this unexpected plot twist. First, while she was in Vancouver her health took a turn for the worse, and she stayed on to have her tonsils removed and recover from that surgery. But more significantly, she learned that her guardian had never had any intention of returning Gerard to the Lindahls or to Kelowna, because Isobel Harvey had determined that Gerard's religiosity was tending toward extremism and needed to be corrected. The solution – to have Gerard stay permanently in Vancouver – seemed punitive to her but it was no doubt made with good intentions. Staying in Vancouver meant that Harvey would be able to supervise Gerard more closely, introduce her to a more reserved expression of Christianity, and provide her with excellent academic experiences. Why Harvey took such a direct and personal interest in Bernice Gerard is unclear, but it is obvious that she saw great potential in this teenager, and she was firmly convinced that the influence of Pentecostals in her life was not a positive one. Gerard was deeply disappointed by this change and she tried to make it clear to Harvey that she did not welcome yet another transition and the upheaval that went with it. She tried to persuade her overseer by building a logical case, citing her happy home life and academic success in Kelowna.

But Harvey remained unmoved. For the first weeks in Vancouver, Gerard was housed at a "receiving home" run by the Vancouver Children's Aid, a site where children stayed for short periods before being placed in more permanent arrangements, either through adoption or foster care. The Children's Aid home was the fourth address where Bernice had lived since leaving Leo Gerard's home, including the Alexandria Orphanage, the Motts' in Summerland, and the Lindahls' in Kelowna. Gerard appreciated the care and attention that was offered to her by the house mother while she recovered from the tonsillitis surgery and had a series of medical consultations with various doctors, but she observed about herself and the other children who were housed there that "what we all needed and wanted most was lacking – to be loved and wanted by someone. But I had in the back of my mind the assurance that I was wanted in the Lindahl home. The sooner I got back there the better!"[2] Of course, that return was not to be, and being uprooted from the first truly happy home setting she had ever experienced was a profound disappointment that left Gerard angry and combative. Despite Harvey's rationale about the advantages afforded by a life in Vancouver, Gerard was convinced that her guardian was no longer her protector, but her persecutor.

Gerard framed this part of her story as an episode of victimization – a tone she had not used in her autobiographies up to this point. "Everything she [Isobel Harvey] told me had caught me by surprise," Gerard reported. "I now knew that I was not going back to Kelowna, that my guardian thought I was developing into a religious fanatic, and that she thought I was about to ruin my life by sticking to the narrow-minded ideas I got in the country. If I didn't have sense enough to save myself from failure – she was going to do it for me."[3] The persecution trope is a familiar one among conservative Christians but it was the first time Gerard employed it. When she wrote her life story she was writing for evangelical readers as her primary audience, and so when she narrated this part of her life she emphasized the ways that she was forced into adopting a position of resistance, thus strengthening her resolve to defend her faith.

The ensuing battles between Gerard and Harvey went on for the remainder of her high school years, reinforced by the fact that Gerard's next set of foster parents were Isobel Harvey's close allies, fully committed to the goal of shaping Bernice into a more moderate believer who conformed more closely to middle-class behaviours of respectability. Her third foster family was Clem and Muriel Hudson and their son "Kim." The Hudsons operated as a very orderly household in one of Vancouver's most privileged neighbourhoods, Jericho Beach. Clem Hudson, who had served as an officer in the First World War, and his British-born wife Muriel, were practising Anglicans. Their ten-year-old son attended St. George's, a local private school near their home. The Hudsons were well-connected in Vancouver's elite business and social circles, and life with them offered many social advantages to a teenager like Bernice. From their home, she attended Lord Byng Secondary School and learned to conform to the Hudsons' high standards of housekeeping, personal discipline, and respect for elders, including the expected "Yes, sir" and "No, sir" that Mr. Hudson demanded in his daily interactions with her. Keeping a watchful eye on who she associated with, the Hudsons clearly hoped that she would become friends with young women in their social circle so that she could embrace the upward mobility that being part of their family offered her. However, what the Hudson family hoped to share, Gerard was not willing to embrace.

In her autobiography, Gerard recounts an awkward moment soon after she moved into the Hudson home. At dinner Mr. Hudson was pleased to announce to the family that he had secured theatre tickets for all of them to attend a production together. While his wife and son were delighted with the news, Gerard searched for a way to explain to her host family that she did not wish to attend because theatre was a worldly pastime and something she could not enjoy. As a conservative Christian, Gerard had been influenced to eschew the theatre and other forms of popular entertainment, because doing so meant she was "taking a stand against worldliness." Denying herself a cultural outing was an act of personal piety and holy living. The Hudsons did not understand, and they found her judgmental attitudes toward middle-class forms of entertainment and recreation to be uncultured and uninformed, even arrogant. In both versions of her life story Gerard recounts a number of these stories that illustrate the gulf that existed between her religiosity and that of the Hudson family.[4]

Another prime example was Gerard's attitude toward alcohol. When she had completed high school and was pursuing her training to become a teacher, the Hudsons were still investing in her social formation, or attempting to. She explains that at this stage of her life, "other girls from our neighbourhood were developing into social belles," and Muriel Hudson, who wished that Gerard would follow their model, praised a young woman from next door because "she takes a cocktail and is learning to move in society."[5] On more than one occasion the Hudsons urged Gerard to accept that social drinking was not sinful but, rather, a mark of sociability, a desirable social grace. Gerard insisted on maintaining her abstinence from all alcohol, and although she did not verbalize her entire rationale to Clem and Muriel Hudson, she did confide to readers of her life story, explaining, "I had seen enough alcohol at Gerards' to last me a lifetime."[6] Muriel Hudson also encouraged Gerard to learn to use makeup, adopting a cruel tone as she quipped, "Anyone as homely as you are should do everything possible to help herself."[7] Yet Gerard's religious subculture emphasized that makeup was worldly and inner beauty was more valuable than physical appearance.[8] The Hudsons were baffled by this young woman who refused to learn the culture and mores of respectable mainstream society.

But for Gerard the list of things being held out to her were not advantages but compromises that challenged her religious convictions. Drinking, dancing, attending theatre, and wearing makeup were some of the practices that Pentecostals and other midcentury evangelicals had rejected as marks of worldliness. Gerard had no interest in adopting those behaviours because she thought they would jeopardize or dilute her commitment to follow Jesus wholeheartedly. For Pentecostals and other conservative faith groups, moral codes and dress codes were common markers that set the faithful apart from their more "worldly" peers. Of course these moral codes were highly gendered, with more strict standards and longer lists of "don'ts" for women than men.[9] But Gerard stood her ground on all of these "sins," refusing to make compromises, although she admitted later in life that she sometimes felt tempted to conform for the sake of avoiding conflict and fitting in. The conflicts in the Hudson household were more than the rebellion of a strong-willed teenager battling well-meaning adults. What was at stake here was Gerard's identity formation and the boundary-making and reinforcement she had adopted through her association with the conservative church subculture that gave her a sense of belonging; it was among like-minded believers that she felt most at home.[10]

Retelling her story with an emphasis on the persecution she felt for the inflexible moral stances she adopted and maintained was a means for Gerard to reinforce her identity. As a recent convert to evangelical faith and to Pentecostalism specifically, she doubled down on issues that became non-negotiable so that she could solidify the bond she felt with believers, first with Layden, later with the Motts, and then with the members of her Kelowna church, especially the beloved Lindahl family. Moreover, Gerard's teenaged convictions belie the fact that so many of the markers of adulthood that Isobel Harvey and Clem and Muriel Hudson were trying to introduce her to were things that Gerard associated with the trauma of her past. She could not imagine alcohol as a means of pleasure or enjoyment when her only associations with it were the abuse she endured whenever Leo Gerard was under the influence. Nor did she put any stock in learning the finer points of social graces that were intended to mark her as an emerging debutante. Gerard wanted to accept the advantages she was being offered very selectively: she welcomed the chance to excel in her academic life, but she wanted to worship in the way that she found meaningful and with the people who gave her an unconditional sense of belonging.

Things her caseworker and foster family intended for her refinement were sources of offence for Gerard. Trying to explain their concern over her involvement with Pentecostalism and the fringe elements of society that it seemed to attract, Clem and Muriel Hudson forced her to read the Sinclair Lewis novel *Elmer Gantry,* hoping she would come to share the view that travelling evangelists and other religious extremists were best avoided because of their duplicitous nature.[11] In one heated exchange Muriel Hudson moralized that Gerard's religious fanaticism was leading her down a dangerous path, potentially leading even to mental illness. "A lot of people who end up at Essondale Psychiatric Hospital were religious fanatics to begin with," Hudson warned. "If you keep going on this religious tangent, that's likely where you'll end up."[12] It was a cruel thing to suggest. When Hudson equated sincere religious conviction with insanity and spoke without a trace of compassion for the mentally ill, Gerard lost even more respect for her foster mother's ideas. A few years later, that remark would resonate even more deeply as Gerard learned more about her own birth mother's story.

After she had lived as part of the Hudson household for the first part of her high school experience at Lord Byng School, Gerard moved to a different foster family when Clem Hudson changed employers. Before he began his new job, the Hudson family took the opportunity to travel internationally for several months and while they were away, Gerard's life was disrupted. Her next two

FIGURE 3.1 Bernice Gerard was academically gifted, excelling in her secondary school, university, and Provincial Normal School training. | *Summit Pacific College, Hudson Memorial Library. Bernice Gerard Collection, uncatalogued.*

foster placements were short-lived, and because she did not form affectionate bonds or have major conflicts with the new families, she does not name these families in her autobiography. She was still under the watchful eye of Isobel Harvey, and she was still placed in care with well-to-do families. However, the next family treated her like hired help, expecting her to perform their domestic work, including laundry detail, caring for the elaborate wardrobes of their children. Gerard reveals that it was her task to iron and starch twenty-one fancy dresses each week because the family's three young daughters wore them as everyday outfits.[13] The unpaid domestic workload became so heavy that it impacted her school performance. When a teacher mentioned to Harvey that her star pupil was falling behind in her schoolwork, the guardian stepped in to make a change and find a new living arrangement.[14]

The second family, also unnamed in Gerard's autobiographies, had the same expectation that Gerard's role in their household was to perform their domestic work. There was no warm family experience awaiting her. Instead, Gerard remembers that her identity as a "welfare case" was reinforced to her in small, everyday ways including being given smaller portions of food at the family table and being denied basic personal care products shared by the children of the household. Instead of toothpaste, she was told to make do with baking soda or salt. These small acts of unkindness make Gerard sound like a Cinderella figure, a girl who was expected to work but not to be treated as a full member of the family. She remarked that later in life those experiences shaped her own practices of generous hospitality. "Silly to remember after all these years? Yes, but to this day any children visiting *our* house can share our toothpaste and help themselves to whatever we are having of dinner, and enjoy the feeling of family."[15]

Even in the midst of these miserable experiences, Gerard's resilience drove her to find some positive aspects to her circumstances. She recalls that when she asked her exploitative foster parents for permission to attend Pentecostal youth activities in the city, they granted it.[16] That freedom to participate in her beloved Pentecostal circles again was the highlight of her time with those families. It meant that Gerard could soothe her feelings of rejection by re-asserting her Pentecostal identity and spending time with like-minded people. In Gerard's mind, that was a refreshing change from her earlier placement with the Hudsons. Although they had welcomed her into their family and expected her to follow their discipline and rules (which she did not mind), she had lamented the fact that they forbid her to practise her Pentecostalism or even to associate with other Pentecostals.

Perhaps it was at Isobel Harvey's insistence, or maybe it was through the persuasive powers of their son, but surprisingly, when the Hudson family returned from their travels and relocated to another home in Point Grey in the University Gates area, Bernice returned to the Hudson household.[17] (Incidentally, this was Gerard's eighth home address since being rescued from her abusive father.) Back with the Hudsons, she was freed from her "housemaid" existence and welcomed back to the family. But being reunited with them also meant that their efforts to socialize her into the mores of respectable, middle-class Vancouver society resumed. It meant that restrictions on her religious practices were enforced and once again she was forbidden to attend meetings or have contact with Pentecostals. When friends, pastors, or anyone else from the Pentecostal groups where she had recently connected reached out to Bernice, Muriel Hudson intervened. Telephone calls to the Hudson residence asking for Bernice were screened. "What is your name, please? And to what church do you belong?" With such direct questions Mrs. Hudson promptly hung up on callers who identified themselves as Pentecostals.[18]

The Hudsons and Harvey had shared misgivings that were partly about religious convictions, but equally troubling to them were the associations of Pentecostals with different ethnicities and lower social classes. When Pastor Catrano from the Kelowna church visited Vancouver and requested permission to see Bernice, Isobel Harvey's attitude was dismissive and even "haughty"; Harvey referred to him as "that little Italian" and restricted the visit to "a few minutes only, as though he were a person of unfit moral character."[19] Later in life, Gerard postulated that those objections to her religious belief were rooted in the superintendent's "Freudian-oriented" approach to social welfare.[20] When Bernice defied her foster parents and her guardian by participating in Pentecostal meetings after sneaking downtown to be with her church friends, she was asserting her independence and reinforcing her Pentecostal identity. What her guardian and her foster family wished for her instead was that she should be part of one of their congregations, either Miss Harvey's beloved United Church congregation, or the Hudsons' Anglican one. With the prompting of Pastor Catrano, she agreed to submit to the restrictions of the child welfare system and her caregivers' rules, chalking the experience up to "a time of testing" where "God was giving me the opportunity to stand up for my convictions in the face of opposition."[21]

Gerard complied. She even taught Sunday school at the Anglican church where the Hudsons worshipped, but the congregation's social class composition only reinforced Gerard's feeling of being an outsider. When children in her Sunday school class returned from family vacations with reports about their European travels, she, "the welfare case," could not relate. She attended the Anglican services and paid close attention to what she heard, critiquing the clergy, whom she did not consider to be good role models. After one sermon on temperance, when the priest recommended the moderate consumption of alcohol, she concluded, "To me his temperance lesson was a flop. To myself I said, 'The Moslems [sic] do better.' Total abstinence from alcohol is commanded in Islam."[22] That opportunity to differentiate herself from her Anglican foster family by taking a moralistic stand and facing opposition for it was something Gerard would practise over and over. The exercise continued well beyond her teenaged years, into her career in ministry, and especially during her foray into municipal politics.

In her autobiography, Gerard reflected on the conundrum that she was facing as her religious convictions collided with her caregivers' expectations of her. As she so aptly put it, "Christ is the great problem solver – but Christ was my problem."[23] The conflict that ensued between Gerard, her foster family, and her guardian was a clash of convictions. "How to stay true to Christ and still please my guardian and the people with whom I lived was a problem impossible of solution. What I believed to be Christian consecration, they thought was narrow-mindedness. They were apparently sincere and so was I."[24] Sincerity and conviction were hallmarks of Gerard's youth. Later in life she did some self-reflection to ask whether she might have been more flexible. "As I look back on it all, I see that in my immaturity I was too certain of the do's and don'ts of Christian living. What exactly was gained or lost, to this day I cannot say with surety, but at the time I was sure that if I gave in on one point and then another, the testimony of a separated Christian life would be lost, and maybe I would be lost too."[25]

While Gerard said she couldn't be sure what was gained or lost in her wilful battles with the adult caregivers in her life, it seems obvious that what she was gaining from her inflexible convictions was a sense of security and a religious identity that tied her firmly to Pentecostalism. By insisting that she was not like her liberal-minded Anglican foster family or her inclusive but controlling United Church guardian, Gerard was carving out and reinforcing the boundary markers of the Pentecostal subculture she had joined. She was staking her claim to a secure identity. Introducing ambiguity, flexibility, or open-mindedness at that stage of her religious development would have only introduced confusion when she was seeking clear and definite boundaries.[26] Given the turmoil of her youth, where she lived in so many different households before she was removed from her abuser by the child welfare authorities, and eight more addresses afterward, it is no wonder that young Bernice was attracted to a belief system with clear boundaries, where her strict adherence to it could give her a sense of stability and control. The fact that Gerard clashed with her caregivers should be read as more than just a battle of wills. Her inflexible convictions indicate that she was reinforcing her fledgling religious identity by rejecting the tempting enticements held out to her by her host family, who patiently tried to encourage her to attend school dances, learn to drink in moderation, enjoy cultural events, and adopt the norms of middle-class respectability.

There were many times when Gerard felt conflicted over these things, including the episode of a year-end party for her high school public-speaking club, the year that she was president. After the banquet, she left the party early to avoid the dance that followed, given her conviction that dancing was wrong. On a lonely streetcar ride home, Gerard was filled with inner turmoil. "Most of the boys and girls I had just left were from good families. Their dress was better than mine. There was no question about their background. They had good reputations and most of them if asked would have said, 'Yes, I am a Christian.' Could it be that I was mistaken? Was I making life harder for myself by tenaciously clinging to strange, narrow-minded ideas?"[27] On these occasions, she did feel tempted by the chance for social acceptance among her peers, but she shunned behaviours that she still associated with the excesses and abuses she had experienced in the Gerard home. She went on to describe a soul-searching

FIGURE 3.2 Gerard was thrilled to learn that secondary school education was a priority within the child welfare system because her adoptive father did not value education for girls and attendance beyond elementary school was still a minority experience for rural students; it signalled Gerard was joining the urban middle class. | *Summit Pacific College, Hudson Memorial Library, Bernice Gerard Nielson Family Scrapbook.*

night of tearful prayer where she tried to settle her doubts by reasserting her faith and asking for direction. While time in prayer reassured Gerard that she was on the right path by taking and reinforcing her position of consecration, the objections from her foster family did not ease up.

Muriel Hudson was relentless in critiquing the choices Gerard was making. After she graduated from high school, Gerard took one year of university and then began her teacher training education at the Vancouver Normal School. Because she refused to attend school or community dances and preferred the company of young adults from the Pentecostal and Holiness Movement churches, "Mrs. H. prophesied that I would be an old maid – an unhappy old maid! Furthermore she declared that it was impossible for me to be a good school teacher as long as I held to my old-fashioned ideas."[28] While Gerard may not have cared much about the absence of romantic prospects, the comment that she would not be an effective educator was a stinging blow. Having met several friends at Normal School who shared her conservative

Christian beliefs, Gerard was finding affirmation there and her career aspirations were evolving. "My vision of preaching the gospel in country schoolhouses had given way to a more dazzling picture of a young career woman with an excellent position and a high salary."[29]

The fact that Gerard had her sights set on a career in education provided her a way out from under the relentless control of her foster family and her guardian. She was still dependent on the provincial authorities for the funds to attend Normal School training. In August 1942 the principal at Lord Byng

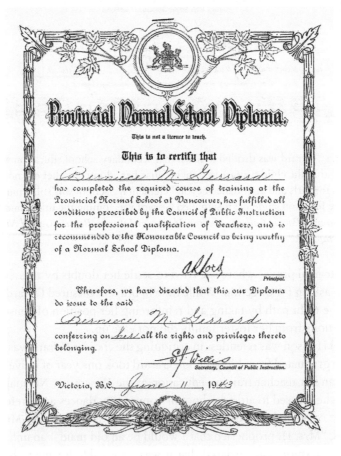

FIGURE 3.3 Because Gerard was pursuing her teacher training during the Second World War, she was recruited to a teaching job even before she had completed the course. | *Summit Pacific College, Hudson Memorial Library, Bernice Gerard Nielson Family Scrapbook.*

Secondary School wrote a letter of support recommending Gerard as an ideal and deserving candidate to receive financial assistance saying, "We have come to know her as a very earnest student, with really good ability. She has entered fully into the work of the school in every possible way ... I have no hesitation in recommending her as a very promising student."[30] On the strength of that reference, Gerard enrolled in the Provincial Normal School for the 1942–43 academic year.

However, Gerard's teacher training would be cut short, partly due to the wartime context of a provincial shortage of teachers, and partly because of a conflict she encountered with the child welfare authorities. In the spring of 1943, when she was nineteen years old and set to "age out" of the child welfare system upon completion of her education, Gerard was presented with an unexpected opportunity. After a dramatic clash with her foster family when she had defied their wishes by attending evangelistic street meetings in downtown Vancouver, where she sang, testified, and preached, Gerard was called to Isobel Harvey's office.

> She wasted no time in getting to the point. I was hardly in the door and seated when she addressed a question to me and then continued talking without waiting for my answer. "What's this I hear about you, down there on the street corner spouting like a soap box orator? Do you think you need a university education to go down and talk to the drunks? Is that what you think I am educating you for?" She made it sound low and vulgar. I appeared to be the most ungrateful wretch alive.[31]

Harvey did not let up, making very personal accusations about how Gerard was squandering the investment that had been made in her.

> You have had wonderful opportunities and I have seen to it that you have had everything you needed. I promised you all the education you could absorb and now I find you using it down on the street corner with vulgar people. With all I have done for you, I asked only one thing of you and that one thing you would not do. I did not ask you to give up religion. I only asked that you follow after a faith that would be more in keeping with intelligence and culture.[32]

The tirade continued,

> I hear that you do well in your psychology studies. I suggest that you try a little introspection. Look into your own mind and examine your mental and emotional

processes. Find out what makes you think and act as you do. When your academic record and your social adjustments are good, why do you have to spoil it all by insisting on going to some mission hall? Why can't you worship God in a mighty church where, as the organ peals out its anthem, you walk down the carpeted aisle, kneel and pray, then quietly arise and go? ... But you have to go to a little church where they pump your hand at the door and say, "God bless you, we are so glad to have you. Will you sing a solo today?" Is it because you have to be the big toad in the puddle?[33]

Exasperated, Harvey did not want to hear Gerard speak in her own defence, and she did not hold out any more chances for resolving their differences. Instead, she made it clear that Gerard had defied her one time too many. With a tone of finality, she exclaimed, "You are through! I have done all I am going to do. You can get out and earn your own living at the first opportunity."[34]

Shocked by the outburst, dejected by the criticism, and sent out the door, Gerard had some soul-searching to do. "Feeling somewhat like the little orphan girl back in the country,"[35] she wondered whether she should go back, apologize, and try to make amends. But again, she could not fathom making a compromise about her religious convictions. So she prayed as she boarded the streetcar, but she did not get an answer to her prayer. "I heard no voice and felt no unusual impression," she recounted. Instead, she recalled a recent church youth meeting where she had made a commitment to serve God wholeheartedly. "I had stood with my hand raised, singing, 'Take the whole world but give me Jesus. I'll not turn back. I'll not turn back.' I had my answer."[36] Gerard's resolve not to turn her back on Jesus was unshakable. But when forced to make a choice, her conviction meant that she could turn her back on the child welfare system – not on her faith.

Just as God had made a way for her to leave the Gerard home, she was filled with gratitude for the next surprising turn of events. Gerard told her Christian friends at the Normal School about how disappointed Mrs. Hudson had been with her at the news that Isobel Harvey was cutting her losses. The situation had reduced "Mrs. H." to a rare display of affection as she cried and accused Bernice of squandering her opportunities. "I treated you as my own daughter. Now I hear you spend your spare time with the drunks in the down-and-out section of the city."[37] Gerard's friends had a different take on the circumstances, assuring her that "nobody ever made a sacrifice for the Lord but that He generously repaid them" and that, as Romans 8:28 promised, "all things work together for good for those who love God and are called according to His purpose."[38] In Gerard's case, that "repayment" came in the form of an early teaching placement, with a good salary.

Gerard's teenaged living arrangements were varied, and so were her religious experiences. She had the opportunity to appreciate the beauty of the Okanagan Valley and to enjoy its bounty and nutritional variety with fruit and vegetables growing at her doorstep. She noted with gratitude the contrast to her earlier home life where, as a small child, she had consumed more than her share of beans and coffee.[39] But she also knew and appreciated the diversity of city life in Vancouver, because she had first-hand experience of its privileges and its hardships. She was very familiar with places where the displaced and desperate tried to find community, from an orphanage and a child welfare receiving home, to downtown street meetings where religious enthusiasts held out hope to the ragtag crowds who gathered to listen to them. But Bernice Gerard spent most of her high school years in some of Vancouver's most privileged neighbourhoods, where she attended Lord Byng Secondary School and worshipped with her middle-class foster families and caseworkers in the imposing architecture of liturgical churches. She thrived in school and regularly took the streetcar downtown to meet with her guardian in an office at the Vancouver Court House. Sometimes she also sneaked downtown to participate in street meetings hosted by her Pentecostal friends, defying her caregivers' strict instructions as they tried to redirect her religious enthusiasm.

Before she reached the age of twenty, having lived in two institutional settings and a variety of foster families, Gerard was a self-confident, young teacher, grateful for the support she had received but far from deferential. Her strong personality reflected her own resilience, honed by all that she had been through, but it was also shored up by her religious convictions. As she navigated through her tumultuous teen years, Bernice Gerard framed her identity in religious terms. She worked out her changing beliefs, reflected deeply on the adults who were guiding her (especially what they believed), and whether she shared their views or not. Sorry to disappoint some of them, eager to learn from the kindest of them, and adamant to defy some others, Gerard emerged as a self-assured young woman who was confident about what she believed and how to take a stand even when it was unpopular. From the wide-eyed schoolgirl under the narrow influence of the Two by Twos and their exclusionary world view to a young professional who was unabashedly Pentecostal, Gerard navigated her teen years with a combative and robust religiosity that defined her sense of self.

Because of the wartime shortage, Normal School students were being placed in teaching jobs even before they had completed the full training. The best placements were awarded based on academic performance in the program and with her outstanding record, Gerard was offered an enviable job in Rossland, British Columbia, filling a vacancy in a large elementary school. When the principal of the Normal School told her of the opportunity, Gerard did not hesitate to send her application by telegram, and the Rossland principal wasted no time with his reply.[40] Before she knew it, Bernice Gerard was on a train out of Vancouver, leaving behind her caregivers and her ties to the provincial child welfare system. What came next would only serve to solidify her religious identity and clarify her life calling.

Chapter 4

FINDING FAMILY

As soon as she stepped inside the door of her new boarding house as Rossland's newest schoolteacher in 1943, Gerard started grilling her land-lady about her options for finding a suitable church. The list of local churches was long, and Gerard recounts that she assumed the woman was starting with the most "respectable" ones as she rhymed off a long list of "the dry, formal churches." Her hostess was a churchwoman herself, and it is probable that she assumed the young teacher, as a newly trained middle-class professional, would share her views about respectable religion. "No doubt she thought she was starting at the top of the list and going down," Gerard recalls, but "I felt she was starting at the bottom and going up."[1] But when the list was exhausted, Gerard had not heard what she was hoping to hear. With her new-found independence, Gerard was looking for a Pentecostal congregation where she could find like-minded believers and worship freely, now that she was out from under the control of Isobel Harvey and her Anglican foster parents. When Gerard asked if there were any other churches, the landlady told her about the local "tabernacle," with a pair of young women served as pastors in Rossland, with a weekly broadcast on the radio station in nearby Trail, British Columbia. Right away, Gerard knew that she had found the right recommendation – these must be Pentecostal women!

In the spring of 1943, Bernice Gerard was about to be introduced to two women who would welcome her into their home, their ministry work, and their lives, giving her a firm sense of belonging. When she met Jean and Velma McColl, Gerard found a family to be part of, and a lifelong professional association. For the next fifteen years, Gerard would travel with the McColl sisters, establishing her organizational credentials with the largest Pentecostal denominations in North America. That base thrust Gerard onto the international stage and from there, she established a global network of Pentecostal contacts. In her partnership with the McColls, Gerard found a sense of family and stability that had eluded her for the first twenty years of her life. She grew so close to Jean and Velma that she called their parents "Dad" and "Mother."[2] At the same time, she solidified her professional and religious identity by committing to a brand of Pentecostalism known as "classical Pentecostalism," which would prove to be a large and enduring movement. As a young adult in her twenties, she expanded her life experiences and her world view, all while building an international reputation in Pentecostal leadership. When she joined with the McColl sisters, Gerard's soul-searching about who she really was and to whom she belonged was settled once and for all.

Being assigned to teach in the school at Rossland was a wonderful opportunity for Gerard, an unexpected perk for new teacher who had technically not even finished her Normal School training. The wartime employment teacher shortage meant that when posts became available, the provincial authorities looked to the Normal School to help them fill the need. Placements were assigned based on academic merit, and because Gerard was at the top of her class, she was offered this very attractive job. The MacLean Elementary School in Rossland, where she stepped into a classroom just two months before the end of the school year, was not typical of small rural Canadian schools in this period.[3] This three-storey school building housed approximately 350 students in multiple grades and a staff of twelve teachers plus the principal. With this teaching assignment, Gerard was not being sent to the backwaters of a rural settlement or a remote, isolated one-room schoolhouse like the one she had attended in her first years of schooling. Instead, she was assigned to a class of thirty-two students, all in the same grade. With approximately eight weeks remaining in the 1942–43 school year when she arrived, she joined an experienced staff as the replacement for a colleague who had to leave before the school year ended.[4]

The other attractive thing about Gerard's new teaching placement was Rossland itself, a West Kootenay mining community that had grown from a tiny settlement to a prosperous town. The local economy was based on gold mining, with a colourful history stretching back more than fifty years to the first prospectors who staked their claims in 1890.[5] At its height, the city boasted a population of seven thousand people with a thriving commercial centre. With a cycle of boom and bust tied to the mining industry, Rossland's population

Figure 4.1 Gerard taught briefly during the Second World War at the MacLean Elementary School, in Rossland, BC, a prosperous community because of the well-paid mining jobs in nearby Trail, BC. | *Summit Pacific College, Hudson Memorial Library, Bernice Gerard Nielson Family Scrapbook.*

fell to around three thousand in the 1930s, but its security had been assured because of the Canadian Mining and Smelting Company of Canada (Cominco) smelter that was built in nearby Trail. Rossland served as a residential town for workers in Trail employed by Cominco. The young teacher was joining a community populated by labouring families who shared her sense of adventure and opportunity. But industry and education were not the only forums for innovation in Rossland: religion was another.

When Gerard first met the pair of female pastors at the tabernacle in Rossland, she encountered two experienced preachers, musicians, and travelling evangelists. Jean and Velma McColl hailed from Regina, Saskatchewan, where their family was part of the Apostolic Mission, affiliated with a form of Pentecostalism known as "Oneness" because of its emphasis on baptisms performed in the name of "Jesus Only" rather than the more common trinitarian theology shared by most Christian traditions.[6] Like other Pentecostal groups in the period, the Apostolic Church of Pentecost welcomed women as preachers and travelling evangelists, endorsing them by granting the "Worker's Licence." This licence, to be renewed annually, certified that women like Jean and Velma McColl were endowed with the authority to "preach the gospel and to perform

FIGURE 4.2 *Left to right:* Velma, Jean, and Bernice. The McColl-Gerard Trio, formed when Gerard volunteered at the church that Jean and Velma McColl started in Rossland, distributed souvenir postcards like this one to those who attended their meetings. | *Author's personal collection, with thanks to Margaret Kechnie.*

such duties that are authorized under this license."[7] The duties that licenced workers were authorized to perform did not include marriages or baptisms, functions that were usually reserved for male ministers with a higher level of certification for ministry.[8] But in spite of these limitations, women like Jean and Velma McColl were valued as popular performers who drew sizable audiences wherever they ministered. Since 1935, the McColl sisters had been holding meetings in various western towns and cities. In Saskatchewan they held their events in Regina, North Battleford, Saskatoon, Rouleau, Swift Current, Indian Head, Mossbank, Estevan, Yorkton, Melfort, Nipawin, Kipling, Kincaid, Hodgeville, Stalwart, and Heward. In Alberta, they had publicized meetings in Edmonton and Calgary. And in British Columbia, they sang and preached in Nelson, Rossland, and Victoria.

Promotional materials for these meetings reinforce the fact that travelling evangelists like Jean and Velma McColl used methods that were common among others in the evangelism business, including handbills, newspaper ads, and press releases.[9] Billed as "Girl Evangelists" who were "singers, musicians, and preachers," the McColls were widely recognized because they had "preached to packed houses from here [Saskatchewan] to the Coast."[10] The copy supplied to local newspapers to promote the McColl sisters' meetings was printed by the Apostolic Mission in Regina, and although meetings were planned for particular dates, usually one week in length, it was common for the meetings to be held over for extended periods when the response was positive.[11] That extended stay is precisely what happened when the McColls visited Rossland in 1940. Due to popular demand, the meetings they began holding in the hall of the local Orange Lodge were extended and moved to a larger venue to accommodate the crowds. Eventually the sisters were persuaded to stay on indefinitely to pastor a new church formed by the followers they attracted. Their sojourn in Rossland turned out to be a five-year stay.[12] In part this longevity may have been a business decision, given the fact that wartime travel became more difficult with the introduction of gas and rubber rationing and restrictions on nonessential travel.

But at the same time Rossland presented good opportunities for growth. The prosperity that residents of Rossland and nearby Trail enjoyed meant that establishing a new church that could support two pastors was financially viable. The McColls chose wisely when they selected Rossland as their new home base because congregants employed in the mining sector were well paid, and that economic stability meant the women could give up their itinerant lifestyle for a more settled one. As Gerard's landlady explained to her when they were discussing church options in area, "The people at that Tabernacle believe in tithing ... When you tithe you give one tenth of your income to the church. They all tithe and most of the men work at the Canadian Mining and Smelting Company, where they get big wages. You can imagine how much money those girls take in!"[13]

Before long, the McColls were collecting a tithe from the new teacher too, as Bernice Gerard became very involved in their church. By the second month of her stay, Gerard's landlady refunded part of her monthly room and board fees explaining, "this month you lived more with the McColl sisters than you did with me."[14] The importance of Gerard's relationship with the McColls cannot be overstated. She described it saying, "In Rossland a new life unfolded to me. There was an immediate bond of comradeship between the McColl sisters and me."[15] As they ministered in the local church in Rossland and did their weekly radio broadcasts together, Jean and Velma McColl quickly recognized what an asset Gerard was to their work. First, she was a skilled public speaker who had honed those skills at Lord Byng Secondary School as president of the school's public-speaking club[16] and then enhanced her ability further with her education to become a teacher. Second, she had an incredibly compelling testimony to recount about her life and faith journey. Gerard was a consummate storyteller and she recounted her life experiences in a dramatic fashion, with humour and candour. And finally, Gerard was musical – quickly picking up various instruments and lending her unusual "lady baritone" singing voice to their live performances at meetings. With Gerard on board, the McColls saw another opportunity for their evangelism enterprise: they recorded their music and distributed records under the label "The McColl-Gerard Trio." Together, they formed a formidable team and when the war eventually ended, the three soulmates would embark on a remarkable series of travel adventures.

But even at the height of the war, Jean, Velma, and Bernice enjoyed a busy schedule of ministry together. In addition to their regular work leading weekly services at the tabernacle, the McColls were radio preachers with a regular broadcast on CJAT, the Trail radio station. Their broadcasts followed a half-hour format, and after Gerard joined them, the programs featured each of the three women by making use of their individual gifts: "Miss Jean and her usual cheery 'Hello' ... the 'Comfort Corner,' the special feature for the shut-ins, then Miss Velma said 'goodbye,'" but first the listeners enjoyed "'Pulpit Proverbs,' with Bernice Gerard in the pulpit – the special feature for those who enjoy a laugh mixed with a little truth."[17] By the 1940s, radio had become a common medium for religious broadcasters and the McColls were in step with some other more well-known preachers who capitalized on the potential of radio to reach listeners in remote and rural locations.[18] Gerard's deep voice made her a natural for radio work and she enjoyed the ministry apprenticeship working with the McColls, learning from them how to put together an entertaining mix of music, inspiration, and preaching.

As a teacher with the summer months free, Gerard had planned to continue her education with additional course work, but her ministry involvement with the McColl-Gerard Trio proved to be a distraction. Devoting her weekends and evenings to volunteer ministry work throughout the school year, Gerard used her summers to join the McColls as they took their ministry farther afield, holding meetings first within British Columbia and eventually branching out much farther. The women made their way to the Maritimes, where they stopped along the way to perform and preach in various communities who welcomed their Pentecostal meetings as a means of promoting revival among local populations and growing their fledgling congregations. For Gerard, this travel expanded her world as she saw the rest of the country for the first time. But it also broadened her experience of Pentecostalism. In New Brunswick, she and the McColls were hosted by another pair of sisters who were twins, Carro and Susie Davis, of Saint John, New Brunswick. The Davises were the pastors of the Full Gospel Assembly of Saint John, the largest Pentecostal church east of

Montreal. Originally from Macon, Georgia, the Davis sisters first established themselves in New Brunswick when they travelled to and led a series of Pentecostal evangelistic meetings across the province in the early 1920s. In 1924 they settled in Saint John, establishing a church where they continued to lead a large congregation for the next four decades.[19] In her autobiography, Gerard recalled that watching these older women who "had pioneered Pentecostal ministry and seen many hundreds come to God, I was wide-eyed and eager to learn."[20] She described the Davis sisters as "women of charm and dignity, shining examples of what the Lord can do with consecrated women."[21]

The Davises were recognized not only for their long-term service, but for influencing and encouraging dozens of younger people to enter the ministry. Most of those they mentored were men, but they had a significant influence on Gerard as well. She recounts, "My part in the meetings was to sing, pray and share my testimony: how, when and where I found faith, and what it took for me to keep it."[22] Encouraging Gerard's youthful enthusiasm and recognizing her giftedness, Susie and Carro did not hesitate to declare that they knew God had a plan for Gerard's life. "The Davis sisters, whose main concern in life was God's harvest field, were sure I should go into the full-time ministry of evangelism. 'The call of the Lord is on your life,' they said confidently."[23] The idea was common among Pentecostals that other people might know, better than (or before) you knew yourself, what your life calling was supposed to be. Indeed, part of the emphasis on spiritual gifting included an understanding that some people had the gift of "discernment" or the gift of "knowledge" that made them privy to the details of God's will for other people. This teaching, taken to its extreme, would lead to controversy among Canadian Pentecostals in the 1940s, but it was a common practice for Pentecostal leaders with social capital and established authority to make pronouncements about other people's futures.[24] Even though the Davis sisters expressed with certainty that Bernice Gerard should give up teaching for a full-time career as a Pentecostal minister, Gerard was not convinced. Indeed, she reflected back on that prediction many years later, remembering, "I was far from sure, notwithstanding that they [the Davises] knew Aimee Semple McPherson personally, and had experience in discerning directions for people's lives."[25] Evidently, the Davises were not alone in their recognition of Gerard's giftedness for public ministry because several others predicted the same future for her. "Over and over again preachers with whom we worked [that summer] expressed surprise that I was going back to school teaching, when we were so effective as an evangelistic team."[26] This kind of endorsement helped Gerard to feel like she really belonged in Pentecostal circles. Although she recalled that she did not feel as sure about

FIGURE 4.3 In addition to their preaching, part of the attraction of the McColl-Gerard Trio was their musicality because the women sang and played a variety of instruments. Velma McColl (*left*) is pictured here with Gerard, circa 1950. | *Summit Pacific College, Hudson Memorial Library, Bernice Gerard Nielson Family Scrapbook.*

her calling as the Davises did, no doubt the suggestion about her potential was affirming for the young woman who had always described herself as an "unwanted child."[27]

With the first teaching experiences in Rossland behind her and feeling accepted and affirmed by the McColls and the cross-country Pentecostal circles in which they moved, Gerard felt ready to start exploring questions about her own family of origin. Believing that her mother had died in childbirth, Gerard began to piece together some clues about her genealogy. Shortly after she arrived in Rossland, Gerard had a visit from Isobel Harvey, who was touring through the area in her role as provincial superintendent of child welfare. Unlike their heated argument in Harvey's office, this encounter was a pleasant one. Gerard remembers that she took the opportunity to thank Harvey once again for all that she had done for her. It must have been a proud moment for the social worker, to see one of her charges who had become a successful young teaching professional. In a brief conversation while the students were on the school playground, Harvey used her training in Freudian psychology to broach the sensitive subject of Gerard's adoption.

> She asked me if I had any idea who my own parents were, saying "You have been rather bitter about your adoption, haven't you? You have been troubled with a feeling of inferiority because you don't know who your parents are." I admitted that was true. Then she said, "I want to assure you that you have no reason to feel bitter or inferior. I am sure your parents were of good stock. It was likely tragedy that separated you from them. Why don't you try to get in touch with them?" She asked if I knew where my adoption papers were drawn up. I said, "Yes. The name of the lawyer was Sullivan. The papers were drawn up in New Westminster." She encouraged me to write to the lawyer, tell him my adoption was a failure, and ask for help in finding my natural parents.[28]

Making this suggestion shows another side to Harvey, displaying much more compassion than Gerard had attributed to her previously. Perhaps Harvey was still hoping that finding her family might help Gerard toward psychological healing and maybe lead her to abandon Pentecostalism for a more respectable expression of her faith. But given Gerard's new life stage as a teaching professional, Harvey's influence was limited to a friendly suggestion rather than a directive to be followed.

Gerard was open to the idea and after Harvey's prompt, she decided to act. She recalled an earlier suggestion from a high school classmate who revealed that her boyfriend, a serviceman, found an uncanny resemblance between Bernice and another woman close in age, originally from northern British Columbia. He wondered if by chance this woman might be related to Bernice. Although it seemed like a long shot, Gerard decided to follow up on the clues because the surname her friend told her did match the family name listed on her adoption papers, and she remembered the name of the New Westminster law firm on those documents she had sneaked a glance at in Leo Gerard's home more than ten years earlier. She wrote two letters: one to Joyce Nielson, whom her friend suspected might be a relation, and one to the adoption lawyer.

To her great delight, not one but three of her siblings wrote back! Confirming that they were indeed sisters, Joyce Nielson, then living in Victoria, British Columbia, was about to get married and she invited Bernice to be a bridesmaid. A brother, Fred Nielson, then serving in the air force, also wrote. A third sibling, Violet, wrote from her address in Vancouver, just a few blocks from where Gerard had lived. Unexpectedly, she also received a telegram from her birth father with a simple but profound message: "Welcome back to the family. Hope we can make up for lost time. Love, Dad."[29] Eventually she heard from other siblings too, and as she recounted in her autobiography, "Each member of the family wrote telling about themselves and their experiences. I was thrilled to know my Father, brothers, and sisters. It was the fulfillment of a wonderful dream."[30] Gerard wrote back to her long-lost family members. "In my letters to them, I rejoiced over my good fortune in finding them and told them about myself. I could not omit an important point: everything good I have is mine because I said 'Yes' to Christ."[31] Even as she grafted a new network of relations into her life, Gerard was careful to introduce herself to them through the lens of her religious identity. Belonging to Christ came first for her, and in her mind every good blessing in her life flowed from there, including the sense of belonging she would forge with the birth family she had not known for the first twenty years of her life.

In her first autobiography, Gerard ends the mention of finding her family on that happy note – that she was finally reunited with siblings and her father, all of whom were eager to meet her. But that was far from the end of the story. Of course, there was a great deal of catching up to do, and when Gerard described in her second autobiography that on finding her siblings and her father she had been "breathless with the excitement of it all,"[32] she also recounted that she was in for a very big surprise. It was her brother, Fred, who introduced her to the family story; she "hung on his every word."[33] Her real curiosity, understandably, was about her mother. Gerard asked her brother to say more about how their mother had died. She was shocked to learn the truth: her birth mother was not dead! Ada Nielson was a long-term patient at the Provincial Mental Hospital, Essondale (later renamed Riverview Hospital), located in Coquitlam. Fred explained, "Mother has been a patient in the psychiatric hospital at Essondale all these years, even more years than you have lived. She was in and out before she was pregnant with you, and in fact was hospitalized even while she was carrying you."[34] The mental health facility was close to the hospital where Bernice had been born, and that is where Mrs. Nielson spent most of her adult life, what Gerard referred to in her autobiography as "a total of almost forty lonely institutionalized years."[35]

Finding Family

To explain how their mother ended up as a long-term mental health patient, Fred recounted that their family had been living in the Peace River District of British Columbia, where the Nielsons owned and operated the Mile Zero Hotel in Dawson Creek, twelve hundred kilometres north of Vancouver. "Fred told me all he could of our family's life in northern British Columbia: Dad had been a telegraph operator, away from home a great deal, Mother bore six children in eight years, and with most of the deliveries she had only an Indian midwife to help her. Life was harsh; the burdens and the loneliness were too much for Swedish-born Ada Nielson to bear."[36] The Nielson family would have quickly run out of options to delay Ada's committal, particularly given the ages of the children, and the nature of Mr. Nielson's work which necessitated frequent travel. But perhaps the most important factor was their remote location.

In 1930, a relative newcomer to the area described Dawson Creek as "a tiny row of shanties, which is expected before the end of this year to blow out into the new *railway terminus* [italics in original]. When that happens, Fort St. John will be only sixty miles [97 km] from the train and we shall be suburban indeed!"[37] Monica Storrs, an Anglican missionary who worked in the Peace River District during the late 1920s and 1930s, wrote a memoir about life in that region. To accomplish her work Storrs travelled, most commonly by horseback, to various settlements in the Peace River District and her account makes clear that the conditions were primitive and challenging. Beyond that general description of life in the north, Storrs makes direct references to the Nielson family. Storrs used the local schoolhouse as the venue for her children's meetings, and because she depended on local residents to help her with logistics including getting the fire started and helping with set up, she describes the Nielson family in her memoir. Mr. Nielson was a school trustee. On one occasion, Storrs recorded her disappointment when, after walking seven miles (11 km; about two-and-one-half hours) in the cold, she arrived to find

> the little school was in a horrible messy condition and of course *icy* cold, and fearfully short of seats – only in fact about twelve desks, several of them small and one or two broken – and there were books and papers and piles of litter all over the table and in every corner. I cleared up as well as I could and then called on the nearest trustee (an agnostic Swede) and got him to promise that the fire should be lighted an hour beforehand on Sunday, and a couple of planks put in for seats.[38]

It is clear that the agnostic Swede[39] Storrs referred to was Gerard's birth father because the details of his life match Bernice's birth family completely: Nielson had two daughters named Joyce and Violet who participated in the Girl Guide meetings Storrs arranged; Nielson was employed as a telegraph operator; and in 1929, Nielson's wife was in an asylum. Storrs also reveals that Nielson coped with his wife's absence by hiring a housekeeper to manage the domestic work and child care for the four youngsters under his roof.[40] The coincidence of all these details confirms that this was, indeed, the birth family of Bernice Gerard.

Storrs gives further insight into community life as she recounts how important social occasions were to collective well-being as they served to break the monotony of isolation. For example, a simple evening of card playing was worthy to be recorded in detail. An evening whist drive, planned by the women's auxiliary of the Anglican church eight miles (13 km) away, was talked about for weeks to come.[41] Yet that happy occasion would have been out of reach for a young mother like Ada Nielson, with her babies and young children under foot and her husband absent for weeks at a time. Storrs describes in some detail the typical living conditions of Peace River settlements in these years – the isolation, the pioneer conditions, and the harsh climate realities that provide context about Ada Nielson's life before she was removed and committed to the asylum.

A 1934 description of the Peace River area's access to technologies reveals that some people had "certain devices which help to break down the isolation of newly settled areas, such as the telephone, the automobile, and the radio," but only 13 percent had access to telephones, and only 17 percent were equipped with radios.[42] Even the most optimistic promoters of settlement in the area admitted that "disillusionment" with the hardships of settlement was a very real concern, and a government-commissioned study of the region ended with the sobering reality "that [some] men and women fail and are weeded out in the rigorous selection of the settlement process is all too evident."[43] Ada Nielson's mental illness, in the midst of this isolated setting, was exacerbated (or perhaps caused?) by the demanding reproductive and domestic work she performed, but she would have been, in the assessment of that writer, a "failure" who was "weeded out" of the settler life.

Historians who have written about British Columbia's provincial mental health facility emphasize that families used the institution as a means of coping with mental illness.[44] The Provincial Mental Hospital, where Ada Nielson lived most of her adult life, is the subject of work by historian Megan J. Davies, who explores the experiences of female patients at the provincial facility from 1920 to 1935. Davies uses case files to establish that women's own perceptions about why they were placed at the facility often differed sharply from the medical and social work professionals who recorded their cases. In the case of "Nellie," doctors deemed her to be a difficult patient because she resisted conforming to the daily routines expected of her. The patient saw herself differently, asserting that she just needed some rest and good nutrition, but it is clear that her husband was the one with the power to make decisions about her care because he signed her out of the facility against her wishes and those of her caregivers.[45] Although we do not know how Nielson felt about her admission to Essondale, it is clear that her husband would have been the one to decide what was in her best interest, and as Bernice's brother explained, Ada made repeat visits to the facility, punctuated by releases and time spent with the family at her husband's discretion. Thus, their mother was admitted to the asylum while she was pregnant with Bernice, because their father determined that she was not coping well as the primary caregiver to their children.

Ada Nielson's experience was in line with that of other female patients at insane asylums whose families decided on their behalf that they needed to be in care. But reaching that decision could not have been easy. Historian Wendy Mitchinson argues that families used mental health institutions when they could no longer safely cope with a person's violence, excitement, depression, or delusions, and she concludes that provincial facilities in southern Ontario offered families a solution to an unmanageable situation when the safety of either the patient or that of other family and community members was at stake.[46] While there is no evidence to suggest that Ada Nielson was violent, it is quite possible that she was depleted by her reproductive work and unable to cope with the demands of motherhood in a frontier setting. Location is one important difference when comparing Nielson's case to those in Toronto, where the asylum "catered to those who could conveniently use it" because of geographic proximity.[47] Northeastern British Columbia in the 1920s was a different story. Although it was hardly "convenient," Nielson was separated from her husband and children on the long-held assumption that "environment was partially responsible for the mental disorder and that removal to a new, controlled environment was the first step towards recovery."[48] Environment probably does serve to explain Nielson's breakdown, but without access to her case record it is impossible to know exactly how her symptoms manifested. Seeking admission to the psychiatric hospital was usually a decision made solely by the family, and given the Nielson family's isolated setting, it is highly probable that expert opinion came only after her husband recognized that for her own safety and the safety of their children, Ada needed professional help.[49] It is safe to assume that her husband's difficult decision to place her in the provincial facility was probably motivated by some combination of love and pragmatism.

While medical professionals and rural sociologists in the 1930s made their assessments about why some people managed to thrive and others failed as settlers in the Peace River District, negative attitudes toward people who succumbed to their mental illness persisted for decades afterward. Well into the 1980s, Gerard reported that her birth family was still operating in silence about Ada Nielson's condition, prompting a younger family member to ask the difficult question, "Why [is] everyone so secretive about Grandmother Nielson?" Although Gerard did not presume to speak for the whole family, she wrote, "I know why it took *me* so many years to establish a relationship with my own neglected mother and I will answer it now: I was frightened. When fear takes over, we behave irrationally."[50]

Irrational fear meant that Gerard could not bring herself to meet her mother right away, even though she attempted a visit in 1945. Gerard was very candid about her own prejudices, writing,

> God knows how I wanted to see her! ... With old wives' tales about mental illness cluttering my mind, bravely bearing my anxieties, I arrived at the psychiatric hospital, and began the long walk up the pathway to the big grey structure with its many barred windows. Some patients were looking out, and I thought I heard some shouting. To this day all I remember then is that my stomach was churning and it seemed impossible to go on; I was too frightened. I covered up my defeat by saying, "Maybe it is better not to know. Maybe it is just too sad, and no one can do anything to help."[51]

Bernice tried again ten years later, with a bit more maturity and the reassuring presence of her friend and former social worker Wini Urquhart at her side. Gerard describes that emotional meeting: "Small and gentle, very quiet, there she stood! At last, I embraced my mother. By that time, she was so thoroughly institutionalized that she was more comfortable in her own familiar surroundings than anywhere else."[52] From that initial meeting until her mother's death a few years later, Gerard visited often, reading to Ada after her eyesight failed, singing, praying, and comforting her.

Whether Ada Nielson was damaged or helped by the provincial care system is a matter of interpretation, but when they finally came to know each other, Bernice recognized that "in those brief years before her death, the reality of knowing and loving my mother face to face, did much to heal my inner person of the wounds of childhood."[53] No doubt Gerard's empathy for her mother's institutionalization was rendered more intense because of her own encounters with state agencies including adoption authorities, the provincial orphanage, and the network of child welfare systems, especially foster care. When she first learned about her mother's situation as a patient at Essondale, Gerard recounted, "That night I cried and cried, and finally drifted off to fitful sleep weeping for my mother."[54] In part those tears were probably linked to the relief of settling a nagging insecurity; until she found her birth family and learned about her mother's situation, Gerard had lived with the shame and rejection that were heaped on children born outside of wedlock. Thinking that she was an "illegitimate child" had weighed her down for years because the unsolved mystery of her family origin led her to believe that she had been born as a "mistake" resulting from a sexual relationship that was not condoned by respectable society in the early twentieth century.

Gerard's comments on her attitudes to mental health are thoughtful, compassionate, and reflective as she wrote, "Why did I not get to my mother's side sooner to kiss her cheek, pat her hand, help her learn to read again, sing with her, pray with her and comfort her? Because the monster of fear and ignorance that plagued my understanding and hindered my compassion needed to be unmasked."[55] That self-reflection reveals a deep level of maturity and the profound depth of compassion that would come to characterize Gerard's ministry among society's outcasts. But that inner growth was years in the making and over the next ten years of her life, Gerard would focus more on external performance in the ever-expanding circles of Pentecostalism she encountered with her full-time career as part of a dynamic travelling trio.

Chapter 5

THE McCOLL-GERARD TRIO
AND PROFESSIONAL BELONGING

BERNICE GERARD MARVELLED at how her life in ministry unfolded. She reminisced, "When Jean, Velma and I began singing together in Rossland, we did not imagine what distant places in the world our melodies would travel."[1] Gerard's networks expanded and her life experiences were rich and rewarding, but at the same time she learned the hard way that working full-time in Christian ministry was no easy path. She never doubted she was called by God to do this work, but her calling was complicated by human realities. "Some people claim guidance from God through dramatic happenings – they hear a voice or see a vision," she mused. But her experience was more grounded. As she observed, "God led me but not in mystical ways."[2] That leading meant that Gerard faced some confusing conundrums as she encountered the political reality of the men who controlled church networks. To be a successful woman in ministry meant facing that reality and learning to operate within the boundaries dictated by human-made structures. She was a wide-eyed and eager idealist when she began her itinerant ministry imagining all that God had in store, but she ended her travels acutely aware that effective ministry required more than enthusiastic spiritual fervour. In the expanding world of Pentecostalism, where competition was real and fellow believers could be mean-spirited, Gerard learned that she needed to be strategic about her alliances. More pragmatic than mystical, Gerard came to recognize the importance of having the right connections because the endorsement of powerful men opened doors that were otherwise closed to women – even women led by God.

When the McColl-Gerard Trio said their goodbyes to Rossland in 1945, adoring parishioners crowded to a farewell event to wish them all the best. In a generous gesture of appreciation, church friends in the Rossland area presented the McColls with the gift of a car, and that vehicle would be put to good use on a demanding travel schedule. For the McColl sisters, launching out to sing, testify, and preach in Pentecostal tent meetings across North America meant they were resuming their familiar itinerant lifestyle that predated their five-year stay in Rossland. But for Bernice Gerard, it meant a whole new life as she gave up her recently launched teaching career and embraced her calling as an evangelist that the Davis sisters and others had been predicting for her.

It was during one of their summer evangelism campaigns in 1945 when Gerard told the McColl sisters that God was asking her to sacrifice her teaching job and join them full-time in their ministry adventures. A providential view of history would explain it exactly that way: God called her to the work, and she accepted the calling. But Gerard's decision was undoubtedly a complex one because she knew that unless she took a bold step to join them, the camaraderie she had enjoyed with Velma and Jean was about to come to an abrupt end. For Gerard, giving up the sense of belonging and inclusion that she was experiencing with her two coworkers undoubtedly would have been a bigger sacrifice than relinquishing her financial security as a teacher. While the trio had enjoyed their ministry together in Rossland and Trail at the church and on the radio, Jean and Velma, who were almost ten years older than Bernice, recognized that they were influencing a woman who was barely twenty years old and that she was making a life-altering choice. They cautioned their young friend that what they were planning to undertake was a difficult vocation, with no fixed address and no guaranteed income. When she insisted that she felt called to join them, Jean and Velma "expressed approval that I had decided to dedicate myself to God's work, with one qualification. 'But please remember, we have not talked you into it. It is your decision, and it's between you and the Lord.'"[3] Gerard hardly needed to be talked into it, given the happiness and acceptance she felt with the McColls. Anticipating an indefinite extension to the time she could spend with them, enjoying an open-ended travel adventure, and finding affirmation for her speaking and singing ability as she performed for appreciative crowds, Gerard eagerly agreed to the gruelling demands of crisscrossing the continent as a gospel worker. During the coming years, in the company of her beloved friends, this work as a preacher, teacher, and musician took Gerard on a circuit of revivalist travel that solidified her Pentecostal identity and expanded her life experience in remarkable ways.

Departing before the onset of a cold Canadian winter, the trio headed for Miami, Florida, where they were booked to preach at a church hosted by one of their ministry contacts. The Rev. Charles Neese and his wife were pastors of the Evangel Temple in Miami who had spent some time as travelling evangelists in Kelowna, British Columbia. On the strength of that friendship, Neese had invited the trio to come to his church for a series of meetings, and he agreed to support their application for "alien resident status" in the United States by underwriting guarantees to satisfy the US immigration department.[4] That kind of gesture was typical of the mutually supportive exchanges that occurred between Canadian and American Pentecostals where the international border allowed for transnational cooperation and ministry collaborations as long as the standard paperwork was completed and filed in good order. Indeed, as Gerard and her ministry partners were about to find out, it was not the political barriers that would pose the greatest challenges for them, but rather church denominations and doctrinal boundaries that were erected to differentiate one "brand" of Pentecostalism from another.

When they set out, Gerard describes her first travel adventures with the giddiness of a coed setting off on an epic road trip, with delicious snacks to tempt her at every stop. "En route to Florida in our Ford V-8, we enthusiastically accepted most challenges as presented. 'Stop! All the orange juice you can drink, only ten cents!' Coconuts, watermelons, grapefruit, oranges, dates and pecans were for sale along the way, not to mention pralines and key lime pie."[5] The novelty of travelling and the sense of freedom the women enjoyed was magnified because wartime travel restrictions and rationing of gas and rubber tires had recently been lifted. For Gerard, the freedom was particularly sweet because she no longer had to answer to any provincial welfare authorities or the scheduling constraints of the school calendar. Postwar car trips and the luxury of the open road meant these three single women were relatively carefree compared to their female peers in postwar America who were rushing to the altar to get married and start families. While the parents of baby boomers took out mortgages, flocked to department stores to furnish and decorate their suburban homes, and bounced babies on their knees, Jean, Velma, and Bernice's lifestyle was minimalist: sleeping in budget hotels and church basements, they kept their schedule flexible as they booked evangelistic meetings upon invitations from Pentecostal pastors, knowing that they might be staying in the next locale anywhere from two to six weeks. Like proverbial "travelling salesmen" the McColl-Gerard Trio did not put down roots in any one place but remained open to the next lead about where they would find an eager crowd of listeners willing to learn about the advantages of their particular brand of the gospel sales pitch.

The idea of travelling evangelists, with roots tracing back to Methodist circuit-riding preachers of an earlier time, was part of the heritage that mid-twentieth-century Pentecostals drew on. As William Kay, professor of theology, explains in his book *Pentecostalism: A Very Short Introduction*, the movement drew heavily from its "immediate roots going back to the 19th century into revivalist Methodism, holiness offshoots of Methodism, Pietism, international missions, and protagonists of divine healing."[6] Given those roots, it would not be misplaced to perceive that when three Pentecostal women set out on their epic postwar road trip adventures, they seemed like a throwback to an earlier time, the era of the circuit-riding preachers of old. However, the fact that it was three *women* on this mission, and that they were travelling by car (and later by airplane) makes this a thoroughly modern, specifically twentieth-century story. The autonomy that automobile travel offered to women had only increased by mid-century and while the idea of women undertaking extended automobile trips without any men along was no longer such a novelty, it did not conform to postwar norms where men were usually the drivers, especially on longer road trips and family vacations.[7]

And while their lifestyle sounds carefree compared to their suburban sisters, gospel work was physically demanding, not only because of the physicality of preaching and singing, but also in the management of material logistics and site preparations when they were hosting tent meetings. All the practical skills that Gerard learned as a self-declared tomboy in her early life on the Fraser River came in handy on the road. She had an aptitude for mechanical problems that inevitably arose with their car after thousands of miles of highway and backroad travels, and she embraced the challenge of the technical and engineering considerations associated with erecting, lighting, and dismantling large meeting tents to accommodate the crowds they hosted. Drawing on help when they needed it, Gerard and the McColl sisters depended on the goodwill and expertise of local church volunteers and friendly mechanics to make their travelling ministry work. The endorsement and cooperation that pastors and churches offered to them was indispensable. Without it, they could not be assured of the crowds to fill the rented halls, or the strong arms to hoist the tents they used to host meetings.

The crowds who attended their meetings were key to making the operation work. The Pentecostal gospel message was what the McColl-Gerard Trio had to offer, and in return, their listeners filled the offering plates. That system of marketing the gospel was very effective. Attendees found the spiritual help they were seeking, and Jean, Velma, and Bernice made a living as gospel workers. Being in the business of evangelism, the McColl-Gerard Trio had an

FIGURE 5.1 *Clockwise from back right in centre of photo:* Bernice Gerard, Frederick Reidenbach, Velma McColl, Jean McColl. Revival meetings held in tents were signature events for the McColl-Gerard Trio as they travelled throughout the United States and Canada. | *Summit Pacific College, Hudson Memorial Library, McColl-Gerard 1949–52, BX8762 Z8 M121 1949.*

entrepreneurial spirit, and by necessity they honed their business and marketing skills. Historian Kevin Kee argues that gospel work was essentially marketing work.[8] Like other revivalists, the McColl-Gerard Trio exhibited a spirit of free enterprise, operated as their own promoters with sophisticated tools of that trade (posters, newspaper advertisements, et cetera), and had to constantly pay attention to their market and their next opportunity. Indeed, considering the business of evangelism that these women plied, and especially the marketing techniques and networks they employed, gives important insight into the gendered aspects of their experience. Kee's study pays little attention to women as travelling evangelists, but historian Thomas Robinson has written extensively about the phenomenon of gospel enterprises run and performed by women.[9]

The McColl-Gerard Trio shares some characteristics with these male entrepreneurs of religion. The women were aware of their market, and they travelled with a well-developed system of marketing through handbills, newspapers ads, and word of mouth. However, there were important differences too. On one hand, they leveraged their gender as a novelty and found to their delight "that 'our all-girl American style act' was not a liability" but an asset.[10] The three women appeared to be independent, even liberated in a proto-feminist "new woman" sense, given their itinerant lifestyle and the ways in which they branded themselves. The McColl-Gerard Trio had its own publications, postcards, and a series of successful gospel music albums that they sold as souvenirs of their meetings and for supplementary income in addition to the cash offerings they collected. The program they created was novel and they knew it: the musicality of their wide-ranging skill with a variety of instruments was a delight, and as they performed familiar hymns and gospel songs, their audiences marvelled at the surprising vocal range of a group that featured the unusual talent of Gerard as a "lady baritone."

But it was not just Gerard's voice that drew people to listen to her. Her singing, her enthusiasm, and her gifted communication style were noteworthy, but her unusual life story was another selling feature. People came by the hundreds to the McColl-Gerard meetings, and many specifically came to hear Gerard tell her compelling story of conversion. When Bernice joined Jean and Velma, she already had a very dramatic tale of conversion, and when she regaled audiences with the story of how she came to accept that Pentecostalism was not a radical heresy, but a deeper level of spirituality, her experience was humorous and persuasive, especially for those who were curious about Pentecostals and their reputation as "holy rollers." It was intriguing to hear Gerard recount her teenaged progression from the fundamentalism of the Two by Twos, whose view of Christianity was restrictive and exclusive, to her acceptance and defence of Pentecostalism as a fuller experience of life in the Spirit. But because that story was also set in the narrative of Gerard's experiences as a survivor of abuse, a ward of the state, and a strong-willed teenager who defied her caregivers' more liberal wishes, her story played well among conservative evangelicals who shared her experience of feeling marginalized, even persecuted, for clinging stubbornly to their conservative social convictions.

When the McColl-Gerard Trio placed newspaper ads promoting their upcoming meetings, they highlighted Gerard's story of being "Converted in the Country" as a saga not to be missed.[11] The idea of sharing testimonies was a familiar ritual among evangelical churchgoers, especially those in the revivalist tradition. One of the rituals of Pentecostal meetings was time set aside during gatherings and church services for oral testimonies to be shared. As historian Virginia Lieson Brereton observes, revivalists tell their personal conversion

FIGURE 5.2 Typical of travelling evangelists, Pentecostal women adopted a variety of marketing strategies to promote their meetings, relying heavily on local print media, such as this ad promoting the upcoming meetings of the McColl-Gerard Trio in the fall of 1954. | Cincinnati Enquirer, September 18, 1954.

tales in a formulaic yet impassioned style.[12] Pentecostal testimony is usually crafted in particularly gendered ways, as women adopt the language of "submitting" to the Spirit because of an irresistible love that is offered to them, while men typically report greater levels of self-control because the Spirit empowers them to more confident expressions of their spirituality, often with great material blessings including greater success in business pursuits and family leadership roles.[13]

Gerard's story included several emotionally compelling elements: losing her mother at birth, an unusual adoption story where she was introduced to her adoptive mother's Stó:lō culture, Annie Gerard's premature death while Bernice was still a toddler, and the alcoholic and abusive adoptive father who made his living fishing on the Fraser River. The critical element in her tale, the point of conversion, came when Gerard was exposed to two women who travelled and preached as itinerants, whose meetings held in the local schoolhouse provided the occasion for Bernice's conversion at age twelve. Immediately after that experience, the young Gerard garnered the courage to expose the fact that she was a victim of her father's abuse, setting in motion a series of foster care arrangements that framed her evolving religious identity.

The horror of her childhood experiences was not lost on Gerard as she took her story on the road as part of the McColl-Gerard Trio. She associated her father's antisocial behaviours of excessive drinking, womanizing, and violence with preconversion, and in a very real sense her religious conversion represented not only a spiritual deliverance, but also a literal rescue from danger. As her religious views developed during her time as a foster child, she clung to the fundamental importance of a "born again" experience. Thus, her life story had many elements of a classic revivalist conversion narrative, and it served as a useful tool in altar calls that characterized the McColl-Gerard meetings. At the same time, her story was an accessible way to communicate to audiences that a Pentecostal experience of Spirit baptism was available to those who chose to seek it out. For churchgoers uncertain about the legitimacy of Pentecostal claims, Gerard's testimony was a reassuring narrative because at first she, too, had rejected the idea of such exuberant and emotional spirituality as heresy. But when she accepted that Pentecostalism was rooted in scriptural truth and surrendered herself to the experience, her hesitations gave way and she embraced a personal Pentecost, complete with physical manifestations including speaking in tongues and physical healing. The McColl-Gerard Trio used that element of the story to invite believers to the altar and to the prayer room so that they could experience the same blessing that gave Gerard the joy she exuded. Thus, by retelling her own story about deliverance from the horrific early years of her childhood, Gerard offered audiences a provocative version of converting, not just to generic evangelicalism, but specifically to Pentecostal spirituality.

The ritualized recounting of Gerard's testimony is in keeping with the gendered patterns that scholars of religion have noted about Pentecostal women's roles in that tradition. Erica Ramirez, a cultural sociologist of religion, argues that the kind of performance Pentecostal and charismatic women perform at the altar, complete with ecstatic experiences of emotionally charged conversion stories, is a familiar charismatic trope.[14] Gerard's story and her dramatic retelling of it are in line with that observation. Her compelling faith story coupled with the musicality of the McColl-Gerard meetings were right in step with midcentury gender norms, where women sang, testified, and warmed up the crowds who came to their tent meetings with their emotional and Spirit-empowered presentations. But for conservative church attenders in postwar America, the more unusual, though hardly rare, part of the travelling evangelists' routine was the fact that these Pentecostal women did more than sing and testify. They preached. Gerard took her turn preaching as well, mentored by the more experienced preachers, Jean and Velma. Where some traditions operated from the conviction that preaching the gospel was work exclusively reserved for men only, Pentecostals still called on gifted women to preach the gospel, especially in the setting of evangelistic meetings. In that regard, the McColl-Gerard meetings represented an extension of the nineteenth-century holiness and evangelical traditions of women as preachers, teachers, and gospel workers with such famous forerunners as Catherine Booth, the mother of the Salvation Army movement.[15] The most well-known Pentecostal of them all, Sister Aimee McPherson, began her ministry adventures in the early years of Pentecostalism, first in rural Ontario, then overseas in a short-lived missionary career, and most famously, as the pastor of the Angelus Temple in Los Angeles and the founder of the Foursquare Pentecostal denomination.

Because Gerard's testimony was so effective as a ministry tool to convince audiences of the need for a conversion and a subsequent Pentecostal experience of Spirit baptism, she and the McColls decided to publish her life story as a book. *Converted in the Country: The Life Story of Bernice Gerard* bore the imprint of the McColl-Gerard brand and they sold it at their meetings and by mail order for radio audiences. As a form of life writing, that autobiography was carefully crafted to communicate the Pentecostal message. Along with postcards, songbooks, and other branded materials, it served as a souvenir for those who attended one of the McColl-Gerard meetings, but the book could also be shared with others who were skeptical about Pentecostal claims. It was a strategically crafted rhetorical tool, and fans of the trio could also be consumers of their product line by buying the book for themselves or as a gift for a loved one.[16]

All these business strategies, including promoting their meetings and selling their gospel wares, made the McColl-Gerard Trio very effective at drawing crowds. However, as the women learned very early in their travels, sometimes it was difficult to keep the crowds coming and to secure the confidence of existing church communities. Pentecostal women like the McColl-Gerard Trio could not be entirely independent entrepreneurs. Their determination to "live by faith" meant that they were "trusting [God] for shelter, food and clothes and for enough through the love offering, the collection for the evangelists on the last night, to get us to the next place."[17] But just how precarious their income security proved to be was made clear to them during their first set of meetings in Miami during the winter of 1945–46. They had been attracting a good crowd and enjoying the success of their meetings when suddenly the crowds just stopped coming. As they soon learned, a local pastor had questioned the orthodoxy of their teaching; attendance at their meetings dropped off immediately, and the financial support evaporated, literally overnight. This pastor, perhaps feeling threatened by the success of their meetings and the fact that the crowds who came to their tent left generous cash offerings behind, or perhaps out of genuine concern for doctrinal orthodoxy, put a stop to their success. With that question mark over their reputation and, specifically, as suspected heresy dogged the women, their success screeched to a halt.

The McColl-Gerard Trio found themselves under careful scrutiny about exactly what they were preaching and who was endorsing them. One interpretation of this careful inquiry is to see it as fear that the popular act was diverting funds into the evangelists' coffers and away from local congregations. Being labelled as unorthodox was a serious problem that could not be ignored.

As Pentecostalism spread, the movement evolved and spawned multiple "brands" that distinguished themselves from each other through particular emphases.[18] For example, in North America, those who were categorized as "classical Pentecostals" worked hard during the postwar years to establish and protect a reputation of respectability that would appeal to families: using a variety of programs that centred on serving nuclear families, their programming catered to every stage of childhood and youth and adopted then-current gendered norms of breadwinning fathers and stay-at-home mothers. Embracing these cultural gender roles meant that with some exceptions, men and women were expected to take up decidedly different roles and functions, not only at home but also in the church, using their spiritual gifts in ways that reinforced the cultural norms. Such churches emphasized the wisdom of having strong governance models in place, claiming that they were abiding by a scriptural instruction to do everything "decently and in order." That order would be assured with male-led church boards and denominational structures. Women would do the work of nurturing children and fostering congregational sociability, and for some exceptional individuals, women could take up public roles as evangelists, but fewer and fewer served in senior pastoral roles during the second half of the twentieth century.[19] Other Pentecostal groups were determined not to be hemmed in by conforming so closely to societal norms or imposing lines of authority through denominational structures. Instead, they emphasized that the Spirit was a wild force who should not be tamed or contained. In these circles, freer expression of more unusual manifestations of the Spirit were welcome, including dancing in the spirit, extended times of vocal and emotional corporate prayer, and fewer structures that posed the risk of "quenching the spirit." In these circles, individual giftings were harder to systematize, and this led to a widespread controversy originating in Saskatchewan known as the Latter Rain issue.[20] In brief, those who followed the Latter Rain emphasized that some individuals were uniquely gifted to have insights and make pronouncements directly from God about the details of other people's lives. This led to clashes about where the authority resided, whether in denominational structures or in individual revelations, and where free-ranging individualism prevailed, extremism could follow. The case from Saskatchewan had wide-ranging consequences for Pentecostals across North America, and denominations like the Pentecostal Assemblies of Canada and its American counterpart, the Assemblies of God, circled their wagons to block any tendencies toward prophetic gifts gone rogue.

In the context of that emerging controversy, rumours and questions began to circulate in Florida's Pentecostal circles about which kind of Pentecostalism Gerard and her coworkers were actually promoting. As she described it, the meetings were going very well and the attendance was high, until suddenly, the numbers plummeted. "A few months after we arrived in Florida, we met with roadblocks. After being well received, and well recommended by pastors in Sanford and Jacksonville, we became the subject of negative gossip."[21] Perhaps it was due to the McColl sisters' roots in a Pentecostal tradition associated with unorthodox views of the trinity that their popularity plummeted. But Gerard was convinced that this downturn was happening because early reports of the brewing controversy about the Latter Rain had started to circulate.

The context for this controversy was larger than the Trio themselves, of course. At this time, within Pentecostal circles there were widespread disagreements about theology, specifically, divergent views on spiritual gifts, the trinity, the authority of scripture, and the role of denominations. The McColl sisters hailed from a Regina church, the Apostolic Mission, that was outside the largest Pentecostal denomination, the Pentecostal Assemblies of Canada. This was a lingering point of division among Pentecostals and, indeed, the question of denominational structures versus more independent "spirit-led" movements remains divisive and controversial among various Pentecostal denominations to the present day.[22] The finer points of those theological disagreements, including the controversy known as "the New Order of the Latter Rain,"[23] are outside the scope of this chapter but suffice it to say that the McColl sisters' ties to Saskatchewan Pentecostalism were at the heart of these debates. Once doubt was cast on the Trio's associations, their very livelihood was in jeopardy until they could take steps to reestablish a reputation of orthodoxy.

As Gerard understood it, the whole misunderstanding that swirled around them in Florida could be traced to one pastor who, "drawing his own conclusions, decided we were off-brand Pentecostals and probably dangerous to the unity of the churches, and therefore should not be allowed to minister."[24] Maybe the local pastors were simply worried about the threat to their own finances if church members became too generous toward the popular Canadians. Most probably it was a combination of all of these factors that led the McColl-Gerard Trio to be investigated. Their friend, the Rev. Charles Neese, the Miami pastor who had supported their immigration file, urged his district superintendent to make inquiries in Canada about the reputation that these women had established there. Assurances came from Pentecostal leaders in British Columbia who wrote to say that "the McColl sisters are good girls, and did a good work in Rossland, B.C."[25] The three women requested a hearing with the Assemblies of God superintendent to give assurances about their orthodoxy, but that request was denied. Losing the confidence of the largest Pentecostal denomination in the United States was not a good omen. Gerard recounts that the gossip campaign had damaged their credibility to the point where they were "virtually on the street."[26]

As they regrouped and strategized about their next steps, Gerard reported that they took on smaller events in order to support themselves. "In Tampa, we preached in a Pentecostal Holiness church, and lived in an improvised apartment, more or less victorious over resident cockroaches. In Deland we rented a school auditorium; in Daytona we were with a small pioneer church. When the Assemblies [of God] churches were closed to us, the Pentecostal Holiness Church invited us to request their credentials instead, and become their state evangelists. We appreciated their kindness, but could not get the peace to say yes."[27] What held these three back from accepting the invitation was the limitation that the Pentecostal Holiness Church was not trinitarian, and making stronger bonds with such a group would close future opportunities with wider Pentecostal circles. The financial uncertainty and character assassination that Gerard was experiencing caused her to wonder whether she had made a wise decision when she took to the road with the McColls. She remembers that in prayer, "I cried, asking the Lord, 'Did I leave teaching for this?' It hurt to be judged unfairly, and falsely accused, with no opportunity for a defense."[28] In the end, Gerard and the McColls decided to return to Canada and sort themselves out. During the drive back, they stopped to hold meetings

94

where they found welcoming hosts in a variety of locations including in New York, New Jersey, and Rhode Island.

Their stay on Rhode Island was important because of the contacts it opened up. Their host there was Christine Amelia Gibson, an educator and pastor who ran the Zion Bible Institute and an associated faith home in East Providence, Rhode Island. Gibson, who had been a widow for over twenty years, operated her school and home on the "faith principle," meaning that she was known to "rely on prayer rather than on advance pledges or fees."[29] For Jean, Velma, and Bernice, this meant Gibson offered them accommodation without having to worry about paying their bill afterward, and in fact, it was Gibson who gave money to the trio, not the other way around. "Pressing several bills into Jean's hand, Sister Gibson, the president and founder of the school said, 'The Lord has impressed me to give you this. I believe He is going to open doors, and bless your ministries richly.'"[30] Gibson's situation was not lost on Gerard, since Gibson had also been orphaned as a child, converted as a young adult, and later immigrated to the United States. Not only did Gibson give money to Gerard and the McColls, but she also gave them a prophetic promise, and she introduced them to some key players in the Canadian Pentecostal world who would help to steer them through a difficult time.

While Gerard and the McColls were with Gibson, they were introduced to a graduate of her school who had returned to his alma mater for a visit. The Rev. E.L. Lassègues hosted a French-language Pentecostal radio program in Montreal, and together with W.L. Bouchard, he is credited with founding the Berea Bible Institute in Montreal, "the first French Pentecostal Bible school in the world."[31] Lassègues invited the McColl-Gerard Trio to come to Montreal for evangelistic meetings there, which they did, holding several weeks of meetings in the French Pentecostal Assembly in Montreal, preaching through an interpreter and singing nightly in meetings that often stretched late into the night, "well after midnight," according to Gerard. It seemed that Sister Gibson's prediction was coming true in those meetings because, "non-believers confessed Jesus Christ as Savior, the demon-possessed were exorcised, and believers empowered."[32] That extended success must have been encouraging to the beleaguered evangelists, but the contacts they made in Quebec through Gibson introducing them to Lassègues went even further.

Over the weeks they spent in Montreal with Bouchard, the three women told him about the troubles they had encountered in Florida when their reputation and doctrinal convictions were called into question. Bouchard suggested that they should spend the coming months at two Pentecostal camps, one in Cobourg, Ontario, and the other – Braeside Camp – near Paris, Ontario.

Bouchard was being very strategic with this suggestion, not only because it would present them with their next set of short-term ministry engagements, but also because it would give them a chance to make connections with some of the most influential Pentecostal leaders in Ontario, who were affiliated with the Pentecostal Assemblies of Canada. Specifically, Bouchard wanted the women to meet the Rev. J.H. Blair, a pastor in Hamilton, Ontario, and a respected leader for the Western Ontario District of the PAOC. Knowing Blair, working in the camp meetings he orchestrated, and having his endorsement would open important doors for the McColl-Gerard Trio.

Blair was delighted with the fine work that Jean, Velma, and Bernice performed at the summer camp meetings, where they ministered to hundreds of people in public services and youth events. Indeed, Blair was so pleased that in August 1948 he agreed to write a letter of introduction on their behalf, enthusiastically vouching for the women's orthodoxy in a period when North American Pentecostals were working hard to quench rumours of heresy in their midst. His letter of introduction was intended to allay the fears of ministers like those in Miami who linked the recent controversy arising among Pentecostals to people originating from Saskatchewan. Blair wrote,

> Their revival meetings in Ontario have been attended by excellent crowds and most gratifying results. Rarely have we met a trio with such well balanced [sic] talent in music, singing and preaching the Word of God. You will find them very cooperative with pastors and loyal to the district in which they labour. Another grand feature of this Trio is the fact that they are thoroughly Pentecostal. They believe in and enjoy the power of God and are sound in doctrine. They keep their meetings free from all controversial subjects and have a great appeal to the strangers.[33]

He assured other ministry leaders that the McColl-Gerard Trio could draw a crowd and that they presented a full and balanced package of music and preaching in their repertoire. More importantly, they were orthodox and they would not pose a threat to male leadership. In a context where Pentecostals were debating points of orthodoxy and seeking to establish a reputable presence in local communities, Blair gave assurance that Gerard and the McColl sisters should be widely promoted. "Don't be afraid to take them into your church and give them a free hand," he exhorted. "They will do you good and your church good."[34]

That kind of professional endorsement is exactly what the McColl-Gerard Trio needed to guarantee their future engagements. The gendered reality of postwar Pentecostal authority should not be lost on us. Although the women were intrepid travellers, experienced preachers, and effective ministers of the gospel, the fact that they were women and that rumours were circulating about their possible association with a heterodox strain of Pentecostalism cast doubt over their legitimacy. With men like Bouchard and Blair promoting them, those doubts could be hushed. Gerard and her ministry partners were rendered legitimate in Pentecostal circles because men with administrative and organizational authority said so. The other thing to note is the deep networking that existed among Pentecostals on both sides of the Canada-US border. From their troubles in Miami, the women worked through a chain of contacts: from Gibson (a woman who, like the trio, lived by faith) to Lassègues, a graduate of her school now running his own Bible institute, to Bouchard, the pastor of a major church in urban Montreal, to Blair, a pastor, founder of camps, and district executive member who wielded a great deal of social capital among leaders and adherents of the Pentecostal Assemblies of Canada. Given all of those entwined connections, the McColl-Gerard Trio were tied to a dense network of Pentecostals.

Still, personal goodwill could take the women only so far. To establish and reinforce their legitimacy and ensure future opportunities, they needed to make their ties to the largest Pentecostal denominations official. In Canada that was the Pentecostal Assemblies of Canada (PAOC), and in the United States it was the Assemblies of God (AG). Because their sights were set on ministry across America and because the AG already had an established history of welcoming women into the ministry, albeit more often as evangelists and missionaries than as senior pastors,[35] Gerard and the McColls applied for ordination with that denomination. While the Pentecostal Assemblies of Canada would still hesitate for four more decades before they offered ordination to women, the American Assemblies of God were already in the habit of ordaining women. On the recommendation of Blair, and through connections the trio made when American speakers shared the stage with them at Ontario camp meetings, Jean, Velma, and Bernice all sought and received the important credential of ordination, solidifying their reputation for orthodoxy. With the brand-recognition of the Assemblies of God, they could now find countless opportunities open to them across the United States of America and beyond.[36]

The misfortune they had experienced in Miami became an episode of their story they would retell often, about how God had opened doors for them through providential intervention. Of course, another way to read that part of their story is through the lens of organizational structures, solidifying denominational identities, and the practice of boundary-making to define, establish, and reinforce authority.[37] As the Pentecostal networks grew and gained strength across North America, the McColl-Gerard Trio became a recognizable part of those networks, with reliable teaching and preaching and an entertaining package of music and testimony. Having won the confidence and secured the endorsement of influential male leaders, Jean, Velma, and Bernice were poised to counter all the rumours of heresy that could be flung at them. Their ordination papers, renewed annually, were proof of their solid reputation. Now they could prove they were Pentecostals associated with a reliable brand.

For Bernice Gerard, this development sealed her professional identity: she belonged among classical Pentecostals like the PAOC and the AG. But for her, the biggest takeaway from this whole controversy about professional belonging went much deeper than "brand loyalty." Looking back with the perspective of forty years of experience, Gerard realized that this had been a formative time where she learned to be more open-minded, not less. "We had learned from our previous experience about the need for well-established credentials. I also determined never to hastily reject a person or ministry simply because they belonged to a different denominational group."[38] That conviction not to rush to hasty judgments meant that Gerard was well ahead of many Pentecostal colleagues who were caught up with preoccupations about loyalty, boundary-making, and doctrinal disputes. While others hesitated, Gerard became an early adopter of an ecumenical outlook, and this episode of professional rejection provides a window into that mindset. For example, when other classical Pentecostals hesitated to embrace the charismatic movement that would burst onto the religious scene in the 1960s, Gerard was curious and affirming. She explained that open posture with reference to the Florida controversy and justified her stance with a Bible verse: "As the Bible says, 'Keep on loving each other as brothers. Do not forget to entertain strangers, for by so doing some people have entertained angels without knowing it.' (Hebrews 13:1,2 NIV.) Not that we were angels – but we *had* [italics in original] experienced rejection as strangers."[39] Gerard was particularly sensitive to rejection given her childhood experiences, but rather than harbour bitterness, as she matured she developed deep empathy for those who were perceived as outsiders.

The McColl-Gerard Trio leveraged their official professional identity and carved out for themselves some incredible opportunities, both domestically and abroad. With their credentials established and the endorsement of the AG, the Trio began building an even more wide-reaching network. Their personal archives are chock full of photographs from those adventures, including tent meetings throughout the United States and Canada, a road trip that extended

FIGURE 5.3 Bernice (*right*) and Velma enjoyed each other's company, and while they kept a demanding travel schedule, they also took time for themselves, as they did on this beach in Acapulco during a mission work trip to Mexico in 1951. | *Summit Pacific College, Hudson Memorial Library, BX8762 Z8 M121 1951.*

into Mexico, and air travel to visit AG mission projects as far south as Bolivia. The photographs include professional depictions of their preaching and singing, group shots of the crowds they attracted, and pictures of them visiting Pentecostal missionary colleagues who were posted throughout Central and South America. Sometimes those photographs depict very personal scenes: one captures the Trio hamming it up as they tried on hats and ponchos at a local market in La Paz, Bolivia, for example, and there are even rare glimpses of the women at leisure, with one photo showing Velma and Bernice relaxing in their bathing suits on a sunny beach in Acapulco (see Figure 5.3).[40] "For fourteen years we travelled as evangelists in North, Central, and South America, in the West Indies, Europe, and the Near East," Gerard recounts.[41] It was a remarkable run, and the name of the "McColl-Gerard Trio" became a household word in North American Pentecostal circles.

Of course, there was more to the work than celebrity status or an endless loop of photo opportunities in exotic locales. This was a spiritual enterprise and the McColl-Gerard Trio was more than a travelling show. "We generally gave ourselves to extended times of prayer and fasting and called the people to do the same ... We all knew the work was the Lord's, and only He could give the increase; nevertheless we worked as though everything depended on us."[42] The work was hard and although their professional association was secure, religious workers are often misunderstood. As Gerard remembers, "Evangelists, in general, have received rather bad press. The truth is that it takes a lot of dedication and courage to get launched and keep afloat on uncharted waters."[43] What the photos depict looks like a joyous, even carefree time, but behind the scenes, the reality was hardly a life of leisure. There was also the logistics of living like campers for extended periods. During one series of meetings that ran for several weeks, they lived "in a rustic dwelling on an abandoned mine site, and travelled the few miles ... to our tent meetings in town."[44] Travelling by car, living in a recreational vehicle, and ministering in portable structures brought particular challenges for three women.

Holding tent meetings across North America as the main event of their enterprise, the McColl-Gerard Trio had the added logistics of managing their portable facilities. The women found themselves dependent on the goodwill of male volunteers who assisted them with the physical work of setting up and tearing down before and after each meeting, but as Gerard explains, "We three women had to learn how to erect the tent, so that we could instruct the volunteers in each new location."[45] Sometimes, given their dependence on good weather, their need for male help was even more pronounced. As the photographic evidence in their own ministry scrapbooks reveals, sometimes the women were caught in the throes of stormy weather. Gerard recalled that on one occasion, "we had just erected the tent, and I was saying to the pastor and a dozen volunteers as we stood inside, 'I think we should tighten up the canvas because it seems a wind is rising,' when a sudden mighty gust caught the tent as though it were a giant umbrella, and dropped it into the next field."[46] That episode made the local news in London, Ontario, and the women needed the help of local men from the church community to help them recover their canvas meeting space. That storm, and others like it, remind us that while the women appeared to be independently managing their evangelism business, the physical logistics of their travelling performances made them dependent not only on the weather, but also on the goodwill and cooperation of local

FIGURE 5.4 The demanding work of travelling evangelists holding tent meetings depended on the work of local supporters to assist with local arrangements, and the challenges of unexpected weather events sometimes posed additional complications. | *Summit Pacific College, Hudson Memorial Library, McColl-Gerard Trio 1949–52. BX8762 Z8 M121 1949.*

supporters (including strong, able-bodied men) who could bring their skills to these practical matters. Again it was pragmatism, not a miraculous turn of events, that carried the day for Gerard and her ministry.

Amid all those logistical challenges, the McColl-Gerard Trio did not work alone. In addition to the all-important local volunteers, all the AG denomination's networks were in place for them to rely on. Whether they were braving the challenges of a road trip into Mexico or boarding a Pan American World Airways flight for destinations in Honduras, Nicaragua, Guatemala, Costa Rica, Belize, Bolivia, or other tropical destinations including Jamaica and the West Indies, they were part of a larger enterprise. Air travel was still a luxury and many of the places they visited were not yet common destinations for tourists.

And while unpredictable events arose, giving rise to what Gerard called "uncharted waters," the McColl-Gerard Trio did not travel as independent agents.

FIGURE 5.5 Velma McColl (*front*) and Bernice Gerard are pictured boarding a flight leaving Costa Rica in 1951. Although postwar air travel was still a luxury beyond the means of most churchgoers, the Assemblies of God flew the McColl-Gerard Trio to a variety of destinations throughout Latin America to visit missionaries and bring back reports that could be shared with the donor base in churches across North America. | *Summit Pacific College, Hudson Memorial Library, McColl-Gerard Trio, 1951. BX8762 Z8 M121 1951.*

Since the 1910s and 1920s, Pentecostals had turned their attention to missionary efforts and by midcentury, larger denominations like the AG had well-established organizational policies and procedures in place and networks of their personnel scattered far and wide. The denomination was counting on Gerard and the McColls to visit existing AG mission posts, minister there as an encouragement to missionary personnel, and bring back encouraging reports, including photographs and films, of the work that was being accomplished. Gerard was rarely

FIGURE 5.6 In an album full of photographs from the McColl-Gerard Trio's travels from Mexico to Bolivia, this picture labelled "Orphans" emphasizes not only the family status of the children who posed with Bernice, but also the story of her troubled childhood, which she retold on countless occasions wherever she went. | *Summit Pacific College, Hudson Memorial Library, McColl-Gerard Trio, 1951. BX8762 Z8 M121 1951.*

without her camera on these excursions and her personal archives include several volumes of photograph albums and scrapbooks that provide a rich record. In effect, this part of Gerard's "life writing" was captured largely in visual texts. In one memorable photograph of Gerard and some children at a Mexican orphanage they visited, the caption in her album simply says "Orphans," making it clear that her empathy for the children she met was tied to her own childhood experience.[47]

The McColl-Gerard Trio members were agents for the expanding reach of the AG, and once they returned to North America they helped to spread the message and procure funds for continuing that work.[48] While they enjoyed the adventure of exploring new places and commanded impressive audiences with their music, testimony, and preaching, the women were forming an important bond among themselves personally, with seasoned believers, and even with curious skeptics. The level of engagement that the McColl-Gerard Trio generated for the Assemblies of God was remarkable, and the invitations for them to appear in various American cities just kept coming. For the denomination, this arrangement meant that they had a fresh and entertaining way to present their missionary efforts to their domestic donor base throughout the United States. The scope of AG contacts opened countless opportunities for taking the McColl-Gerard show on the road and keeping it there with remarkable longevity. Gerard's world was broadening in step with the ever-expanding reach of Pentecostalism itself. And that reach was far wider than the Americas.

As the work of Allan Anderson, professor of mission and Pentecostal studies, has established Pentecostalism has always been a global phenomenon, with multiple sites of origin and an early and abiding commitment to missionary work.[49] In the spirit of postwar internationalism, Pentecostals from around the world came together after the end of the Second World War to create the World Pentecostal Conference (known from 1958 on as the Pentecostal World Conference). The reason for organizing was to hold triennial, international ecumenical gatherings of Pentecostals. Talk of uniting Pentecostals worldwide had been circulating for many years, but the progress toward global cooperation was slowed by a combination of factors, including the world wars and divisions that rose from "issues of polity, doctrine, mores, and personalities."[50] But efforts spearheaded by the Assemblies of God and individuals including international leaders like David du Plessis of South Africa[51] and Donald Gee from the UK finally came to fruition when the World Pentecostal Conference (WPC) met for the first time in Zurich, Switzerland, in 1947. Gee was the long-time editor of the WPC periodical *Pentecost* (1947–66) and an advocate of Pentecostal cooperation who argued that "the Pentecostal revival is a diverse worldwide movement, transcending national interest and united by shared experience."[52]

As well-travelled and well-respected Pentecostals, the McColl-Gerard Trio attended the second WPC when it was convened in Paris, France, in 1950. Gerard describes how "as the years passed, we were led, step by step, into ever-expanding fields of ministry. Our first overseas venture included a plan to spend two months in England and continental Europe."[53] When they announced their plans, they encountered many naysayers, whom their mentor and defender, J.H. Blair, called the "impossibility thinkers." Such people suggested that what the women had to offer would not resonate with British audiences. They heard warnings, including "'The British will never receive women,' and 'The Brits are very conservative; they won't like your music.'"[54] But the critics were wrong, and the Trio was very well received, "Whatever fears we had concerning our reception by conservative English congregations disappeared early in our tour. From London onward, our American-style gospel music and all-girl preaching team proved a genuine asset rather than a liability."[55] Not only did they have a successful tour prior to the WPC, but once the conference began, Gerard reports, "We were invited to sing almost every night at the Paris Conference where evenings were devoted to worship and preaching, and music played an inspiring part."[56]

The kind of exposure they had from that international stage meant that they, in Gerard's words, "were deluged with invitations."[57] Attendees at the WPC had gathered from thirty-five countries, and although the three women "could not get everywhere we were invited" they expanded their Pentecostal circles a great deal, and "we did preach in Belgium, Germany, Denmark, Italy, Switzerland and Sweden."[58] The historic WPC gatherings with Pentecostals from across the geographic and theological spectrum was a remarkable phenomenon given the deep divisions and heated disagreements that usually characterized, what Gerard called, the "highly separatist" groups they represented. As a young woman in her twenties, Gerard admits she was so enthralled with the adventure of international travel and the thrill of singing in front of groups composed of such diverse people, that the significance of those gatherings was lost on her at the time. Only later did she realize how important those meetings really were, and how significant some of the contacts she made would prove to be.

> As for me, my youth and inexperience were the only possible defense for the fact that I was oblivious to the ecumenical dimension of that [Paris] gathering, little dreaming that years later I would come to know as a personal friend, and actually work with "Mr. Pentecost," David du Plessis, the prime mover for the conference, who saw the need and had the courage to eventually bring the fractious Pentecostals together.[59]

Gerard's later encounters with du Plessis came about because of their mutual involvement in the charismatic movement, when their efforts to promote ecumenism were deeply misunderstood by other Pentecostals. David du Plessis was famously ousted from the AG for his acceptance of Roman Catholic charismatics in particular.[60] In retrospect, Gerard was amazed by the fact that she had been introduced to and worked closely with so many Pentecostal leaders from around the world. The transnational exposure she had to Pentecostalism was deeply formative in ways she could not have predicted.

The Trio returned a second time to Europe just a few years later, and this time they took an American film with them, *Venture into Faith*, for use in their meetings. The film was a creation of Oral Roberts, and by using it they were promoting the ministry of one of America's best-known faith healers and Pentecostal preachers.[61] Gerard and the McColl sisters met with Roberts before they left to be clear about their cooperation with him. "In our conversation with Oral Roberts in Sacramento, California, we stated our objectives: ours was to be a soul-winning effort in every detail. The film would be shown one-third of the time. When the SS *United States* set sail from New York, everything we needed for the British tour was stowed away in the hold: the movie projector, several hundred of our own gospel recordings, gospel literature and our Pontiac which was to carry us over forty British cities and continental Europe."[62] Gerard's "road trip" adventures expanded well beyond the escape to Florida that is familiar to Canadian "snow birds," to include driving through Europe and beyond.

The third meeting of the WPC was held in London, United Kingdom, in 1952, and the women planned their travels on this second trip to coincide with that gathering, although Gerard does not go into detail about it. What captured her attention on this transatlantic trip was the tremendous response to their meetings throughout England. Gerard marvelled, "The four months in England were one of the most fruitful periods of our ministry. Everywhere the auditoriums and churches overflowed. We saw hundreds of people take their stand for Christ at the altars."[63]

After that success, an even bigger travel adventure followed: "From England we crossed the channel to Cherbourg and then drove in our own automobile to southern Italy. In the two months that followed, we were to preach in Egypt, Lebanon and Trans-Jordan, and visit the new State of Israel."[64] After successful meetings with missionaries cooperating in a variety of locations, culminating in Beirut where "once again we saw an outpouring of the Holy Spirit," the women celebrated that they had witnessed what was purported to be the first public service in the Middle East where anyone had experienced the baptism of the Holy Spirit.[65]

All that success was building, as Gerard's autobiographical accounts make clear, toward their ultimate destination: a trip to Jerusalem and the Holy Land. So taken was she with her visit there that Gerard wrote a separate book titled *The Holy Land: Guide to Faith!*[66] Gerard would make many more return trips to Israel over the course of her lifetime, but her first visit marked her deeply and reinforced her faith. As she wrote in the preface to her book, "I reverently sought out the footsteps of Jesus. This [book] is written to tell you what we saw and what it did for us. We were not disappointed! The Holy Land has a message for the world today, 'Have faith in God – Jesus is coming soon!'"[67] Gerard's affinity for Israel continued for the rest of her life. No doubt her interest was tied to her understanding of the end times, namely a premillennial eschatology with its certainty about how the nation of Israel would play a central role in future world affairs and be the site of important events during the "last days." While that view of Israel was commonly shared among Pentecostals and evangelicals more generally, suffice it to say that Gerard took a special interest in the place. From her first visit she was completely captivated, and she and Velma would return many more times, leading tours of other believers with them to share the wonder of the place.

The scope of Gerard's travels with the McColls and the broad international networks they joined were truly remarkable. From her first teaching assignment in the West Kootenay region of British Columbia, when she met and teamed up with Jean and Velma, their travels took them crisscrossing North America multiple times. By extension, Gerard's world expanded to international destinations too. At first, this was part of the network she joined by her professional affiliation with the Assemblies of God, where she was introduced to the missionary efforts that tied North American Pentecostals to places that seemed exotic in the early postwar years before international travel was a common experience for most. Gerard came to appreciate the wide reach of the Pentecostal movement through the auspices of denominations like the AG and the PAOC, whose missionaries were scattered across the globe. Her first tastes of transatlantic travel introduced her to the World Pentecostal Conference and Pentecostal believers in England, across Europe, and into the Middle East, including the Holy Land. The McColl-Gerard Trio gained an international reputation and Gerard's Pentecostal world expanded, not just in terms of geography, but by virtue of the many different kinds of Pentecostals she encountered.

This period of Gerard's life was characterized by her developing sense of belonging on multiple levels. First, she settled the questions about her sense of personal belonging through two important developments: when she teamed up with the McColls in Rossland and when she established connections with her birth family. From that point on, she had a new-found confidence about who she was and to whom she belonged. Second, on the professional front, she gave up her teaching career to become a travelling evangelist. Doing so meant she had her first taste of the complexities of itinerant ministry work and she discovered the need to affiliate with a reliable "brand" of Pentecostalism. When she sought and received ordination by the Assemblies of God, she found a professional identity that endowed her with the credibility of belonging to a respected denomination that seemed to offer unlimited ministry possibilities for her. Together with Jean and Velma, Bernice was affirmed and endorsed by leaders who vouched for their solid reputation. From that point on there was no question that Gerard felt she belonged in the midst of Pentecostal gatherings wherever the ministry schedule took her. Finally, with international travel opportunities, she not only enjoyed adventures but also was embraced by a growing international Pentecostal network of leaders who affirmed that she belonged as part of their movement.

Ministering in large and successful meetings across Europe and attending historic gatherings where she was introduced to the leading Pentecostal ecumenists of the time, Gerard clearly belonged to something much, much bigger than she could have ever imagined. It was a far cry from her early experience as a young girl growing up on the Fraser River who first heard the gospel preached in a remote rural schoolhouse by women who led her to believe that real Christians were part of a very small and exclusive circle. After fourteen years of travel and moving in the ever-expanding circles of a growing global Pentecostal movement, Gerard was transformed into an intrepid international traveller, approaching middle age as a woman who was confident in her religious identity and her place in the larger Pentecostal community.

The Pentecostal World Conference came to Toronto in 1958, and although Gerard had anticipated it with excitement, that year also marked a significant set of transitions both professionally and personally. While the conference would offer her the chance to enjoy reunions with many people she had encountered through her earlier travels, Gerard's life was at a crossroads. Her career as an international itinerant evangelist ended when each of the McColl sisters accepted marriage proposals and settled into conventional domestic lives. As she imagined her future, Bernice had some soul-searching to do about her personal life.

Chapter 6

CAMPUS LIFE

By 1958 the McColl-Gerard Trio had disbanded. When the World Pentecostal Conference (WPC) met in Toronto that year, Jean McColl was already married to her American husband and settled into a postwar suburban life. Meanwhile, Velma and Bernice had been on the road together since that wedding, living in a thirty-two-foot recreational vehicle, travelling and ministering in the United States and Canada as an evangelistic party of two. But that happy phase of ministry life was short-lived, coming to an abrupt end at the WPC conference in Toronto when Velma accepted a marriage proposal from Dick Chapman, a prominent Vancouver Pentecostal businessman. Velma's marriage thrust Bernice into a season of soul-searching as she tried to imagine what her future might hold as the woman she had been sharing her life with brought her new husband into the mix. The Chapmans were very welcoming to Bernice, even sharing their home with her as they offered her a place to live in Vancouver.

Gerard welcomed the stability of sharing an address with Velma and Dick Chapman, but accepting their offer came after a season of inner turmoil for Gerard. "I wanted to get married myself," she confided to readers of her autobiography. "I was head over heels in love with a man, and he with me," she recounted.[1] Although she says very little about it except for a few paragraphs in her second autobiography, her archived photo albums contain two photographs of "Bill": one, a professional portrait that he signed "With love, Bill" and the other, a picture of the happy couple side by side, with the caption "B & B."[2] Gerard did reveal the depth of her struggle when she wrote, "The object of my passion was in my opinion very attractive; the chemistry was right, and I thanked God he was sincerely living a Christian life ... There seemed no end to my capacity for rationalization, that is, thinking up good reasons for bad deeds, in this case for choosing a marriage which was out of bounds for me."[3] Like a woman deeply in love, she remembered that "his red roses, phone calls and love letters kept coming! I was wearing his ring and in the mood for marriage. But I also knew I was not thinking straight. We broke off the engagement by mutual consent, and the wedding did not take place. I cried, but not for long."[4] Gerard was forced into that choice, giving up her heteronormative desire, to protect any future ministry opportunities that might arise. It was not that her fiancé, Bill, disapproved of his future wife doing that kind of work, but "I knew full well that my denominational fellowship would lose no time in lifting my Missouri District [Assemblies of God ordination] credentials, if I married a divorced man."[5] Velma was free to marry the widower who proposed to her, but Bernice could not do likewise because Bill was a divorcee.

Gerard opted to return to UBC as a mature student. Picking up the studies she had abandoned when she accepted a wartime teaching job, Gerard took the leap and enrolled as a second-year arts student, almost twice the age of her classmates. During frosh week, when she lined up with hundreds of other students for the in-person registration process, Gerard had a conversation with Dr. Malcolm MacGregor, head of the Classics Department, whom she describes as a "personality-about-campus." As he helped her choose her courses, he struck up a casual conversation:

MM: "When did you do your first year?"
BG: "Sixteen years ago."
MM: "Have you had any philosophy or psychology?"
BG: "Not much."
MM: "What have you been doing since you left school?"
BG: "I have been an evangelist."
MM: "You have been an evangelist! Heavens above, you *do* need help. Here, I'll get you into Professor Rowan's class. He'll help you sort things out."[6]

Gerard would come to learn that Professor MacGregor – and Professor Rowan, whose class he recommended – liked to throw out challenges to incoming students. As she completed her registration process that day, MacGregor sent her on her way with a tone of condescension, promising, "We aim to make you literate." Gerard remembers that "as he looked at me, wishing me well, I sensed that he felt a certain pleasure in knowing that I was going to be given a good shaking up at UBC."[7]

Indeed, Gerard would be shaken up by her university experience, but not in a way that her professors predicted or that left her feeling intimidated. Returning to university studies as a mature student, Gerard came with a wealth of life experience so that she was hardly a typical undergraduate. Not shy or introverted, but nervous all the same, Gerard recognized the privilege that she would enjoy as a postsecondary student and she relished the prospect. "The idea of a life of constant intellectual exploration where everything is subject to critical evaluation and nothing held sacred was a concept that fired my imagination," she wrote. "It had taken years to get here and now, come what may, I wanted to play the game."[8] No one, including Gerard herself, could have imagined that she would play that game of intellectual pursuit and campus involvement so well or so long.

Pursuing higher education from a public university set Gerard apart from most Pentecostal ministers in Canada in this period. As *Maclean's* magazine reported in 1962, "The Pentecostal policy makers have a strong aversion to higher education, to what they call 'book learnin' [*sic*]' and to liberal arts courses even for the ministry."[9] A leading denominational figure, W.E. McAlister, told the *Maclean's* journalist that "too much education encourages skepticism and skepticism is ungodly."[10] With that fear in mind, and in order to immerse prospective ministers into its own subculture, the Pentecostal Assemblies of Canada (PAOC) had established a network of its own Bible schools to train leaders rather than encourage them to enrol at public universities or colleges.[11] But Gerard was not typical and she was not afraid of hard questions. She never did graduate from a Pentecostal Bible school although, as a UBC graduate student, she was a part-time instructor at Western Pentecostal Bible College, where she taught English and Church history.[12] Unlike the educational pattern of most PAOC ministers, especially the men, Gerard had completed one year of university at UBC followed by her Normal School training in 1942–43. After she returned to her studies at UBC in the fall of 1958, she earned two degrees: an undergraduate degree in 1962, and a master's degree in English in 1967. Her graduate thesis on Milton's *Paradise Lost* explored the question of Milton's orthodoxy.[13]

But earning those degrees was only one part of what occupied Gerard's time in these years after her travelling ministry ended. By 1963 she was working on the campus as a member of the university chaplaincy team, a position she would continue to occupy until 1985.[14] In that role, she worked to understand the needs and mindsets of students – both religious and irreligious – and she joined a team of chaplains from six other Christian churches, offering her another opportunity to revisit her prejudices about who should be considered a "real believer." Learning to make allowances for denominational differences meant that Gerard was predisposed to be somewhat open-minded when the charismatic movement emerged and rumours about new spiritual experiences surfaced among believers in historic churches outside of classical Pentecostal circles.[15] Gerard's studies and her campus networks meant that she was fully integrated into the campus, feeling very much at home there during a period when the role of religion on public university campuses was being debated and significant shifts toward secularization in Canadian society were under way.[16] Gerard embraced the campus experience completely, working to make change and, at the same time, being changed herself. Her time at the university expanded her thinking in some unexpected ways.

When Gerard travelled internationally as an evangelist, her world had expanded geographically and her Pentecostal associations broadened, but during this phase of life at the university, she expanded her mind. Her intellectual world was widening because of her studies, stretching her religious ideas as she grappled with the complexities of creating and sustaining meaningful engagement with her professors, fellow students, colleagues, and community members. As Gerard quickly came to recognize, each of those groups she interacted with included people who were religious and people who were not. Indeed, she sorted her contacts into mental categories of believers and unbelievers, and just as she had done as a teenager, she modified her definition of who could be regarded as a "real Christian." She recognized that despite some differences, Christians had much more in common with each other than the gatekeepers in some groups cared to admit. As a Pentecostal working with chaplains from the more traditional churches, Gerard respected her peers and coworkers, remaining curious and open to see where the Spirit might be moving in new or unusual ways. Among the believers she met, many were changed by their encounters with her, but she was changed by them too. Gerard continued to apply the insight she had gained from her earlier experiences. Her own evolving religious identity and her professional encounters had taught her that no one group had a monopoly on truth. And yet, she maintained her commitment to two fundamentals: the evangelical conviction that everyone needed the experience of being "born again," and the Pentecostal insistence that encounters with the Holy Spirit led to deeper spirituality. In other words, she liberalized some of her views about inclusion as she expanded her network to include Christians from historic denominations, but at the same time she doubled down on her core beliefs about conversion and Spirit baptism.

From the late 1950s and for the next three decades, Gerard's campus experiences entwined with other aspects of her life as she came to embrace not only the world of learning, but also the evolving religious landscape. Irreligion was becoming more prevalent on campus and in the wider society yet at the same time a wide variety of people, including those in the mainline churches, were having new spiritual experiences as the charismatic movement swept through the North American religious scene.[17] Gerard's interior world expanded because of her studies and her campus chaplaincy work, and this led her into her initial encounters with ecumenism beyond her Pentecostal networks. At the same time she clung to and reinforced the fundamental truths that defined her Pentecostal identity because those ideas gave her ballast as she sailed through some uncharted waters.

In her autobiography, she admits that because she was coming "from a religious milieu [as a newly returned travelling evangelist], it occurred to me that even for me, with so many years logged in Christian service, the university could be a risky place. Suppose someone presented me with the proof that God did not exist, what would I do then? At that point I had no clear idea what would be required for such a proof, or if anyone had come up with evidence that would satisfy the demands of rational argument."[18] The rhetoric about university campuses being "risky" or "dangerous" places for conservative Christian students is a trope that Gerard used in her autobiography because it would have resonated with readers. As Antony Ferry had reported in *Maclean's*, Pentecostals worried about the influence of skepticism on young adults and the very real possibility that they might lose their faith.[19] University training, especially in the liberal arts, does encourage students to think outside their established world views, and many conservative Christians still find that exercise threatening, even pushing them to claim that postsecondary educational institutions are a site of "persecution" for evangelicals.[20]

In her first semester of studies, Gerard found herself in a classroom with Dr. Rowan, whom she describes as "a good teacher and very funny." In his philosophy classes, where "God was laughed off the campus," Gerard waited for several weeks before she mustered the courage to challenge the professor and point out to him that his humour about Christianity revealed cracks in his own logic. Gerard began, "Professor, you are not as rational in your arguments as you claim to be. You insist that Jesus is a good man, and His disciples honorable men, yet you at the same time refuse to accept the New Testament account of what Jesus did ... Sir, you say Jesus was a good man, and yet, according to the principles of rational discussion, He cannot be both good and bad, true and false, at one and the same time. He is either what He and His faithful disciples say He is, or He is deceived, or a madman, or a liar!"[21] The professor invited Gerard to debate him, and she declined, saying earnestly, "No sir, I do not feel competent, but I simply had to point out that you are not being fair to the Christian witness."[22] With that remark, Gerard was not being arrogant or disrespectful, but she would not admit defeat or concede to this dynamic instructor. She was earnestly insisting that the professor must respect his own principles of logic and, at the same time, refrain from mocking the legitimacy of faith. She wanted to communicate, for his sake, but also for the sake of her fellow students, that Christian faith was a legitimate world view that should not be mocked.

The fact that Gerard was willing to take such a public stand, rising to her feet in a classroom setting to address the popular professor, impressed her classmates. She describes the scene after the class when a group of evangelical Christian students found each other in the hallway outside the classroom saying, "We had not realized there were so many of us in the class, and that we had all been feeling the same way."[23] When Gerard saw how many other students shared her views, she not only felt supported, but she also realized that there was a need to create community among conservative Christians on the campus. She took up that role formally the year after she finished her own undergraduate studies, meeting the requirement that chaplains should have at least a bachelor's degree.

However, as she completed her own degree work, Gerard was defined by more than taking a defensive stand of "contending for the faith," as evangelicals might express it, or resisting the new information and world views she was encountering. She embraced the opportunity for intellectual exploration as she completed a variety of courses (including world religions) to deepen her understanding about other ways of seeing the world. She wrote papers on a variety of religious texts, not just Christian ones. Her penchant for clear communication meant she earned high marks even as she adopted relatively conservative interpretations of the material she was mastering. In a paper titled "The Good News of the Bhagavad-Gita," that she wrote for her third-year religion class, Gerard earned a grade of A−. The handwritten comments on that paper praised her scholarship with this feedback: "Good essay. Thoughtful − Discriminating − well arranged and well expressed."[24] Gerard was a serious student and she applied herself to mastering mundane tasks such as academic conventions, including proper citation styles, which she confessed were a struggle for her.[25] More importantly, as Gerard studied, she filtered the material through her Christian lens, looking for parallels and differences between her own beliefs and the texts she was reading. Her personal copy of *The Song of*

God: Bhagavad-Gita contains her markings on the text, including underlining of some passages she used in the paper, but also marginalia including references to New Testament scriptures that occurred to her as she read. In the last section of the book, "The Yoga of Renunciation," when Arjuna asks Krishna for clarification about renunciation and nonattachment, ten pages of teaching follow, concluding with this instruction: "You must never tell this holy truth to anyone who lacks self-control and devotion, or who despises his teacher and mocks at me."[26] Beside this paragraph, Gerard wrote "pearls before swine," a reference to the New Testament Sermon on the Mount, when Jesus instructed His followers "Do not give what is holy to the dogs; nor cast your pearls before swine, lest they trample them under their feet, and turn and tear you in pieces" (Matthew 7:6). Gerard called to mind these parallels between her own religion and the Eastern religions she was studying, and her archived sermon notes from this period are sprinkled with references that illustrate her mastery of the material and her skill at making this content accessible to her parishioners and her radio audiences.

Gerard's graduate work provides another form of her life writing that offers insight into her intellectual formation and approach to ministry. In her master's thesis, Gerard grapples with issues of theology, history, and orthodoxy, displaying her ability to think critically, wrestle with complex intellectual puzzles, and formulate a compelling argument. Her thesis, "Milton's Orthodoxy and Its Relation to the Form of *Paradise Lost*," encompassed a wide range of subjects and approaches including literary criticism, Church history, apologetics, and theology. Clearly, she had been shaped by that undergraduate philosophy class in logic because her thesis provides a well-structured and logical defence of Milton without falling into the trap of dismissing counterarguments. The thesis tackles the problem of Milton's unorthodox views about creation, mortality, and the trinity. Those are key Christian doctrines, and it was a serious charge against Milton that he played with those issues and held to positions outside of the views established by the Church fathers and codified in the creeds. Gerard builds her case in defence of Milton by arguing that on many more items, he was solidly orthodox, including his approach to history, which she found to be "providential, universalistic, epochal, and teleological," characteristics that align completely with her Christian view. She also found his views on Christian marriage were orthodox, though she tempered her admiration for Milton when she pointed to her disappointment with his patriarchal antiwoman stance. He was a product of his time, she conceded. The main argument Gerard used to establish Milton's orthodoxy rests on the fact that he emphasizes God's supreme authority and praiseworthiness while presenting the way of salvation in a classically Christocentric manner. In other words, Gerard declares Milton was no heretic. Rather, she praises him for the creative way that he communicated the Christian gospel message, because according to Gerard, Milton faced a particular challenge as a poet-apologist trying to present a "Christian theme in a pagan and classical form."[27]

Gerard's graduate work should be seen as a form of her life writing because this was more than an intellectual exercise for her. She admires Milton for his presentation of the gospel message in a form and to an audience that challenges the boundaries established by systematic theology set down in the creeds by the Church fathers. She finds him inspirational in this regard, and it could be argued that in many ways her own ministry was framed as an imitation of Milton, because challenging some established orthodoxies in order to promote others was Gerard's way too. She nimbly used her creative intellectual abilities to find ways of presenting the gospel message in forms that broke rank with traditional Christian institutions, including some classical Pentecostals. Yet, as she did so, she held tightly to the core tenets of the gospel. Without overstating Gerard's effectiveness, it is not an exaggeration to say that as an apologist for the Christian gospel (specifically the Pentecostal version of that gospel) she, too, was a master of adopting different forms to communicate to the broader culture and did so at the risk of being misunderstood by her religious peers. Early in her ministry career while travelling in Florida, Gerard had already been suspected of being unorthodox herself, and as she wove tighter networks with other Christian believers through the charismatic networks she developed, she would be suspected again. At the same time, like Milton, she was creative in the forms she was willing to adopt in order to connect with the broader culture and communicate an essentially conservative religious message. Here, Gerard echoes what historian Grant Wacker observed about Pentecostals, that they are pragmatic adopters of modern means, while remaining conservative in their core revivalist messaging.[28] While more conservative critics judged Milton unorthodox because of his views on creation, mortality, and the trinity, Gerard concludes that in *Paradise Lost*, there is no reason to dismiss Milton as a heretic because after a careful reading of his work, she found "nothing but well and fair."[29]

Indeed, thinking about Gerard's graduate thesis as a piece of life writing, one sees that she not only clears Milton of all charges of unorthodoxy, but she admires his creative approach to communicating the Christian gospel in a literary form attractive to those outside the church. She calls him "surprisingly ingenious" and "astonishingly successful" with the daunting task of translating the Christian gospel into a "pagan and classical form."[30] His poetic genius was something she hoped to imitate in her own gospel work. While Gerard was critical of Milton on some issues, including his views about women, she thought his cultural engagement was laudable and his intellectual nimbleness worthy of imitation. Gerard found Milton compelling for his creativity in communicating the gospel message through a particular literary form, thus reaching an audience who might not otherwise be interested in exploring Christian themes of redemption and deliverance.

By devoting herself to university studies, including graduate work, Gerard was not a typical Pentecostal. While most Canadian Pentecostals steered clear of higher education, except for the vocational training offered in their own Bible colleges, Gerard embraced it. She loved literature and she loved learning. For her, education and religion were never in competition. As she studied, she relished the opportunity to grapple with complex ideas, and she contemplated how she could become more skilled in communicating the gospel message to an even wider audience. Writing a graduate thesis about orthodoxy was a far cry from giving an altar call at an evangelistic tent meeting, but to Gerard, the two settings were linked because she brought her Pentecostal world view to her studies, and she realized that people who attended religious meetings or heard her speak on the radio were grappling with some of the same profound questions about the human condition that were at the heart of academic debate. Gerard embraced her studies enthusiastically, but her love of learning never precluded her sense of call to reach people with the gospel. Her intellectual life only deepened her quest to understand the human condition and address the longings she saw in people's lives. She leveraged her academic training in her gospel work, both on campus and beyond. In part, Milton appealed to her because she was intrigued by a writer who communicated Christian themes to a wide audience, even if it meant pushing the bounds of orthodoxy. While Gerard did not stray from her identity as a Pentecostal, she was not hemmed in by a particular set of Pentecostal doctrinal boundaries. Therefore, when her creative communication strategies took her outside the circles where other evangelicals and classical Pentecostals felt safe, Gerard became an early adopter of ecumenical impulses. Her years of travel and international experiences left her with an appreciation for how broad the Pentecostal family was in all its expressions. Her confidence rested on the fundamentals of her faith, and she was ready to be generous about the finer points of doctrinal disputes as she grappled with the tension of how to be "in the world but not of the world."[31] For more than two decades, Gerard's world revolved around the university campus, as a student and a chaplain.

When she was invited to speak at the 1971 meeting of the Pentecostal Fellowship of North America about how to approach campus ministry, Gerard had a ready answer.

> What is the most helpful idea that ever struck you concerning the university campus and the presence there of Pentecostal students, professors, and campus ministers? My answer, wrung out of more than ten years [of] experience as a Pentecostal university chaplain is, "That Jesus Christ is Lord of the campus!" There are, of course, many other Biblical insights which help make university days an exciting venture in faith, but just thinking of Him and His attitude toward our campus and its people does great things for my outlook. Often I have walked over our scenic, impressively modern campus and prayed, "Lord help me see what you see, and love as you love." Thanks be to God, He has given me some insights and convictions about campus ministry which have proven marvellously fruitful.[32]

Although she framed that opening remark in providential terms, Gerard's philosophy of ministry among postsecondary students clearly was something she had pondered in depth; it was much more than uttering one-line prayers and finding simple answers. As she revealed, she had insights and convictions about the task, but these were rooted in ideas and convictions that matched her interior world and were developed from her reflections and readings on the question. By examining how she explained her campus ministry, we find another example of how her thinking was shaped by complexities. While she claimed that God gave her those ideas and that is why they were successful, it helps to see the way her success was grounded in a particular time and place and was tied to her own experiences and thinking.

After her first few years back at university, Gerard recognized that religion was certainly not absent from the campus, as many Pentecostal believers imagined. Indeed, she noted that there was a large and varied team of university chaplains present at UBC and Simon Fraser University (SFU), with at least six different Christian denominations represented. Among the clergy who were available to provide counselling to university students were Roman Catholic, Anglican, Lutheran, United Church, and Baptist chaplains.[33] Gerard found it strange that Pentecostals were not represented among the chaplains, and so she decided to inquire about it with the PAOC national leadership. Evidently, they heard her. "On my recommendation, the Pentecostal Assemblies [of Canada] decided to appoint an official chaplain, and, to my surprise, they selected me.

FIGURE 6.1 Pictured alongside representatives of several historic denominations, Gerard served as the only female chaplain on the campuses of UBC and Simon Fraser, where her appreciation of ecumenism grew as the charismatic movement was emerging. | *Summit Pacific College, Hudson Memorial Library, Bernice Gerard Nielson Family Scrapbook.*

The Anglican chaplain, Alan Jackson, made me welcome in his office, and the Assemblies [PAOC] paid my expenses."[34]

To find a Pentecostal minister (especially an ordained female!) serving in the capacity of chaplain at a public university in Canada during the turbulent decades of the 1960s and 1970s is surprising for two reasons. First, unlike some other Canadian universities, UBC was not founded by church colleges collaborating, and second, British Columbia is widely recognized as the most irreligious province in all of Canada.[35] The university, prestigiously regarded and publicly funded as the only provincial university in BC from its founding in 1915 until the mid-1960s, was the second largest university in Canada next to the University of Toronto. A few years after her initial appointment at UBC, Gerard was also named to serve as a chaplain at SFU, which opened in 1965 after being hastily organized to help alleviate the bulging postwar enrolment crisis. SFU was widely regarded as one of the most radical and irreligious university campuses in the country. These were unlikely postings, indeed, for a Pentecostal chaplain, but especially so for Gerard as a middle-aged woman and a former itinerant evangelist.

In the 1960s and 1970s, Canadian universities expanded rapidly as baby boomers came of age and participation rates in postsecondary education increased. British Columbia was no exception to those demographic trends. UBC had been recognized since its founding as the provincial university;[36] by the early 1960s, however, it was clear that one university did not have the capacity to meet the increasing demand for postsecondary education and by 1963, the University of Victoria was created, with Simon Fraser University following only two years later. SFU was sometimes referred to as "the instant university" because it was conceived, built, and operating within less than three years.[37] The haste in creating this new university left no time to consider the incongruence of an authoritarian model of university governance and the world views of the students and faculty who would populate the new campus. Still, that new university included chaplains representing half a dozen Christian denominations as part of its student services.

The story of Bernice Gerard's work as a university chaplain gives a glimpse into how Canadian Pentecostals were attempting to intersect with campus life when traditional expressions of liberal Protestantism on campuses were in decline, irreligion was on the rise, and tumultuous social upheaval was dominating youth culture. Conservative evangelicals inserted themselves into campus ministries in that context. On Canadian university campuses this was a period of radical political action as students demanded participation in university governance and challenged previously accepted social mores, attitudes, and behaviours, balking at the *in loco parentis* principle the university administration assumed over student lifestyles, rules, and governance of campus life.[38]

The students' demand for increased participation in governance coincided with the expansion of postsecondary education that was unfolding against a backdrop of major social change in the 1960s in Canada.[39] Ideologically, a shift was occurring toward the left, and more liberal attitudes were exhibited across Canadian culture. Among youth, the social unrest manifested as a rejection of the materialism that dominated their parents' postwar suburban ideals. Social critics pointed to the rise of an industrial-military complex, and the voice of antiwar protesters gained strength as the Vietnam War dragged on and American draft dodgers flocked north of the border. Socially, sexual mores were liberalizing with demand for more open access to abortion, a greater acceptance of premarital sexual expression, and in Vancouver specifically, a greater open-mindedness toward public nudity and forms of popular culture that pushed the limits of what had previously been considered "decent" according to shared ideas of community standards. On the federal political scene, Trudeaumania swept the nation, and the hip, "young" prime minister wasted no time in bringing about sweeping changes to Canadian laws that included the decriminalization of homosexuality and birth control, and liberalized attitudes toward and access to abortion and divorce. University campuses were sites where many of these new social mores were promoted and reinforced. To cite but one well-known example, a McGill University student group in Montreal published *The Birth Control Handbook* in 1968, a publication that was widely circulated across the campuses of Canada and the United States containing detailed information about various birth control methods and promoting sexual experimentation as a new norm among young adults.[40]

That period of tumultuous social change was the backdrop for campus life when Bernice Gerard took up her calling as a chaplain. Yet, amid the radicalism that was unfolding, religion was still a prominent feature of campus life, as historian Catherine Gidney reminds us in *A Long Eclipse: Liberal Protestant Religion and the Canadian University, 1920–1970*. Gidney establishes that contrary to what previous scholarship about the rise of secularism claimed, religion was still alive and well on Canadian campuses up to the late 1960s although it was evolving.[41] Gidney focuses on liberal Protestantism but she acknowledges the growing presence of evangelical student subcultures on campuses during and after the 1960s, pointing to the growing divide that existed between liberal Protestantism on the one hand and an increasingly strong evangelical campus presence on the other. According to Gidney, liberal Protestants lost ground in the 1960s when campus groups like the Student Christian Movement found themselves sharing space with other religions and even atheists. But at the same time, liberal Christianity found a new challenger in what Gidney calls the "aggressive" expansion of more conservative evangelicals on campus such as the expanding networks of Inter-Varsity Christian Fellowship and Campus Crusade for Christ. Such movements gained momentum in the postwar years because of the rising fortunes and media presence of North American evangelicalism, perhaps most famously embodied by the American evangelist, Billy Graham.[42] The aggressive evangelical presence was represented on the campuses of UBC and SFU, and Gerard was part of the emerging evangelical alliance in Canada that John Stackhouse and others have traced to this same period.[43]

Although Gerard was the first PAOC university chaplain in Canada, she was not alone in the work and she read widely about what was happening on other campuses.[44] When she took on the role, accepting it as part of her calling to serve God, Gerard had already become very comfortable on the campus; having completed her undergraduate studies, she was in the midst of her graduate program and had served on several university-level committees including the university senate. One of those committees, the Senate Committee on Religion on Campus, dealt with questions surrounding the relationship between religion and the university. Moreover, Gerard made history in 1972 when she became the first woman ever to officiate at a UBC Baccalaureate service.[45]

Not only did she participate in committee work, but Gerard also did her homework to learn about the students who would be at the centre of her "mission" on campus. In 1963 when she began the work, UBC had almost fifteen thousand students. Gerard took steps to find out how many of those students were Pentecostals. By her calculation, the answer was approximately ninety students. She knew this because she held events including informal social gatherings and shared meals where she used guest books and asked students to sign them, not only as a record of attendance but to provide contact information, including their church affiliations. In this way, Gerard collected data about who was frequenting her gatherings and she learned quickly about the students' networks.[46] It is clear that she saw campus ministry as a means to develop Christian students in their own faith journeys, and also as a means of urging them to evangelize their peers. In her autobiography, Gerard reflects on the balance she was trying to strike as she encouraged Christian students to take their studies and their faith seriously:

> I was eager to see Christian students pull out all the stops and go for all the university experience had to offer, but not to the detriment of their walk with God. We had to be ready to take up the cross of agonizing over intellectual difficulties. In the midst of uncertainties, when in all honesty we see our own resources to be far from adequate, we must be willing to share what we know to be true. A clearly reasoned presentation of the gospel is important, not as a rational substitute for faith, but as a *ground* for faith.[47]

She saw her chaplaincy role as a mentorship, where her own experiences, like the formative one she had in that undergraduate philosophy course, shaped the way she worked with students.

However, as a forty-year-old graduate student, Gerard was not really a peer to the young students she was shepherding, and she did judge them from the perspective of a middle-aged person:

> Many Christian freshman come on campus in a fog. They do not know what of theirs to be proud of, or what, if anything, to apologize for. It is some time before they see the campus as it really is. How to do an honest job as a student and at the same time develop one's own potential (spirit, soul and body) is something they need to consider. Some neglect their studies as they busy themselves in religious activities; some study hard and are glad to hide in the stacks because they fear they will lose their souls if they dare to face university life square on.[48]

However, Gerard did not blame the students for their shortcomings. Instead, she thought their families and their churches had failed to give them a good grounding in their faith. She wanted to encourage Christian students to drop their fear, embrace the privilege of education, and find some balance between their faith and their academic life. Gerard worked to create opportunities for students to network and meet each other in social settings so that they could create a sense of community, but she was not insular in limiting her contacts only to students who already professed a strong faith or had ties to Pentecostalism. She was casting her net much wider than that. Gerard used several different strategies to structure her work with students including the infrastructure of seeking PAOC sponsorship to make her chaplaincy official.

From her role as part of the chaplaincy team, Gerard could begin to establish some measure of how university students were thinking about religion and the ways this should shape her campus work. One of the methods she used to collect data was a campus survey. In September 1968, Gerard and her fellow chaplains used a questionnaire at SFU during the student registration week. They asked students to complete a card providing information about their religious affiliations and invited them to add any additional comments they had. Gerard collated the results, paying particular attention to the remarks that students provided. She reported to her radio listeners, "You must realize of course that 1000's of students voluntarily gave their names, addresses and phone numbers, and their church affiliation ... [ellipsis in original] and felt no need to put anything in the space that invited comment. But here for you[r] consideration is a random sample of the comments ..."[49] What Gerard offered were ninety-eight of those "random" responses that students offered, and she used that qualitative data as a basis for strategizing about her work. Her handwritten notes on the list show that she was thinking about the categories of students she was likely to encounter, including "sarcastic cynics," "committed believers," and "thoughtful seekers."[50]

Gerard's list included some hostile remarks: "Don't start pestering me"; "This is an idiotic form and wastes time"; "Is this any of the university's business?"; "I fail to see the point of this questionnaire"; "Why?"; and "Sickening!"[51] These responses were in step with what recent scholarship has revealed about irreligion in British Columbia. The work of historians Lynne Marks and Tina Block demonstrates that the 1960s were a critical period when the ranks of irreligion swelled as increasing numbers of people stopped attending church.[52] Scholars of irreligion use oral history to explore the personal stories and experiences behind the statistical reality of declining church involvement and cultural perceptions of the West Coast region as a hotbed of atheism and alternate lifestyles.[53] In the realm of belief and spirituality, it is noteworthy that Marks and Block explore the rise and influence of alternate communities, including groups like the Humanist League, to understand where people turned when they abandoned the churches. Gerard was eager to offer a sense of community to students, whether they were believers or not.

The study of irreligion serves as a foil to another reality that was developing in the same period: while students were calling for greater diversity and inclusion, other students were engaging with religious fundamentalism. While all these lines of thinking were represented on the campus, Gerard's work was tied to the more conservative strain. The campus survey revealed that religious views were quite varied, from the dismissive to the positive. That range included both liberal and conservative leanings: "Thank you for being interested"; "Would be interested in an ecumenical interest group." Yet another wrote, "Any philosophy that creates enlightenment is worth making the effort to understand its ideas. All of these religions have ideas of value." And others: "Eastern religions should receive greater emphasis"; "Happy with our church. United"; "Services welcome"; "There are not activities on campus for Jewish students – and there is no rabbi on campus – even part time"; "Great service to campus!"; "Glad to see this"; and "Good idea."[54] It would be students in this "positive" category that Gerard worked most closely with on initiatives that involved challenging unorthodox ideas like extremely liberal theology.

Gerard's synopsis shows that she was particularly intrigued by comments that, although brief, were thoughtful. She was drawn to those that showed a religious inclination, as these examples illustrate: "In reality scepticism is my real faith. No group seems to have answers in harmony with knowledge obtained at S.F.U." Several admitted to uncertainty or ambivalence such as "I don't believe in any rigid doctrine"; "Not a regular church goer. Rather dubious of any Christian Faiths"; "Perhaps you should have a column 'undecided'";

"Only a family religion. Very undecided as an individual"; "Just not sure about God yet"; "There is a growing interest among students in Philosophies such as Zen Buddhism and forms of Hinduism. I am very much attracted to these myself although I do not belong formally to any organized group or church."[55] While this was hardly scientific data, Gerard relished the rich insights she was gaining from this qualitative evidence, preparing her for the variety of students she would encounter. She thought about the responses as opportunities for evangelism, especially in this third group of comments among students who were curious but not convinced.

Gerard was not an interloper to campus life with the sole purpose of evangelism. Instead, she was a thinker and an integral part of the community who took the academy and intellectual work seriously. In her 1971 talk titled "Bringing Christ on Campus" Gerard declared: "There is no question in my mind that God is calling Pentecostals to a special ministry in the secular universities. Which means some of us will have to be hard-working academics, taking seriously that the quest for and sharing of truth is a primary vocation of the university."[56] Gerard did not hold an idealistic view of the academy, and she offered criticisms that resonated with her religious audiences when she shared her insight that "the academic community prides itself on its objectivity and impartiality and often worships some highly questionable idols: the goddess of success, scientific materialism, mere intellectualism and the spirit of this age."[57] At the same time, she valued higher education and encouraged reluctant conservative Christians not to discount the benefits of university training.

Gerard's life writing gives important clues about how she approached her calling as a chaplain and her purpose on the university campus. These same records provide insight about how she translated her ideology into strategies and concrete plans of action. She worked among conservative religious students on several initiatives, hosting gatherings for them in her home, encouraging them to embrace their studies and speak up about their beliefs. She was especially deliberate in her work with Pentecostal students who were studying on the campuses of UBC and SFU. She wished to shake these students out of complacency and equip them to be effective witnesses both on the campus and after their graduation. Students who came from classical Pentecostal churches faced a particular set of challenges, especially before the charismatic movement took hold. About such students, Gerard asserted,

> Often they came labouring under a severe "fear" complex. Higher education was held by many of their pastors and parents to be dangerous; in the churches there was a fairly common, brash and unthinking anti-intellectualism which

ill-equipped the student for his campus pilgrimage. Not the least of these fears had to do with apprehension over what others thought about Pentecostals. Definitely for Pentecostals arrival on the university campus provoked a crisis of identity.[58]

Warned by their parents and pastors (who were steeped in anti-intellectualism) that university was a dangerous place where they might lose their faith, these students felt they needed to be on the alert to withstand the dangers of secular humanism. Even when Pentecostal students mingled with other Christian students on campus, Gerard observed that they downplayed their distinctive beliefs and experiences about Spirit baptism because they wanted to fit in with believers from other evangelical subcultures. Pentecostals in Canada were working to gain respectability in this period, both with the larger culture and among other evangelical believers, shaking off the popular perception that they engaged in strange and outlandish behaviours given their reputation as "holy rollers."[59] Gerard was frustrated by the Pentecostal students' hesitation to embrace and promote their distinctive faith practices. It was clear in her mind that every born-again Christian needed a subsequent experience of Spirit baptism following their conversion. Without that spirit of empowerment, living the Christian life was a struggle; with the Spirit there were new levels of boldness, power, and giftedness that would increase the Christian's effectiveness and joy in service. One of Gerard's typical expressions was exactly that: "There is joy in serving Jesus!"[60]

Gerard was free to express that joy at UBC and SFU because even though the universities were wrestling with the question of religion's place in their institutional life, the presence of chaplains on campus was still normalized. Chaplains were billed as a part of student services; they were religious figures who would provide counselling for students seeking them out. In 1979 journalist Eleanor Wachtel, now a well-known national CBC radio personality but at the time a freelance journalist, wrote a feature article for the UBC alumni magazine about campus chaplains. Wachtel observed that "UBC regards them with benign neglect" and that "chaplains are on the fringe of the campus – both literally and figuratively."[61] Yet despite their location at the edge of the UBC campus (a chaplaincy office was located at 10th Avenue and Wesbrook), Wachtel admired the nimbleness required of chaplains as they juggled conversations on everything from personal crises to metaphysical questions. Wachtel was not critiquing the chaplains' presence but offering a respectful portrait of a challenging role where these spiritual leaders made themselves available for conversation and guidance without a formal agenda of trying to convert anyone.

Their role, she said, was to be "generalists in an age of specialization."[62] Gerard certainly embodied that nimble ability to range from topic to topic, and she leveraged it with her live radio programming. Yet Wachtel's reference to marginalization was apt because chaplains were not university employees. Each denomination appointed their own chaplains and paid their salaries; they were forerunners to the mental health professionals and counsellors now commonly employed as campus staff members.

Gerard was not concerned that chaplains might be regarded as marginal, or that universities were working hard to reflect the growing secularism that called for definite separation of church and state by removing religion from universities. Indeed, as someone who wanted to embrace less formal approaches in her work with students, Gerard welcomed the freedom of throwing off church structures and organizational models borrowed from the business world. In Gerard's mind, those mechanisms stood in the way of more organic and relational approaches to sharing the love of God. Critical of denominational leaders who measured their successes with metrics borrowed from the corporate world, Gerard asserted, "But it must be born in mind that the 'brick and mortar mentality' (how many churches have you built?), 'the denominational drive' (how many new members this year?), and the competitive, often schismatic spirit (my church against your church) that has pulled down so many spiritual endeavours has no part in our unique inheritance."[63]

Through the lens of gender analysis, it is clear that Gerard's critique of the businessman's approach to ministry would touch a nerve. She held her denominational affiliations loosely and did not endorse the subculture of male church leaders who competed for measurable results to satisfy church boards, donors, and constituents looking for good return on their ministry investments.[64] Instead, Gerard suggested that her model of valuing relationships over denominational competition was more in step with the leading of the Spirit. Indeed, as a Pentecostal, the main premise of her campus ministry philosophy was Spirit empowerment. She suggested that the secret to success was being "able to move in the university world under the Holy Spirit's guidance. Therein lies the key to our most fruitful ministries on campus and elsewhere."[65]

Yet while she claimed to rely on the Holy Spirit, Gerard had also thought deeply about how to approach her campus ministry and that included reading scholarly literature about religion, specifically the work of anthropologists and other social scientists. She was striving to understand the psychological and sociological aspects of religious conversion experiences as she framed her philosophy of campus ministry. One 1968 article from the *Journal for the Scientific Study of Religion,* titled "Five Factors Crucial to the Growth and

Spread of a Modern Religious Movement,"[66] proved to be particularly influential to Gerard's thinking. The study focused on the growing popularity of Pentecostalism, especially the emerging charismatic movement, and Gerard was intrigued. Luther P. Gerlach and Virginia H. Hine, two anthropologists from the University of Minnesota, challenged notions about Pentecostalism as a sect that appealed only to society's most marginalized. Instead, the researchers emphasized that individual Pentecostals had personal "charisma" that served in part to explain the rapid spread of their ideas. They did not depend on top-down organization. They used pre-existing relationships to recruit new members. They emphasized acts of commitment and experience (being born again and baptized in the Spirit). They operated with a change-oriented ideology. And finally, they had a shared perception of opposition.[67] Gerard considered each of those characteristics and found them to be true of Pentecostal experience. Just as she had read the texts from other world religions in her undergraduate studies, Gerard read this social science paper with interest through the lens of her own faith experiences. Anticipating objections from critics who might question her use of secular sources as a way of framing her approach to ministry, Gerard admitted that the academics "quoted no Bible verses, but a Biblically literate Christian has no difficulty making the identification."[68]

Gerard leveraged the idea that growing religious movements could expect to face opposition. For example, she worked with students who shared her frustration about the claims arising out of the "god is dead" controversy. She recounts that when one of her fellow chaplains "came on strong as a god-is-dead theologian," she was very disappointed that he would promote such an idea as a viable belief for university students to adopt. The chaplain in question was removed from his campus post, or "hung up by his bishop" as she put it, but there was a positive outcome because the episode "helped the Pentecostals to get into action." As Gerard explained, "In answer to prayer, the Lord gave me the idea of having students buy pages for publication inside the radical, frequently vulgar student newspaper."[69] Again, while this was clearly a strategic rhetorical move, Gerard framed it as a providential, spirit-led initiative.

Gerard's foray into print using the UBC campus paper, the *Ubyssey*, gives further insight into her thinking about campus ministry. While she told her listeners in 1971 that it was an idea the Lord gave to her, support for purchasing publication space also came from some prominent and well-endowed BC Pentecostals, including members of the Gaglardi family. On March 3, 1966, Gerard and the students she was working with made their debut in print. The four-page insert in the campus paper was called the *Wayfarer*. In its pages, Gerard and her followers identified themselves, explaining that "*The Wayfarer* is published by the Associated Full Gospel Students for the purpose of Christian witness. We believe that the claims of Jesus Christ have been too summarily dismissed by too many students. Letters to the editor should be sent to Box 46, Brock Hall."[70] The editorial team was listed as Ken Gaglardi, editor, and John Rathjen, associate editor, along with twenty-one names of assistants listed in alphabetic order after Bernice Gerard's name at the top of that list. The individual columns were signed by some of the assistants, as they wrote making the case for Christian faith, debating the relationship between faith and science, describing a drug rehabilitation program, and reviewing books. The content had an earnest, "preachy" tone to it, urging readers to consider the claims of Christ ("Relationships with Him Are on a Personal Basis"), the possibility that speaking in tongues really was a sign of God at work ("Holy Spirit – God?"), and the success of Christian ministries that were helping people struggling with addictions ("Home Cures 80 Per Cent of Addicts").

The other purpose of the insert was to announce upcoming campus events sponsored by the Associated Full Gospel Students. One of the announcements in the first edition of the *Wayfarer* is noteworthy for what it reveals about this student group's affiliations. A feature titled "Ministers Come to Talk Religion" announced that two guests were scheduled to visit the campus later that month. One of them was the Rev. John (Jack) Pitt, an Anglican affiliated with the Full Gospel Business Men's Fellowship, from New Westminster, BC, and the other was the Honourable P.A. (Phil) Gaglardi, the BC minister of highways from 1952 to 1972 and a member of the provincial cabinet under Social Credit premier, W.A.C. Bennett.

The Social Credit Party held power in BC from 1952 to 1991, with only one interruption when the New Democratic Party unseated them for three years, from 1972 to 1975. As Jean Barman explains in her history of BC, the Social Credit's rise to power was the first time that evangelical Christians had a significant involvement in provincial politics, as several of Bennett's caucus members were adherents of evangelical faith groups. The most well-known among those members was Gaglardi, also known as "Flying Phil," a Pentecostal minister and successful businessman from Kamloops. According to a 2022 report, Gaglardi's son Bob, with business holdings including the Sandman hotel chain and several restaurants, had a net worth of over $3 billion, ranking them among the top twenty-five in the list of Canada's wealthiest individuals and families.[71] In his first speech in the legislature after the 1952 election, Phil Gaglardi declared he was "not only a minister of the Crown, of the Queen, but also of the King of Kings."[72] Gaglardi was a colourful individual. As the *Wayfarer* explained in the announcement that he was coming to the UBC campus, he would be "speak[ing] as a minister of the gospel but it is not expected that his presentation will be 'stuffy' (even if it is religious) because there is nothing stale about Mr. Gaglardi."[73]

Gerard's ties to the Gaglardis are significant for two reasons. First, they give insight into her political leanings as the Social Credit Party was notorious for its conservative social policies and its close ties to industry and business. And second, these networks demonstrate that the Pentecostal connections Gerard was fostering among sympathetic supporters included increasingly successful businesspeople. As Pentecostalism gained strength in numbers (the Canadian census data shows that just over 500 Canadians identified as Pentecostals in 1911, and by 1971, that number ballooned to 222,390[74]), they were also gaining social and cultural capital. With friends like the Gaglardis whose pockets were very deep, Gerard was aligning with influential sympathizers who could lend material and political support to the kinds of initiatives she hoped to undertake in her campus ministry and beyond.

On the campus of a public university like UBC, the conservative and aggressively evangelistic tone that the Associated Full Gospel Students held forth in this publication and the events they promoted would not go unchallenged. After the first issue of the *Wayfarer* appeared in print, vigorous objections arose. The following week, a letter to the editor of the *Ubyssey* appeared: "We object – we object to the inclusion of a blatantly evangelical publication in a supposedly nondenominational newspaper. If this publication, The Wayfarer, was paid for by the Full Gospellers then its status as an advertisement should be clarified."[75] The editorialists continued to build their case, writing "Regardless of the puerile content and invidious implications inherent in the Wayfarer, the real objection must lie in the fact that this [university] is a non-religious institution. The personal religious convictions of a small minority group, sincere though they may be, have no place in a publication sanctioned by the Alma Mater Society."[76] It was not an overstatement to call the *Wayfarer*'s content puerile. On the masthead of a later issue, the paper declared "Our God Lives. Sorry About Yours."[77] It was clearly meant as a cheap shot at the "god is dead" theologians but undoubtedly came across sounding smug, petty, and exclusive to those who were not following the intricacies of the theological mudslinging.

The objectors were raising an important point. They were right to question why the student newspaper, funded by student fees, was being used as a religious vehicle to privilege and promote particularly conservative views. The editor replied, defending the inclusion of this paid supplement simply as a business decision and service to a campus student club. The editor's defence pointed out that other student groups distributed their inserts inside the *Ubyssey*

FIGURE 6.2 Even while she called herself a feminist, Gerard was well-known as an outspoken antiabortion protester, and she is pictured here identifying herself as a member of the UBC campus with the placard she was carrying during the Walk for Life event held on Parliament Hill, Ottawa, November 3, 1973. | *Summit Pacific College, Hudson Memorial Library, Bernice Gerard Nielson Family Scrapbook.*

because it was an efficient and convenient way to do so, including the education undergraduate society ("the Edussy"), the agriculture student club ("the Moobyssey"), and the frosh ("The Oddyssey"). The objectors were quite correct to point out, however, that nowhere did the paper make clear that the *Wayfarer* was a paid insert to the student newspaper. The *Ubyssey* editor made the case that the decision to include the insert was not an endorsement "any more than an Eaton's furniture sale insert in a downtown paper is 'sanctioned' by the publishers of that downtown paper."[78] Still, with Eaton's flyers, readers could easily recognize the brand and know that the insert was a paid advertisement. That had not been made clear with the *Wayfarer*. The objectors' argument worked. Although the *Wayfarer* continued to be published in the *Ubyssey*, by 1967, the word "Advertisement" was prominently displayed at the top of each page.

The publication that Gerard and the Associated Full Gospel Students worked on was not mainly about defending orthodoxy or taking reactionary stances. The main purpose of the publication was to promote events and guest speakers that Gerard was bringing to the UBC campus. And many of those guests, who were associated with the charismatic movement, came with messages about how the Spirit was moving in miraculous ways. Gerard did not spar often with those from the mainline churches, reserving her harshest criticisms for fellow evangelicals who did not share her views about spiritual gifts or public engagement. At the same time, she consistently nudged classical Pentecostals reticent to disclose the importance of their personal experiences of Spirit baptism, to speak up about how Spirit empowerment was crucial for the ways it empowered them for service, increased their love for God and people, and set them apart from nominal believers.

As a chaplain, doubling down in defence of the truth was not Gerard's main focus. Her primary interest was paying attention to how the Spirit was moving. Rather than take a rigid stance to protect a denomination or doctrinal statement, Gerard was openly critical of Pentecostal churches that failed to prepare their youth for campus life. She oriented herself with an open curiosity about what the Spirit might be doing or saying through circumstances, people, and trends. What surprised her the most was how much she saw the Spirit working through characters and organizations she had previously dismissed. Throughout her time as a chaplain, Gerard adopted a growing openness to various Christian denominations. She had come a long way from her adolescent years when she had been convinced that the circle of "true believers" was very small and very narrow. By the 1960s, Gerard had seen enough to know that sometimes God moves in mysterious ways, using the most unlikely people, and she was poised to enthusiastically embrace the emerging charismatic movement.

An evangelical presence on public university campuses in Canada persists to the present. The PAOC continues to sponsor a program called "Serve Campus Network," and in 2024 their website declared that the ministry is "positioned on dozens of campuses across our nation," with "many more yet to be reached."[79] Sometimes Pentecostals attempt to draw a straight line from Gerard's chaplaincy at UBC and SFU to the work the denomination now sponsors. While there is no doubt that Gerard's work was pioneering and there might be lessons to learn from what she did in campus ministry, tracing a direct line between Gerard and twenty-first-century programs of campus outreach and mission efforts, such as those hosted by the PAOC, is an exaggeration even if her campus ministry work seems suggestive for twenty-first-century Pentecostals strategizing ways to relate effectively with students and colleagues at institutions of higher learning. However, there are important caveats that should be noted. Gerard was in step with the continuing urge to evangelize the "lost" and she saw potential to make converts on university campuses because "the students themselves for the most part were open, idealistic, and ready to be won for Jesus Christ."[80] Sentiments like that are still held by twenty-first-century strategists who hope that Gerard's work as a campus chaplain might guide them on questions about what Pentecostals and other evangelicals currently express as "how to be 'missional' in a secular campus setting."[81] What is often overlooked by Pentecostals eager to evangelize on university campuses is the fact that Gerard did not parachute into the university milieu as an outsider hoping to protect Christian youth from the hard work of challenging the views they had learned in their families and home churches.

Bernice Gerard embraced her campus experiences as a time of growth and intellectual stimulation. She appreciated the privilege that postsecondary education represented, and she welcomed the chance to engage with ideas and grapple with academic puzzles. She excelled at logic and brought her critical thinking to her studies at both the undergraduate and graduate levels. When she engaged with ideas, she looked at them through the lens of her Pentecostal faith. She noticed that young undergraduates, especially those from Pentecostal churches, were not sure of themselves or their church heritage, and she took her role as chaplain very seriously, hoping to both support and challenge young adults in their faith. She wanted young believers to recognize that doing serious academic work was not incompatible with their Christian life and practices. And at the same time she urged them to see their campus as a mission field where they could share the good news of the Christian gospel with others. To help students do that, Gerard had several strategies, including using the student newspaper to offer an alternate world view, hosting numerous events to build a sense of community, and inviting guests to the campus to expose students to the transformative potential of Christianity, especially its Pentecostal-charismatic expressions. Partly as a sign of her own expanding world view, and partly in hopes of fostering broader collaborations, Gerard reached out and built networks with charismatics who were emerging from within the historic churches, finding common ground with them in their encounters with the Holy Spirit. This open-minded curiosity about what was unfolding meant that Gerard crossed boundaries and built bridges with like-minded believers that left some in her religious circles feeling very uncomfortable. Her affinity with charismatic Catholics, for example, was misunderstood among many in her PAOC circles. Yet Gerard saw no problem going where she felt the Spirit was leading her. She was convinced that the Spirit was leading her to forge new ties with her Christian "siblings" as she discovered that the family of God was much more inclusive than she had realized.

The professor who had predicted that Gerard would be shaken up by her university experience was absolutely right. But that shakeup took on dimensions neither he nor Gerard could have predicted. She developed intellectually, and she looked for creative ways to do campus outreach, but perhaps the biggest shakeup of all came from her close encounters with charismatic Christians from a variety of church backgrounds that caused her once again to adjust her definition of who was a real believer. As much as Gerard enjoyed her life on campus, she never confined herself to the ivory tower, and in her attempts to preach the full gospel to unconventional audiences in unconventional ways, Gerard turned to radio, beginning while she was still a chaplain.

Chapter 7

ON THE RADIO

In the fall of 1973, Gerard asked her radio listeners to write in telling her why they enjoyed her programming. One admiring fan from Victoria, BC, wrote a systematic explanation about why he found her broadcasts so compelling. He explained that the strength of the radio program could be found in what he called "the Magnetism of Encounter"; specifically, he pinned it to Gerard herself and her personality, suggesting that it took a special kind of talent to do what she did: "To be a radio openliner takes rare ability and knowledge, far more than any professor needs. Very few men can do it. For a lady to be so good at it is a far greater rarity. In this sense you have double appeal."[1] The writer explained that "as a woman pastor you are in a pretty rare niche." He admired Gerard's strong stance on controversial questions telling her she was "a great spiritual rarity also in that you stick to your guns. In the case of heavy fire you hold to your position. The world is now filled with flabby people and you stand out like a beacon in your strength."[2] But the number one reason the writer offered to explain Gerard's appeal was her intellect. "You bring something desperately needed by mankind, the power of the fully developed *female* [emphasis in the original] mind, its balance and invigoration. Your personality has courage, wisdom and experience as reflected in your voice, steadfastness and dedication. But it is the power of your developed mind that seems to win."[3] Given Gerard's commitment to feminism, including her personal conviction that Jesus was a feminist and that Gerard's gender by no means hampered her calling, she would have been particularly pleased when the listener asserted that "Christianity has a strong element of the female mind within

FIGURE 7.1 Gerard had an engaging radio persona, and her late-night phone-in show was popular with listeners across the Lower Mainland and into Washington State. | *Summit Pacific College, Hudson Memorial Library, Bernice Gerard Collection, uncatalogued.*

its wonderful fabric. And you, as a developed female mind, seem truly at home there."[4] Maybe his glowing review of her work explains why she kept that letter among her personal papers, but gender definitely shaped her radio work.

By the mid-1970s when that adoring fan from Victoria wrote to her, Gerard had been involved in radio broadcasting for three decades, and her Vancouver broadcast had grown from a five-minute feature to live programming where she interacted with callers for more than four hours every Sunday.[5] Gerard's first introduction to radio ministry dated back to her volunteer work while she was a teacher in Rossland, when she joined the McColl sisters for their weekly wartime broadcasts on the local radio station at Trail, BC. Throughout the postwar years when the McColl-Gerard Trio travelled extensively, they often spent time in radio studios cooperating with the churches and ministries that hosted them across North America and internationally. As a university chaplain in the 1960s, Gerard hosted a phone-in show called *Ask the Chaplain*, where she took calls on the local radio station from listeners. Her discussions ranged across a wide gamut of topics, attracting a broad and faithful following of eclectic listeners. As her popularity grew, Gerard spent more time on the air and rebranded the broadcast as *Sunday Line*, using a mix of live studio interviews, calls from listeners, and prerecorded material from her own preaching at her local Vancouver church. Given her proximity to the Canada-US border, Gerard's radio broadcasts were also picked up by American stations in Washington State. By 1979, *Sunday Line* evolved to launch a television ministry, and the reach of her media ministry expanded even further.[6]

When Bernice Gerard embraced radio as a ministry tool, she was part of a long line of other Pentecostals who were early adopters of this modern technology, beginning in the 1920s. Historian Michael Stamm makes the point that Pentecostals and fundamentalists outpaced the mainline churches in their adoption and effective use of electronic media.[7] One of the earliest and most well-known North American religious radio personalities was Aimee Semple McPherson, whose station "KFSG was the third radio station established in Los Angeles. Sister Aimee was the first woman to hold a Federal Communications Commission broadcaster's license."[8] In her book *Redeeming the Dial,* media historian Tona J. Hangen argues that McPherson "remains a fascinating example of the way religion functions as a form of popular culture entertainment in America and how faithful believers – religion's spokespeople – became transformed through their relationship with media into objects of intense interest, ranging from ridicule to reverence."[9] Hangen aptly characterizes the tone of McPherson's broadcasts as a "cheerful version of Pentecostal Christianity,"[10] while historian David Clark noted that "Sister Aimee also gave entertainment and assistance to many and provided a feminine symbol of daring and 'chutzpah' appropriate to Los Angeles."[11] Thinking more deeply about McPherson's gendered performance, historian of American religion Leah Payne explores the way Sister Aimee constructed and leveraged a particular expression of femininity by identifying herself as "the Bride of Christ," complete with her signature white gown and red roses reminiscent of traditional wedding attire.[12] That hyperfeminine, even sexy, imagery was obviously not a viable persona for all women in ministry and it certainly was not what Gerard aspired to convey. But just as Aimee Semple McPherson can best be seen through the lens of gender history, there is a gendered aspect to the radio personality that Bernice Gerard represented, and some of her listeners articulated that this was the secret to her large listenership.

Canadian Pentecostals made wide use of radio too, as *Pentecostal Testimony,* the magazine of Pentecostal Assemblies of Canada (PAOC) illustrates. In December 1963, the publication ran a feature called "Canadian Revivaltime," about C.M. Ward, a Canadian who had become the voice of the American Assemblies of God radio voice and broadcaster. In his tone, Ward resembled other radio preachers with a familiar preaching format and a revivalist message. Ward's program had an impressive reach, "released over more than 445 stations – fifty-one of which are outside the United States – and reaches an estimated audience of 12 million in the United States, with many more being reached abroad. Yet the broadcast has only reached a fraction of its potential audience."[13] PAOC leaders were convinced that radio was "one of the best ways to transmit our Pentecostal message to the remotest areas where it may be heard by the most hardened sinners." Therefore, they promoted *Revivaltime* as a "soul-winning arm of the local church. It reaches those in your community you cannot reach ... [because it] goes beyond the closed door and pierces the heart of the indifferent listener who 'accidentally' tunes in for the first time."[14] In that same issue, the PAOC was announcing that it was possible to get the Canadian version of the *Revivaltime* broadcast on local stations because their national office had a radio department that could help to facilitate a contract arrangement with local stations and provide taped content.

While Bernice Gerard was in step with other classical Pentecostals in her use of radio, she used the medium differently by promoting interdenominational cooperation. Through her campus chaplaincy, Gerard found herself in conversation with voices of the charismatic movement long before her own denomination accepted the legitimacy of the reported move of the Spirit taking place among the historic denominations. Gerard had overcome those hesitations quite soon after the movement emerged, and she welcomed charismatic leaders with enthusiasm and curiosity. For that reason, her story invites comparisons with Canadian Pentecostal David Mainse, who built multifaceted broadcast ministries in the same period through a similar combination of ecumenical spirit, charismatic conviction, and evangelical impulse.[15] At the same time, Gerard's gender set her apart from the male models of broadcasting that Ward and Mainse represented, and the difference showed not only in the tone of her programming, but also in the level of listener engagement, especially among those who were not regular churchgoers.

While the PAOC offered Ward's prepackaged radio content for circulation on local stations, and Mainse had national appeal, Gerard took a unique approach because she started with the assumption that the city of Vancouver and its university campuses were her mission field. She embraced opportunities for her radio broadcasts to intersect with her chaplaincy work and her expanding involvement in local charismatic circles. Her content was focused on her listeners' needs and was very wide-ranging in scope, but at the same time, Gerard spoke and wrote about the strategic ways that all churches should think about embracing technologies.

In the late 1980s, she wrote a paper, "Electronic Evangelism and the Local Church," where she claimed that "the availability of electronic media to our generation has launched a revolution as dramatic as when the 95 theses were nailed to the door of Wittenburg Cathedral. Never before in the history of the world has it been possible to take the message of Jesus Christ to so many people, to cut across man-made barriers, international boundary lines including iron and bamboo curtains, and right in our own cities enter double-bolted doors to apartments and private residences."[16] Ever the evangelist, Gerard agreed with her denomination in their unbounded enthusiasm for technology's potential to reach people with the gospel message. Gerard's radio broadcasts and the accompanying archival materials where she reflected on this part of her work support the idea that part of the explanation for her wide appeal was her gender. Specifically, Gerard engaged empathetically with a variety of callers and listeners to hear their concerns and offer counsel.

As a radio host, one of Gerard's hallmarks was her effectiveness at attracting a broad range of listeners well beyond her own campuses and well beyond the churches. Her weekly phone-in show on public radio in Vancouver attracted a wide variety of listeners and put Gerard on the radar as an entertaining and engaging religious broadcaster who enjoyed a wide audience in her own province and beyond. No doubt it was partly on the strength of her popular media presence that the *Vancouver Sun* declared Gerard the most influential religious figure of the twentieth century in BC. Writing about religious broadcasting, Hangen argues that "religious radio changed the evangelical movement's self-perception and strategic position in American life from marginalized outsider to ubiquitous cultural presence, preparing the way for an aggressive assault on moral and political fronts in the latter half of the twentieth century."[17] Exploring Gerard's media personality and presence shows that she was not a typical radio preacher using aggressive pressure tactics to persuade listeners but instead she cultivated an inviting airspace where listeners felt they shared an intimate bond with her. She gently asked her listeners,

> Are you in trouble? Would you like to present your problem and allow me to help you find an answer? We can certainly help you explore possible solutions. And then as you tell your story, a host of warm-hearted people who believe in prayer will be listening and sharing with you in a constructive way.[18]

Gerard had the air of a compassionate and trusted friend, and she made clear that she was part of a wider community of people who cared; in this way, her media persona was highly gendered, as the letter from her Victoria fan pointed out. She did promise to provide answers, but the intimacy and trust she established with her listeners was offered with genuine concern for people's circumstances. And listeners who felt that care learned to trust her.

Gerard began with her campus work, but she paid attention to making the content of her programming accessible to all listeners. For example, when her sermon included material based on an academic study about religion, she took extra care to make the language simple. At the same time, she recognized that university colleagues might be listening and explained one of her sources saying, "He gave the big words and I'm translating them ... What amused me about this man's English is, he says, they are 'even less amenable to quantification.' [He means] it's hard to count them. I trust that some of you academic types are not going to be offended because I'm making jokes about your academic language."[19] Gerard had recently completed her graduate studies at UBC, but she worked hard at connecting with her listeners by making academic ideas simple and clear. And no matter what their education levels, she hoped all her listeners would enjoy thinking through the various issues and themes her programs raised.

Gerard revealed her motivations for going on the air: "I give my five minutes every day on this station and know that there are thousands upon thousands who are influenced consciously or perhaps even unconsciously. My goal is to excite people over the marvellous privilege of giving everything in service to Jesus Christ. Also it seems to me absolutely necessary that Christians today should be intellectually aware and challenged."[20] At first she would offer five-minute segments in answer to listeners' questions, and Gerard asked her listeners to wade in and offer their opinions about her format. "I understand that five minutes of this kind beside a news broadcast is considered a prime time," she said. "I would be interested to hear from some of you who have been listening to 'Ask the Chaplain' if you find the five minutes provocative and helpful." She continued with her reflections on audience engagement saying, "For one thing, it is not just how much you say but how much is heard that makes the difference between just filling up spaces on the air and actually communicating." When she called for listeners to write to her, Gerard explained that it was essential for her to hear what people thought of her broadcasts because "real communication requires that information flow both ways. In order for an individual to communicate he must also be able to listen. That is one reason why I am very anxious to receive mail from you, the listener. What is the effect of a provocative five minutes?"[21] She hoped that her time on air was not just entertaining, but that it also caused people from all walks of life to think deeply about a variety of issues.

140   *Pentecostal Preacher Woman*

While it is impossible to know how many of Gerard's listeners were among the "academic types," her archived correspondence does contain many letters from listeners over the years, and they demonstrate that while their literacy levels varied, listeners made deep connections with their radio host. Even when her time on air was short at first, Gerard knew that she was still having an impact. "It is true isn't it that people who do not listen for long periods of time to Gospel broadcasts will listen for a few minutes if the topic is such as to interest them."[22] Audaciously, she suggested there was a parallel between her broadcasts and the Pope's brief words from the Vatican balcony on Sundays, noting that the Pope bore a great responsibility because many of the people who crowd into St. Peter's Square are faithful Catholics "willing to accept his spiritual leadership."[23] Gerard took her radio ministry seriously for a similar reason, knowing that her listeners looked to her for spiritual direction and she was responsible for whatever she said during her time on air.

With high levels of audience engagement, Gerard's broadcasts grew in popularity and in length; by the early 1970s, she was doing four and a half hours of open-line programming on Sundays.[24] As she explained,

> I've received letters from young and old, male and female – a nice cross-sectional representation of CJOR's listening community. The letters, with comments and contributions were most encouraging. If you haven't written yet, but are listening, and thinking as you listen, please write ... this week.[25]

Topics for Gerard's shows were based in part on a variety of issues the callers had been thinking about, including theological and ethical questions, drug culture, sexuality, and Eastern religions. Gerard was surprisingly respectful of those who did not share her views, and her listenership grew as she broadened her medium to a cross-border audience in the American northwest.

Bernice Gerard shared the evangelistic agenda of other American radio preachers, but her tone was not the aggressive manner of a male preacher. Nor was it the "cheerful" message of Sister Aimee's hyperfeminine manner. And while Gerard remained unabashedly Pentecostal, her broadcasts were not in the tradition of stereotypical Pentecostal radio preachers who invited listeners to put their hand on the radio to receive their healing, mysteriously transmitted through some mystical exchange made possible by the airwaves. Gerard did not offer "dazzling religious theatrics," like McPherson.[26] Instead, Gerard used the radio to extend the conversations she was already having with various leaders and converts of the charismatic movement she had joined through her campus contacts and beyond. Her very first radio guest was Kevin Ranaghan, the Catholic theology student who had invited her to Notre Dame for the Catholic-Pentecostal dialogue meeting.[27] Her eclectic network of charismatics, classical Pentecostals, and chaplaincy colleagues gave Gerard a lot of possibilities when she planned who she might invite into the studio to share the broadcast. She aimed to create provocative programming that would make her listeners think about a variety of issues.

Probably one of Gerard's most infamous programming decisions was to invite the Singing Addicts, a group from New York City, to visit Vancouver, speak on campus, and appear on the radio with her. In conjunction with David Wilkerson, who founded Teen Challenge, a New York–based organization that worked to reach gang members and drug addicts, this travelling spectacle was not just for entertainment, but also to tell personal stories of deliverance from lives of crime and addiction. Led by John Gimenez, a former addict who became an influential American Pentecostal leader, the group toured widely, and Gerard was pleased to book their visit to her city. Promoting the campus visits in the *Ubyssey* student newspaper,[28] Gerard explained in her autobiography,

> [this plan] received a great deal of publicity in Vancouver, partly because [the Singing Addicts] were subject to a deportation order because of previous criminal convictions at the time they attempted to enter Canada. Our Associated Full Gospel Students Society helped the group appeal, and Canadian Immigration Minister Jean Marchand reversed the order, so the singers were able to present their dramatized version of the horrors of drug addiction.[29]

Sadly, Gerard learned that shortly after their visit to Vancouver, several of the group members returned to their previous lifestyles and succumbed to their addictions. While that news called into question the validity of Gerard's guests, she was happy to note that Gimenez, the leader of this touring group, maintained his new lifestyle for the long term. As Gerard declared, "Twenty years later John's miracle is still good."[30] Gimenez became the influential pastor of Rock Church, a large Pentecostal congregation in Virginia Beach where he also headed the Rock Satellite Network and chaired Jesus rallies in Washington, DC.[31]

When she invited such provocative guests to her broadcasts, it was clear that Gerard was using the radio program to communicate with a wide audience. She wanted all her listeners to be inspired by the power of the conversion stories they heard, but specifically she hoped older people, especially churchgoers, would realize that some of the social movements afoot among youth were more easily understood if one took the time to listen. A newspaper headline from the summer of 1968 referenced Gerard's campus work and billed her as the chaplain who "Learned Students' Jargon." Describing her thoughts about working with students and young adults in the midst of the turbulent 1960s, the journalist reported, "Miss Bernice Gerard thinks that if people have something to say, we should listen to them, no matter whether they are a square or a hippie."[32] Speaking at a women's luncheon, Gerard addressed the problem of how to bridge the so-called generation gap by listening to the ideas behind youth rebellion. "The people of the community must not shut out the young people just because their hair is long. Some of the hippies have good things to say: they are, for instance, against our materialistic society."[33]

Still on the topic of hippie culture, in December 1968, Gerard welcomed three guests to her CJOR Sunday morning radio show and explained to her listeners that these three young men "have been involved in the hippie movement."[34] Gerard's motive in presenting various topics, including Eastern religions and hallucinogenic drugs, was not to open people's minds to other religious views, but rather to explore what the felt needs were of various groups and use their own expressions to find new ways of articulating the gospel message of repentance and conversion. While it was clear that Gerard was by no means a social rebel, she was creative and intellectually curious, eager to engage with individuals who expressed views and behaviours that were unlike her own. For that reason, she welcomed guests to her radio studio whose personal experiences would serve to enlarge her listeners' understanding and appreciation of what motivated social protest.

Given the time period and the youth culture where Gerard ministered as a campus chaplain, it comes as no surprise that she should offer a program on the topic of "hippie culture." Working on campus Gerard had come to the realization that "students for the most part were aware that scientific materialism, long the religion of the majority, had been weighed in the balance and found wanting. A nation's well-fed, affluent, and metaphysically starving youth began reaching out for beatific visions in the only way they knew – with a five dollar bill and a few grains of L.S.D. There was, and still is, an amazing new openness for religious experiences. Very evidently now our task is to show students the way to take that one trip that will bring them to reality instead of providing an escape from it."[35]

What Gerard attempted when she welcomed young counterculture activists to come on air parallels historian Bruce Douville's findings in his study of charismatic and evangelical engagement with Toronto's youth counterculture in the 1960s and 1970s.[36] Douville explores how liberal Protestant churches as well as charismatic Pentecostals ministered among hippies, gangs, and displaced youth living in communal spaces in Toronto's Yorkville. Young believers involved with the "Jesus Movement" agreed with irreligious hippie peers in their critiques of middle-class conventions and scientific materialism. Yet in the realm of social experiences and cultural engagement Douville argues that these young believers were also surprisingly conservative. Because of their personal stories of recovery from addictions, and for many their previous work in the sex trade, Yorkville's "Jesus People," who operated communes and coffeehouses in 1960s and 1970s Toronto, clung to a gospel that concentrated more on individual conversion experiences than engagement in social causes. While Douville's study was situated among downtown mainline churches including some university venues, most of the believers he traces were not direct participants in higher education, unlike the postsecondary students Gerard was reaching.

"What is a hippie," Gerard asked her studio guests, "and why did you decide to adopt the hippie lifestyle?" In response, her guest, "Jacob," explained that hippie culture was an extension of youth protest and a critique of the middle-class establishment. "We call ourselves 'hippies'" he explained, "because we are the products of parents who are hypocrites. When pigs have offspring, they are called 'piggies,'" her guest explained. "And when middle-class hypocrites have children, they should rightly be called 'hippies.'"[37] In the interview, Gerard probed into the deeper motivation of what had caused her guests to reject the middle-class lifestyle that their parents' world offered to them. In Gerard's mind, it was an oversimplification to explain the so-called generation gap as a form of rebellion without probing deeper. The guest, who had come to faith in Christ, explained that his main motivation was to reject the materialism of mainstream society. The chaplain editorialized that she thought what drove most young people to reject their parents' culture was their spiritual hunger. Gerard understood that in her role as chaplain and radio pastor, her purpose was to help her listeners learn from the experiences of her guests. When her listeners experienced existential crises, Gerard felt she could help them realize that what they really needed was to accept Christ and experience the baptism of the Holy Spirit. Ever the Pentecostal evangelist, Gerard was striving to bring clarity and certainty to people's uncertainties.

After asking her hippie guests about why they were attracted to an alternate lifestyle, she probed more deeply into their experiences with using drugs to try to understand what benefits they and their peers found in drug culture. Her guests were carefully selected, of course (all three had since overcome their addictions and embraced a religious faith that was evangelical), but they remained vocal about the conservative middle-class values they were rejecting and the deeper meaning of life they had come to appreciate through experimenting with drugs. There was definitely an entertainment factor to this content when Gerard, the Pentecostal pastor, a well-meaning middle-aged woman, got into conversation with guests whose experiences were so foreign to her. Like a naive but affectionate old auntie, Gerard plunged into unfamiliar territory:

B: Now, Joe ... would you say you thought you were a hippie?
JOE: Well, I imagine I did. I didn't consider myself to be a hippie, but I did consider myself to be hip.
B: Hip?
JOE: It's a thing where you think that you know where it's at, and a lot of other people are sort of missing the point by being under all kinds of illusions and this type of thing.[38]

When Gerard interviewed Joe to ask him how he first became a drug user, he explained that it started while he was a student at Simon Fraser University.

JOE: Well, when I was in university, I developed an interest in LSD, and thought I'd like to experiment with it and find out what it was all about. And so I read a few articles and a book on it and I just went ahead and tried it. This was my first exposure to it. After that, I was out of it for a while.
BERNICE: May we ask, did you have a good trip?
J: Yuh, it was good. It was interesting.
B: What do you mean? Like going to the moon, or a big mystical religious experience?
J: No, it's an insight into what you're doing yourself, it's an insight into your motivations, and what makes you do the things you do.
B: What did you like? Did you like yourself better after?
J: Well, not exactly that. It was just that it was an enjoyable experience to find out what seemed to be the truth about myself.
B: The search for meaning then?
J: Right. About a year later I was exposed to marijuana, and I tried that a few times, LSD a few times again, and this is how I got involved in it.[39]

When Gerard asked another guest, Jacob, about the time he lived in a "hippie house," he clarified that it wasn't a house, but yes, he had had an apartment of his own, what he called a "crash pad" where people could come and find temporary housing.

BERNICE:	You had your own [place]. You were what you'd call a capitalist then.
JACOB:	Capitalist?
B:	If you had your own crash pad, man.
J:	I was a dealer. I could afford it.[40]

With no concern that she might sound silly, Gerard engaged with her guests to ask questions about a lifestyle for which she and many of her religious listeners had no frame of reference.

Indeed, during this interview, a listener called in and Gerard put them on the air so they could ask a question: "I'd like these three gentlemen to explain their motivation for appearing on your programme."[41] Gerard intercepted the question, answering that they were there because she invited them to be there. There was, of course, a reason for Gerard's invitation to these three guests in particular: each of them had recently had a profound religious experience. One of the guest's, George, offered the caller an explanation, saying, "We were invited to be on the programme to sort of air our ideas, I imagine, and I thought that by being here and saying what I feel, maybe I could give some other people an insight. I've accepted Christ because I found that I needed something to hang on to, to lean on in this world, and I've tried a lot of different things, and I've done a few different things, and I found that Christ was the answer for me."[42] Jacob explained that where he had previously felt life was meaningless and he wanted to drop out of everything, he had come to realize that he risked losing himself as well. "Dropping acid, smoking grass was, for me, looking for the way out, and it was there, right in front of my nose, all the time. It was in the person of Jesus Christ ... It's the experience of the reality of Christ. And it's the experience I've tried to find in drugs. It's the baptism of the Holy Spirit."[43] Gerard affirmed Jacob's testimony, commenting, "Now you feel you've got a spiritual dimension that seems the same as, only better than the other stuff you'd been trying for before." Jacob replied: "Right. I should say this: LSD, marijuana, and hash are Satan's counterfeits for the baptism of the Holy Spirit."[44] Although the stories these men told about rebellion and experimenting with drugs were obviously outside of Gerard's own life experiences, their religious encounters were completely in step with her own Pentecostal world view. And that is why she had invited them to her show.

Gerard was very aware that her audience was mixed, and as she moved toward closing the interview with Joe, George, and Jacob, she gestured toward concerned parents with the comment, "It's just about time for us to go off the air. I really believe you boys have made a wonderful contribution by airing some of your ideas. I know there are people out there who have kids in the family who are exploring, and scaring their parents right out of their wits because some of them are getting ready to opt out."[45] At the same time, she knew her audience might include others who were experimenting with drugs, including students on her own campuses. Perhaps in a comment directed to them, or perhaps to the church audience and those who sponsored her chaplaincy work, she remarked, "Looking at the student population at both S.F.U. and U.B.C., I'd say that there are a lot of people in need."[46] Interestingly, she did not close the program with any kind of altar call or pressure tactic. Instead, she acknowledged the fear that parents felt for their young adult children and the questions that people entertained as they searched for meaning in their own lives. Gerard's answers were not typical of bombastic radio preachers. While her exchanges were obviously framed in traditional beliefs about the need for conversion and for Pentecostal Spirit baptism, they were also grounded in compassion for the people who listened to her show. To Gerard, what people lacked was obvious: they needed to experience the transcendent. And that was available to all through one means – the baptism of the Holy Spirit.

Although Gerard's answer about finding meaning was clearly a reductionist one, her broadcasts offered listeners the chance to ponder ideas, engage imaginatively, and grapple with difficult questions. In effect, as her letters from listeners reveal, her radio programs engaged people's minds. Unlike television with its visual aesthetic, radio "left all of this information to the imagination of the listener" [47] and, therefore, it engaged the audience at a deeper level with what was being said, without distractions such as the visual appeal of the television studio. Gerard capitalized on the combination of her oral communication skills and radio's potential to engage "the individual's imagination."[48] As one listener told his favourite radio preacher, "it thrills me to hear the fine music, but I can also hear the congregation think."[49]

When listeners wrote letters to Gerard, it was usually with the familiar salutation "Dear Bernice." They wrote to tell their very personal stories of moral and spiritual struggles as if they were confiding in a trusted sister or a sympathetic aunt. As Hangen establishes, this was radio's special appeal, that listeners "often mentioned in fan mail to radio preachers how they felt singled out for personal attention by a message and how close the experience of listening to radio was to having an actual religious advisor by their side. Radio shrunk distances, collapsing time and space with unseen power."[50] The power of radio as a medium was not just in its wide reach, but in its very personal touch. Hangen asserts that "a radio sermon – unlike attendance at an enormous

FIGURE 7.2 Portrait of Bernice Gerard in CJOR radio studio. In 2000, Gerard was named the most influential spiritual figure of the twentieth century in BC, and there is no doubt that her media presence was a factor in building that reputation. | *Summit Pacific College, Hudson Memorial Library, Bernice Gerard Collection, uncatalogued.*

mass meeting – could be experienced by a single listener like a personal chat. Radio religion often made best use of the medium's ability to speak to listeners as if in a one-on-one conversation."[51] Here, Gerard was typical of radio personalities who established surprisingly strong bonds with their audiences. The level of trust and intimacy that Gerard established with listeners leaps from the pages of the archived letters in which people bared their souls to tell their favourite radio host some of their deepest personal secrets. This kind of disclosure was undoubtedly more common for Gerard because she was a woman.

Gerard's gender was a factor in establishing a level of trust with listeners that evoked secrets from them; they wrote to tell her things that they had never told anyone before, not even their spouses or parents. Given her own troubled childhood and her mother's mental illness Gerard had learned the importance of compassion. Although she spoke with clarity and assurance that Christ was the answer to every problem, in fact Gerard had come to realize and appreciate that all people (whether they sat faithfully in the pews or never darkened the door of a church) were struggling with things that continued to plague them, including addictions, issues around sexuality, and past hurt caused by their families and their churches. She was painfully aware that while people found themselves in very challenging circumstances, sometimes church leaders and religious organizations were a big part of the problem as they continued to draw lines of exclusion. She had experienced it herself. That is why she was not afraid to be critical of church cultures – both liberal and conservative ones. Gerard bonded with her radio audiences in ways that were emotionally intimate even while she maintained her commitment to fundamental truths like the need for conversion and the advantages of Spirit baptism.

In December 1979, after hearing Gerard's *Sunday Line* radio program, one writer positioned herself as a "born again Christian and spirit filled, [I] am so much in Love with Jesus." The woman prefaced her confession of sexual sin, saying, "no one knows this but Jesus, I've already let him know How I feel, and been reading in psalm 51 and asked to be forgive! [*sic*]" [52] She disclosed that in the fall, through her church circles, she met and fell in love with a man. Things escalated quickly, and "I fell in my own trape [*sic*]. We both Did, we had sex four different times." Conflicted about it, the listener went on to explain that she had broken off the relationship and the man had since moved away.[53] To further illustrate the level of trust that the writer felt with Gerard, she revealed that "My Mother is a Christian and we are very close, but I just couldn't share with her about this deep part! She knows him too!"[54] And as she concluded the letter, the writer included her personal telephone number, hoping that the radio preacher would respond with a call and a personal counselling session. While it is rare to find Gerard's written replies to listener letters in her correspondence files, there is evidence that she frequently did reach out to respond by telephone. Several letters demonstrate this, with telephone numbers circled or scrawled across the letters offering proof that Gerard or someone on her staff attempted to make contact.

Confessions about premarital and extramarital sex were not the only kinds of stories that Gerard heard. Listeners who struggled with same-sex attraction also made their confessions to the radio preacher. One woman wrote to explain,

> I came to the gay liberation movement early in 1970 in San Francisco, at the age of 20. My choice to identify myself as a woman homosexual was motivated by several personal factors I won't go into at this time ... I gave myself unconditionally to the cause of gay liberation. I know I alienated myself from the wider society but only gay liberation appeared to offer me freedom.[55]

The woman had written to Gerard a few years earlier, enclosing a "small gift for Sunday Line" and explaining that she had "come to Christ." Although she had tried to deny her sexual orientation, she confessed, "I'm not trying very hard to be straight; I view that as an impossibility, and choose to pursue a life of celibacy. My feelings are not fading into the past but nevertheless, I continue to avoid openly gay situations."[56] However, as she explained when she wrote back four years later, "I withdrew, dissociated myself from the gay lifestyle. I became silent. The inner contradiction did not go away. I experienced it daily. It was outside me like a large beast looming omnipresent in front of me. Internally, like a crab with serrating pincers, it gnawed at me."[57] She was writing to tell Gerard that she agreed with the pastor's objections to the creation of another "homosexual nightclub." "You expressed yourself beautifully," the woman wrote, because "Vancouver doesn't need another such establishment."[58] The conviction that creating more social spaces for homosexuals was a bad idea was based on her own youthful experiences. She recounted, "In the clubs & bars, I was introduced to LSD, cocaine, astral projection, tarot cards, satanic worship, astrology, Spiritism, profane utterances, martial arts, scientology, the weatherman left-wing political party, the young socialists, the drug trade, gun-running, etc ... etc ..."[59] For this woman, a recent convert to conservative Christianity, all manner of evil was associated with same-sex social spaces. Yet, while she could stop frequenting such establishments, she could not change her sexual orientation. Nevertheless, she wrote to encourage the radio preacher not to be discouraged by the opposition she inevitably received from gay activists. The listener explained to Gerard, "You arouse their contempt; some mock you and even go so far as to cultivate this with care & pride. On their behalf, and representing the hundreds of silent gay people ... I ask you to please forgive the sin they harbor in their hearts."[60]

Another lesbian who wrote to Gerard focused on a different set of complications. While she, too, had resigned herself to a life of celibacy, she had not resolved the contradictions between her sexual orientation and the conservative church culture that Gerard represented. This writer revealed the deep dissatisfaction and psychological angst that pervaded her life as she tried to deny her sexual orientation. She explained, "I feel very lonely sometimes, even in a room full of people. I want to love, give love, receive love, but see myself living on the surface of living, loving. Not knowing which way to turn."[61] To complicate matters even more, she feared the social injustice of her situation as a mother.

> Bernice I am a lesbian, but in the first place a woman and because of this I can
> be jailed or have my children taken away from me. Because I am a lesbian I can

150   *Pentecostal Preacher Woman*

lose that job because the people around me are threatened by my very existence, and in their eyes I am a misfit, a genetic fault in a smoothly running biological reality. I am abnormal, sick. I may not be curable.[62]

That looming injustice was also attended and exacerbated by her spiritual crisis: "This [injustice] all I can fight or except [*sic*] or understand. Bernice, I have prayed and asked God to guide my life, but I cannot find him, maybe because I do not know *how* to find him [emphasis in original]."[63] Listening to the radio preacher made the woman's crisis more acute, but rather than suffer through her existential crisis alone, she reached out to Gerard, saying, "I take your words into my mind and into my heart – but by doing this I end up in a fighting battle, with my own thoughts, my own feelings."[64] The fact that Gerard preserved the letter is evidence that this heartbreaking situation moved her, suggesting she felt compassion for the writer. Perhaps her compassion was directed toward the children because she knew first-hand how devastating it could be for a child to be removed from their mother's care.

An elderly woman wrote to Gerard confessing, "I am not really a Christian." Yet at eighty-one years of age, she respected Gerard's work so she wrote to ask, "When I die, I would like very much for you to conduct a service at my funeral. I have no close relatives here ... but no doubt some of my people would come out from Winnipeg."[65] The old woman confessed that she had regrets in the way she had lived her life, but she praised Gerard, explaining that she wrote "to thank you for all your good works, Bernice and to wish you much happiness now and always. What a satisfaction it must be to know how much you have accomplished."[66] That correspondent was also an insomniac; her letter recorded that she was writing at 1:45 a.m., and she opened her letter saying, "Have just finished listening to Sunday Line."[67] Gerard's broadcasts invited such interactions since her program aired twice on Sundays, once in the morning and again for late-night listeners between 11:00 p.m. and 1:00 a.m.

Another of Gerard's correspondents wrote from prison to respond to what he had heard on air. His letter reinforces the emotional tie he felt with Gerard and his gratitude for her pastoral care over the radio. He explained, "I'm writing in reference to your request of correspondence from Sunday Line listeners. In no way could they possibly ever take you off the air. Anyone that values life can understand that. In more ways than one, you are responsible for saving people."[68] The inmate went on to explain more about his personal profile, revealing, "At the moment I'm in prison facing a life sentence if I'm convicted. I'm an American sailor that's seen his whole life change overnight due to liquor and a tremendous amount of ignorance."[69] Gerard's correspondent, only twenty years old, engaged with what he had heard and expressed how deeply indebted he felt to the radio pastor.

> Putting the Bible aside I can honestly say your the only [one] that's given me the courage and the understanding to survive these past few months. God willing after my trial in two weeks I can call you long distance and thank you. Too many people depend on you so please don't ever stop doing what it is your doing. I needed a good straightening out but this is just a little to hard to believe. I only hope these past few months have been enough to make up for my mistakes ... Too much babbling. I can only say your loved and we all need you. I'll never ever backslide again and I thank you for that.[70] [spelling errors in original]

Whether the writer's resolution never to backslide again was realized or not, Gerard followed his case with interest because her archives include a newspaper clipping that covered his ongoing trial.[71] The young inmate provides further evidence that Gerard engaged deeply with her correspondents and thought about their circumstances.

Indeed, with at least one inmate, she kept up an ongoing exchange of letters.

> I received your letter yesterday morning, and was very happy to hear from you. It had been awile since I had heard from you. And I figured that you had lost hope for me. But that's the way I've been for a long time, I jump to conclusions to fast. I should know by now, that you wouldn't just up and drop me as hopeless. The only two friends that I really have left, is you and my little boy." The man reflected on Gerard's appeal, saying "Keep up the good work. Your a good person Bernice, that's why I like you, I've learned some pretty good things off you. Even if I've never put them in practice. They may help me later on in life. You've always been frank and honest with me like a real gambler, you've always layed your cards face up on the table, and not down. I appreciate that, Bernice, and I've very sincere when I say this. I've always been honest with you. I don't think I could ever lie to you, for the simple reason that you've always been straightforward.[72] [spelling errors in original]

He closed the letter with a familiar tone, "Write soon and hang in there Partner. Don't forget to put the right name on the envelope."[73] No doubt writers like these reaffirmed Gerard's conviction that the medium of radio had unlimited reach, going behind locked doors and into the very hearts and minds of listeners in crisis.

Another of Gerard's repeat correspondents opened his letter saying, "First I thank you for your generosity, love and understanding toward human beings. You have always given of yourself unselfishly to those in need of prayer & guidance."[74] From a northern BC logging camp, he was writing to say he hoped to maintain his connection with her even though he was in a location too remote to hear her broadcasts:

> We can't pick up your programme here in our locality and I miss you. But I know in my heart and mind that you will carry on with your work for God and man kind. And that is a great comfort to me. I wish for you happiness and health. I thank you again for your patience and understanding with me. When I come down from camp I'm going to come to your Church and ask you to pray with me and teach me to pray for thanks that God has allowed me more chance to make up for my sinfull and yes, evil past life. Until I come back to town, take good care of Yourself and Yours' Bernice. God Bless You.[75] [spelling errors in original]

Gerard's reply to this writer reveals that through her radio ministry she established a sense of community. When she wrote back to him, she told the logger, "I received your letter with joy, and shared [it] with the radio audience at the time that I had heard from you."[76] In her reply, she explained that after he had originally called in,

> there were quite a number of people who phoned to ask how you were, or if I had heard from you, and some mentioned in letters that they were concerned and wanted me to let them know when you got in touch. In other words, as a result of the phone call when you were so discouraged, there were a lot of people who joined in prayer and who had like I did a real hope that you were going to be on the way up soon because of God's grace and mercy.[77]

The sense of community that Gerard established with her listeners replicated a congregation of caring individuals who offered mutual support through prayer and social connection. She wrote back to this man.

> In hope that you are still at that logging camp, and not transferred to another one somewhere, I am mailing you under a separate cover a copy of the New Testament, called *Good News for Modern Man*. Believe me [name withheld], I look forward to seeing you in Vancouver and to having a good chance to visit and talk over some of the things you've mentioned in your letter. I hope you'll answer me and I will try to answer more promptly next time.[78]

She also let him know that her travel schedule would take her away from Vancouver for a month, in case he came during those dates and would miss connecting with her. Then she closed with an affectionate gesture, reassuring him, "In the meantime you are in my thoughts and prayers."[79]

One correspondent wrote to say that their addictions had driven them to desperation and they were contemplating suicide.

> Bernice, as you know, I am a drug addict and have been for quite a few years. Lately my life has become unbearable, I can't tell you in words how lonely, wretched and wracked I am in both Spirit & soul. I contemplated suicide quite sincerely a number of times, but each time I ended up realizing it was a cowards way out. But then I went back to heroin and it's own private hell, and found myself deeper in the pit of fear and helplessness; and more miserable than ever. So I've decided Bernice, I want to go to GOD ... I don't know if you understand what I've said in this letter Bernice, but simply I'm asking you for help out of my hell. If you send me to someone or send someone to me, I'd be most greatful. Before it's too late.[80] [spelling errors in original]

No doubt it was alarming to receive that letter, and this desperate call for help was something Gerard took very seriously. Although it is impossible to know how quickly she responded, there are telephone numbers written on the letter that indicate attempts were made to reach out to the desperate writer. Later letters in the archive indicate that the individual did not take their own life because they wrote to say they had found work outside of Vancouver and the next time they returned to the city they hoped to come to Gerard's church to see her.

While many listeners wrote because they had no other church to turn to, others wrote to describe the pain and grief that their churches had caused them. One particularly heart-wrenching episode is recounted in the letters written by a woman who confided in the radio pastor about how the conservative attitudes in her family and church community collided with her personal circumstances and tore her life apart. Revealing that she had never told her story to anyone, the writer disclosed that in the months before their marriage, the young couple discovered they were pregnant and decided together to have an abortion. "I took the life of our child only because he would have been born seven months after our wedding celebration. [My fiancé's] mother was very Victorian in her outlook on sex."[81] That decision was complicated by the fact that they were deeply in love and planned to be married, but at the same time, they recognized the stigma and shame that his family attached to premarital sex. In an effort to protect the future mother-in-law from the embarrassment

154   *Pentecostal Preacher Woman*

and disappointment they predicted would be expressed toward them, abortion seemed like the path of least resistance. Many years had passed but the woman confided she had never recovered from the trauma of sacrificing her unborn baby in order to keep peace in the family and the church. While the marriage survived, the woman had suffered in silence for years and endured a great deal of moral anguish over her decision.

When she heard Gerard on the radio espousing her antiabortion stance, the woman felt compelled to write in.[82] She did not write the letter in anger toward Gerard and she was not interested in debating the issue of abortion. For her, the time for argument had long passed. She made her position clear when she explained she could see many situations when an abortion could be justified, "I can understand a woman or girl seeking an abortion in a case of incest, rape, financial burdens, the burden of an already large family or even being single."[83] Instead, this woman wrote to reveal the depth of her own regret for having an abortion simply to appease her in-laws' conservative beliefs. She described the horror of the procedure in some detail,

> The abortion itself was probably as bad as any you have read about. It was performed in a rundown old house near Stanley Park. There was a great blood loss, a three day labour and an infection. [We] stayed in a hotel and the doctor who was called in wouldn't hospitalize me for fear of the police being called. Our fear and remorse then is understandable. There we were, only a few days married and criminals according to law and God's word. That was our honeymoon.[84]

The writer felt she could not forgive herself because in her own mind, her situation did not justify having an abortion; the young couple only decided to abort because an overly harsh family and church subculture forced them into what they thought was an impossible moral dilemma. Because Gerard always prefaced her remarks about why she opposed abortion with her own deeply personal story about being an "unwanted" child and a product of the child welfare system, that narrative invited the kind of emotional engagement her troubled listener offered.

This broken-hearted woman chose not to argue whether abortion was right or wrong, but she did want Gerard to recognize that taking non-negotiable stances on the question usually only led to further problems. In this tragic case the choice to protect the family reputation from the shame of a baby conceived before the church wedding led to the woman's continued mental suffering decades after her youthful decision.[85] Unfortunately, the archive does not include a written response from Gerard so it is impossible to know what comfort or counsel she may have offered to this tortured soul. But the fact that Gerard preserved this letter in her personal papers illustrates that she must have been moved by the woman's story. Maybe she kept it as proof of regret after the abortion, or maybe because it revealed the impossible dilemmas people inevitably faced in such circumstances.

Like the woman who regretted her abortion, other listeners pushed back when they felt Gerard was oversimplifying things by reducing every topic to a simple answer derived from a literal reading of scripture. In answer to a caller's question about reincarnation, for example, Gerard had been unequivocal, declaring that the Bible clearly says "it is appointed unto a man *once* to die, but after this the judgment, (Hebrews 9:27)" [emphasis in original]. For Gerard that meant the discussion was closed: reincarnation was not possible within a biblical world view. One of her callers, who had found himself tongue-tied on air, followed up by writing to Gerard:

> I expect there are a number of people who listen to your programme who are also interested in meditation, yoga, and some of the various Eastern religious concepts that are gaining popularity these days – and I pictured in my mind young people who could be torn between their experiences through meditation, (which may be valid states of consciousness that are meaningful experiences of the experiencer) – and their ties to Christianity through their upbringing. It was my hope to resolve what seems to be a contradiction; unfortunately I don't think I got my point across.[86]

Moreover, the writer indicated that Gerard had opened her next program with reference to this caller's remarks, stating that listeners should heed the advice in scripture about testing the spirits, thus diminishing her conversation partner's position. The written rebuttal began there, conceding that testing the spirits was indeed important but challenging Gerard with the validity of his own experience.

> I could not agree more – but ... I am certain that the spiritual guidance I have received [through Eastern religious practices] ... is of God, as the results have been an increase in Faith in God, and an awareness of His ever-presence and my spiritual awakening to it; an increased love for the Christ; a love for my fellow men which is best described as compassion; a dedication of my life to

moment by moment obedience to the Will of God ... and repeated insights into
the inner meaning of the Holy Scriptures which come to me unawares and not
as a result of mental wrestling with it.[87]

The writer went on to affirm his belief in some of the central doctrines of the
church, including the virgin birth. And yet, he asserted that he could not echo
Gerard's certainty about dismissing reincarnation. Open to the idea, the writer
said, "I expect that I may reach that state of awareness one day. But till then I
just simply don't want to see young could-be Christians being turned off
Christianity by a certain interpretation of the meaning of the phrase 'it is given
unto man once to die and after that the judgement.'"[88] In effect, her listener
was reminding Gerard not to be so dismissive of opposing points of view.

This interaction reinforces the fact that Gerard's audiences were drawn to
her program because they were wrestling with intellectual and spiritual questions. Another evidence of this is the number of letters she received from
churchgoers who were embroiled in debates with family members over the
best expressions of their faith. Numerous people wrote to tell Gerard about
their disagreements with family members, especially parents and in-laws.
Frequently, these debates centred on the question of religious expression,
particularly whether Pentecostalism was within the bounds of orthodoxy because of the emotionalism often associated with its practice. These listeners
felt validated by Gerard's affirmation of charismatic experiences that the older
generation could not accept. They appreciated Gerard's clear pronouncements
on debated questions.

The letter from a listener that opens this chapter points to the fact that
Gerard's success as a radio host was due in part to the fact she was a woman
– a woman with a good mind. For that fan, Gerard's gender explained the
intimate connections she created with listeners who trusted her to hear their
secrets and received her sound advice without being subjected to the boisterous
tone that characterized so many male televangelists. The gender question offers
an intriguing explanation for some of Gerard's appeal. The sense of intimacy
that she created with her listeners meant that people wrote to her prepared to
divulge very personal information in great detail as they would with a trusted
confidante. When her correspondents used her first name to address her, it
reveals a certain level of trust and comfort they felt in sharing their stories with
Bernice as a maternal or sisterly figure.

Reading the correspondence in Gerard's personal archives feels voyeuristic
because the nature of the moral and ethical dilemmas contained there make
one privy to a level of confidentiality that parallels a confessional booth or a

conversation overheard through the counsellor's office door. Gerard's audience was surprisingly eclectic and surprisingly overt about their dilemmas: prisoners awaiting judgment, drug addicts contemplating suicide, lesbians worried about losing their jobs or custody of their children, elderly insomniacs planning their funerals, young women confessing their sexual indiscretions, and conflicted women forced to choose abortions to preserve the family reputation. In each of these cases, the troubled listener turned to Bernice as a confidante, pastor, and sympathetic friend. For other listeners, grappling with ideas about religion explained why they enjoyed her program. From the man who urged Gerard not to be so literal in her hermeneutics because Eastern religious practices could be helpful for Christians too, to a young wife who grappled with how to maintain family unity in spite of her in-laws' disapproval about her choice of church, correspondents were troubled by ideas more than by behaviours or ethical questions. They revealed the angst and interpersonal conflict that resulted when religion was wielded like a weapon.

As Gerard's admirers wrote to explain, it was her warm personality, her reassuring feminine presence, and her sharp intellect that attracted them to her. People turned to Gerard for answers because they felt she could be trusted with their secrets. They hoped that she would write them back, call them, or send reading materials so that they could continue to build their relationship with her and find the help they were seeking. Radio provided Gerard with the medium to foster that intimate and pastoral relationship.

Bernice Gerard was a woman with a deep mastery of media. She attracted large and mixed audiences as listeners tuned in to see where Gerard would go in her unscripted responses to such an eclectic group of callers. When people heard her broadcasts, it is probable that reactions varied from amusement to aggravation as she offered her self-assured responses. While some people probably found her earnestness amusing, others appreciated her compassionate and thoughtful approach to the topics raised by her guests and callers. If they thought she was being dismissive or too simplistic, they told her so. The listener who wrote in to praise her savvy on-air personality was convinced that because of her gender, Gerard was especially effective. He appreciated her intellect, her clear communication, and her compassion for her guests and callers. Gerard did care deeply for people, and as that letter pointed out, her emotional engagement came through on the air like a sisterly spiritual guide one could trust with deeply personal secrets and concerns. Gerard connected with her audiences in intimate ways, as her personal archives illustrate. Letters from her listeners show the kind of intimate pastoral relationship that Gerard cultivated through her media persona. Moreover, the letters show the range of experiences that her listeners chose to write about, including premarital sex, abortion, hallucinogenic drugs, hippie culture, and their adoption of Eastern religions including practices like meditation and yoga and beliefs including reincarnation.

Gerard was a spiritual sister to many, but she was also a pastor of the Fraserview Assembly in Vancouver, a PAOC church that she co-led from 1964 to 1985 with her long-time ministry partner Velma McColl Chapman. Velma and Bernice had both been ordained Pentecostal ministers since the mid-1940s, and for them, the question of whether women could or should take on leadership roles in ministry was a moot point given their decades of experience in a variety of Pentecostal circles. That question, along with the issue of how to relate to charismatics from other traditions, was not new for Gerard. While her own denomination questioned the wisdom of cooperating with other traditions and the legitimacy of women in church leadership, Gerard's ideas proved to be much more open-minded than many of her peers. Her thinking about ecumenism and feminism meant that her relationship with the Pentecostal Assemblies of Canada was complicated.

Chapter 8

CHALLENGING PATRIARCHAL AUTHORITIES

"WOE IS ME, WHAT will our people think, when they hear that I am working with a Roman Catholic?"[1] That was Bernice Gerard's internal monologue on the day she went to the Vancouver airport to pick up a guest she had invited to come to the campus. She was shocked when her guest arrived that he was accompanied by a priest. Gerard was right to worry about being seen with a Roman Catholic. After that visit, a fellow Pentecostal minister confronted her directly. "What are you doing? Our students tell me you had a Roman Catholic priest at the student gathering [at UBC], and you were all praying together!"[2] Gerard hastened to explain that working with the priest was not her idea initially. However, her further explanation was no doubt troubling to the inquirer. "He wasn't there by my invitation, Pastor; to my surprise, he arrived at the airport with Tommy Tyson; it was kind of a package deal."[3] Working with her cross-border networks, Gerard had arranged for the Rev. Tommy Tyson, a United Methodist Church evangelist and the director of spiritual life at the new Oral Roberts University in Tulsa, Oklahoma, to be her guest at the university. Tyson was one of the first South Methodist clergy to have had a charismatic experience. But his cooperation with a Catholic priest caught Gerard off guard. However, as she explained to her interrogator, "When I heard he was born again and filled with the Holy Spirit, I received him as a brother."[4] That kind of ecumenical overture was problematic. In the 1960s (and for some time after), Gerard's denomination was fundamentally opposed to cooperating with Catholics, and she would have to answer for ignoring that fact.

This was not the only problem area for Gerard as she squared off with denominational officials. Women's place in church leadership was a second major issue where Gerard's position was problematic to some of her peers within the Pentecostal Assemblies of Canada (PAOC). And to be fair, the question of women's roles in the church was not limited to her Pentecostal brothers; apparently the visiting priest was equally surprised upon his arrival at the airport. As Gerard explained, that priest "was having his own problems about working with a Pentecostal woman minister."[5] On that point, the Catholic priest resembled many Pentecostal brothers who were of two minds about women's place in church and lay leadership. Gerard sparred with denominational authorities and Pentecostal laypeople alike over her ecumenism as an early adopter of the charismatic movement and over the legitimacy of her ordination status as the PAOC reopened debate about the limits to women's leadership.

Gerard recounted feeling intrigued when one of her friends in ministry asked her, "Can you believe it, now some of the old line denominational clergy are speaking in tongues, and praising God like Pentecostals do?" The chapter "Something New Is Happening," in her 1988 autobiography, traces Gerard's involvement with the charismatic movement, explaining how she came to embrace the new charismatics as a genuine move of God and came to terms with the ecumenism that accompanied it.[6] Some Pentecostals were slow to accept that the new charismatic movement was a genuine work of God, especially when those members of historic denominations reported encounters with the Holy Spirit but refused to leave their own churches to identify exclusively as Pentecostals.

Peter D. Hocken, a Roman Catholic historian and theologian who has written extensively about the charismatic movement, defines the phenomenon this way:

> The term *charismatic movement* (CM) is here understood in its most common usage to designate what ... [is] called "the new Pentecost," namely the occurrence of distinctively Pentecostal blessings and phenomena, experience of infilling/empowerment with the Holy Spirit (generally termed baptism in the Holy Spirit) with the spiritual gifts of 1 Cor. 12:8–10, outside a denominational and/or confessional Pentecostal framework. Although the designation CM was originally applied to this work of the Spirit within the historic church traditions, it came to be used in a wider sense to include nondenominational patterns of charismatic Christianity.[7]

According to Hocken, the movement emerged in the years 1960–67, and took shape over the next decade (1967–77). Those dates overlap with Gerard's most active years as a university chaplain, and as her life writing and other supporting sources make clear, she was a curious participant and promoter of the new developments. Gerard was witnessing first-hand what Hocken explains about the 1960s when "the new movement was distinguished from the Pentecostal movement primarily by the formation of groupings affirming Pentecostal experience and gifts *within* historic denominations. At the outset, there were also nondenominational groupings witnessing to baptism in the Spirit and the spiritual gifts, but the facet attracting greater attention was the combination of Pentecostal grace and historic church affiliation."[8] Gerard was in the midst of all this, herself a devoted Pentecostal, adamantly protecting orthodoxy against liberal theology movements like "god is dead" thinking, and at the same time serving as part of an interdenominational campus chaplaincy service. From that vantage point she watched with amazement to see how this new emphasis on the Holy Spirit was unfolding.

But she was more than a passive observer from the sidelines. Gerard worried about what people would think if they saw her picking up a priest at the airport, because whether or not to work with Catholics was a conundrum widely shared among Pentecostals and other evangelicals in the early days of the charismatic movement. The divide between Protestants and Catholics was still very pronounced in Canadian church cultures, particularly in the more conservative churches, and the transition years around Vatican II in the mid-1960s until the 1980s and after, were fraught with division on this issue. An example from Gerard's PAOC world illustrates this quite well. David Mainse was a well-known Canadian Pentecostal, ordained by the PAOC, who exerted a wide influence with his foray into Christian television broadcasting as founder of the media organization Crossroads Christian Communications. Having begun in 1962 with a fifteen-minute segment for local television stations, Mainse resigned from the pastorate in Sudbury, Ontario, in 1970 to grow his media organization into a vast network with programming released on more than 150 stations by 1976. The spread and popularity of Crossroad's signature show, *100 Huntley Street*, was partly due to the way that Mainse had tapped into the growing charismatic movement and the curiosity that viewers shared to learn more about that movement and its effects in individual lives. When Mainse chose a Roman Catholic priest, Father Bob MacDougall, as his co-host for the show, it was because of their deep connections born of the charismatic movement that was sweeping North America and Mainse's long-standing connections across denominational lines. But seeing Mainse and MacDougall share the camera frame was widely misunderstood by more conservative classical Pentecostals.[9] While some of that controversy was likely to do with competition for donor

FIGURE 8.1 Gerard was an early adopter of ecumenism and like David Mainse (*on Gerard's right*), the founder of Crossroads Ministries and television host of *100 Huntley Street*; her openness to work with Roman Catholics and others caused no small stir among fellow Pentecostals. | *Summit Pacific College, Hudson Memorial Library, Bernice Gerard Collection, uncatalogued.*

resources, at its root was the fact that many people in the PAOC, leaders and laypeople alike, were uncomfortable with Mainse's ecumenical overtures. While they welcomed the wondrous thing that the Spirit was doing among those in the historic Christian churches, many Pentecostals were convinced that working with Catholics was simply going too far. It was common parlance among Pentecostals (and evangelicals generally) to say that Catholics who had had a charismatic experience had "become Christians." And, they maintained, if one had really been born again and had a genuine Spirit baptism, they would leave their "dead church" and make a formal move to join a Pentecostal one. As historian Ewen Butler has argued, there is a certain irony in the PAOC posture as the gatekeeper of orthodoxy and denominational loyalty in the face of competition from the charismatic movement, since it was only fifty years earlier that the PAOC itself was born out of a very eclectic spiritual genealogy when its own members had been misunderstood by the churches they were leaving. Yet now the PAOC was an established church itself, and any departure from their ranks to join something new was frowned on.[10]

Like David Mainse, Gerard found herself under scrutiny for her cooperation with Roman Catholics. A 1968 newspaper reported on a talk that Gerard gave to a women's conference in Ontario when she referenced her openness to ecumenical initiatives. She suggested that "Christian women [need] to communicate with people in other churches, to have interchurch dialogue. She said the Pentecostals had to find out what the Catholics, the Baptists and the United Church [of Canada] members were doing. People cannot ignore others just because they have a different belief."[11] While such a suggestion hardly sounds radical to a liberal-minded person in the twenty-first century, ecumenical dialogue was cause for concern among conservative Pentecostals in this period. As a result of her views, Gerard became the subject of controversy for the national leaders of the PAOC. That concern persisted for decades. Among Gerard's personal archives is a copy of a letter written in 1987 by the Rev. James M. MacKnight, general superintendent of the PAOC, about Gerard's involvement with the International Roman Catholic/Pentecostal Dialogue. Gerard's involvement had drawn the attention of a ministry colleague from South Africa, who wrote to MacKnight to commend him for choosing Gerard to speak on behalf of that denomination. The writer was impressed with Gerard's eloquent and thoughtful understanding of the issues surrounding ecumenical initiatives. In his response, MacKnight praised Gerard's "competence and sensitivity to the things of God," but he unequivocally reinforced the position of the PAOC that even twenty-five years after the charismatic movement had begun, there still was "no approval from our office for any official endorsement to appoint an individual to dialogue with Roman Catholics."[12]

Gerard was clearly out of step with her denomination's national leadership. Or perhaps it is more accurate to say that Gerard was years ahead of the PAOC leaders. Sixteen years before MacKnight wrote to reassert that his Pentecostals did not talk to Catholics, Gerard was already doing just that. In 1971 she wrote a personal letter to an American colleague confirming her plans to attend a Roman Catholic conference scheduled for the early summer and explained that she had been hosting an open-line radio program for more than three years "which has made quite a contribution to the understanding of the charismatic renewal on the part of many people in the denominational churches."[13] While she might have been commended for that broadcast work that was serving to spread the Pentecostal message of charismatic renewal, she crossed a line in the minds of many Pentecostals when she declared, "I am quite convinced that the Lord is leading me to work with the Roman Catholics who are sincerely endeavoring to move within the circle of their own church ... There has definitely been conflict here, but in my own mind I have no doubt ..."[14]

Gerard had settled her doubts through a series of involvements. She recounts the trepidation she felt when she accepted her first invitation to attend the Roman Catholic-Pentecostal Conference at the University of Notre Dame in Indiana.

> At first, the impressive baroque domes and abundance of decorative crosses somewhat unnerved me. I said to myself, "I am not going to feel at home here. They won't like it that I have come." Instead of feeling confident, even joyous, I was depressed by the beautiful campus and the sight of priests and nuns greeting one another with the kiss of peace. I felt myself in an alien culture.[15]

Perhaps Gerard was having flashbacks to her childhood and her Roman Catholic aunt's funeral, when she found the rituals of the service mysterious and made the faux pas of drinking the holy water when she entered the church. But that feeling of not belonging was compounded now by the fact that she knew what she was doing: meeting with Catholics was controversial and would probably be misunderstood by all sides. Given the inner turmoil she was experiencing, she turned to prayer to settle herself:

> Alone in my room at the Morris Inn, I knelt to pray and take account of what was going on in my own soul: I was here at Notre Dame to learn. Every day in recent months I had been challenged with evidence as to different ways in which God's mercy was being shown. He was upsetting some of my old ideas, but I wanted to move with His direction. Beside[s] that, the Notre Dame adventure could be an interesting fact-finding tour. If the Heavenly Father is doing something new with the Roman Catholics, we too ought to know about it. My meditation finished with a prayer of commitment: "Lord, you know why I am here. If I am to go quietly about the campus and say nothing all weekend, I'll do it. If you want me to minister to someone, I'll do it. If you want someone to minister to me, I'll receive it. Please guide me, Lord."[16]

It probably came as a great relief to Gerard that the Lord was not asking her to be silent all weekend. Soon after she concluded that private prayer session, it was time to attend the first evening meeting. Alone in the dark on an unfamiliar campus, Gerard recounts that her unease about finding her way at this conference continued, both literally and figuratively. She asked for directions from a group of fellow attendees who introduced themselves as four Jesuit priests and two Sisters of Mercy. Gerard quipped in her autobiography, "'Mercy is just what I need,' thought I gratefully, 'How perfectly appropriate.'"[17]

Finding a warm acceptance among these first contacts, Gerard was put at ease, reporting "They took me into their circle so I did not end up lacking friends at Notre Dame."[18]

One reason why Gerard made so many friends among those Catholics was the expertise she brought to the gathering about Pentecostalism and the social capital she already enjoyed among other charismatics. While many among the group had personally experienced the new move of the Spirit, they had no context to help understand what was happening. As Gerard said, "They knew nothing of the Pentecostal movement, Roman Catholic or otherwise. In fact, I knew more about the Catholic Pentecostals than they did. But they were eager to help me understand the Roman Catholic side of things and I was excited to ... see how the Catholics carried on."[19] When the conference opened with a sharing meeting, Gerard introduced herself as the chaplain of UBC and Simon Fraser University, and "at that moment Abbot Father Columban Hawkins of the Trappist Monastery in Lafayette, Oregon, got up out of his seat, came toward me in the aisle, and gave me the kiss of peace."[20] It turns out that Gerard had been part of a prayer team at a retreat in Portland, Oregon, the year before, where the Abbot had "received an overflowing anointing of the Holy Spirit."[21] Evidently, he remembered her from that occasion, and when he told the gathering about his connection to her and her role in his charismatic experience, Gerard said "it was as though my passport to complete freedom in this Roman Catholic conference had been firmly validated. The conference, on hearing a few words from the Abbot, gave me a tremendous clap of welcome so that the lonely insecure Pentecostal had reason to be ashamed for having doubted the leading of the Lord in providing the Notre Dame visit."[22] When she bravely stepped into Catholic circles, Gerard enjoyed the Abbot's endorsement, his kiss of peace, the conference public applause, and the stirring corporate worship. As she had done at earlier points in her life, Gerard took it as a very positive sign when she felt a sense of belonging; it confirmed to her that her evolving religious views and networks were indeed legitimate.

In her teenage years she had struggled with the idea of expanding her definition of a real believer to include those beyond the confines of one narrow set of beliefs. During her years on the road as an evangelist whose orthodoxy was called into question, she garnered the endorsement of important Pentecostal leaders, received ordination credentials, and participated in transnational circles of fellowship. All of that confirmed that she belonged in the big, wide family of international Pentecostalism. Now, as a middle-aged chaplain, Gerard was testing the idea that classical Pentecostals might not have a monopoly on what the Holy Spirit was doing. Once again, she expanded her views and embraced the charismatic movement along with an even more inclusive definition about whom she should regard as her spiritual brothers and sisters. She described her evolving views about greater inclusion in her autobiography:

> As time went on, the school of hard knocks and the experience of being on the receiving end of bigotry made me want to be as broad in sympathies as possible – but not to the point of being broader than Jesus. The major turning point for me was the experience of prayer and worship with people of other communions through the renewal. The fresh winds of the Spirit were influencing us to a new application of old familiar Scripture passages.[23]

The Notre Dame conference was not an isolated event and back in Vancouver, Gerard was in the thick of things as the charismatic movement unfolded there. She regularly attended and participated in charismatic Catholic gatherings, and she invited key international figures from the charismatic movement to come to her church, her home, and her campuses. The list of guests she helped to sponsor for visits to the campus and the city read like a veritable who's who of the charismatic movement. Many of those same individuals were guests of Gerard on her radio shows, including Kevin and Dorothy Ranaghan, the Catholics who had first invited Gerard to Notre Dame,[24] and David Wilkerson, a former Assemblies of God (AG) pastor and author of *The Cross and the Switchblade,* who famously worked with street gangs, drug addicts, and troubled youth in New York City, eventually founding the Teen Challenge organization.[25] And finally, Gerard counted as a personal friend David du Plessis, the South African Pentecostal known as "Mr. Pentecost," whom Gerard had met in Paris in 1950, when he organized the early meetings of the Pentecostal World Fellowship while she was travelling as a member of the McColl-Gerard Trio.[26] Du Plessis was now playing a key role in the North American charismatic movement and she regarded him as a friend and fellow traveller. Like Gerard, du Plessis embraced Catholic charismatics, and for that reason he was disciplined by the American Assemblies of God and stripped of his ordination credentials.[27] The story of du Plessis's conflict with the AG authorities serves to reinforce that Gerard was taking risks by being so ecumenical.

The largest investment of time that Gerard made in the local charismatic movement in Vancouver was her ongoing involvement with weekly Roman Catholic prayer meetings in Sunshine Hills, just outside Vancouver. For eight years during the 1970s she was also part of those home-based prayer meetings hosted by Bill and Lorraine Baldwin, who sought her out at her Simon Fraser University chaplain's office to ask if she would join their group where charismatics gathered for singing, worship, and prayer. Again, Gerard was moving outside her personal comfort zone and certainly outside the norms of PAOC church subcultures. She described how the meetings were typically held in smoke-filled rooms, and one time she was praying "for a man to receive the anointing of the Spirit. He seemed tired after all his praying, and maybe a little discouraged, so he lit up a cigarette. I thought, 'Thank God our church can't see me now. They'd wonder what we're doing, trying to minister God's Word in this cloud of smoke.'"[28] The prayer gatherings attracted an eclectic mix of people, and Gerard recalls them with fondness: "Hundreds of people poured through the weekly prayer meeting: nuns, priests, some sharing the ministry; hippies, ex-convicts, university people, neighbors, friends, anyone, everyone – people who were seekers. Wonderful things were done in the Name of Jesus."[29] She only stopped attending those meetings when she was elected as a city alderman in 1977 and had to redirect her time and energy elsewhere. Gerard's campus ministry had led her into these charismatic circles, and her ecumenical overtures were yet another step in the evolution of her faith as she once again expanded her definition of who belonged as a true believer. But her expansive outlook was not shared by her own denomination, and while the national superintendent respected her sensitivity to God's leading, he could not endorse her cooperation with Catholics or her early embrace of the new charismatic movement. Gerard's involvement with the charismatic movement was further evidence of her evolving faith. She had come a long way from the little girl in the schoolhouse who held such narrow views about who qualified to be part of that very small circle of "real" believers. Gerard's experiences with charismatic believers expanded her networks, enriched her spirituality, and reinforced her confidence that God was working outside the lines of denominational boundaries.

At the same time, Gerard was convinced that some of the boundary-making that went on within her own denomination should be challenged, especially where patriarchal structures put limits on the roles of women. Life experience had taught her that women could be powerful leaders, both inside and outside the church, and she had no patience for those who worked to limit and silence women. While her convictions about women's equality rested on decades of experience, some people within her denomination in the 1970s and 1980s worried that speaking out in favour of women's equality meant selling out to "worldly" feminist influences. To counter that cultural development, they emphasized a literal interpretation of selected biblical passages to support their views. Gerard had no patience for weaponizing the scriptures as a means of suppressing women and limiting their spiritual authority. Indeed, in her mind it was such patriarchal manoeuvres that were the real sign of "worldliness," not feminism per se.

Pentecostalism has a long and complicated history of women's leadership.[30] While early Pentecostals welcomed women to their pulpits and tent meetings as evangelists, as the twentieth century unfolded, women's roles in many Pentecostal churches became more limited.[31] For the PAOC, the issue of women's ordination surfaced in the 1970s and 1980s, and the formal decision to grant full ordination to women came into effect following the 1984 General Conference in Saint John, New Brunswick. However, what seemed like a victory for Pentecostal women was not a unanimous decision.

A great deal of controversy arose in the aftermath of the 1984 conference, fostering division among PAOC members, both clergy and parishioners, for years afterward. Several letters to the editor of the *Pentecostal Testimony* expressed the fear that delegates to the general conference had made the wrong decision in granting ordination to women. At the root of this objection was a fear that modern-day feminism had infiltrated the ranks of the PAOC, putting the denomination on a slippery slope toward worldliness.[32] Pentecostals were not alone in those worries; as Allison Murray argues, the fear of feminism infiltrating church circles was widely shared among evangelicals in this period, and the perceived incompatibility of feminism and conservative faith groups is a much-debated topic among scholars of religion.[33] But Gerard saw no contradiction between her faith and her particular expression of feminism. Objectors writing to *Pentecostal Testimony* couched their concerns about women's ordination in their high regard for the Bible and insisted that the idea of women's ordination was not biblical. Quick to point out that according to their literal understanding of the Bible there were only twelve male apostles, these editorialists concluded, therefore, that women did not belong in church leadership because "Jesus called only men."[34] Another writer accused the PAOC magazine of bowing to the culture around them, claiming that a previous issue had "a worldly cover" because it proclaimed "The Gospel Has No Gender ... Either" and depicted a female construction worker. Adding to the offence, the issue in question was for the month of December, and readers would have expected an inspirational Christmas image rather than this jarring cultural statement.[35] The division was not limited to the pages of the denomination's magazine because the issue of women's ordination repeatedly came to the floor of the general conferences during the 1980s and 1990s.

Gerard attended these conferences and consistently spoke in favour of women's ordination and including both sexes in governance roles. She herself had been ordained more than forty years earlier in the United States, and for more than twenty years she had been the co-pastor of a Vancouver PAOC church alongside her female ministry partner. For Bernice, any objections to women's full participation in ministry were out of bounds and particularly outside what she considered normal Pentecostal practice. She was convinced that Pentecostalism had always been welcoming to women preachers. Over more than four decades of ministry work Gerard had proven herself to be a capable evangelist, preacher, pastor, administrator, counsellor, and spiritual guide to students, parishioners, and radio listeners alike. Moreover, her earliest childhood faith experiences were influenced by women in ministry, not all of them Pentecostals. Shortly after she began to do ministry work with the McColl sisters in the mid-1940s, other Pentecostal women, including the Davis sisters in New Brunswick, endorsed her ministry potential and predicted she was destined to a life of preaching the gospel. Her sex had never been a hindrance; indeed, when she travelled through Europe to preach and sing with the McColl sisters, Gerard had reported that their "all-girl" act was deemed to be an asset, not a liability, and many doors of opportunity opened up for them. Therefore, it is understandable that as a woman in her sixties, with a lifetime of ministry experience to her credit, Gerard would feel weary and disrespected when she found it necessary to rise on the conference floor to speak in favour of an initiative that could clear the way for more women to take up ordination credentials and do what she and countless other Pentecostal women had already been doing for decades.

Given what Gerard endured in the context of her own denomination's proceedings, it is no wonder that she had little patience for those who insisted on reopening a debate about women's roles in ministry. When pressed to declare where she stood on the controversial questions surrounding women in church leadership and governance, Gerard wrote in her 1988 autobiography, "Please understand me, I am not belligerent on this subject. I am bored, bored as a black person is bored with discussing what's wrong with apartheid."[36] At sixty-five years of age and with more than forty years of ministry behind her, it is no wonder that Gerard was bored, and a little impatient with fellow believers who were stalled on the issue of whether or not women should take up formal roles in ministry.

The issue of ordination was entwined with conservatives' fear about secular feminism. Given the context of the second-wave women's movement and Gerard's progressive views about women's equality, she was often asked to clarify where she stood on feminism. In a media interview in 1974 Gerard explained, "I'm not a women's libber in the sense of Germaine Greer but I do want to be a free and full person."[37] Identifying how divisive feminism was,

FIGURE 8.2 Certificate of Ordination, Bernice Margaret Gerard, Assemblies of God, 1948–49. After their orthodoxy was called into question, Gerard and the McColl sisters followed the advice of a trusted mentor to align themselves with a recognized "brand" of Pentecostalism by seeking ordination with the Assemblies of God (AG) in the United States; this was almost four decades before the PAOC renewed its debate about granting ordination to women. | *Summit Pacific College, Hudson Memorial Library, Bernice Gerard Collection, uncatalogued.*

especially among conservative Christians, Gerard declared "I feel deeply about discrimination against women."[38]

Those feelings of discrimination would only grow in the next decade, leading Gerard to spar with colleagues and fellow delegates at conferences of her church denomination throughout the 1970s and 1980s. She acknowledged how explosive the issue was: "When you say women's liberation, some people go up in smoke ... The extremists have done damage to the cause, but, I do not think they can alter the change that is occurring in women's status."[39] At the time when she made these remarks, Gerard was in Regina to attend the PAOC's 1974 biennial General Conference. The city newspaper, *The Leader-Post,* reported that the conference "is considering a resolution that will allow women ministers to be ordained in Canada, and Miss Gerard is all for it."[40] Gerard was being optimistic when she had told reporters in advance of the vote that she was confident it should pass:

> The Pentecostals are absolutely superb as far as women's lib because women are allowed to preach, but we are encumbered by a bit of verbiage in the constitution. If churches (all churches) don't clean up their affairs, they are going to lose a generation of young women ... All those statements [in church constitutions] that suggest women belong to some other race – they should all be removed.[41]

But the statements were not all removed. Gerard's wish that the resolution would pass was dashed. After several failed attempts to remove the motion by sending it to committee for study, a vote was taken. Although the result was 149 in favour and 143 opposed, the motion was defeated because it was a bylaw change that required a two-thirds majority.[42] Evidently, not all PAOC delegates saw the issue the way Gerard did.

After the 1974 motion was defeated, a committee was formed to study the issues around the ministry of women with a mandate to report back to the next general conference in two years. The committee members consisted of two women and five men, including Robert M. Argue as chair. One of the women was Marion Parkinson, the national leader of the Women's Missionary Council (later called Women's Ministries). Another member was Homer J. Cantelon, a delegate from the Western Ontario District, who infamously made his position opposing women's ordination imminently clear on repeated occasions.[43] The committee's report considered six areas in depth: the present status of women in the PAOC; the past policies and practices; the policies of National Home Missions and Overseas Missions Departments; the policies and experiences of other denominations; the future prospects of women in the PAOC; and the biblical position.[44] On the last point, the question of what the Bible had to say about all this, the committee reported "there was divergent opinion within the Committee and across the Fellowship on this subject."[45] Indeed the debates over how to interpret biblical passages that seem contradictory, sometimes affirming women's leadership roles in the church and sometimes apparently silencing them, were at the heart of this controversy for all Christian churches whether they were conservative, liberal, evangelical, or Pentecostal.[46]

The committee's report went further and their research led to the conclusion that "there does not presently appear to be an expanding opportunity for the ministry of women within the PAOC."[47] That declining trend was reinforced by the committee's two recommendations about ministry training for women when they suggested that Bible colleges should offer "full theology for those [women] called to the ministry," and "subjects specifically designed for supportive ministry ... such as bookkeeping, typing, music, Christian Education, counselling, supportive roles of 'Women in Ministry,' PAOC departmental programs and policies."[48] These recommendations were clearly designed to reinforce binary gender roles. While women might be called to ministry roles, especially missionary work, in Canadian PAOC churches, men were cast as leaders in the pulpit and the boardroom, with capable and practical "helpmate" wives at their side. If women did not take Bible College training, the committee recommended that "our girls be encouraged to prepare themselves for school teaching, nursing, full business training, and music teaching."[49] That list of suggested career paths would provide good training for women to become missionaries or pastors' wives. Although the report did not make the claim overtly, it was also true that if a woman had professional training she could be counted on as a second breadwinner to supplement the income of a pastor, especially if he was working in a smaller church where PAOC pastors did not earn a living wage. All of this was premised on the assumption that PAOC ministers were heterosexual married men, of course. That model, complete with its required Bible college training, did not describe Bernice Gerard or other women like her, who were single and never attended a PAOC training school.

When Gerard sensibly had suggested in 1974 that it was just a matter of cleaning up "a bit of verbiage" in some church constitutions to make way for Pentecostal women to be ordained, she sounded very reasonable. But she was wrong. When she said that Pentecostals were "superb" on women in leadership, she was referencing the movement's long-standing practices of women in pulpits, tent meetings, and churches in the first fifty years of the Pentecostal movement. She was also referencing her own ministry experience over more than thirty years. But things had changed in light of a perceived feminist threat, and Gerard was underestimating the backlash that groups like the PAOC's special committee on women in ministry represented. Even as Canadian society was becoming more liberal in its views about women in the last part of the twentieth century, it seems the PAOC and other conservative evangelicals were trending in the opposite direction. And for Gerard, this meant her views would be overruled, her experiences would be underestimated, and her voice would be challenged. It must have come as somewhat of a shock to her that she should be so widely respected in other circles, including the charismatic movement, public university campuses, and Vancouver city council chambers, and yet her own denomination would call into question whether women like her should be welcomed into leadership and decision-making roles.

Gerard was not alone in the PAOC with her views about women in ministry, but the denomination was deeply divided on the issue. The 1976 report that recommended diminished roles for women did not go unchallenged. At the 1978 General Conference, a motion passed asking for further study of the issue and that another resolution on the question come to the 1980 meeting. Moreover, it was moved, seconded, and carried that "the reports of all committees called for by the General Conference be circularized intact as they come from the committees, including minority reports where applicable."[50] The need for such a motion indicates that some delegates felt they were not receiving full information; no doubt they suspected that the more conservative voices were being privileged over those calling for greater egalitarianism.

Resolutions were prepared for the 1980 General Conference meeting in Hamilton, Ontario, and once again the question of women's ordination came to the conference floor. The divisions meant debate was heated at times, and when the final vote was taken by secret ballot, the result was a narrow majority supporting women's ordination with 216 in favour, 211 opposed. But once again, the motion failed because it fell short of the requisite two-thirds majority. Several people who attended that meeting remember that the tone of the debate was quite emotional and delegates needed to be reminded to exercise decorum in their remarks and responses to those on the other side of the question.[51]

Once again, in 1984, at the biennial General Conference held in Saint John, New Brunswick, a motion to ordain women was presented. This time, the preamble referenced the fact that many PAOC women were already doing the work of ordained ministers, and it was time for the policy to catch up to the reality: "WHEREAS there are women ministers in our fellowship who are in full-time pastoral, evangelistic and Bible college ministry, and earning their livelihood from the same, BE IT RESOLVED that those persons may be ordained,"[52] and the bylaw wording be amended to reflect that change. Debate on this motion began on the Saturday of the conference and when it was not settled, the meeting adjourned for a day of worship and rest on the Sunday without having resolved the issue. One can only imagine the discussions that dominated around the dinner tables that evening as delegates halted the business of the conference, attended Sunday worship, and met over brunch after church during this pause in the work of the conference.

On Monday morning, debate resumed. A series of motions to make amendments and to limit debate were defeated. Meanwhile, the other business of the conference was interspersed, with election of officers taking place and audiovisual presentations about missions and emergency relief programs being offered as delegates made their way through the balloting processes. Close to four hundred delegates were casting ballots on the election of officers, but when the vote on women's ordination finally came, it is clear that many delegates chose to abstain. The result was 254 in favour, 26 against: the requisite two-thirds majority of delegates finally had been achieved. The minutes record "Miss L.M. Ellis expressed her thanks on behalf of all women in the fellowship. The session adjourned at 12:08 p.m."[53] But given the significantly reduced number of ballots cast, it seems that almost one hundred delegates must have left early for lunch, without voting at all. Technically it was a victory for women in the PAOC, but not a resounding one. The issue was far from settled.

Two years later, the question of women's leadership was back on the agenda in two different items for discussion. First, the delegates considered wording about electing officers and members-at-large to the general executive committee. Descriptions of suitable candidates stated they should be "men of mature experience and ability." Delegates were quick to notice that this might exclude women from serving and "the Chairman was asked by a member of the house if the term 'men' was generic or inclusive. The Chairman responded that 'a man meant a male.'"[54] The question reflected the fact that gender was top of mind for the delegates and the answer reinforced the practice that PAOC's national leadership privileged men to the exclusion of women. While the ordination issue had passed two years earlier, this discussion made it clear that women's leadership roles would not extend beyond congregational roles to include district or national governance.

When Gerard rose to speak on the conference floor (perhaps it was she who questioned whether "men" was generic or inclusive?) she was heckled. Suggesting that Gerard should cease and desist from expressing her views, a male delegate yelled, "Bernice, you need a man." The rudeness and disrespect were noted by some attendees who were shocked by the remark. However, the chair of the meeting, General Superintendent James MacKnight, did not acknowledge the comment nor did he seek to silence the heckler. By failing to hush the heckler or insist on maintaining proper decorum in the formal setting of the business meeting, the chair was essentially overlooking the abuse being hurled at Gerard (and by extension, at other women like her). After I learned about this incident, I suggested to an interviewee for this project, who shared Gerard's views about women, that Bernice had sparred with her ministerial peers on this occasion. But they were quick to retort, "They were not her peers or equals. They were small-minded rednecks."[55] What my source was emphasizing was the enormous gap that existed between Gerard and some other PAOC ministers. She had decades of ministry experience, a long list of international networks and travel experiences, and a reputation for intellectual depth. But meanwhile, younger, small-town, machoistic colleagues were hardly a match for her level of education, life experience, or intellect. Perhaps they felt threatened by a powerful woman who spoke with unflappable confidence? But clearly, they thought it was acceptable, even funny, to take potshots at an older woman, protected by the patriarchal assumptions that dominated the general conference. With regret for that unchecked rudeness and disrespect, twenty years later at the 2006 General Conference, in Winnipeg, David Wells sought a formal apology for Gerard and all the women who had been ridiculed and dismissed by their own faith group during these divisive meetings in the 1980s.[56]

In 1988 the question of women's ordination was up for debate once again as delegates considered this motion: "BE IT RESOLVED that Resolution #6 of the 1984 Conference be rescinded and a committee be appointed to formulate a new resolution for women's ordination which clearly demonstrates its scriptural authority and basis."[57] The preamble to the motion makes clear that the proposers' discontent sprang from a commitment to literal interpretations of the Bible:

> WHEREAS our most fundamental belief is that "the whole Bible ... is ... absolutely supreme and sufficient in authority in all matters of faith and practice" ... [and] WHEREAS ... the ordination of women in the PAOC, passed in 1984 at the 36th General Conference in Saint John, New Brunswick, makes no reference whatsoever to Scripture, ... and WHEREAS the passage of such a resolution, as it stands, clearly violates our belief in the authority, supremacy and sufficiency of Scripture in all matters of faith and practice.[58]

The minutes do not record who proposed or seconded the motion and it is unclear how much support this proposal garnered. The minutes only record that the motion was defeated.[59] The margin of support is questionable, but those who dismissed the legitimacy of women's leadership persisted. Ten years later the 1998 General Conference voted in favour of affirming women's equality in ministry and governance, making women eligible to serve at all levels of leadership, including as members of the national executive. While that vote could affirm an official position, the local autonomy of congregations meant that it could not dictate local priorities, nor could it erase the battle scars that persisted in PAOC circles from these fierce debates on gender.

The issue still divides congregations and leadership at various levels of the organization.

The PAOC's own statistics consistently reveal that only 5 to 6 percent of credentialed lead pastors in congregational ministry are women.[60] Well into the twenty-first century, the national executive, a group of approximately two dozen members, still includes very few women (4 of 23 in 2020, 6 of 26 in 2024).[61] As with other evangelical subcultures, the idea of privileging men's leadership over women's equality persists. The PAOC's official statement on women's equality in ministry confesses "there is a gap between our official position and our lived reality."[62] That reality is the legacy of debates waged throughout the 1970s, 1980s, and 1990s that divided the general conferences and shaped the next generation of leaders.

Bernice Gerard held her convictions about faith and feminism so firmly that she was willing to defy denominational authorities and refuse to compromise with patriarchal colleagues in the PAOC. She welcomed opportunities to work with Catholic believers (and a variety of historic denominations) long before her Pentecostal peers were persuaded to accept the legitimacy of the charismatic movement. She insisted that women's authority and callings were God-given, even when others suspected she was caving to the influences of secularism. Gerard often found herself under attack from other Pentecostals who doubted her legitimacy and questioned her orthodoxy. Yet she stood her ground.

Chapter 9

FEMINISM, FOOTNOTES,
AND FAMILY

THE CONFERENCE FLOOR, where delegates wrestled with setting national church policy on Pentecostal women's roles, was a very public site of debate. Against that backdrop of enduring public disrespect and heckling for her stance, Gerard's life writing reveals the complexities of her inner world as she navigated and processed her experience as a woman in public ministry and in private life. Ever the thinker, Gerard encouraged readers of her 1988 autobiography to lean in as she confided her thoughts about the matter:

> The question of women in ministry is not a simple one, nor one I can avoid any longer as I tell my own story. My first impulse has been to ignore this complex issue and write as the majority of ministers would write, that is, as a man would write. One finds no explanations, no justifications, no apologies for being "mere men" in the ministry. However, for many years I have done what some say is a "man's job only." In some cases they mean, "It's a man's job, so get out of the pulpit!" In others, they are attempting a compliment, as in "You preach like a man." Just as, in another context, they might say "You drive real good, just like a man."[1]

She finally took up her pen to address the woman question in the fourteenth chapter of her autobiography, beginning by saying that "for friend and foe, I force myself to collect my thoughts, and share how I, as a woman, pastored the same church for twenty-one beautiful years, preached twice on Sundays and midweek, ministered the communion, baptized believers, performed

FIGURE 9.1 *Left to right*: Rev. Frederick Reidenbach (Assemblies of God, Scranton, PA), Bernice Gerard, Velma McColl, Jean McColl. The McColl-Gerard Trio travelled throughout North America as professional evangelists, gaining the trust and sharing the pulpits of hundreds of Pentecostal ministers who engaged them to lead revivals and boost the local church membership, as they did in Scranton, Pennsylvania. | *Summit Pacific College, Hudson Memorial Library, Bernice Gerard Nielson Family Scrapbook.*

wedding ceremonies, counseled the living, buried the dead, acted as chairman of the board and chief administrative officer, and then, with a peaceful heart, chose to shift gears and go full time into writing and radio and television ministry."[2] She reflected deeply and wrote about the problems that attend women in public ministry, leaving good clues about the intellectual and experiential processes that shaped her convictions.

By her own admission, Gerard's experiences in Vancouver and particularly on the campuses of the University of British Columbia and Simon Fraser University shaped her profoundly. The influence of academics is evident in her thinking on a wide range of issues, and especially on the question of women's roles in the church. As she explained, "to the students whose sincere questioning demanded on behalf of the church an answer that represents Jesus more adequately than in the past, I owe the development of many insights."[3] For readers who might be interested in understanding the development of those insights and her intellectual formation more generally, Gerard confided "my own interests led me to the works of radical secular feminists, as well as those of Bible-believing evangelical scholars, male and female." She held out this challenge: "I would urge the reader who is interested in studying these issues to check out my footnotes for recommended reading."[4]

Challenge accepted! Following Gerard's instruction, I proposed to do just as she had suggested by tracking her footnotes and uncovering the authors and ideas she referenced. My goal was to understand how the works she read shaped her thinking. What quickly became evident is that Bernice Gerard was very much a product of her times, as she studied and ministered during the rise of the second-wave women's movement in Canada and through the years when debates about women in ministry were reaching a crescendo in evangelical circles, including the Pentecostal Assemblies of Canada. Drawing on her autobiography, the works she cited there, and her personal papers and correspondence, one sees more clearly the various ideological influences that converged in Gerard's views about women in the church.

Given the target audience for her autobiography (one assumes she was writing her life story mainly for evangelical and charismatic Christians), it is not surprising that her footnotes show far more reliance on evangelical scholarship than on secular sources. Sixteen footnotes accompany her chapter on women in ministry, and all but three of those sources point readers to evangelical writers. The remaining three sources include one reference to the *New English Bible,* and two references to prominent figures in Canadian women's history: Emily Murphy and Nellie McClung. The remaining thirteen notes include references to two classic texts concerning women and ministry, including Catherine Booth's 1859 work *Female Ministry; or, Woman's Right to Preach the Gospel* and Katharine C. Bushnell's *God's Word to Women,* originally published in 1912, along with more contemporary authors from the 1970s and 1980s. Unfortunately, the footnotes to her chapter can only take one so far in a quest to track her intellectual formation, but by piecing those together with the papers and correspondence in her personal archives, a more complete picture of what influenced her thinking emerges. And those influences were unquestionably feminist in orientation. Reading Gerard's personal papers in conjunction with her autobiography, it becomes clear that a variety of feminist influences are entwined throughout Gerard's writing, correspondence, and speaking notes including evangelical feminism, ecumenical feminism, and secular feminism.

As religious studies scholar Pamela Cochran explained in her 2005 book, *Evangelical Feminism: A History*,

> For most people today, much less in the 1980s, the terms "evangelical" and "feminism" are contradictory. "Evangelicalism" ... known for its strict or "literal" interpretation of the Bible ... conjures up images of right-wing politics and social conservatism, including support for "traditional" gender roles. So how could an evangelical also support feminism, a movement that seeks, at its most basic level, to redress the inequalities, injustice, and discrimination that women face because of their sex?[5]

Despite those seeming contradictions, Cochran traces how a historic gathering of young evangelicals in 1973 gave rise to a group known as the Evangelical Women's Caucus and a movement "characterized by the belief that when interpreted correctly, the Bible teaches the equality of women and men."[6] That view is one that Bernice Gerard shared and was the conviction on which she based her thinking and her career in ministry.

The most widely circulated publication that emerged from evangelical feminists in the 1970s is Letha Scanzoni and Nancy Hardesty's *All We're Meant to Be: A Biblical Approach to Women's Liberation*, published in 1974.[7] Cochran pointed to the significance of that book, indicating that its argument was constructed both theologically and historically to assert that the call to use women's gifts in leadership was an important part of authentic Christianity. Taking that historical and theological base, the authors "hoped to divert complaints that [they were] just adding a feminist veneer to Christianity."[8] Gerard cited Scanzoni and Hardesty in the footnotes of her autobiography and took from them a critical reference, her working definition of liberation. Gerard explained that "liberation for a Christian woman is not a movement or an organization but 'a state of mind in which a woman comes to view herself as Jesus Christ sees her – as a person created in God's image whom he wants to make free to be whole, to grow, to learn, to utilize fully the talents and gifts God has given her as a unique individual.'"[9]

Scanzoni and Hardesty were important leading voices in the emerging debates about feminism in evangelical circles, and at the time they were writing their book, the idea of an "evangelical feminism" was perceived to be quite radical and daring, for many even an oxymoron.[10] The fact that Gerard cites Hardesty and Scanzoni in her footnote is a cue to readers that she had read and been influenced by their now-classic text. Gerard was not merely a casual reader of their ideas; it is clear they had a profound influence on her. Gerard's personal archives include some copies of the newsletter *Daughters of Sarah*, published by the People's Christian Coalition. In the September 1975 issue of that newsletter, which Gerard kept in her files, there were references to Hardesty and Scanzoni's book, but also book reviews of other publications dealing with themes of biblical feminism, including a review of Fuller Theological Seminary professor Paul K. Jewett's 1975 book *Man as Male and Female: A Study in Sexual Relationships from a Theological Point of View*.[11] The newsletter also featured announcements about upcoming events concerning biblical feminism, International Women's Year, and conferences of interest to its readers as well as news about a newly published directory of biblical feminists issued by the Evangelical Women's Caucus. The fact that Gerard was reading this material, and that she preserved it among her personal papers for more than thirty years, lends weight to the idea that she was shaped by the lively debates engendered by these early American evangelical feminists.

In following the scholarship of these two leaders of evangelical feminism there is no doubt that Gerard had also read Scanzoni's 1973 article "The Feminists and the Bible," where Scanzoni pointed out that American feminists from the first-wave women's movement who fought for women's right to vote were Bible-believing Christians.[12] Gerard took that model of tying her feminist thought to women's history when she opened the chapter on women in her autobiography with a parallel account of early Canadian feminists whose faith had spurred them to argue for equality for women in public life. Devoting six paragraphs to a short history, Gerard recounted how, in 1929, after an extended court battle and a series of appeals, Canadian women came to be recognized as persons under the British North America Act because of the campaign waged by the Alberta Five, including Emily Murphy and Nellie McClung, who fought tirelessly on behalf of Canadian women's right to a political voice. Gerard made the point that these were women with active connections to church life.

Indeed, Gerard quoted McClung, a celebrated author and satirist, who mocked turn-of-the-century church structures when she quipped, "Women may lift the mortgages, or build churches, or any other light work, but the real heavy work of church, such as moving resolutions in the general conferences ... must be done by strong, hardy men."[13] More important than citing the amusing bits of McClung's writing, though, was the fact that here Gerard was tying early Canadian feminist initiatives for women to enter into public, political life to their life of faith and involvement in church politics. Gerard wanted her readers to see the logic behind this fact: women's rights, including voting in elections and occupying political office, were widely accepted among

Canadians. And the women who had won those victories on behalf of their fellow citizens were churchwomen.

Having established those facts of Canadian history, Gerard went on to question, in unabashedly feminist terms, why, several decades later evangelical churches were one of the last bastions of male chauvinism with their patriarchal church leadership and governance practices. While she professed boredom with the question of why it was acceptable for women to provide leadership in church ministry after a long, successful career as an evangelist and then as a pastor she simply stated, "I have no time for debate with those who raise the subject of women's ministries with the intent to silence or harass women. There is a lot of meanness in people that finds ready expression in targeting persecuted minorities."[14] This could be interpreted as pragmatism; Gerard had simply decided not to waste precious time to engage in sparring over the question. After all, like the prophet Nehemiah, whom she cited, she maintained, "I am carrying on a great project ... why should I leave it and go down to you?" (Neh. 6:3, NIV). Although she reported that she had been "endlessly challenged, questioned, cajoled, and condemned,"[15] it was clear she had long since settled in her own mind that she was called of God to do what she was doing and had done for decades.

Moreover, a closer look at her rationale shows that she was, in fact, following a hermeneutic that was in step with that of evangelical feminists in the 1970s and early 1980s. Rather than merely debating the exegesis of certain passages of scripture, she invoked the language of the feminist movement. She claimed that she only wanted to share with her readers "what is presently foundational in my own understanding," what she believed to be true, and significantly, what "[I] find liberating to me as a person."[16] Clearly she was incorporating language and ideas from evangelical feminist thinkers who, according to Cochran, "came to rely on personal experience as authoritative in their interpretation of Scripture, thereby weakening their commitment to external, transcendent authority."[17]

Gerard's greatest reliance for her chapter on women in ministry came from one author in particular, Charles Trombley, and his 1985 book *Who Said Women Can't Teach?* Gerard admired Trombley's work for its clear communication as he tackled the three parts of the biblical record at the heart of the woman question: the creation account, Jesus and his treatment of women, and the teachings of the apostle Paul. As she explained, when Trombley came to the question "Should Women Be Silent in the Church?" his "answer to that question concur[red] with reliable scholarship,"[18] and Gerard used it to give direction to her readers seeking to understand the key Bible passages that were typically offered to refute feminism. This was significant because by the mid-1980s some of the evangelical feminist scholars Gerard had admired ten years earlier had taken up controversial positions on social questions, including Hardesty who came out as a lesbian.[19] When Gerard found a publication like Trombley's, which gave a feminist reading of the most commonly debated scriptures, she would have been relieved, because it allowed her to sidestep the question of homosexuality as she sought to establish her position on women in ministry without being dismissed by readers who discounted more liberal, progressive, and radical feminists.

It would be misleading, however, to create the impression that Gerard always played it safe with her own reading choices or intellectual associations. The second group of writers that shaped her thinking on women in the church illustrates this clearly. Although it was obviously outside the boundaries of what her readers and the PAOC executive at the time could endorse, Gerard was heavily influenced by, and an enthusiastic participant in, ecumenical initiatives and interchurch dialogue. Just as her various connections with other denominations led her to be open-minded on issues like the charismatic movement, she also encountered and embraced some views on the woman question expressed by scholars within the historical mainline churches.

Following her admonition to reference her footnotes, the careful reader of Gerard's autobiography cannot ignore that to support her position on feminism's place in the church she pointed to Catholic scholarship, specifically the work of Leonard J. Swidler, professor of Catholic Thought and Interreligious Dialogue at Temple University in Philadelphia, Pennsylvania. In 1971, *Catholic World* published Swidler's paper "Jesus Was a Feminist," an oft-cited article that is now regarded as a classic feminist text.[20] The fact that Gerard was following Catholic thinkers on this topic is another example of the wide-ranging influences that were shaping her views at the time.

On the question of women and the church Gerard was particularly drawn to Swidler's historical scholarship because of the way he contextualizes Jesus's interactions with women in light of the status of women in Jewish and Roman culture at the time of Christ. Based on his understanding of the restricted views that characterized the lives of women during the lifetime of Jesus, Swidler argues that Jesus was unquestionably feminist in his dealings with women because he ignored the cultural norms about gender and religion. Swidler cites several of the well-known episodes of Jesus interacting with women in affirming ways, including the woman at the well, the woman with the issue of blood, the woman who wiped Jesus' feet with her hair, and Mary and Martha.

Swidler argues that Jesus ignored the conventions of the day. First, he disregarded ethnic and gender restrictions that would have prohibited him from conversation with the Samaritan woman; by engaging with her, he actually entrusted her with news about his true identity. She was the first person to whom he disclosed that he was the long-awaited Messiah, and the gospel message was actually spread to her entire community through her reports of their conversation. Second, when Jesus made a public scene by pointing out that the woman who had been healed from the issue of blood had touched him, Swidler argues that Jesus was calling attention to the fact that her physical touch had not contaminated him. On the contrary, he commended her for her act of faith and challenged the conventions that had been created to block women from accessing religious leaders. Third, Swidler writes about the woman of ill repute who wiped Jesus's feet with her tears and her hair. He accepted her action and, Swidler argues, did not dismiss her as a sex object despite her reputation as a sex trade worker; instead, he blessed her and modelled for the men around him a different way to interact with women by refusing to objectify her and to reduce her to a one-dimensional being. And, finally, Swidler argues that Jesus elevated the place of women when he validated Mary, the sister of Martha, for her choice to leave off housekeeping concerns and opt instead to sit at his feet to listen to the teaching and to enjoy a spiritual encounter with Him. Gerard emphasized that in so doing Jesus opened the possibility for women to enter fully into intellectual and spiritual life by sharing with men the act of loving God with their minds.

Publishing this argument in 1988, only one year after her general superintendent had firmly stated that the PAOC was not officially involved in any dialogue with Roman Catholics, Gerard must have surprised some readers of her autobiography by pointing to Catholic feminist scholarship work to defend her stance on women in ministry. As a *Toronto Star* journalist had remarked about Gerard a few years earlier, "In a denomination not known for making waves on social issues, Miss Gerard has a tendency to rock the boat."[21] Apparently, she had been rocking the boat, not just on social issues, but also by entering into dialogue with Catholics against the wishes of the national PAOC office when she had been reading Catholic feminist scholarship for more than fifteen years.

The third expression of feminism that shaped Gerard's views was perhaps the most surprising of all: secular feminism. On August 26, 1968, the *Windsor Star* reported on a talk that Gerard had given at the 1968 General Conference of the PAOC. The newspaper reported Gerard was urging the PAOC delegates to the women's meeting that they needed to grasp the opportunities that were all around them. She reportedly said, "Women should not say, 'I am only a woman.' We must realize we are people too. We all have to give an account of ourselves as persons."[22] Invoking Canadian history to remind women of their position in society, she said, "It is not that long back when women didn't have the vote and it isn't that long back when they couldn't keep the money they earned. We women today can move into areas where we are needed and do our part as Christian women."[23] The reporter added that "Miss Gerard said women must pull up their socks because they are missing a lot of their opportunities."[24] Gerard's speaking notes for that Windsor talk are preserved in the archives. In eight pages of handwritten notes, Gerard emphasized that "Christian women need to see themselves as persons."[25] She elaborated on this point in her notes with the remark that "there is nothing especially Christian about an exaggerated meekness that allows a woman to draw back from the challenges of real living saying, 'I'm only a woman.'"[26] To support that point, she quoted scripture in her notes, specifically Acts 2, which cites the prophet Joel predicting that God would pour out His Spirit "upon all flesh" (Acts 2:17; Joel 2:28 KJV) and that "your sons and your daughters shall prophesy" (Acts 2:17; Joel 2:28 KJV), and Galatians 3:28 (KJV) where the apostle Paul declared, "There is neither Jew nor Greek, there is neither bond nor free, there is neither male nor female for ye are one in Christ Jesus."[27] Gerard continued making her notes with references to history:

> Canadian Women Have Unlimited Opportunities To Develope Their Full Potential (1) position vastly different from those in Greek culture to whom Paul wrote (2) or even those of 19th Cent. (no right to vote, own property, keep the money they earned by their own labour). The 19th and 20th centuries brought a revolution in the status of women, but some revolutionary concepts have yet to be grasped by many of our Christian women ... [28] [spelling errors in original]

For Gerard to invoke these references to societal reform accomplished by the first-wave women's movement is noteworthy; so, too, were her multiple references to second-wave feminism as it was playing out through then-current events, namely the work of the Royal Commission on the Status of Women in Canada, an inquiry launched by the government of Canada in 1967 to explore the place of women in Canadian society.[29]

In February 1972, Gerard preached a sermon at Fraserview Assembly, the church where she was co-pastor, titled "Diamonds Are Forever." That slogan was from a jewellery company and was also the title of a recent James Bond movie. But Gerard argued for women to realize that, in fact, diamonds are *not* forever because husbands can die or stray and are sometimes stolen from you. She was making the point that true security cannot be found in earthly possessions, social positions, or human relationships. The only source of lasting security, Gerard concluded, was in a relationship to God. In her sermon notes, Gerard included elements of Germaine Greer's text *The Female Eunuch* that resonated with her.[30] For example, the reference to husbands being lost or stolen paraphrases Greer.[31] Gerard agreed, for example, that people are trapped by the demands of the culture and the ways that they set out to create false security for themselves. She quoted Greer directly saying, "Probably the only place where a man can feel really secure is in a maximum security prison, except for the imminent threat of release."[32]

While Gerard obviously did not agree with the coarse language or sexual prescriptions in Greer's work, she did take up some of the same sentiments that Greer urged on women when she told her listeners to stop bowing to the dictates of men but also to stop blaming men for their lot in life. Greer famously said, "Those miserable women who blame the men who let them down for their misery and isolation enact every day the initial mistake of sacrificing their personal responsibility for themselves."[33] Gerard took that same sentiment and told the Pentecostal women she addressed that they needed to take personal responsibility for themselves and stop projecting what she called "an exaggerated meekness." Instead, she exhorted every woman in the church to recognize herself as "a whole person for whom Christ died" and realize that "you will be called upon to give an account of yourself: what you did with what you had."[34] Gerard's challenge to churchwomen was not to take too passive a position and abdicate to any man (husband or father) the responsibility for her own spiritual life and work. Pentecostals agreed that every woman had God-given gifts, and Gerard emphasized that they were expected to use those gifts. Although Gerard's exhortation to churchwomen to exercise personal responsibility was a theme she had been preaching even before Germaine Greer's classic feminist text was published in 1971, it is significant that Gerard incorporated direct quotes from this prominent secular feminist into her speaking notes to urge Pentecostal women to find their security outside of their relationships with men. Moreover, it is clear that Gerard's impatience with churchwomen who deferred too much to men was only reinforced by what she found in Greer's secular feminism. Like her secular counterpart, Gerard was calling women to stop sacrificing their personal responsibility and to step up into the roles that they were called to take up. For Gerard, unlike Greer and other secular feminists, there was an eternal consequence to this since she taught that

Christian women would be judged in the next life for their failure to fully embrace the gifts and opportunities available to them in this life.

Portrayals of Gerard in the media and in Pentecostal church circles as a popular (and often controversial) preacher, broadcaster, and municipal politician have tended to overshadow the fact that she was an academically inclined woman who read widely, enjoyed academic exchanges, and thought carefully about how she could arrive at a synthesis between her faith and her feminism. She managed this so skilfully, almost subversively, that many of her listeners, readers, and parishioners might balk at the very idea of applying the label *feminist* to her. Certainly, her instruction to simply "check the footnotes" in her book belie the complexity of ideological influences that converged as she adopted and adapted ideas from various sources to arrive at her conclusions about the role of women in the church.

The heckler at the PAOC general conference who had suggested Gerard needed a man was wrong on many levels, of course. When he implied that if she were in a heterosexual marriage, Gerard would be less vocal about women in leadership, he was articulating a commonly held view among conservative Christians, where family structure is premised on the model of the man as head of the woman, and the woman in submission to the man. The logic of the heckler was that Gerard needed to practise being in submission to a man, because maybe then she would stop being so vocal about women in church leadership. But Gerard did not need a husband; she had broken off an engagement thirty years earlier when she recognized that marriage to a divorced man would jeopardize her ministry opportunities. Perhaps more importantly, Gerard did not need a husband because she already had a partner. She had someone who had been her partner in ministry and in life since the 1940s.

Gerard's private life is intriguing, especially her domestic arrangements and the loving relationship she had with Velma McColl Chapman, her partner in ministry and life over more than sixty years. Throughout Bernice's adult life, Velma was a constant presence, and the nature of their partnership is a puzzle. Together, Bernice Gerard and Velma McColl Chapman were a dynamic duo who shared a happy home life and an enduring legacy in ministry. Yet, like the challenge she left her readers to "follow the footnotes" on her feminist ideas, Gerard also left intriguing clues about the complexity of the domestic life that she shared with Velma.

Dilemmas about Pentecostal leadership couples usually centre on binary questions of heteronormative gender relations and rhetoric about complementarian versus egalitarian views. But what if both members of a leadership couple are women? Velma and Bernice shared a ministry that spanned more than sixty

FIGURE 9.2 *Left to right:* Dick Chapman, Velma McColl Chapman, and Gerard. Velma McColl accepted a marriage proposal from Dick Chapman in 1958, and the couple welcomed Bernice to share their home, making them a household of three. | *Summit Pacific College, Hudson Memorial Library, Bernice Gerard Collection, uncatalogued.*

years beginning in the 1940s. Theirs was a long and complex partnership. The two women were coworkers who enjoyed a special relationship of affection and mutual support. Their partnership is intriguing because it defies existing gender constructs. In North American Pentecostal leadership today, men dominate. Heterosexual couples are the norm, patriarchal organizational structures are common, and homosocial relationships can be deemed problematic. For all those reasons, the long-standing ministry partnership and intimate friendship of Bernice and Velma is a fascinating case study to explore questions of gender and authority. While it was not uncommon for two women to team up in ministry during the twentieth century, that same pattern is very rare today. In the hypermasculinized and homophobic subcultures of North American Pentecostalism today, it is unlikely that the future will include other same-sex leadership couples like Velma and Bernice.

When I refer to Gerard and her partner as a case study of a same-sex leadership couple I do not mean to suggest that Velma and Bernice were lovers or that their partnership was sexual in nature. Where the sources are silent, the historian cannot presume to know. However, where the sources are clear and even emphatic, it is the historian's job to ask why particular emphases were made. In this case, there are direct and deliberate declarations which assert and reinforce that both these women were heterosexual. Velma (McColl) Chapman was married to Dick Chapman, a Vancouver businessman, from 1959 until his death in 1978. Bernice Gerard, who remained single for her whole life, asserted her own heterosexual desires when she recounted that as her female friends were accepting marriage proposals in the 1950s, "I wanted to get married myself. I was head over heels in love with a man, and he with me – before I knew he was divorced."[35] The taboo of divorce forced Gerard to choose ministry and singleness over marriage because, as she explained, "I knew full well my denominational fellowship would lose no time in lifting my ... credentials if I married a divorced man."[36] And with that, Gerard set aside her heterosexual desires.

The one partnership that predated, endured, and outlasted Bernice and Velma's romantic episodes with men was their relationship with each other. Archival sources, including photographs from their personal collections, make it very clear that Velma and Bernice's ties were much deeper than a professional and public partnership. Gerard dedicated her 1988 autobiography to Chapman saying, "With thanks to God for Velma Chapman and the gift of her friendship and partnership in ministry."[37] Velma's 2007 obituary mentioned that she was predeceased by her husband Dick and his daughter, but before listing her immediate family members, the death notice declared "Velma leaves [behind] her life-long ministry partner, [the] Rev. Bernice Gerard."[38] Gerard's acknowledgment of Velma as God's gift to her, and Velma's obituary naming Gerard as the one she left behind, provide clear evidence of the depth of affection the women shared until death separated them; they died just over a year apart (in 2007 and 2008) and they are buried together with a shared cemetery plot in Burnaby, BC.[39] Because their relationship and ministry model defied existing gender constructs and deviated from heteronormative models of Pentecostal ministry leadership, it begs an exploration through a critical gender lens. To do this, it is useful to think about the dynamics that existed between these two Pentecostal women ministers in three phases of their lives: before, during, and after Velma's marriage.

Bernice Gerard and Velma McColl came from very different families of origin, and they occupied different, but complementary roles in ministry. Gerard's tumultuous childhood in state care stood in stark contrast to the McColl family's affectionate household. Jean and Velma McColl hailed from Regina, Saskatchewan, and they had grown up Pentecostal, following their father's conversion experience in the early days of the movement when they were small children. In contrast to Bernice's troubled childhood experiences as a ward of the state, the McColls enjoyed a warm and happy family life, and as adults they looked forward to their annual visits home to spend time with their aging parents. Gerard was embraced and welcomed by the entire family, and she grew very fond of the whole clan, even calling Velma's parents Mother and Dad.[40]

It was common in the first decades of Canadian Pentecostalism for pairs of women to travel together as evangelists and pastors, and examples abound including the Argue sisters from Winnipeg, the Davis sisters in New Brunswick, and the Forsey sisters in Newfoundland, to name but three. The McColl sisters were a typical duo with complementary ministry gifts: Jean was described as "the preacher [and] Velma was the diplomat and negotiator. Together they sang."[41] When Bernice joined the McColl sisters to form the trio, she was described in their promotional materials as "the singing lady baritone." Adding Gerard's talents to the McColls' repertoire, they recorded albums of their music and published books of Jean's poetry, Bernice's dramatic childhood conversion story, and their inspirational travelogues about the Holy Land. But the three-some could not last indefinitely. Jean McColl accepted a marriage proposal, and in 1957, the three became two. Because Jean had always been billed as the lead "preacher" of the group, with Velma and Bernice speaking occasionally, adjustments needed to be made. According to Gerard's memoir, Jean did not leave before "casting her preaching mantle upon me."[42]

Now it was just Velma and Bernice. The pair happily continued their work, sharing their busy itinerary and their efficient travel trailer, along with a large, inflatable tent that drew attention in every locale where they stopped for meetings. Velma's graceful feminine ways and endearing personality, her lovely voice, and her skill for interacting with people both on stage and off, proved perfectly complementary to Bernice's baritone singing, her testimony of a rough and rugged upbringing, and her commanding pulpit presence. They were still just two women on the road, but their gifts and persona echoed the typical gendered dynamics of a married heterosexual couple, with Velma as the "lovely musician/wife" and Bernice in the role of the "authoritative preacher/husband" character. That binary model of husband and wife/helpmate would continue to endure for heterosexual Pentecostal couples in North American ministry circles as gendered notions about appropriate roles for women and men solidified around the complementarian model in the postwar years.

Canada hosted the World Pentecostal Conference in Toronto in 1958, an event that Velma and Bernice would have anticipated as a chance for reunions with their far-flung Pentecostal acquaintances. But Bernice could not have anticipated how much her personal world would be shaken by what happened there when Dick Chapman, a Vancouver widower and businessman, made a marriage proposal to Velma. Fifteen years after her relationship with Velma began, Bernice was about to lose her partner and friend. Sensitive to the close relationship that his fiancée shared with her ministry partner, Chapman broached the subject with Gerard. She recounted the episode in detail in her memoir:

> As we were taking Dick to his hotel, sitting three abreast in the front of our automobile, he leaned a little toward me in the driver's seat to say, "I am going to be taking Velma away to be my wife. I know you have worked closely together for many years, and you will miss her. You will always be welcome in our home." Without a moment's warning a flood of tears literally gushed from my eyes and down my cheeks. "May God's will be done," said I, trying hard to contain my emotions. Velma dug her elbow into my side, "I haven't said yes yet!" she whispered.[43]

But in fact, Velma would say yes. And true to his word, Dick Chapman did make Bernice welcome in their home. Typically, Christian marriage is described as "the two becoming one"; in this case, it was "two becoming three" – that is, a household of three. Gerard shared a home with the Chapmans from 1958 onward.

While Velma settled into her new role as a married woman, Bernice returned to her studies at UBC and started her work as a university chaplain by 1963. Gerard busied herself with organizing activities for students, both on campus and off. She used the home she shared with the Chapmans as one of the regular sites of student gatherings where, she recounted, "I too, at Chapman's residence, saw dozens and dozens of students in our home for meals and fellowship."[44] As Bernice launched her radio phone-in show, Velma did administrative work for the radio program and reviewed and edited the scripts, so although she was not playing such a front-line role, Velma was obviously more than simply a silent partner and gracious host for Bernice's student gatherings.

In 1964, attempting to reach students and socially marginalized people, the PAOC proposed to start a new church in Vancouver South. Having noticed how effective Gerard was in the campus milieu and open-line radio medium, and given their vast experience in ministry together, the denomination approached Bernice and Velma, inviting them to become the founding co-pastors of the Fraserview Assembly, a new PAOC congregation. Their work in the church and on the radio was entwined as Bernice took up the role of on-air host and public voice, while Velma was the producer, working in the background with the editing pencil and managing the details of the broadcasts.

FIGURE 9.3 *Right to left:* Bernice, Velma, and Dick are pictured in their home, which Velma and Bernice continued to use as their base for ministry while Bernice did her campus work, radio broadcasts, and church ministry even after Dick passed away. | *Summit Pacific College, Hudson Memorial Library, Bernice Gerard Collection, uncatalogued.*

Pastor Bernice and Pastor Velma welcomed a wide variety of speakers to their pulpit, regularly featuring the same guests on their weekly broadcasts and at church services. Given the pair's complementary leadership skills, on one hand, it is not surprising that the PAOC endorsed them as co-pastors, yet on the other hand, it is surprising. The Fraserview Assembly's establishment in 1964 was twenty years before the PAOC would officially endorse the ordination of women. But because Velma and Bernice already held ordination credentials from the Missouri District of the Assemblies of God, since the 1940s, they were fully equipped to provide pastoral leadership, including serving communion, performing marriages, and officiating at funerals. Gender aside, for the PAOC, these two seemed like a safe bet as pastors.

There was one more thing that made this new church venture a low-risk proposition: the financial backing and business acumen that Velma's husband, Dick Chapman, brought to the table. Chapman, born in 1901 and fourteen years older than Velma, had become a Pentecostal during one of the earliest tent meetings held in Vancouver and ever since he had proven himself to be a loyal, generous man; he was a fixture of Vancouver Pentecostalism. Together with his first wife, Gladys,[45] Dick Chapman had been very involved in the 1923 Charles Price revival meetings in Vancouver, which were significant for the growth of the Sixth Avenue Pentecostal Tabernacle (later renamed Broadway Tabernacle), the city's flagship PAOC church.[46] Having served as a ministering deacon for thirty-five years, and as the long-time treasurer of the Broadway Church, when the new Fraserview congregation was proposed, "Dick gave his full support to the venture."[47] No doubt the nature of his support was financial because Chapman was a successful businessman, with decades of financial and church experience. He was in the printing business, and by 1943 he had launched his own successful company, Chapman Printing and Die Works. But perhaps even more important, Chapman gave his full support to the new church when he endorsed the idea of two female pastors leading the work: his wife, the Rev. Velma Chapman, and her ministry partner and housemate, the Rev. Bernice Gerard.

This was not the first time that Dick Chapman had shown his endorsement for women in ministry. Chapman's Methodist mother had been a strong influence in his life, and his testimony included his childhood conversion experience at her knee. Chapman's donations to support mission work were generous and widespread. His gifts had led to the establishment of the Evangel Press in Nairobi, which was purported in the late 1970s to be the largest African gospel press. He donated funds to name a chapel in Antigua in honour of his first wife, Gladys Dawson Chapman. And it was revealed at his funeral that for twenty years he had personally financed the mission work of Coralee Haist, a Canadian PAOC missionary in China.[48] Chapman Printing was also the corporate sponsor of Gerard's radio programs. So, when the PAOC tapped his wife and her long-standing ministry partner to take up the work as founding co-pastors of a new church in Vancouver, Dick Chapman enthusiastically demonstrated his support. He transferred his church membership from Broadway to the new congregation and played an important role in the business affairs of that church from its very beginning until the end of his life, in 1978. He was, as his eulogy described him, "the founding father" of the Fraserview Assembly, and with his passing, it was declared, "All ministers have lost a special friend, especially all these years of his life, women ministers."[49] Fittingly, the minister who officiated at his funeral was his wife's closest confidante and ministry partner, the Rev. Bernice Gerard.

Dick Chapman died twenty years after his marriage proposal to Velma. And once again, for Velma and Bernice, a ministry trio became a party of two. Just as Dick had honoured the passing of his first wife with funds to name a chapel in her honour, Velma and Bernice would honour Chapman himself through a new building at their church, Fraserview Assembly. In a 1979 report published in *Pentecostal Testimony,* Pastor Velma and Pastor Bernice are pictured with their all-male church board at a groundbreaking ceremony announcing that one part of the new church facility would be named "The Dick Chapman Memorial Hall."[50] After Dick's passing, Velma and Bernice carried on. Their church was expanding, their late-night *Sunday Line* phone-in radio program was the talk of the town, they had expanded their media work to include television ministry, and Gerard had recently made a successful run for a seat on the Vancouver city council, where she served as a municipal politician from 1977 to 1981.[51] Velma and Bernice were not slowing down. They continued to co-pastor the Fraserview Assembly for several more years, retiring in 1985 after celebrating twenty-one years in the pulpit.

The end of pastoring did not mean retirement for this leadership couple. Instead, Velma and Bernice continued to pour their energy into ministry work. By the end of their lives, they had visited the Holy Land no less than thirty-three times – leading tours and introducing other believers, both in person and through their travel reports, to sites where they "sought out the footsteps of Jesus." Gerard had written in her first guidebook to the Holy Land that the place "has a message for the world today, 'Have faith in God – Jesus Christ is coming soon.'"[52] From her earliest writing about the Holy Land to her second autobiography published in 1988, Gerard's perspective on the Middle East did not change – she saw in her travels there assurances that the promises of God about Christ's second coming were true and imminently about to be fulfilled. In those views, Gerard was typical of other conservative Christians, with their dispensational views of the coming "end times" and the critical role that the nation of Israel would play in those developments. The campaign "Trees for Israel" is just one example of the fundraising and promotional work Velma

FIGURE 9.4 Bernice and Velma pastored the Fraserview Assembly, a PAOC church they co-founded, where they shared a pulpit and led the congregation from the late 1960s until they retired more than twenty years later. | *Summit Pacific College, Hudson Memorial Library, Bernice Gerard Nielson Family Scrapbook.*

and Bernice undertook later in life. As Bernice and Velma aged, their commitment to ministry work did not waver.

How should we understand the remarkable story of Velma and Bernice, specifically how they devoted their lives to ministry and to each other? There is no question that they made a powerful leadership couple and that they loved each other deeply. Speculations about the nature of their relationship might be titillating, but I am not declaring their relationship was a sexual one. What I am asserting is that they were devoted to one another for more than sixty years and, like an old married couple, they supported one another in their declining years until death parted them.

While labelling Gerard a lesbian would be going too far, it should be noted that Gerard was never as strident against gays and lesbians as some of her contemporaries. When radio listeners wrote to Gerard about coming out as lesbians, she saved their letters among her personal papers and responded with compassion to the anguish these women experienced, especially within their churches. Gerard did distance herself from evangelical feminists like Hardesty who came out as queer, but she also distanced herself from the most strident antigay voices that were dominating church circles in the last quarter of the twentieth century. For example, when Anita Bryant, the American anti–gay rights activist, visited Vancouver in 1968,[53] Gerard did not participate in her meetings. Ten years later, when David Mainse held meetings at the Orpheum Theatre in Vancouver, LGBTQ+ activists suspected that he might be planning to have Bryant make a surprise appearance on stage with him.[54] He had no such plan, but protesters blocked the entrance to the theatre, and when Gerard attempted to make her way through the crowd, she recalls "a young woman with a placard ... spat full in my face, her saliva streaking down the upper front of my jet black fur coat."[55] Gerard attempted to have a conversation, but when she tried to engage with the protester, "she gave me another mouthful!" and continued chanting "Down with born-again hate!"[56] Gerard took the opportunity to assert that she felt no such hate, and she silently called to mind the words of Jesus from the gospel of Matthew "Love your enemies, and pray for those who persecute you." Gerard resolved to express love on this occasion but once she was safely inside the venue, she did call the Vancouver police to ask them to clear the crowd away from the theatre doors so that Mainse's audience could arrive unhampered. That call might not have looked like love to the protesters. Her mixed response only serves to muddy the waters and add to the ambiguity of Gerard's position on gay rights.

Ten years later, Gerard reflected on the incident at the Orpheum Theatre, trying to make sense of it in her autobiographical writing. "My public profile as an active community-minded Christian made some of the gays try to cast me in an Anita Bryant role," Gerard recalled, "but I knew that Gerard and Bryant were very different people."[57] Exactly what she meant by underscoring the difference between herself and Bryant is not at all clear. Reminiscing about her encounter with the angry crowd that evening, she reasoned "they needed a scapegoat," and she understood that was why she was targeted. She quickly added, however, that she did not appreciate the assumption she was just like Bryant, saying, "I resist being told by them or anyone else but the

Lord what my calling is."[58] Without reading too much into her remark about how different she was from Anita Bryant, it is true that Gerard was surprisingly compassionate toward lesbians who wrote to her as faithful listeners to her radio show, a response that Bryant would certainly not have shared. Yet hints of Gerard's compassion for people who felt ostracized from church communities because of their sexual orientation should not be overstated because Gerard certainly did not publicly endorse homosexuality. To do so would have jeopardized her own support base from evangelical donors, including Pentecostal ones, and it would have strained her alliances with Roman Catholics who took clear positions opposing gay rights. What we can say is that her sermons and statements about sexual orientation did not exhibit the same vitriolic language that was commonly expressed by some other religious conservatives like Bryant.[59]

Perhaps Gerard's softer tone about homosexuality sprang from her own experience of sharing her life with another woman? Bernice and Velma spent more than sixty years together in ministry, travel adventures, and at their home in Vancouver. Whether they were lovers, I do not know, and I do not think it is important to know. What we do know is that they loved each other deeply, to the end of their lives. Academic inquiry into women's same-sex relationships in Canada broaches the subject of women who loved each other by suggesting that for historians, respect and humility are in order. Historian Cameron Duder, in their book *Awfully Devoted Women: Lesbian Lives in Canada, 1900–65*, addresses the ambiguities that persist as scholars debate questions of terminology, and in particular the question of who really should be counted as a lesbian. At the heart of the question about who to include and who to exclude "is whether we can prove that a relationship between two women had a physical, particularly genital, component."[60] I have no such proof about Velma and Bernice. What her archives do reveal is photographic evidence of the physical affection they displayed during those photo shoots, where one of them typically had a hand on the other's shoulder. Of course, we should be careful not to read too much into those photographs, but during the period when Velma was married to Dick, they had several pictures taken showing the three of them together (perhaps for Christmas greetings?) and in each of those photographs, Velma and Bernice are touching each other. Velma and Bernice pose together on one side of the piano (Bernice's hand on Velma's shoulder) while Dick is on the other side of the piano with the dog (see Figure 9.3) There is no mistaking the intimacy and fondness in these photographs, whether one reads them with a queer eye or not.[61]

People who knew Velma and Bernice remember the two women as inseparable. In conversations with some of their former ministry partners, I asked what their relationship was like and how they worked together.[62] In each case, people were quick to point out how different the two women were: Velma always presented herself in a very feminine manner, with attention to her appearance and fashionable dress; Bernice, a self-professed tomboy most comfortable in jeans and rubber boots as a child, had grown up to become a woman with broad shoulders, a very deep voice, and a proclivity for attention to the engineering details of tents and automobiles. In terms of the skills and gifts they brought to their work, Velma was the one who took care of details, sang sweetly, and exhibited hospitality. Bernice was the public voice of the team with an irascible sense of humour, unflinchingly defending her firm principles and leveraging her extraordinary public-speaking skill. As Bernice recounted, she was often congratulated for her ability to "preach like a man."[63] One pastor who knew the pair during their retirement years described his impressions after visiting their home, noting that Velma's bedroom was decorated with flair and a penchant for frill and feminine details, while Bernice's room resembled what he imagined a cloistered nun's quarters might be like: a room with a single bed and a nightstand and, overall, a spartan decor. Gerard's admirers cautioned me about speculating on the nature of Bernice and Velma's private relationship, but they were intrigued by the photographic evidence I offered with displays of affection very much in evidence. One person, entertaining my suggestion that perhaps the relationship was more than it appeared, remarked thoughtfully, "Well, maybe ... but she would have had to have been *so* discreet!" Then they repeated that in all the years they knew them, there was never a public hint of sexual liaison between the two women.

The idea that a historian would even follow such a line of inquiry is a reflection of our times more than of Bernice and Velma's. One did not speak about sexuality in polite company, especially conservative religious company, and it is only in the context of the mainstream homophile movement and lesbian-gay rights that it seems normative to speculate or focus on the idea that female partners in ministry and life may have shared more than what was on public display. Moreover, Duder makes the important point that as historians "we cannot 'know' how our historical subjects thought about themselves and ... we must remember that categories of sexual orientation are neither cross-cultural nor transhistorical."[64] That is an important reminder – ways of thinking about and expressing same-sex love are not timeless, but time-bound. *Awfully Devoted Women* is a study based on letters and interviews and the author highlights the problems of labelling, saying, "the women whose letters I discuss here never described themselves as lesbians, homosexuals, or sexual inverts. The interview narrators now describe themselves as lesbian, but in the period under study

Feminism, Footnotes, and Family

many did not." One of Duder's contributions to the scholarship is to add "a Canadian perspective to the large literature on the transition in women's relationships from the romantic friendship to the modern lesbian."[65]

I predict that some readers will take offence with my raising these questions about Velma and Bernice's relationship. And that objection is predictable, given the Pentecostal and evangelical subcultures where homophobic stances are still reinforced as churches struggle to accept, let alone affirm marriage equality. It was common in the twentieth century to find Pentecostal women travelling and ministering in pairs. Most commonly they did this as young, single women who abandoned their same-sex travels after marriage. Often the pair were biological sisters who stayed together if they both became lifelong spinsters. What is unusual about Bernice and Velma is that their partnership spanned the periods before, during, and after Velma's marriage to Dick Chapman. It is hard to imagine a return to such a pattern of female ministry in circles dominated by patriarchal church structures and congregations that function with historic notions of nuclear family at their centres. In those settings, it seems unlikely that same-sex leadership couples could gain acceptance again. While twenty-first-century conservative churches cling to preoccupations about heteronormative sexuality, the possibility of a return to the model of twosomes like Velma and Bernice seems highly unlikely. Lesbian and gay persons are scarcely made to feel welcome in most Pentecostal circles and, therefore, women as devoted to one another as Velma and Bernice were might have trouble finding endorsement among Pentecostal supporters today.[66] In hypersexualized church cultures where strict adherence to gender prescriptions prevails, questions would surely be raised about whether deeply shared affection between women leaders could really be above reproach.

Gerard sparred with her church over appropriate roles for women even as she and her partner Velma got on with their ministry and their private lives. Meanwhile, as successful Pentecostal pastors of a Vancouver church, gender was central to that experience. Alongside Velma, Bernice preached, led the church's business affairs, and cared for her parishioners while leading communion, weddings, and funerals. Their church attracted a wide variety of people because of Gerard's wide networks of campus ministry, radio audiences, and local charismatic circles. In a period before her own denomination officially ordained women, and while the PAOC's general conferences saw fiercely divisive debates on the issue of whether women should be in ministry leadership or not, Gerard simply took up her pastoral work and carried on. Always a voracious reader and a self-reflective thinker, Gerard was also a pragmatist, so she invoked the American ordination credentials that she and

Velma both held and simply got on with the work of ministry. While she led her church, Gerard also participated in the PAOC's biennial conferences, where she was a strong voice in favour of women's ordination and leadership. For taking that stance she was misunderstood and disrespected by the more conservative PAOC members who raised misogynistic and hermeneutical objections to her convictions and her very presence on the conference floor. Still, she soldiered on. When she wrote her autobiography, she reflected deeply on why she was bored with debating the patriarchy about the legitimacy of women in ministry.

It is significant that Gerard did not lead her Vancouver church single-handedly. Together with Velma McColl Chapman, Bernice Gerard offers us an example of a dynamic ministry couple. They worked together very effectively because while Bernice was the booming public voice behind the microphone and in the pulpit, Velma took care of administrative details, hospitality, and a bit of preaching of her own. They were both musical, playing a variety of instruments and singing harmonies, much to everyone's delight. And because they lived together, the two women also shared their private lives. Before, during, and after the Chapmans' marriage, Bernice and Velma were inseparable. The exact nature of their relationship was complex and, ultimately, private. While it is tempting to speculate on how their family life worked, what we do know for sure is that over their lifetimes, Velma and Bernice loved each other deeply, only to be separated by death when Velma passed in 2007. Bernice died a year later.

While Velma and Bernice were constantly together, the one part of public life where Gerard was alone in the spotlight was during her time as an elected municipal politician. But even then, Gerard's personal convictions, pastoral work, and private life were entwined. Velma was taking up extra church duties (and no doubt, praying fervently!) while Bernice stood up for a variety of causes and became the subject of controversial headlines in the Vancouver papers.

Chapter 10

PUBLIC ENGAGEMENT

IN JANUARY 1977, THE front page of Vancouver's alternative weekly newspaper the *Georgia Straight* featured a political cartoon of Bernice Gerard with a large rubber stamp in her hand marked CENSORED. The headline proclaimed the recent municipal election results: "Anti-porn Queen Bernice Gerard & Other New Rightists [are now] on City Council."[1] Of course, the cartoon was not flattering; Gerard looked very severe, dressed in a frumpy three-piece suit and wearing combat boots, with frown lines on her face and her hand on her hip. The satirist forcefully conveyed that nothing immoral would escape Gerard's careful scrutiny. And the cartoonist was not wrong. Gerard took her role as a municipal politician very seriously, reinforcing her reputation as a moral crusader while she served as an alderman from 1977 to 1981. A few months after that cartoon appeared Gerard would take her famous walk on a Point Grey beach in a silent protest about public nudity. Meanwhile the Vancouver Status of Women group had been following Gerard closely, fearing that she might leverage her new political position to act out her antiabortion stance by influencing the selection of directors for the Vancouver General Hospital's therapeutic abortion committee. Toward the end of her time in office, Gerard was filmed as she protested the screening of the movie *Caligula*, calling its depictions of violent sex "hard core pornography,"[2] and arguing that it violated community standards for decency. No wonder then, that she became the subject of political satire. And yet, as with other aspects of Gerard's life story, her public engagement and short-lived political career were not as simple as they first

FIGURE 10.1 Billed as the "anti-porn queen," Gerard defied categorization: she aligned with politicians on the far right, but her emphasis on compassion meant she supported social justice initiatives including affordable housing, Indigenous cultural centres, and refugees arriving from Vietnam. While political satire was amusing, the *Georgia Straight* admitted that they were not sure how to categorize her, saying, "the jury was still out" on Gerard as a politician. | *Rand Holmes, cartoonist.* Georgia Straight, *January 27–February 2, 1977, cover.*

appear. One thing is clear: what motivated her brief flirtation with elected office was not politics per se, but her deep religious convictions.[3]

When she spoke out on a variety of issues, Gerard was identifying with a cohort of social conservatives who were resisting the liberalization of attitudes, values, and behaviours in Canadian society that gathered momentum during the 1970s. Her short but colourful career in public life, including the episodes that made her so widely recognized across the province and beyond, provides a case study of Pentecostal engagement with culture. Indeed, one could read these incidents as evidence of a religious right in Canada, a subject that deserves more scholarly attention.[4] Significantly, at the same time Gerard justified her actions of protest, she also critiqued the passive, often silent, stance that other evangelicals around her had adopted, offering evidence that evangelicalism was (and is) by no means homogenous. Pentecostalism is not homogenous either. As I have argued, Gerard was a Pentecostal woman with a rich interior life, and her activism offers yet another example of the complexities conservative religious women negotiate as they live out their calling. Gerard's life writing offers clues about why she thought she was being misunderstood for her actions both outside and inside the church. She defended herself by describing her involvements as acts of prophetic engagement with the culture around her. In her own mind, it was perfectly clear what she was doing. She was acting like a spirit-led Pentecostal "prophet," and exactly what she meant by that is the focus of this chapter.

Gerard's election to Vancouver city council must be understood within the larger contexts of national, provincial, and municipal politics. In Ottawa, the Liberal Party of Canada was dominating the federal political scene, and during the 1970s, perhaps their most enduring social legacy was the Trudeau government's efforts to liberalize the Criminal Code of Canada, including greater access to abortion and divorce and wider acceptance of homosexuality, in keeping with progressive Canadian social mores. Ongoing debates ensued as conservative and liberal value systems clashed. Alarmed by this turn away from traditional values, some conservative Christians expressed their concern by lobbying or establishing organizations that would give voice to their concerns while denominational authorities dithered about whether they should speak up to challenge government policies or quietly disengage from public life and the turn away from the familiar values their parents and grandparents had taken for granted. The 1970s and 1980s saw the rise of political lobby groups in the United States, and while Canadian religious conservatives were smaller and far less vocal compared with their American cousins, media personalities like David Mainse and denominations like the Pentecostal Assemblies of Canada made forays into political activism. Gerard was associated with many of those efforts.[5]

Provincially, from 1952 to 1991, the Social Credit Party held power in British Columbia, with only a brief interlude under the New Democratic Party from 1972 to 1975.[6] According to historian Bob McDonald, to understand BC provincial politics in the period leading up to the 1970s, it is helpful to recognize that "political discourse aligned along a left-right continuum, supporting the view that class considerations fueled BC politics."[7] The Social Credit and New Democrats were commonly perceived to occupy opposing places along the political spectrum; therefore, given some of Gerard's support networks, it is not surprising that under the headline announcing her election as an alderman, she was grouped with the "rightists." It is a handy distinction, McDonald suggests, to think of the Social Credit as "a populist party slightly to the right of centre" and the NDP "a populist party slightly to the left"[8]; however, he insists that populism itself only serves to provide a partial explanation of how BC politics (including Vancouver local politics) functioned. In his book *A Long Way to Paradise: A New History of British Columbia Politics,* McDonald set out "to offer up a new history of the province's polarized political culture"[9] by focusing on how competing ideologies, not simply colourful personalities, shaped the past. Therefore, he calls for attention to be paid to liberalism, and specifically "how society should respond to social inequity in an industrializing and modernizing world."[10] As he traces provincial politics from BC's entry into Confederation up to the NDP election victory in 1972, McDonald works from the premise that "ideology lies at the heart of the province's political fault lines."[11] In short, people perceive the NDP to be concerned with equity and social justice issues, while the Social Credit is commonly associated with private enterprise and development initiatives, all with an eye toward profit making by capitalist investors.

Although McDonald's book ends just a few years before the Social Credit Party returned to office and Bernice Gerard began her brief political career in 1977, his focus on ideologies does establish just how complex and contested BC's political landscape was in this period. Like the province itself, and like so many other aspects of her life, Gerard defies easy categorization because while she did have ties to and supporters from the populist right, she was also a champion of the marginalized. Gerard's conservative world view and her association with wealthy capitalist developers did not preclude her concern for refugees and people experiencing homelessness.[12] Her populist appeal, informed by religious views on the right, and her deep compassion for the less privileged was not out of place in the tumultuous context of her province.

The Vancouver press, especially the liberal *Vancouver Sun,* largely dismissed Gerard the politician as simply "the ideological sidekick" of Mayor Jack Volrich,[13] because they both found most of their support from the so-called Non-Partisan Association (NPA). As Vancouver historian Daniel Francis explains, the NPA was a civic group dating back to the 1930s, and while "the new group might have been non-partisan in the sense that it drew from both Liberal and Conservative camps, had no formal platform of its own and generally favoured 'good government,' ... it was decidedly partisan in its determined opposition to the CCF. And it worked. Candidates with NPA backing dominated civic politics for decades to come."[14] Gerard was influential at city hall, and those who remember her as a public figure in this role remember her unwavering criticisms and very public rants on questions of public morality.

On other questions, she was perceived as a follower of Volrich and the NPA priorities. One journalist dismissed her as rather ineffective: "Gerard usually follows the party line supporting large developments and measures aimed at enhancing the business climate and protecting property rights. She sees herself as a protector of the family and reserves most of her aggressive debating tone for matters of morality. Otherwise, she appears not to have done her homework, and contributes little enlightenment to debates."[15] That harsh assessment of Gerard's political record may be accurate because it is clear that Gerard's motivation for getting into municipal politics was narrowly focused: she felt it was her calling to enforce morality. She had very little to say about the ethics of development and urban renewal (leading some to conclude she had not done her homework or was simply toeing the party line); however, she did make contributions that should not be forgotten. She took up causes that capitalists involved with the Social Credit were not known to promote, including her support for a "native Indian cultural centre."[16] Gerard voted in favour of that project even when local residents were opposed, and it is probable that she did so as a way of honouring her adoptive mother Annie, her Grandma Edwards, and their Stó:lō culture, and because she understood from experience the harsh realities of Indigenous populations, especially residential school survivors, who grappled with poverty and substance abuse. Another part of Gerard's legacy, something she worked toward later in her life, sounds more in line with NDP priorities than Socred ones: she and Velma established the Shiloh Project, an affordable housing complex near Vancouver's Downtown East Side.[17] These two initiatives are hard to square with the accusation that Gerard always toed the party line of the NPA and the interests of her conservative (and wealthy!) friends and supporters.[18]

When Gerard was elected to office in Vancouver, the city was a colourful place. As Francis observes, "The city was awash in paisley and bell-bottoms, the sound of electric rock and the aroma of marijuana."[19] Gerard tried very hard to engage with youth, the counterculture, and student culture generally. But the spirit of protest was not limited to the university campuses, and student activists joined with community groups and others concerned about the urban renewal that investors with ties to the NPA were proposing for the downtown. Again, the paradoxes of Gerard's position were in evidence because she had financial and moral support from the conservative NPA camp, but she was working hard to understand student protest and their challenge to unbridled capitalism and middle-class interests. As we have seen, Gerard wanted her radio listeners to understand that hippies' critiques of their parents' complacency and materialism were not misplaced, and those concerns should be heard and respected.

Although Gerard the alderman was commonly perceived as an unbending champion of the right, when she took her place at the council table, she represented a complicated mix of priorities and she insisted that she was motivated by her desire to help people. As one journalist quipped, "Bernice Gerard picks up labels ... [and] is known as an anti-abortionist, a radio evangelist, and a right-winger. She is a teacher, a minister, a freelance broadcaster and now – an alderman."[20] That writer's headline, "Gerard Out to Change Image of the NPA," made it clear that the new alderman hoped to break down the silos of opinion represented on the council because she was "out to shatter the image of the NPA as an uncaring organization for the affluent."[21] The clash of ideologies that historian Bob McDonald referenced were fully in play at the Vancouver city council table.

Gerard recognized that council had the responsibility to be fiscally responsible, something she associated with conservative investors, saying, "we need people on council who can balance the books."[22] But she quickly qualified that thought, saying, "at the same time, if Vancouver is to be a truly great city, it must be culturally rich. And we should have a space in our budget for the poor."[23] Gerard invoked her own childhood story of poverty, abuse, and social welfare to emphasize that she knew first-hand what it was like to rise out of unfortunate circumstances because of the love and care extended to her through government agencies. She asserted that her bid for elected office came out of her sincere wish to help people. "Everybody says they care about people but it doesn't necessarily follow in what they do. I do honestly hope I do turn out to be one of those people who is genuinely caring."[24] Even the *Georgia Straight*, with its satirical cover image of Gerard as the judgmental "Anti-porn Queen," admitted that while Gerard was a "new rightist" with many convictions they found troubling, her compassion for the disadvantaged, the poor, and the elderly was noteworthy. While their editors claimed "it is fairly simple to dig out the political leanings of most of the new council members," they confessed that "Gerard is an unknown quantity" and therefore, as she took office the paper simply said, "We reserve judgement on Gerard."[25]

This was also the backdrop to Vancouver's municipal scene where Gerard's conservative social, religious, and political circles were entwined. When Gerard ran for office, she did not run to represent a particular corner of the city because Vancouver elections were not based on a ward system, but on an at-large system of representation. In this regard, Gerard's media presence was an advantage, given her wide exposure on the airwaves. The city council represented echoes of the larger provincial and national preoccupations as aldermen drawn from the political left and right sparred over issues in their work of local government.

Running as a candidate with support from the NPA, Gerard was aligned with ideological conservatives, many of whom had clear ties to the Social Credit Party and economic interests in urban development and provincial infrastructure projects. A moderate group of reform-minded voters known as The Electors Action Movement (TEAM) called for more popular representation in decision making around development projects, including advocating on behalf of residents displaced by new housing developments, and groups opposing freeway construction. A third group, further left along the political spectrum, was the Committee of Progressive Electors (COPE).[26] Given these competing views, McDonald's claim about the centrality of ideologies in BC politics rings true at the municipal level as well. When Alderman Gerard joined her political colleagues and rivals as a member of city council, she became part of a very complex political mix.

Despite all that complexity, Gerard maintained that the timing seemed right in 1977 to run for office as a city alderman for three reasons. First, as she reveals in her memoir, several Catholics within her networks and, specifically, a columnist from *BC Catholic* were the first to suggest she should enter politics. Keen to endorse her, they were convinced she would make a very articulate and effective politician to represent their socially conservative views.[27] Second, running for office can be an expensive proposition, and Gerard had supporters with money. In *The West beyond the West,* BC historian Jean Barman notes that conservative evangelicals had an increasing presence in BC's provincial politics during the Social Credit era, and one of the most prominent individuals was Philip Gaglardi, the long-serving minister of public works in Premier W.A.C. Bennett's cabinet. He was an outspoken Pentecostal minister from Kamloops, and members of the Gaglardi family had been working closely with Gerard in her campus ministry efforts, funding the guests she invited to campus, to her church, and to her radio show. Knowing she had support from their deep pockets must have figured into her political calculations. And third, by the late 1970s, Gerard had been on the radio for more than a dozen years, and she had wide name recognition throughout Vancouver and beyond because of her popular and provocative broadcasts.

But within the tumult of the wider political context, and beyond the practical considerations of successfully getting the vote out, Gerard had a personal motivation to take up social activism and run for office. It is clear from her life writing that she acted out of conviction. And those convictions were a complex mix. Influenced by her deep spirituality and her lived experience, Gerard was motivated by more than just a stubborn commitment to intransigent religious and social conservativism as the political cartoonists suggested. Before we turn to an exploration of Gerard's inner world to understand what she was thinking as she entered politics and became the infamous public crusader, a brief synopsis of her most infamous causes is in order.

Three unforgettable incidents in Gerard's public life thrust her into the headlines. The first instance revolved around her stance on abortion. In the very same decade that Canadians were coming to grips with the liberalization of measures to make abortion more accessible, Gerard stood for the entrenchment of very conservative positions. Like many other Christians in the pro-life camp, the idea of protecting the rights of the unborn was a matter of conscience and principle for her. Yet Gerard's strong conviction on the issue had very personal roots. Adopted at birth and placed in a series of foster homes, only later in life did she manage to reunite with her siblings and meet her birth mother. Gerard frequently recounted that if abortion had been accessible at the time of her birth, because her mother was institutionalized she would probably never have been born. That fact was a driving motivation for Gerard to speak out against abortion and she did so as a tireless crusader. Her work on behalf of the unborn was motivated by that personal story, but also by her conviction that the 1970s argument "every child should be a wanted child" was nonsense. While that ideal sounded reasonable, Gerard pointed out that just because a pregnancy was unplanned or inconvenient and the cost of raising a child was high, these reasons did not justify turning to abortion. Raised by a series of foster families after her adoptive family proved to be unsuitable and abusive, she countered the logic of the pro-choice movement saying that although her early childhood years were far from ideal, the argument was never made (by her or her caregivers) that she would be better off dead than adopted or placed in foster care.

However, in the decade after the Canadian federal government had removed abortion from the criminal code and figures like Dr. Henry Morgentaler were calling for even greater liberalization of the law, Gerard and her fellow protesters had reason to fear that they were losing ground on the abortion issue. Indeed, recent research is pointing to the fact that Gerard was probably more conservative on this question than some of her fellow Canadian Pentecostals who did not unanimously take an antiabortion stance.[28] When Gerard was running for municipal office in 1977, feminists on the Vancouver Status of Women Committee had been keeping a watchful eye on the influential pastor and media personality. The group hosted a conversation with Alderman Marguerite Ford, a fellow supporter of abortion, and according to an undated, handwritten note in their archives these pro-choice feminists were tracking Gerard's strategic moves. Ford alerted the Status of Women members to be vigilant: "Marguerite warned us that Bernice Gerard is launching another antiabortion campaign at VGH [Vancouver General Hospital] to influence election of directors in May 77."[29] They suspected Gerard would attempt to influence the hospital board, doctors, and decision makers at the Vancouver General Hospital to curb their approval for cases brought before the therapeutic abortion committee. They were wise to pay attention to Gerard because she proved to be a formidable and unrelenting opponent of abortion, all the while maintaining the seemingly paradoxical stance that she was a feminist with women's and children's best interests at heart.

The second incident that thrust Gerard into the public view was her protest over the increasing acceptance of public nudity. Vancouver boasts several public beaches along the Point Grey Peninsula west of the city, near Pacific Spirit Regional Park, and one of them, a seven-kilometre stretch known as Wreck Beach, is clothing optional. As a city councillor, Gerard was concerned because citizens were writing to tell her, as their elected representative, that nudists were increasingly making use of all these beaches, not repecting the boundaries of Wreck Beach. As a university chaplain she also had a vested interest in the issue because of Wreck Beach's proximity to the campus of the University of British Columbia. In response, Gerard took a public stand to protest the spread of public nudity to other Vancouver beaches: in July 1977 she decided to lead her silent protest march along the beach. Two very different versions of this episode exist. The public media had a heyday with the fact that Pastor Gerard, the outspoken alderman who was sometimes likened to a staunch version of the literary Mrs. Grundy, was going to walk the beach – that beach! However, Gerard insists she never went near the nude beach, but only walked the public beach adjoining it. According to Gerard, that was the point – not to stop the nudists from enjoying their own area but to make a statement that the spread of nudity beyond that one beach was not acceptable.

Gerard was certainly not alone in her concern over public nudity, and a range of views on the issue were expressed during the summer of 1977, some of them in response to Gerard's infamous beach walk. Vancouver Mayor Jack Volrich received several letters about Wreck Beach, prompting him to ask the Vancouver Police Department to provide him with "a brief report as to any complaints which have been made or brought to your attention in this matter and no doubt you will check with the R.C.M.P University detachment."[30] Acting Chief Constable Dixon replied to the mayor's request, and his answer reflects the fact that various levels of government legislation were at play, from municipal bylaws to provincial laws, up to the highest courts of the land. According to Dixon the Vancouver police had "received no complaints of nudity as outlined in Section 170, Criminal Code of Canada, and there have been no charges laid under that Section."[31] Dixon went on to explain that "it is fairly common" to have "incidents of 'Man Exposing', which comes under Section 169 Criminal Code of Canada, where the offender, if caught, is usually charged with Indecent Act. The incidence of this offence has no connection with Wreck Beach, but are spread throughout the city."[32] Having communicated with the campus police, Dixon reported further that "they have only two cases where there are named complaints. However, they have received numerous verbal complaints of incidents in their area," and the university detachment had "plans to inspect the area of Wreck Beach by helicopter" and report the findings to the attorney-general.[33]

While the police file on the issue was thin, the mayor's office could not say the same thing because they received a lot of letters on the subject. The people who were most angry wrote to say they appreciated Gerard's protest walk, and they used inflammatory language, referring to nudists as "misfits," and "arrogant people flaunting the law" whose behaviours threatened to cause "a moral landslide," as the complainant linked nudism to pornography and sexual predation. "Is organized Crime producing porno or kiddie porno on our beaches?" one writer wondered.[34] One accused nudists of "laziness" because although Wreck Beach was understood to be "clothing optional," more and more people were opting for the easily accessible beaches rather than making the challenging climb down the steep trail leading to Wreck Beach itself. Writers with these views were incredulous that the mayor and city council did not simply use a heavy hand and heighten law enforcement. "We were amazed at the position [of inaction] you took," one said, enclosing a copy of the city's parks bylaws, highlighting section 20, "Bathing Beaches and Swimming Pools," which calls for swimmers to be "properly clothed in a bathing suit."[35] Some who complained were older citizens, like the couple who had lived in Vancouver for more than sixty years and wondered if the area could perhaps be designated as "a military zone," presumably to allow for greater surveillance.[36] Another writer was a philosophy student who asked incredulously, "You are not actually going to allow nude bathing on public beaches, are you?"[37] One dismissively suggested that nudists were not respectable citizens and the mayor should not bow to their will because "not many votes there, Mr. Volrich – in fact, it is doubtful if they are even property owners."[38] Such voices were united by their self-righteous tone and their conviction that the issue was a simple one, only requiring some political will on the part of municipal politicians.

In fact, the issue was not at all simple and Gerard recognized that fact. As historian Mary-Ann Shantz argues in *What Nudism Exposes: An Unconventional*

History of Postwar Canada, nudism raises a plethora of questions about "the body's position at the intersection of nature and culture, the individual and the social, the private and the public."[39] All of those issues were at play as Gerard and other local politicians grappled with the complexities that faced them. Several people wrote explaining in nuanced ways that they appreciated the issue was not black and white. Nude bathing should be allowed on Wreck Beach, many reasoned. And while at least one asserted that this was a nonissue and politicians should concentrate on real social problems like the use and abuse of drugs in Vancouver,[40] most who agreed that nudists should be free to express themselves with their bodies still called for clear boundaries. One mother explained that she and her family had enjoyed the beaches, but "with the increase of naked people there, our visits have stopped. We do not like to be confronted by nudists, and our sons who are 18, 16, and 15 are embarrassed also."[41] She, and some others, suggested that nudists should be limited to private property, not public spaces. But others were more accommodating, saying they didn't mind Wreck Beach being on public land, but they wished to see the clothing-optional beach clearly marked with signage and even fencing. Enforcing boundaries and applying consequences were required, they argued, both to protect "the right of the nudists to sunbath[e]" but also to "protect the rights of others who like to relax at the beach too."[42] Another writer expressed essentially the same idea, saying, "This would be fair both to those who are devotees of nudism as it would allow them all the space they need and to those who are offended by nudity and yet are entitled to the use of the beach just west of Spanish Banks."[43] This moderate position is actually the one that Gerard was calling for, though of course political satirists missed any nuance in their depictions of her.

Two archival letters on this subject offer a deeply personal perspective that would resonate with Gerard, the abuse survivor, because they raised the question of sexual danger. One woman described her confrontation with a nudist who disrupted a wedding she was part of in a Vancouver public garden. She suspected the man was "a stray from the nudist colonies at the nearby beaches" and recounted that "he wasn't a streaker as he walked very nonchalantly through the gate towards the main gathering of wedding guests." Eventually, the RCMP's university detachment was called to respond, and the intruder was removed. But the woman was shaken by the experience. "An hour earlier I was sitting, alone, in one of the shelters in the centre of the Gardens. If this man had appeared then, I would have been very upset. As it is, I am very angry that such an incident could occur." The woman explained what prompted her to write to the mayor. "You were quoted in the Vancouver Sun as saying you wouldn't take any action in regards to beach nudity until you received complaints. This very definitely is a complaint."[44]

Another woman's encounter led her to write to the mayor expressing overtly the fear she felt and explaining how she had gone down to the beach in front of her house to enjoy the sunshine on a recent early fall day. "I sat on a log relaxing & feeling good when along came a nude man [who] lay down fifteen feet from me. Nothing wrong with that," she explained, except that it was clear the man was sexually aroused. "I couldn't stay & relax in the sun and bask anymore. I had to get up and go away. I turned to go back up the path when I saw a thunderous young man nude except for shoes & socks standing at the head of the path. I could not go right up to him, so I thought I would continue down the beach & go home that way but the way was blocked by more nude men." She explained "I think of myself as a liberal thinker, nevertheless, I did not feel comfortable (I felt threatened) at the beach in front of our house." The woman reported that her neighbours felt the same way and that her husband was very upset by her story. To communicate that her fear was gender-based, she challenged the mayor, saying, "Try to imagine how it feels to be the only one of one sex surrounded by nude members of the other sex – Or maybe it doesn't have the same effect in reverse?"[45] The possibility of sexual danger was certainly on her mind, as it was on Gerard's, and the letter writer argued that public nudity on the beaches so close to the university campus was not acceptable. "Girl students cannot be comfortable – or relax at the beach as it is."[46] As a survivor of sexual assault, Bernice Gerard could certainly imagine the feeling of threat this woman was trying to express.

Like her stands on abortion and public nudity, the third theme of Gerard's protest activity was no less public and no less controversial: standards of decency in popular entertainment. There were two notorious occasions when Gerard took a stand against what she perceived as obscene content on the stage and screen in Vancouver's popular culture scene. The play *Oh! Calcutta!* was staged in a Vancouver theatre in the summer of 1977 and the movie *Caligula* screened in Vancouver in the summer of 1981. Both productions were infamous for pushing the limits of public morality. In both cases, Gerard and her supporters protested outside the theatres, and media coverage about their objections was widespread. As she described it, "We got into it. We acted. We went down and picketed the theatre. It was an ugly scene because the lewd ones were there. They broke the signs over our heads."[47] Yet, despite that opposition, Gerard was pleased to report in her autobiography that good had come of all this because she and her team "led several people to Christ" on the sidewalk outside the theatre.

FIGURE 10.2 Gerard protested the depiction of violence and sexuality in the film *Caligula* because she regarded it as pornography. Her own history of abuse continued to trouble her into her old age, and the consternation in her face resembles her teenaged countenance. | *City of Vancouver Archives.*

"I recall getting involved with great reluctance in the protest against the showing of *Caligula*, the first hard-core pornographic film to run in a commercial theatre in Vancouver," Gerard wrote in her autobiography. "I knew there was a law against it. I knew that we Christians should speak up and I didn't want to. But as I went to prayer about it I was mightily convicted."[48] Out of that conviction, Gerard proceeded with the protest outside the theatre, and the event was recorded on film for posterity. That film footage captures Gerard's stern demeanour, but it also underlines the fact that the protest was intended to be a silent one, and she worked hard to ensure that her supporters did not engage in debate or acts of incivility.[49]

In fairness to Gerard, it should be noted that she rarely spoke in anger and many of her protests, including the famous beach walk, were silent marches. Her protests about the theatres in Vancouver were silent ones too, and although she was happy to speak with reporters about what they were protesting and why, she encouraged her supporters and fellow protesters to remain respectful and silent.

When inevitable skirmishes arose between the protesters and those who opposed them, Gerard worked to silence her own team, asking them not to engage in verbal battles but simply to walk, holding their signs and their tongues. When she spoke out as a city alderman in opposition to public nudity, she never argued that Wreck Beach should not exist as a clothing-optional beach. Her argument was that public nudity should be contained to that one beach and not be allowed on other public beaches. Again, as the vignette that opens this book demonstrates, her presence at protests could easily be misconstrued, because the complexity of her motivations could hardly be appreciated by casual observers.

But in fact, Gerard was not an intransigent or irrational individual when it came to public affairs. As an alderman for the city of Vancouver, she explained that her personal views were not uppermost, and indeed, she did not always vote in ways that her fellow believers might have predicted. She gave the example of her work on the council's Community Service Committee:

> Did I, a teetotaler, always vote down a liquor license application? Some said, "As a Christian you should never vote yes to a liquor license." Granted, I know [from my own childhood experiences] the horrendous damage done by excess of alcohol. But my view is that the alderman is not there to make up the laws on an *ad hoc* basis as he/she goes along. As a Council we have put by-laws in place. If the application meets the criteria for acceptance, my personal abstemiousness should not hinder the other person's business or personal interests.[50]

Here Gerard was making it clear that her position was neither arbitrary nor predetermined. She did not always vote like a conservative trapped in the past striving to keep in step with fundamentalist Christians; indeed, many of her decisions were puzzling to her fellow believers, because she did not use her office as an alderman to promote only one view. As she explained, she tried to work within the existing bylaws, call for change to the laws when she felt it necessary, and always to be a voice of reason and a representative of her constituents. She used her university training in critical thinking and logic to appeal to common sense and common law, and she was convinced that the Christian politician's role was to ensure that the laws of the land were being followed.

Given Gerard's reticence to do this work, then what motivated her? As she reveals with her comment that when she prayed about it she felt "mightily convicted," she was putting her spirituality at the centre. She was convinced she should do it, and to refuse to do so would be a matter of conscience because she felt God was asking her to take a stand. But of course, there was more to her activism than a simple prayer session giving her direction to become involved. Once again, she reveals the complexity of her inner world on this matter through her life writing.

Gerard reports that she was moved to run for city council in part because of her supporters' encouragement when they saw that she was a strong, articulate, and recognized voice for the right who could be an effective spokesperson for antiabortion and other issues they found morally objectionable. She had many friends and supporters among Roman Catholics, especially the charismatic Catholics who became her friends and associates. At the same time, she was part of a wing in her own denomination, the PAOC, who believed they had the responsibility to stand for righteousness on the social issues of the day. As a result, when the PAOC created its national Social Concerns Committee she was more than willing to participate and promote the work of challenging government on increasingly liberal policies around sexuality, especially. But rather than just serve through the committee her church executives were creating, Gerard took local actions too. She famously is remembered for opposing many local initiatives in Vancouver, but at the same time, even some of her most vocal critics had to concede that Gerard was doing a lot of good for the city. While she was an alderman, Mayor Volrich appointed Gerard to chair the Vancouver Refugee Committee, a group that coordinated efforts to help new Canadians to settle and begin new lives in the Vancouver region and beyond. Gerard recounted that Canadian Senator and former broadcaster Laurier LaPierre, "has not always blessed me," but when he interviewed her about her refugee work, he kissed her hand before she left the studio.[51]

Debates about evangelicals' involvement in cultural affairs stem from the dilemma that believers face in trying to be true to the admonition to be "in the world but not of the world." As Wilkinson and Ambrose argue in *After the Revival: Pentecostalism and the Making of a Canadian Church*, Gerard's denomination (the PAOC) put significant effort and resources into engagement with public issues of morality when, in 1978, they created their Social Concerns Committee, at first called the National Committee on Moral Standards, under the leadership of the Rev. Hudson T. Hilsden.[52] Gerard served as a member of that committee and supported the initiatives that moved the PAOC toward exercising greater political engagement. The existence of the Social Concerns Committee was short-lived, and by the mid-1990s, the PAOC dismantled this department and relied more heavily on the Evangelical Fellowship of Canada to be the mouthpiece for its political and social concerns. While some

Pentecostals, including Gerard, regretted any initiative that seemed to be a retreat from public engagement, it made sense to align with the broader evangelical sector to leverage strength in numbers.

As that larger evangelical group was taking shape Gerard stepped forward to assist Brian Stiller when he took up the role of leading the new Evangelical Fellowship of Canada (EFC). Stiller expresses very high regard for Gerard, not only for her convictions and effectiveness as a voice in public engagement, but also for her skills as a strategist, organizer, and administrator. "She was my partner in the EFC," Stiller recounts.[53] When pressed to explain this since she had no formal role or office in the EFC, Stiller points to the ways that Gerard modelled for him how to motivate people to support the same causes, and the practical steps of coordinating a group that had so many constituent parts. Those who shared the same conservative views about social issues were drawn from such a variety of backgrounds that they would indeed be a difficult bunch to wrangle. Gerard's wide experience of moving in different faith groups served as a great asset to Stiller and the EFC as the group emerged to speak with one voice for political and social views from the right.

Sam Reimer, sociologist of religion, explores how the evangelical "right" in Canada is similar to and different from its American counterpart, with one key difference being that Canadians are typically more likely than their American counterparts to drop denominational differences to seek consensus.[54] For Gerard, having a presence in the "world" led her to enter municipal politics and take very public stances on questions of morality, and her convictions caused her to take actions that fellow believers could not condone. She invoked her own life story as her best argument against abortion, attempting to counter the logic that if a child was not "wanted" they should not be born. While many would have supported her stance on that question, clearly not everyone within PAOC circles was convinced that abortion should never be an option under any circumstances, including some of Gerard's radio audience.[55] Nor could all Canadian Pentecostals condone her controversial action of going to the beaches where nude sunbathers greeted her and her entourage as they made their silent protest. Yet Gerard insisted that to protect public beaches for the use of families and concerned citizens, she needed to endure some unpleasant encounters and even personal harassment. When she argued that depicting sexual violence in popular culture was abhorrent, she was suggesting a rating system should be implemented to warn audiences in advance about offensive content that violated community standards of decency. Gerard was not alone in this view because others, including some secular feminists, were divided in their views about pornography. The issue was not a simple one and not limited to the divide between the religious and irreligious.[56] But when Gerard made it clear that she had viewed the film *Caligula* herself, that was going too far for many church folks who were uncomfortable that a Pentecostal pastor had exposed herself to the popular media content she had declared "obscene." Gerard defended her action on that occasion saying that it was disingenuous to protest a film that she herself had not seen.

The fact that Gerard was controversial is hardly surprising. Given the context of Canadian social history during the 1970s, her resistance to the liberalization of sexual mores was sure to invite criticism from the public media and secular society. Gerard fully expected that her stance on these questions of morality would invite ridicule. As she explained, "non-believers ... [who] were apprehensive of 'born again Christians' achieving political power, imagined that behind every born-again politician is a monolithic, oppressive, power-hungry church structure."[57] A Vancouver journalist writing about Gerard in 1979 observed, "At the height of her career both as an evangelist and a politician, the thing Bernice Gerard fears most is that she will become a caricature of herself. It may already be too late."[58] Indeed, Gerard accepted that being ridiculed was part of the prophet's lot in life. As she recounted in her autobiography, "The truth is that Christians will be spoken against as evil-doers whether they deserve it or not." Her consolation, however, was that "trouble because one is faithful to God is only a short-term problem."[59] Gerard recognized that opposition from unbelievers was to be expected; playfully she even included a satirical cartoon in her autobiography to illustrate how she was regarded for her conservative stance as an alderman (see Figure 10.3). In a *Vancouver Sun* cartoon, a citizen applying for a business licence is told that he will have to wait for approval because everything first has to pass before the watchful eyes of Bernice Gerard. "Take a pew ... while I invoke the wisdom of the mayor and Alderman Gerard," the applicant is told.[60]

But while she acted locally, Gerard was thinking globally, and she took courage from the fact that she was not alone in voicing her righteous indignation. In 1984, when she gave a keynote address to the PAOC general conference, she explained that she had been working across international networks and that moral decline was worldwide. "Soho in London had become a filthy rotten Hell because of all the garbage the purveyors of pornography were dumping. It was coming in from Denmark, in Denmark with their live sex shows, women had sex with animals and the Humane Society protested on behalf of the horse. But who spoke on behalf of the woman? No one."[61]

"Take a pew... while I invoke the wisdom of the mayor and Alderman Gerard..."

FIGURE 10.3 Gerard's moralistic stance on a variety of issues carried over to her time in municipal politics, and although she was easy to mock, her political positions were usually more complex and nuanced than her critics admitted. | Vancouver Sun, *August 16, 1977*, 4. Len Norris, cartoonist.

Hoping to persuade her Canadian audience, she related that similar protests had taken place in Australia and Great Britain.

> But now there is an international network of us. When they act in Australia they let me know in Vancouver. When something good happens in Great Britain we want to communicate. It's not a local problem, although it can be very ugly on the local scene. But what thrills me is the Festival of Light in Great Britain ... That was my introduction to all of them. It is encouraging that somehow, God, by his spirit, is using Christians as salt.[62]

Gerard was establishing that with that global backing, her local fight to uphold "community standards" in Vancouver was certainly not the act of an outdated moralizer acting alone but, rather, part of a worldwide effort on the part of publicly minded Christian citizens.

From that global base, Gerard urged other believers to adopt a religious-political strategy, calling on politicians and lawmakers to uphold the existing laws prohibiting obscenity when local legislation called for community standards to be upheld. Encouraging fellow Pentecostals to get involved, Gerard reminded listeners that simply writing to local authorities could have a big impact because "you often hear it said among the politicians, nobody protested. We never got any letters of complaint. So you can see how we need so much to be led by the Spirit and declare ourselves willing to take action."[63] And while Gerard was not surprised to be a minority voice among the wider population when she was speaking out on these matters, she was surprised and disappointed by the reactions of other evangelical Christians who sometimes echoed public amusement about her activism. But for Gerard, the question of Christians taking a stand on matters of morality was no laughing matter. While her own congregation at the Fraserview Assembly was consistently supportive of her foray into municipal affairs, she was fully aware that other believers felt differently. "Some of my Christian critics were particularly concerned that I, as a minister of the gospel in the political arena, would receive a great deal of persecution simply for who I was. More difficult for me to deal with was the fact that some people believed that ordinary believers in our metropolitan area, and particularly those in my own congregation would have to 'take persecution' on my account. Their idea seemed to be that if we all keep reasonably quiet and inactive in community affairs, we will save ourselves a lot of trouble."[64]

Recognizing that fellow believers might have trouble accepting not only her actions, but also her rationale for acting, Gerard explained: "I literally preached myself into politics, shocking as the idea may be to many conservative other-worldly evangelicals."[65] It is intriguing that Gerard drew this distinction between herself as a Pentecostal and a group she called "conservative other-worldly evangelicals." She expected that latter group to be uncomfortable, even shocked at her explanation for how she came to take up these very public acts of political involvement and protest.

Beyond her networks of conservative Christians devoted to varying degrees of public engagement, Gerard's Pentecostal spirituality provides a second piece to the puzzle about her motivation for civic engagement. Since Gerard referenced that she had "preached herself into politics," I set out to explore her sermon notes to see what they could reveal about her motivations for entering public life. In 1973 she had preached a series of sermons she called "Too Much Wilderness, Too Few Prophets," based on her study of several leaders in the Hebrew scriptures.[66] She focused on Moses, who led the children of Israel through the wilderness to the Promised Land, because she related to

Moses personally as she highlighted the parallels she saw between his life and hers. Like her, Moses was adopted. Moses moved between two different cultures. Educated by Egyptians, he understood that dominant culture before he returned to lead the Israelites. Gerard felt like a cultural go-between too. With postgraduate education in a public university, she felt she could explain Canadian culture-at-large to Pentecostal, charismatic, and evangelical believers who tried to be "in the world, but not of the world." And like Moses, she expected that she would encounter detractors, even within her own ranks. Moreover, just as Moses had Aaron to support him when he became weary in this calling, Bernice had Velma. In her own mind, the parallels between her and Moses were striking!

Gerard's teaching and sermon notes from that series make clear her understanding about what prophets do and how they operate. And, in true Pentecostal fashion, when a scripture resonated so deeply with her, Gerard assumed that the Holy Spirit was directing her attention to it. She recounted that it was "in preaching on Exodus, I took a long hard look at a fully developed prophetic ministry as demonstrated in the life of Moses."[67] And, sensing that God was calling her to operate as a present-day prophet, she found a model in Moses that she tried to emulate because, as she noted, he had been described in Deuteronomy 34:10 as "the greatest of Israel's prophets."

But what exactly did Gerard mean by prophecy and taking up a prophet's role? Many evangelicals invoke the word *prophecy* when they reference eschatological themes about how world history will conclude "in the last days." Like other conservative Christians in the late twentieth century, Gerard shared a dispensational understanding of world history and of things yet to come, and some of her sermon notes include teachings that addressed future events depicted in the book of Revelation, for example. But when she identified with Moses and preached about his life as a model for her own calling to be prophet, she was very clear to emphasize that the role of prophet was not restricted to predicting future events or demystifying apocalyptic themes.[68] Rather, Gerard emphasized that prophets spoke up as critics of the culture around them. She asserted that prophets were not only called to bring God's message to fellow believers, but also to challenge the culture around them. "We Bible believers today understand the urgency of the Great Commission," she told readers of her autobiography, "but are frequently guilty of taking an either/or approach when we should be saying, 'Yes, let us preach the good news for the salvation of the lost, *and* explore every possible means to act and speak prophetically to our contemporaries.'"[69] For Gerard, speaking "prophetically" included speaking publicly whenever the opportunity arose, and she found there was no end of opportunities! As she told a national gathering of Canadian Pentecostals in 1984, "I am loaded with examples. I just get out of one thing and I'm into another. I don't seek it. And I don't think you really need to seek. I think what you need to do is pray and don't do anything that you don't feel you really must do. But if we took seriously the prophetic side of it I believe we would find ourselves activated more than we imagine."[70]

Gerard accepted that the role as prophet meant her activism would surely be misunderstood. The public media portrayals and municipal records might lead a historian to endorse the caricature of Gerard as a right-wing crusader who set out to curb civil liberties and freedom of expression. Yet her life writing, including her notes from speaking engagements and sermon series, reveals that she understood the actions she was taking to be part of her calling. She concluded, "When it comes to those things that concern God's commands for us and our living out the life of Jesus, we are going to have to have a prophetic function. I don't see how we can avoid it," and "In this world ... we are under obligation to stand with the truth and ... we're fools if we think we are going to get popular because we did it."[71]

Popularity was not top of mind for Gerard because, as she explained, her involvement in public affairs, political life, and protest movements came from a place of deep conviction. She understood her involvements as the acts of one who was called of God as a prophet. Moreover, she lamented, "Unfortunately, Christians often shrink from the prophetic task and somehow see the 'condemning of ungodliness' as embarrassing to themselves and their church, and as an end in itself whereas righteous living is a part of God's redemptive action and a proper expression of His love (Ephesians 5:6–11)."[72]

From the story of Moses leading the children of Israel out of captivity in Egypt, Gerard drew several important points that shaped her own ministry work and public engagement. She identified the characteristics of a prophet. She noted that humility (and even reluctance) was common for prophets when they first considered their role of fulfilling God's calling. Moses hesitated about appearing before Pharoah because of his speech impairment, and Gerard hesitated about running for office and staging such public protests because she knew those actions would seem strange to those around. She pointed out that prophecy was not about condemning others, but rather about speaking from a place of deep compassion for people who, like the Israelites of old, were in bondage. In her own context, Gerard perceived that many citizens of Vancouver were in bondage to inappropriate moral conduct. She also concluded that sometimes prophets underwent an "identity crisis," as Moses did. He had been raised in Pharaoh's household and he identified with Egyptian culture, yet he chose to identify with the suffering of the children of Israel and return to the culture of his birth mother. Gerard, similarly, had grown up in foster care and trained at a public university, but she chose to identify with religious conservatives rather than with mainstream middle-class society, and with people who were marginalized in the secular society.

When Gerard wrestled with what she sensed God was asking her to do, she took direction from the case of Moses, the reluctant prophet, who was finally convinced to do what he was being asked to do. Gerard preached that Moses was empowered by God for the task, that he relied on God's presence and directive. Moses was instructed that if authorities objected to his boldness, he was to "tell him I AM has sent you" (Exodus 3:14). Gerard interpreted that as a model for her own public engagement; she would have to rely on the Holy Spirit's empowerment and gifting as she took up the role of prophet. It was all part of her Pentecostal identity.

Gerard dwelt on the point about spiritual gifts and empowerment to draw distinctions between Pentecostals and other charismatics exercising the gift of prophecy and other evangelicals who frequently preached about the end of the world and the imminent return of Christ but did not subscribe to the idea that prophecy was a spiritual gift or a role to be taken up for the current day. Such people might attempt political activism, Gerard reasoned, but without the power of the Holy Spirit to guide and empower them, they were not likely to make much of an impact. Gerard defended her public actions and protests about controversial issues because she was convinced that the Holy Spirit was prompting her to act. Indeed, whether her actions translated into changed behaviours and policies or not, she was convinced that even if only for the sake of conscience, it was important to act. She wanted to be able to recount, when questioned by young people in the future about what she had done, that she had been obedient to the prompting of the Holy Spirit in the steps she had taken to stand up for righteousness.

Sometimes taking a stand meant objecting to popular culture when it crossed the line and became indecent. Gerard was very clear about this, saying, "*Caligula* is hard-core pornography and everybody, including the media critics, admitted it. Mass sex orgies, decapitation, castration, every sexual perversion with violence done with hundreds of beautiful men and women obviously filmed in some foreign land, unspeakable things and there were those clergy and those professors who stuck up for it saying that it was history."[73] Gerard was clear to say that it did not qualify to be valued as culturally important, and her role as a prophet compelled her to speak out about it.

That kind of cultural critique emphasizes that for Gerard, prophetic ministry was not about predicting the future but, rather, about the "equally important prophetic task [of] 'forthtelling,' that is 'telling forth the will of God for the situation.' With an understanding that this is for every believer, we move easily into involvement with social and ethical concerns, right conduct and right relationships."[74] Moreover, in declaring herself to be acting like a prophet, she did not wish to imply that she was superior to other believers, lording her authority over them. On the contrary, she was pleading with fellow believers to take seriously the idea that God still used ordinary people as prophets, as part of the list of spiritual gifts that were in operation among the spirit-baptized. For Gerard, the point of prophesying or operating in any of the other gifts of the Spirit, was not to condemn but to offer a message of love and of hope. Of course, this is not usually how she was perceived. Instead, she was mocked and ridiculed for her hypermoralistic stance on issues. When Gerard claimed that she "preached herself into politics," she meant that her own study of scriptures drove her to the logical conclusion that she must be engaged with the culture around her. She explained that preaching about Moses translated into a personal recognition of her social responsibilities and she also taught her parishioners to think in the same terms.

> We gain an insight into our responsibility as Christians when we realize that, because of the Incarnation, everywhere we go, Jesus goes. We are indwelt by the Holy Spirit. Therefore, at the marketplace, the school, waterfront, bank, bakery, farm, fish cannery or Parliament, our daily lives have a "prophetic" impact. Since our lifestyle is made up of various components, each of which reflects our value system, whether we think of it or not, each of us is a prophetic word to our contemporaries.[75]

Pentecostalism is not homogenous, and Gerard was sometimes misunderstood, even within the PAOC. The rationale that Gerard offered for her actions represents the ties she maintained outside the more conservative expressions of faith typically found in classical Pentecostalism. With her emphasis on "spirit-led" activism, Gerard was embracing a more charismatic expression of Pentecostalism, sometimes referred to as neocharismatics.[76] Gerard revealed in a 1984 talk that she and Velma Chapman had recently taken a course on the gifts of the Holy Spirit at Fuller Theological Seminary with John Wimber.[77]

The founder of the Vineyard movement, Wimber represents a brand of Pentecostalism that originated in California with an emphasis on "signs and wonders." The course that Bernice and Velma took is one that Wimber taught from 1982 to 1986, and course notes reveal that he gave instruction to students about a variety of ways that people could be healed, including healing from past hurts, something that would surely have resonated with Gerard and her childhood trauma.

Gerard emphasized that Wimber's teaching reinforced a variety of Pentecostal principles, including the important reminder that whether it was healing or public engagement, any attempt to do prophetic work or influence society using one's own strength or force of personality would come to nothing. She admitted that she was prone to an addiction to work, but Wimber's course reinforced to her that it was not human effort that would get results in the church or society. Lasting impact required a return to the exercise of the gifts of the Spirit; that kind of supernatural empowerment was the source of the "signs and wonders," the outcomes commonly associated with Wimber and the Vineyard movement that he taught his students to seek. Gerard was committed to this view and she became quite critical of fellow Pentecostals who shied away from public engagement and did not share her neo-charismatic convictions, ridiculing some of her male colleagues who hesitated to take up public engagement and political work, calling them "limp men."[78]

Gerard's motivations for activism were complex. She acted alongside other conservative Christians to resist the changing morality in Canadian society. And she did so out of her Pentecostal convictions about calling and spiritual gifts. But there is another explanation that is even more deeply personal. Gerard became involved in public affairs because her lived experience as a survivor of abuse shaped her profoundly. Beyond the promise of achieving results, Gerard was undoubtedly drawn to teaching like Wimber's because of his emphasis on healing from past hurts. The lasting impact of abuse followed her to the end of her life. In photographs of Gerard from the period when she served as a city alderman, she appears angry and combative. Visual texts from the period reinforce the severe tone of Gerard's stance. Photographs and film footage document Gerard protesting outside a Vancouver theatre and calling for rating systems and standards of morality to be applied in order to question the obscenity that frequented the stages and screens in Vancouver.[79] In all of the visual archives of Gerard (e.g., photographs, videos), it is only in this period and in her roles as protester and politician that her angry, severe demeanour comes across. When I compare the face of Gerard the combative protester to that of the little girl rescued from abuse, the same angry countenance is evident.

Most observers saw this side of Gerard and concluded, like the editorialists in *Georgia Straight*, that she was a conservative battleaxe character, but the anger that Gerard expressed was more complicated. The one other occasion when her face belied the same kind of anger was in her childhood school picture at age thirteen (compare Figures 2.1 and 10.2) That photograph, taken at the time of her rescue from sexual abuse, matches the angry protester/politician that Gerard became in the late 1970s. The link back to her childhood is an important one. Having escaped abuse herself, she was adamant about standing up for the victimized because she empathized with the oppressed. Forms of entertainment depicting sexual violence or sadomasochism were triggers for Gerard. The rage she had experienced as a child came flooding back, and she rose up in protest to be a voice for the voiceless. Her reactions were complex, of course. On one hand, she was the angry defender of the abused. On the other hand, she saw abuse where others might not. Her perception of sex trade workers, for example, was one-sided: women in that profession must be victims, she concluded. Her perspective on the edgy, raw sexuality depicted in *Oh! Calcutta!* and *Caligula* was that these were simply disgusting glorifications of abuse that should not be granted the dignity of a public audience or condoned as acceptable forms of entertainment for "open-minded" people.

Yet, to be clear, Gerard's goal was not to abolish these forms of entertainment entirely, as disgusting as she found them to be. Rather, she hoped to introduce a rating system that would forewarn audiences about disturbing scenes and mature themes. So, while she was cast as a reactionary right-wing extremist (and given elements of her position, that is fair) her goal was a more modest one: to tell audiences in advance what they are about to view and experience, and make sure that what was offered for consumption did not violate community standards. This unflinching public demeanour is what led political cartoonists to mock her.

Beneath that harsh exterior, Gerard was fuelled by compassion as she reflected deeply on a variety of broad ranging issues. Once again her life writing gives insights into her thinking, complicating the impression that she was simply a reactionary conservative with her mind made up on every issue in advance. Unquestionably, Gerard's public responses were angry ones. But her anger was understandable, even logical, given her childhood trauma, and she made connections in her mind between several different issues. She was deeply disturbed by the mere thought of eugenics and her antiabortion stance was entwined with those concerns and others, including racism. After she read *Black Like Me*, she was deeply impacted.[80] Although that book has since been criticized and dismissed by many as an awkward example of cultural appropriation, Gerard remembered her own youthful ignorance when she was first exposed to racial tensions while travelling through the rural American south in the early postwar years. Gerard was moved by the book to a posture of seeking justice on behalf of the victims of racism, believing that healing race relations would take a supernatural move of the Spirit.

In the same way, although Gerard's unquestioning fondness for Israel is troubling to us in light of current events, specifically the genocidal atrocities committed in Gaza, Gerard was concerned that antisemitism and the trauma experienced by Holocaust survivors needed to be addressed. And again, she was convinced that healing would require spiritual intervention. Deeply impacted by her visit to the Holocaust Museum in Jerusalem, where she had the emotional experience of walking through the exhibits, especially the children's memorial, Gerard's compassion and empathy were aroused. She knew from her family experiences that society's castaways were often left powerless in the face of evil policies including cultural genocide and dangerous attitudes toward those with disabilities. She identified deeply with those victims. Her own childhood framed her understanding, including her empathy for her disabled mother and her childhood roots of being a child no one wanted. Gerard transferred those experiences of abandonment and mistreatment to her perception of a variety of issues, entwined with, but not limited to sexual abuse. On her repeated visits to Israel, she adopted the rhetoric that was common to evangelical believers informed by a dispensational understanding of history and the importance of the nation of Israel for the teleological purposes of seeing God's hand in history. However, unlike some others who were driven to positions of stubborn, intransigent support for Israel as a political ally, Gerard's takeaway was different. What moved her about Israel was the history of how Jewish people, particularly women and children, were dehumanized and murdered. She recounted, "My first in-depth experience with the Holocaust documentary and memorial known as Yad Vashem in Jerusalem, when I was leading a Holy Land tour, left me horrified." It was the children's plight that she could not forget. "In particular, the sadness of the little boy with the large brown eyes, dressed in a greatcoat, hands raised over his head in the face of the Nazi officer's gun, lingered on in my thoughts," she explained. And following that first emotional encounter with the memorials, when she led tours of pilgrims to Israel, she saw "the task of raising people's awareness of human history's darkest hour as an important part of our pilgrimage."[81] Gerard's activism was far-reaching. She was not as simply fixated on questions of sexual morality, as some have suggested, but her actions and reactions on behalf of Holocaust survivors, refugees, the mentally ill, and other victims of injustice consistently circled back to the abuse of women and children.

The fact that Gerard was a survivor of abuse marked her deeply. Yes, she seemed prudish about all manner of issues, especially sexual questions, but her views were grounded in opposition to sexual expressions that she perceived to be victimizing women or children. "We protest against all conditions, circumstances and social pressures," she explained, "that serve to keep people in bondage. We don't insist that every person act in the same way we do. But society should recognize the legitimacy of our conviction."[82] Gerard often cited examples of women who were in bondage, and that is why she spoke out against entertainment that she judged to be obscene or pornographic – because it centred on the sexual exploitation of women.

Of course there is more than one way to think about women who work in the entertainment industry, and as Becki Ross asserts in her book *Burlesque West: Showgirls, Sex, and Sin in Postwar Vancouver,* "striptease was not prostitution, but near it; it was not pornography, but near it; it was not consummated sex, but near it."[83] While some "vocal feminists, including Canadian filmmaker Bonnie Sherr Klein, dismissed erotic dancers as dupes of a debasing, misogynist plot,"[84] dancers saw their work differently. Based on interviews with women who had retired from their dancing careers, Ross reminds readers that these women were "well-paid, glamorous entertainers, [who] earned, on average, more than other female workers in the service sector's pink ghetto."[85] Yet their work challenged respectability because it was risqué, sometimes even dangerous. And women recounted that they lived with a certain ambiguity about being entertainers; while they "found some measure of empowered sexual subjectivity" it was not lost on them that they had struck a deal with "the patriarchal devil" because they were "capitulating, as all dancers did, to employers' and customers' demands for fantasy fulfillment."[86] Hardly passive victims, these women clearly understood the complexity of their social position.

But Gerard was not interested in thinking about this entertainment with any nuance. For her, it was clear that women who worked as exotic dancers or appeared in burlesque shows were being exploited. She refused to see it any other way: female entertainers were in bondage. Themes of bondage came up again when Gerard considered the question of municipal liquor licences, because alcohol and entertainment were entwined. As a teetotaller herself, it was not drinking per se that disturbed her but, rather, the exploitation of women she associated with alcohol consumption. No doubt her own abuser's alcoholic tendencies influenced her thinking here too.

228   *Pentecostal Preacher Woman*

At one point when I was judging these matters there were enough liquor outlets in Vancouver for two-thirds of the drinking population to sit down together at one time. When there are too many proprietors of booze outlets competing with each other for customers, in order to get ahead of the competitors, certain places offer live sex shows, with nude women cavorting, whips in hand, to entertain male customers. On tour with other Council members who were investigating a certain hotel, I saw girls gyrating in the nude in front of mirrors before an audience of men who sat drooling into their beer at mid-day. Needless to say, I voted no every chance I got to these ugly, exploitative watering holes that trafficked in female flesh. My prayer was always, "Oh God, where are the reformers? David Livingstone, who fought the slave trade, we need you now to help set the captives free!"[87]

In 1984 Gerard recounted that she recently had been asked what she thought of exotic dancers. In response she told her audience, "Well, I happened to have seen that when I was an Alderman. We went down at noon hour to Hastings Street [in Vancouver] and I nearly upchucked. Oh, it was awful. Those poor girls! Talk about progress. We have gone back to the jungle. So I said, well, first of all, there's nothing exotic about it. Let's clean up the language. It's filthy. It's exploitative. It's downgrading [*sic* degrading?] to women."[88] Because of Gerard's unequivocal condemnation of such forms of entertainment, she was confronted directly by an exotic dancer who asked, "When are you going to leave us alone?" When the woman identified herself and her profession, Gerard challenged her. "I said, 'Oh really. What's exotic about it?' And I talked to her about it. And I said you know the reason I don't approve is because it's not right for you ... And I spoke to her in the love of God."[89] There is no question that one of Gerard's most profound and enduring experiences of God's love was her own deliverance from her drunken abuser. Her internal narrative about sexual exploitation meant she wished the same deliverance for other women. She was a survivor with a keen sense of mission to rescue others from similar emotional and spiritual pain.

The media's caricatures of Gerard the activist were quite funny, as she freely admitted later in life. She was an easy target for the political satirists because of her causes and because of her stern, even puritanical appearance. In hindsight, she could see that too. But while humorists delighted in mocking women like Gerard, such amusing depictions belie the complexity of Gerard's inner world. Her commitment to resist the liberalization of Canadian social and sexual mores was a goal she shared with other conservatively minded people, whether they were churchgoers or not. British Columbia was a deeply divided place in the 1970s as the provincial and municipal political scenes attest. And Gerard's right-wing stance, seemingly easy to label and even easier to mock, was in step with the social engagement that religiously minded people took up in the same period that Gerard held public office in Vancouver. Yet even the religious right was not unanimous on how best to engage with the larger society around them and because of her very public demonstrations and decisions, Gerard was sometimes at odds with church folks who declined to embrace public engagement. Despite that fact, there is no doubt that Gerard took motivation from her networks of like-minded believers and even from those she regarded as too complacent. Tracing her associations with Catholics it comes as no surprise that she was an ardent antiabortionist. Knowing that her own denomination was organizing ways to influence public life and resist changing sexual mores, it is logical that Gerard would stand up for causes of public morality and oppose things she found to be indecent, like public nudity and uncensored violent sexual content in popular media.

What is much harder to see is Gerard's personal and private motivation for acting as she did. Using her life writing to guide my conclusions, I offer explanations that arise from considering her complex interior world. Gerard's sermon notes offer some of the best insights and evidence about her mindset. As a Pentecostal thought leader, of course she was motivated by her deep spirituality. She references the fact that she resolved to be involved because she felt "mightily convicted" and that she formulated her plans of action after spending time in prayer. None of that is surprising, given her roles as chaplain and pastor. But the form of spirituality that she practised is important.

Gerard was Pentecostal. And Pentecostals, especially those with neo-charismatic affinities, are convinced that each believer is given particular spiritual gifts that empower them to act effectively in specific situations. Gerard was convinced that the Holy Spirit had tapped her specifically to be a modern-day prophet. Gerard took inspiration from her study of Moses, whom God called to lead the people of Israel. In Moses, Gerard found parallels to her own life as an adopted child living between two cultures. And she took Moses as a role model for her opposition to the wider culture. While Moses took on the Egyptian Pharaohs, Gerard stood up to Canadian public policy. At the same time, she recognized that Moses had to deal with dissension in the ranks of his followers and Gerard was disappointed, but not surprised, to realize that not all Christians (not even all Pentecostals) shared her activist convictions. Yet, she persisted with her public engagement because she felt called to the role of prophet.

Beyond her spirituality, I suggest that Gerard had more private motivations for expressing her anger and disapproval about particular issues. As a survivor of sexual assault, Gerard turned her anger toward individuals and ideologies that condoned the exploitation and abuse of women. She opposed sex work in Vancouver because she could not imagine it as a life any woman would choose. She abhorred the depiction of violent sex on the stage and screen because she was disgusted by men (especially men under the influence of alcohol) who exploited women for pleasure. And she questioned whether the sexual revolution was really in the best interests of women and children when sexual freedoms were often attended by complicated and unintended consequences. She feared that abortion did not represent true choice, but involved heartbreaking options, possibly even serving as a weapon of eugenics. Gerard's logic about these issues came out of her personal story and lived experience.

The well-known incidents of Gerard's protests on the streets, in the council chambers, and on the beach should not be oversimplified. Explaining what motivated her to act requires us to consider the complicated networks she inhabited, the specific expression of spirituality she practised, and the lingering trauma of her own abuse. All these factors serve to complicate and contextualize her actions and reactions. At first glance she seems so easy to dismiss as a comical extremist. But for Gerard, public activism was a serious matter born out of her context, calling, and life experience.

CONCLUSION

IN THE YEAR 2000 the *Vancouver Sun* named the Rev. Bernice Gerard number one on a list of the twenty-five most influential spiritual leaders in British Columbia in the twentieth century. As he defended that ranking, journalist Douglas Todd explained, "The veteran evangelist has made Greater Vancouver a stronghold of charismatic worship, spreading its super-emotional, arm-waving style to mainline Protestant, Anglican, and Catholic congregations. In addition to founding some of BC's 200 Pentecostal churches and a Christian TV network, Gerard's gravelly voice has reached hundreds of thousands of people through her radio and TV shows."[1] Indeed, over her lifetime of ministry, Gerard operated in a wide variety of roles and gifts including that of pastor, teacher, evangelist, and prophet.

Bernice Gerard led a complicated life. Careful reading of her autobiography and other life writing demonstrates that Gerard's thinking about her Pentecostal faith impacted all the areas of her life and her very identity. She was beloved by many but mocked and misunderstood by others. Easy to caricature, she was the frequent subject of political satire because she was a strange mix, given her booming baritone voice, her engaging media presence on late-night radio, and her combative way of taking a conservative stance on social questions. Exploring her life through her autobiographical writing, sermon notes, and personal archives, I conclude that her inner life was rich and complex. Her faith, conservative by most measures, was certainly not static. Her evolving beliefs led her to establish and foster an expansive series of networks that crossed denominational lines, offered her a multitude of international travel adventures, and defined her very identity. When Gerard began seeing herself as a prophet like Moses, it was more than a spiritual metaphor. As her faith evolved, she continued to be a product of her own early childhood experience. A sexual assault survivor, she maintained a fierce and unflinching opposition to all forms of violence against women and children. She challenged progressive social conventions because she was convinced that sometimes those liberal ideas and behaviours were a thin veneer, disguising abusive situations that trapped women and children into some form of bondage. Her Pentecostal spirituality meant she felt grateful to have been delivered from an abusive childhood but reticent to adopt the conventions her middle-class caregivers modelled for her. And while she might have resisted being so public about her values and opinions, she felt compelled, because of God's call on her life, to identify sites of potential bondage for other people.

Bernice Gerard has been commemorated in in a variety of ways, including the "Gerard House," a facility adjacent to the UBC campus, which was intended to mark her engagement with the campus because the house provided a base from which campus ministry could operate. The location of the house was symbolic of the influence Pentecostals have had on the UBC campus for more than sixty years. As Eleanor Wachtel suggested in the 1970s, campus chaplains were on the fringes of campus life even then. This seemed like a fitting legacy but as a way of remembering Gerard, the operation of the facility was problematic. It served as a residence for students involved in campus ministry, but the last occupants of the house were all male – hardly a fitting tribute to Gerard's feminism or her ministry partnership with Velma. Moreover, the costs of maintaining the house became prohibitive because the house needed repairs, and in the spring of 2024, the once beloved "G House" was demolished.[2]

While Gerard's domestic life remains an enigma, the impact of their shared work together persists. Together Bernice forged and maintained deep personal ties with Velma who was her confidante, ministry partner, and lifelong companion. In 2004, when Velma was eight-nine and Bernice was eighty (sixty-one years after they had first met in Rossland, BC) they posed together for a picture to celebrate the fifth anniversary of their work in child rescue and to promote the good work being accomplished by investments generated from their ministry, Sunday Line and World Ministries. Sunday Line Communications Society continues today as a registered charity reporting to Revenue Canada. In recent years, the organization has reported assets totalling just over $350,000, and disbursements to a range of other ministry organizations that account for the donations received.[3] The charitable organizations receiving funds from

Sunday Line represent the kinds of work that characterized Velma and Bernice's ministry and their shared values including the denomination they reported to, child rescue efforts including feeding and education, international relief, and Christian media.[4]

The board of directors for Sunday Line still manages funds originally generated by Bernice and Velma's ministries, and they direct money to organizations and causes that resonate with Gerard's life story. For example, in 2018 one of the projects they helped to fund was a group in the Philippines offering a daily feeding program of hot meals to twenty-two hundred children from a facility called the "Gerard-Chapman Benevolence Kitchen." It was a fitting tribute to two women who shared a home for many decades, always seeking to ensure that their personal kitchen was a site of generous hospitality. Here again, echoes of Gerard's childhood shape the ministry priorities, especially the years she spent in foster care. She wrote in her autobiography that the ill treatment she had received as a child led her to emphasize generous hospitality: "I remember vowing that if I ever was the mother of household I would see to it that everyone at the dinner table was welcome to a fair share of whatever food was there."[5] Another group in receipt of Sunday Line funds in 2018 was the House of Hope, in Bethlehem. This organization, founded in 1963 by an Arab Christian woman named Aunty May, serves children who are blind.[6] No doubt Gerard visited this charity several times when she travelled to the Holy Land to see the work first-hand. Again, it echoes her own story, because although she was never blind, when Gerard was a young adult, her eyesight was miraculously restored and for many years she did not need to wear glasses, until her advanced age required them once again.[7] Helping children who were disadvantaged by poverty or family circumstances remained her lifelong passion, a clear reminder of her own early childhood experiences. And while she sometimes sparred with colleagues in her own denomination over women's roles in ministry and her early ecumenism, Gerard maintained her connection to the PAOC, and even after her death, with the donations Sunday Line distributes in her memory, the PAOC and some of its affiliated ministries continue to benefit from the legacy of the work she and Velma did together.

Long before a religion writer declared Gerard's significance as a spiritual influencer in British Columbia, Gerard herself knew she had lived an extraordinary life and she felt compelled to republish her life story. In the spring of 1988, one of Gerard's academic friends, after he had reviewed the manuscript for her forthcoming autobiography, praised the way she had "elaborated on the multiplicity of roles available to women."[8] Moreover he concluded by saying,

FIGURE C.1 Bernice and Velma led tours to Israel on multiple occasions, and their views about "the end times" aligned with typical late-twentieth-century evangelical views about eschatology. | *Summit Pacific College, Hudson Memorial Library, Bernice Gerard Collection, uncatalogued.*

> The strongest case for the potential of the female sector of the human race, however, is the entire autobiography; you yourself are your own best argument. If an individual with such diverse interests and attributes as yours had lived in the sixteenth or seventeenth century, he would have been called a "Renaissance Man." ... but I think I have met a modern "Renaissance Woman" who, apparently was raised on the banks of the muddy Fraser River in British Columbia before she emerged to make an impact on our society in our time.[9]

While that professor's praise for Gerard and her book bordered on hyperbole, there is no denying that Bernice Gerard was a woman with many interests and that her ideas were influenced by a surprisingly broad spectrum of thought. Gerard was a product of her time and her life experiences but having the opportunity to delve into her interior world offers rich insight into her Pentecostal thought and how she navigated through a series of life stages and a variety of public roles. After a long and debilitating battle with Parkinson's disease, Bernice Gerard died in Vancouver in 2008.

Writing this book over the course of several years, I have had many occasions to reflect on what drew me to this project and what held my interest to bring it to completion. Always curious as a reader and writer of biography myself, I was intrigued when I read one scholar's assertion that "a biographer's own life story necessarily plays into the creation of biography. In other words, there is 'autobiography in biography'[... that] encompasses voices from the biographer's own life history."[10] Reading that stopped me in my tracks because I wondered to myself, "What has Bernice Gerard to do with me?" And is it true that my own experience is somehow "entangled" with Bernice Gerard, through the complexities of the biographer-subject relationship?[11] On reflection, I could see how Bernice Gerard had impacted my friend Margaret, who first encountered her in the pews of a Pentecostal revival meeting. Prominent leaders in the Canadian Pentecostal and evangelical world like David Wells and Brian Stiller think of Gerard as a personal mentor whom they fondly remember because she invested in each of them and encouraged them in their ministry careers. At the other end of the spectrum, it was easy to see that for folks like Scott, the Vancouverite, Gerard was an unforgettable figure, easy to mock. And for religion writer Douglas Todd of the *Vancouver Sun*, Gerard was important enough to top his list of twentieth-century spiritual influencers in BC. But me? I never even met Bernice Gerard in person and I didn't think about her as a subject for a biography until someone suggested the project to me, after Gerard's death.

So, what possible "entanglements" did I have with Gerard's story? First, I will say that in many ways, our lives could not be more different. As a child, I was never orphaned, adopted, or sexually abused. I did grow up in a rural household with a precarious income base, and I lived in a complex, multigenerational household for a good part of my growing up time. My childhood encounters with substance abuse among some of the adults in my life pale in comparison with what Gerard recounts. Yet some of Bernice's childhood anxieties do feel familiar to me. She was taken into state care while I had the privilege of a stable home setting. We both walked a certain distance every day to attend school (uphill both ways!) in rural schoolhouses that served as multipurpose venues for community life. But I grew up in 1960s Ontario, in the picturesque Beaver Valley, near Blue Mountains, just as the province's rural schools were consolidating into larger school boards, and Gerard's family home in the 1920s and 1930s was a float house on the Fraser River. By her teenage years Bernice was a city girl, walking to a Vancouver high school with neighbour children from the solidly middle-class community where she lived with her foster family. I took a bus to a nearby town for secondary school, along with lots of other rural and small-town peers. Moreover, Bernice and I are from very different cohorts – she was from my parents' generation and I am a late baby boomer. My parents never had the luxury of a secondary school education, but Gerard finished at the top of her class and went on to university life at UBC. Four and a half decades later than her, I was the first in my family to venture off to postsecondary education. She loved campus life, and so did/do I! She returned as a mature student and immersed herself in her work as a contract teacher and campus chaplain; I became a tenured professor and enjoyed rich relationships with colleagues and students. So, Bernice and I have some things in common despite our age differences, and in other things we are from different worlds in terms of generation, geography, and social context.

But what about religion? The beliefs that animated Gerard's interior life were core to her identity, and I have argued throughout this book that her whole life orbited around her evolving beliefs, where she found her purpose and forged a sense of belonging. Religion was her work – as an evangelist, pastor, media personality, and chaplain – providing the foundation of her identity and defining her professional life. While I am a person of faith, my religion has never been so entwined with my professional identity. I have never been ordained by any denomination, although I have maintained high levels of voluntary involvement in a variety of congregations. Like Bernice, from a young age I did take religion as a central part of my identity formation including phases of fundamentalist thought, especially during my teenaged and student years. I too experienced an important conversion experience as a young teen growing up in a disaffiliated household, and from my youth through adulthood, I gradually expanded my sense of ecumenism as I threw off the most restrictive of my early beliefs to make way for an expanding range of exposure to different denominational practices. I also had a Pentecostal phase as part of my religious experience, although for me this was much later in life than Bernice's. Subsequently, I was introduced to charismatic circles, and for a time I found a new church home within a PAOC congregation. As a layperson, I served one congregation as the first woman ever elected to the church board and the first woman to chair that board, and in multiple congregations I have offered adult education classes and facilitated discussion groups for youth, young adults, and older adults. Despite these high levels of voluntarism and a religious belief system that has provided frameworks for my life, my identity has never been entirely defined by the church I attend, and Pentecostalism is not the core of my identity.

Like Gerard, I have often clashed with the patriarchy that is so ingrained in Pentecostal (and other evangelical) churches. That explains why I was so curious about Gerard's battles within her own denomination about women's roles. The rhetorical posturing and ambiguity of groups that claim to embrace egalitarian gender roles get my attention every time questions about the limits of women's involvement are raised. My leadership, confined to local levels of the church, was unlike that of Gerard, who rose to national and international recognition. Yet I have been regularly subjected to "mansplaining" encounters when men my own age and younger tried to make me understand that my involvement as chair of the church board or adult educator in the congregation were transgressions. According to my detractors, women were never meant to take on leadership in church governance, and the extent to which they should become teachers of men was debatable. These views, arising from a literal reading of sacred texts, were so incompatible with my own experiences as a university educator and administrator for more than three decades that I was shocked to be subjected to these misogynist views. Indeed, whenever I was confronted in this way, I found myself wondering if I had entered some strange portal of time travel back to a period when separate spheres were the norm and women were deemed unsuited to politics, public life, higher education, or governance roles. Had I been transported back to the era when women were not even considered to be persons? Yet the views such men (and some women) espoused are not uncommon in twenty-first-century evangelical circles, and during one memorable encounter, two male colleagues from the church board stood by without challenging my critic's misogynist view, delivered in a very threatening tone. They told me later that I was overreacting, and I needed to calm down because everyone knew the critic had a bad temper and besides, most men did not share his view. Even in the moment I recognized this for what it was: another layer of the paternalistic church subculture, a form of victim blaming known as "gaslighting," when my board colleagues let the angry critic's dismissal of my leadership go unchallenged. So, when I learned about Gerard being subjected to heckling as she rose to speak in favour of women's equality on a Pentecostal convention floor, her experience felt familiar to me.

Unlike Gerard, I have not had a lifelong commitment to one denomination. But in common with her, I have formed networks of relationships across denominational lines. My own evolving faith has seen me circle back to liberal Protestantism and membership in the United Church of Canada after decades of dabbling in different expressions of evangelicalism ranging from those with a decidedly fundamentalist tone during my youth, to experiences of charismatic and Pentecostal Christianity more recently. Gerard's loyalties to the PAOC (and also to the Assemblies of God) ran very deep, both professionally and personally. After my unpleasant encounters with fellow parishioners and their antiwoman views, I cut my ties with the PAOC and evangelicalism as I navigated the sixth decade of my life. But unlike many others in Canadian society whose disenchantment with conservative Christianity led them to abandon church life altogether, I did not join the ranks of the "nones," although I have a profound respect for those whose experiences have led them to that conclusion. Instead, I returned to the church of my family roots, and in the United Church of Canada and its liberal Protestant views, I have found a spiritual and intellectual home as part of a vibrant community of believers who are tenacious in their commitment to social justice, with inclusion, equity, and diversity as core values. As a grandmother approaching retirement, I find my faith has taken a decided turn away from dogma and drama and toward the embrace of mystery and wonder.

And how I would dearly welcome the chance to chat with Bernice Gerard about all of this! I am drawn to her story of evolving faith for so many reasons: her emergence from a troubled childhood of poverty and isolation to join the middle class; her expanding appreciation of the wider Christian community; her suspicion of those who dogmatically defend denominational boundaries; her love of intellectual life on campus and off; her ongoing attempts to reconcile her spiritual and intellectual views; her clashes with the church patriarchy; her outrageous, yet somehow moderate, adventures in public engagement; her friendships with other women; and her late-life reflections on where her life had taken her. I suspect that several days to chat with her would hardly be enough! And I would love to know her thoughts about the trend toward disaffiliation as former evangelical, charismatic, and Pentecostal believers find they simply cannot continue to associate with churches that are becoming more deeply entrenched in patriarchal expressions of social conservatism within their own walls, looking more and more like their American cousins on the far right.

These questions of why and how people, especially women, are deconstructing their evangelical faith and distancing themselves from conservative church cultures intrigue me. I am certain Gerard would have things to say about this. And while she might cling tenaciously to her quips about finding "joy in serving Jesus," I am convinced she would be critical of simplistic formulas for church growth, weaponized biblical literalism, and the toxic positivity of the "best life now" prosperity gospel. In the culture wars that are dividing conservative churches, I suspect Gerard would tip toward embracing social justice issues. Surely, she would be deeply invested in the #MeToo and #ChurchToo initiatives to expose the abuses (sexual and otherwise) that have plagued patriarchal institutions, especially those of a Pentecostal-charismatic persuasion, for far too long. Even after immersing myself in Gerard's story for so many years while writing this book, I am still curious to think about how she might situate herself in the context of post-pandemic, twenty-first-century Christianity. She

FIGURE C.2 Bernice Gerard remained loyal to her denomination, the PAOC, despite sparring with patriarchal structures and individuals who questioned her authority as a woman. Gerard is depicted here, engaged in a friendly conversation, at the PAOC General Conference in Regina in 1974, when she somewhat naively expected the meeting would easily pass a resolution about female ordination. | *"General Conference, 1974,"* The Pentecostal Testimony, *November 1974, 15. Photographer: E.N.O. Kulbeck.*

rose to prominence while the charismatic movement was having its moment. What would she do and say about the current mass exodus from organized religion? On so many occasions, I find myself wondering WWBD: What would Bernice do?

That reflection question intrigues me, of course, because I have invested so much time in this research about her. But more broadly, the question behind that question is one that grapples with how a woman, whose life experiences have been rooted in evangelical Christianity, can make her way through the existential questions that Christians have faced for millennia in their individual journeys of faith. But I also think about this question on more than an individual level. How do women of faith as a collective committed to living out their beliefs with intelligence, empathy, and conviction negotiate the inevitable roadblocks that arise along the way? What is the inner conversation, the self-narration, and the application of faith that can address the cognitive dissonance that women experience in their congregational lives? WWBD? And other than abandoning the church to enforce some boundaries and centre ourselves, what are disenchanted people of faith to do? This is the age-old question of Christians over the centuries: What do those directives laid out in the sacred texts say to us? How are we to live out our callings? I would dearly love to see Bernice Gerard in conversation with other twenty-first-century Christian thought leaders whose evolving faith often makes them the subjects of public ridicule, both inside the churches and in the wider culture.[12] I am convinced that Bernice Gerard could speak to such questions with conviction and clarity. But I wonder, if she could offer us some direction for a post-pandemic world in the second quarter of the twenty-first century, would her insights resonate with me and others like me? Or are we too far removed from her world and from the coherent internal script she wrote to explain herself to herself and to others?

When we caricature other people we diminish them, whether the pictures we paint of them are negative ones like Gerard's hecklers, or overly positive, sanitized ones like those who champion her as a prototype for women in ministry. Simplistic explanations about "why they act like that" might make our own internal narratives more coherent, but they do not begin to plumb the depths of why people act and think as they do. To assume that one successful woman's ministry career is a blueprint for all the women who might follow is a vast oversimplification of Gerard's complex life story. On the other hand, to assume that Gerard was just a hypermoralistic crusader is a vast oversimplification of a different sort. Stopping to listen to other people, how they justify themselves, what they are silent about, and how they frame their self-narration can take us a long way to understanding one another. As a historian, I am convinced that placing characters into the context of their times brings clarity and richness to our understanding of them. When I consume biographies about other peoples' lives, and especially when I read their autobiographical accounts, I often wonder why the stories are being told that way. What is being emphasized and what is being downplayed or left out altogether? And why? At the same time, reading other people's stories makes me reflect on the stories I tell about myself to myself and to others. Why do I tell them the way I do? I've observed that my own reflection on these existential matters becomes easier and feels richer as I age and as I continue to make connections between my academic work and my lived experience.

I WENT TO WRECK BEACH in the late spring of 2019. I made the steep trek down, 490 steps in all, leading to the rocky beach below. And then I endured the very challenging climb back up that feels much longer! I went there because

I wanted to put myself where Gerard had been.[13] I wanted to imagine what she might have been thinking on that summer day in 1977 when she made her silent protest. I was trying to understand the firmly held convictions that caused her to do something so public and so dramatic, especially when she knew she would endure a great deal of mocking afterward. On my walk along the beach that day, there was only a solitary individual whose relaxed demeanour led me to believe they were probably a regular visitor to the place. I thought about Bernice Gerard, and I remembered the letters in the archives from those with very strong views on many sides of the issues connected to that beach. Some wrote to say they were worried about public decency in Vancouver and others wrote to defend themselves and their nudist community, urging Gerard to keep an open mind and not be too quick to condemn lifestyles that did not match her own. In the end, Gerard took a moderate stance on the Wreck Beach question, respecting that those who enjoyed the clothing-optional beach had every right to do so but also insisting that Vancouverites who wished to stroll along other public beaches should not have to worry about unexpected encounters with naked people. In other words, Gerard took a moderate position. The political cartoonists did not capture that nuance, of course, because satire and subtlety are unlikely partners.

I took three smooth stones from the beach that day as a souvenir: a white one, a black one, and a grey one. Those little stones now sit on my desk. They remind me that when I am writing history, things are rarely black and white. There are always more than two sides to every story. Spending all this time with Bernice Gerard and her life stories, I have come to realize that the same thing is true when we craft our own inner narratives too. Like those little stones, worn smooth by time and tide, a life is never quite as simple or easily categorized as it might first appear to those looking on. People who navigate and negotiate their way through evolving belief systems inevitably make and remake meaning through the stories they tell themselves and others. And as it was for Bernice Gerard, so it is for each of us – when we make meaning from our life stories, it's complicated.

NOTES

Introduction

1 Ros Oberlyn, "Barely Anybody Around for Gerard's March," *Vancouver Sun*, July 11, 1977. Media discussion of the issue and of Gerard's silent protest includes Peter Walls, "Wreck Beach Nudies Eye Passing Parade," *Vancouver Province*, July 11, 1977; "Wrath at Wreck Beach," editorial, *Vancouver Sun*, June 29, 1977; "Naked Averages," editorial, *Vancouver Sun*, June 29, 1977; and "Average Citizen Loses in 'Nudist Takeover,'" *Vancouver Sun*, July 9, 1977.

2 Quoted in Bernice Gerard, *Bernice Gerard: Today and for Life* (Vancouver: Sunday Line Communications, 1988), 195.

3 Douglas Todd, "British Columbia's 25 Most Influential Spiritual Leaders," *Vancouver Sun*, April 21, 2000.

4 Bernice Gerard, *Bernice Gerard*, 163. By 1972, Gerard's broadcast on CJOR 600, a historic Vancouver radio station, had expanded to four-and-one-half hours of open-line programming. The Bernice Gerard archives at Summit Pacific College contain several collections of personal correspondence between her and her listeners on a wide range of topics.

5 Sarah Bessey, *Jesus Feminist: An Invitation to Revisit the Bible's View of Women* (New York: Howard Books, 2013); Rachel Held Evans, *Searching for Sunday: Loving, Leaving, and Finding the Church* (Nashville, TN: Thomas Nelson Books, 2015). Other writers who address these disenchanted "exvangelicals" include Diana Butler Bass, *Christianity after Religion: The End of Church and the Birth of a Spiritual Awakening* (New York: HarperOne, 2013); Diana Butler Bass, *Freeing Jesus: Rediscovering Jesus as Friend, Teacher, Savior, Lord, Way, and Presence* (New York: HarperOne, 2021); Sue Monk Kidd, *The Dance of the Dissident Daughter: A Woman's Journey from Christian Tradition to the Sacred Feminine* (New York: HarperOne, 2016); and Brian D. McLaren, *Faith after Doubt: Why Your Beliefs Stopped Working and What to Do about It* (New York: St. Martin's Essentials, 2021).

6 Sarah Bessey and her associate, Jeff Chu, have carried on with this work since the passing of Rachel Held Evans, hosting conferences that are branded as "Evolving Faith." See the organization's website: https://evolvingfaith.com/about.

7 Susan P. Wells, interview by Zoom with author, September 22, 2020.

8 Paul Bramadat, "Introduction: Religion, Spirituality, and Irreligion in the Best Place on Earth," in *Religion at the Edge: Nature, Spirituality, and Secularity in the Pacific Northwest*, ed. Paul Bramadat, Patricia O'Connell Killen, and Sarah Wilkins-Laflamme (Vancouver: UBC Press, 2022), 4, 13–14.

9 See Robert A.J. McDonald, *A Long Way to Paradise: A New History of British Columbia Politics* (Vancouver: UBC Press, 2021); Jean Barman, *The West beyond the West: A History of British Columbia*, rev. ed. (Toronto: University of Toronto Press, 1996), 270–96; Robert Burkinshaw, "Evangelicalism in British Columbia: Conservatism and Adaptability," *Journal of the Canadian Church Historical Society* 38 (1996): 77–100; and Robert Burkinshaw, *Pilgrims in Lotus Land: Conservative Protestantism in British Columbia, 1917–1981* (Montreal/Kingston: McGill-Queen's University Press, 1995).

10 Sam Reimer, *Evangelicals and the Continental Divide: The Conservative Protestant Subculture in Canada and the United States* (Montreal/Kingston: McGill-Queen's University Press, 2003).

11 See Joel Thiessen, *The Meaning of Sunday: The Practice of Belief in a Secular Age* (Montreal/Kingston: McGill-Queen's University Press, 2015); Joel Thiessen and Sarah Wilkins-Laflamme, *None of the Above: Nonreligious Identity in the US and Canada* (Regina, SK: University of Regina Press, 2020); and Paul Bramadat, Patricia O'Connell Killen, and Sarah Wilkins-Laflamme, eds., *Religion at the Edge: Nature, Spirituality, and Secularity in the Pacific Northwest* (Vancouver: UBC Press, 2022).

12 See, for example, Lynne Marks, *Infidels and the Damn Churches: Irreligion and Religion in Settler British Columbia* (Vancouver: UBC Press, 2017); and Tina Block, *The Secular North-West: Religion and Irreligion in Everyday Postwar Life* (Vancouver: UBC Press, 2017).

13 Brian Stiller, interview by Zoom with author, August 20, 2020; David Wells, interview by Zoom with author, September 17, 2020.

14 David Mainse, *100: An Inspiring Journey of a Life Dedicated to the Call of God* (Burlington, ON: Crossroads Christian Communications, 1999); David Mainse, *100 Huntley Street: The Exciting Success Story from the Host of Canada's Popular Television Program* (Toronto: G.R. Welch, 1979).

15 See Phyllis D. Airhart, *A Church with the Soul of a Nation: Making and Remaking the United Church of Canada* (Kingston/Montreal: McGill-Queen's University Press, 2014), 200–2, 264–67; and Kevin Flatt, *After Evangelism: The Sixties and the United Church of Canada* (Kingston/Montreal: McGill-Queen's University Press, 2013), 104–43.

16 See, for example, McColl-Gerard Trio, "I've Been with Jesus," MG1005-A, n.d., YouTube audiopost, accessed July 31, 2020, https://www.youtube.com/watch?v=CnTH6s1h-T0.

17 Bob Skinner, "Next Generation of Women in Ministry Please Stand Up!" *Pentecostal Testimony*, June 1991, 2.

18 Pentecostal Assemblies of Canada, "Fellowship Stats 2023 at 6 Feb 2024," https://www.paoc.org/services/desk-of-the-general-secretary-treasurer/fellowship-statistics.

19 For a popular and sympathetic treatment of McPherson, see Daniel Mark Epstein, *Sister Aimee: The Life of Aimee Semple McPherson* (New York: Harcourt Brace, 1993). Academic studies include Edith Blumhofer, *Aimee Semple McPherson: Everybody's Sister* (Grand Rapids, MI: Eerdmans, 1993); Matthew Avery Sutton, *Aimee Semple McPherson and the*

Resurrection of Christian America (Cambridge, MA: Harvard University Press, 2007); and Leah Payne, *Gender and Pentecostal Revivalism: Making a Female Ministry in the Early Twentieth Century* (New York: Palgrave Macmillan, 2015).

20 See Linda M. Ambrose, "Gender History in Newfoundland Pentecostalism: Alice Belle Garrigus and Beyond," *PentecoStudies* 15, 2 (2016): 172–99; Burton K. Janes, *The Lady Who Came: The Biography of Alice Belle Garrigus, Newfoundland's First Pentecostal Pioneer*, vol. 1, *1858–1908* (St. John's, NL: Good Tidings Press, 1982); and Burton K. Janes, *The Lady Who Stayed: The Biography of Alice Belle Garrigus, Newfoundland's First Pentecostal Pioneer*, vol. 2, *1908–1949* (St. John's, NL: Good Tidings Press, 1983).

21 Linda M. Ambrose, "Pentecostal Historiography in Canada: The History behind the Histories," in Michael Wilkinson and Linda M. Ambrose, eds., *The Canadian Pentecostal Experience* (Leiden: Brill, forthcoming 2024), chapter 1; previously published in *Canadian Journal of Pentecostal-Charismatic Christianity* 10 (2019): 15–36. The PAOC has published several volumes of its own history including Gloria Kulbeck, *What God Hath Wrought: A History of the Pentecostal Assemblies of Canada* (Toronto: Pentecostal Assemblies of Canada, 1958); Gordon F. Atter, *The Third Force*, 3rd ed. (Caledonia, ON: Acts Books, 1970; Peterborough, ON: College Press, 1962); Thomas William Miller, *Canadian Pentecostals: A History of the Pentecostal Assemblies of Canada* (Mississauga, ON: Full Gospel Publishing House, 1994); and Douglas Rudd, *When the Spirit Came upon Them: Highlights from the Early Years of the Pentecostal Movement in Canada* (Mississauga, ON: Pentecostal Assemblies of Canada, 2002).

22 Michael Wilkinson, ed., *Canadian Pentecostalism: Transition and Transformation* (Montreal/Kingston: McGill-Queen's University Press, 2009); Michael Wilkinson and Peter Althouse, *Winds from the North: Canadian Contributions to the Pentecostal Movement* (Leiden, NL: Brill, 2010).

23 Michael Wilkinson and Linda M. Ambrose, *After the Revival: Pentecostalism and the Making of a Canadian Church* (Montreal/Kingston: McGill-Queen's University Press, 2020).

24 *Canadian Journal of Pentecostal-Charismatic Christianity* ceased publication with vol. 10 in 2019, but the content is available online: https://journal.twu.ca/index.php/cjpc/index.

25 Michael Wilkinson and Linda M. Ambrose, eds., *The Canadian Pentecostal Experience* (Leiden, NL: Brill, forthcoming 2024).

26 Andrew Gabriel, Adam Stewart, and Kevin Shanahan, "Changing Conceptions of Speaking in Tongues and Spirit Baptism among Canadian Pentecostal Clergy," *Canadian Journal of Pentecostal-Charismatic Christianity* 7 (2016): 1–24.

27 See Adam Stewart, *The New Canadian Pentecostals* (Waterloo: Wilfrid Laurier University Press, 2015); Sam Reimer and Michael Wilkinson, *A Culture of Faith: Evangelical Congregations in Canada* (Montreal/Kingston: McGill-Queen's University Press, 2015).

28 See Linda M. Ambrose, "Gender," in *Brill's Encyclopedia of Global Pentecostalism*, ed. Michael Wilkinson (Leiden, NL: Brill, 2021), 244–48, along with biographies of significant Pentecostal women including Aimee Semple McPherson, Ellen Hebden, Alice Belle Garrigus, and others.

29 Charles H. Barfoot and Gerald T. Sheppard, "Prophetic vs. Priestly Religion: The Changing Role of Women Clergy in Classical Pentecostal Churches," *Review of Religious Research* 22 (1980): 2–17.

30 See Kimberly Ervin Alexander and James P. Bowers, *What Women Want: Pentecostal Women Ministers Speak for Themselves* (Lanham, MD: The Seymour Press, 2013); and

Estrelda Alexander and Amos Yong, eds., *Philip's Daughters: Women in Pentecostal-Charismatic Leadership* (Eugene, OR: Pickwick Publications, 2009).

31 Bernice Gerard, *Bernice Gerard*, 142–62.

32 Bernice Gerard, *Bernice Gerard*, 142–62.

33 See Bernice Gerard, "Communicate in '68 WMC Windsor August 24, 1968," speaking notes for Communicate in '68, uncatalogued, Summit Pacific College, Bernice Gerard Collection (hereafter SPC BGC); and Michael McAteer, "Woman Pentecostal May Rock the Boat," *Toronto Star*, August 16, 1980.

34 Allison Murray, "Creating the Feminist Boogey Woman: Popular Evangelical Authors' Portrayal of Feminist Ideas, 1970–2010," paper presented at the American Society of Church History, New York, January 2020.

35 On the paradoxical relationship of feminism and religion, see Linda Woodhead, "Feminism and the Sociology of Religion: From Gender-Blindness to Gendered Difference," in *The Blackwell Companion to Sociology of Religion*, ed. Richard K. Fenn (Oxford: Blackwell, 2003), 72.

36 Orit Avishai, "Theorizing Gender from Religion Cases: Agency, Feminist Activism, and Masculinity," *Sociology of Religion: A Quarterly Review* 77, 3 (2016): 262.

37 Ori Avishai, "Theorizing Gender from Religion," 263.

38 See Dawn Llewellyn and Marta Trzebiatowska, "Secular and Religious Feminisms: A Future of Disconnection?" *Feminist Theology* 21, 3 (2013): 244–58; Linda M. Ambrose, Tina Block, and Lynne Marks, "Forum Introduction: Challenging Orthodoxies: Religion, Secularism and Feminism among English-Canadian Women, 1960s–1990s," *Gender & History* 34, 2 (2022): 317–24; Christel Manning, *God Gave Us the Right: Conservative Catholic, Evangelical Protestant, and Orthodox Jewish Women Grapple with Feminism* (New Brunswick, NJ: Rutgers University Press, 1999); Niamh Reilly, "Rethinking the Interplay of Feminism and Secularism in a Neo-secular Age," *Feminist Review* 97 (2011): 12; Rosa Bruno-Jofré, Heidi MacDonald, and Elizabeth Smyth, *Vatican II and Beyond: The Changing Mission and Identity of Canadian Women Religious* (Toronto/Kingston: McGill-Queen's University Press, 2017); Carol Williams, "Reproductive Self-Determination and the Persistence of 'Family Values' in Alberta from the 1960s to the 1990s," in *Compelled to Act: Histories of Women's Activism in Western Canada*, ed. Sarah Carter and Nanci Langford (Winnipeg: University of Manitoba, 2020), 364–414; Erica Dyck and Karissa Patton, "Activists in the 'Bible Belt': Conservatism, Religion, and Recognizing Reproductive Rights in 1970s Southern Alberta," in *Compelled to Act*, ed. Carter and Langford, 289–316; and Rachel Rinaldo, *Mobilizing Piety: Islam and Feminism in Indonesia* (New York: Oxford University Press, 2013).

39 Ruth Compton Brouwer, "Transcending the 'Unacknowledged Quarantine': Putting Religion into English-Canadian Women's History," *Journal of Canadian Studies* 17, 3 (1992): 47–61.

40 Orit Avishai, "Theorizing Gender from Religion," 268.

41 See, for example, Orit Avishai, "'Doing Religion' in a Secular World: Women in Conservative Religions and the Question of Agency," *Gender & Society* 22, 4 (August 2008): 409–33; Rachel Rinaldo, *Mobilizing Piety*; Orit Avishai, "Theorizing Gender," 270; Elizabeth Weiss Ozorak, "The Power, but Not the Glory: How Women Empower Themselves through Religion," *Journal for the Scientific Study of Religion* 35, 1 (1996): 17–29; and Linda M. Ambrose, "A Messy Mix: Religion, Feminism, and Pentecostals," *Gender & History* 34, 2 (2022): 369–83.

42 Orit Avishai, "Theorizing Gender from Religion," 264.

43 Elizabeth Weiss Ozorak, "The Power, but Not the Glory."

44 Orit Avishai, "'Doing Religion,'" 413.

45 Orit Avishai, "'Doing Religion,'" 413.

46 Orit Avishai, "Theorizing Gender from Religion," 270.

47 Orit Avishai, "'Doing Religion,'" 413.

48 Bernice Gerard, *Converted in the Country: The Life Story of Bernice Gerard* (Jacksonville, FL: McColl-Gerard Publications, 1956), 103.

49 Orit Avishai, "'Doing Religion,'" 413.

50 Barbara Cain, *Biography and History* (London: Red Globe Press, 2019), 67.

51 Bernice Gerard, *Converted in the Country*.

52 For a brief and accessible text to understand Pentecostalism, see William K. Kay, *Pentecostalism: A Very Short Introduction* (Oxford: Oxford University Press, 2011).

53 David M. Csinos, *Little Theologians: Children, Culture, and the Making of Theological Meaning* (Montreal/Kingston: McGill-Queen's University Press, 2020).

54 Susan E. Henking, "The Personal Is the Theological: Autobiographical Acts in Contemporary Feminist Theology," *Journal of the American Academy of Religion* 59, 3 (Autumn 1991): 511. See also James Wm. McClendon Jr., *Biography as Theology: How Life Stories Can Remake Today's Theology* (Eugene, OR: Wipf and Stock, 2002).

55 Bernice Gerard, *Bernice Gerard*.

56 Susan E. Henking, "The Personal Is the Theological," 517.

57 Bernice Gerard, *Bernice Gerard*, 144.

58 See Elizabeth Hanscombe, "Now That I'm Old: Writing, Women, and Ageing," *Life Writing* 16,1 (2019): 127–38; and Margaret O'Neill and Michaela Schrage-Früh, "Women and Ageing: Private Meaning, Social Lives," *Life Writing* 16, 1 (2019): 1–8.

59 See Elaine Lawless, "Rescripting Their Lives as Narratives: Spiritual Life Stories of Pentecostal Women Preachers," *Journal of Feminist Studies in Religion* 7, 1 (1991): 53–71; and Linda M. Ambrose, "Aimee Semple McPherson: Gender Theory, Worship, and the Arts," *Pneuma: The Journal of the Society for Pentecostal Studies* 39 (2017): 105–22.

60 Bernice M. Gerard, *The Holy Land: Guide to Faith!* (Jacksonville, FL: McColl-Gerard Publications, n.d. [c. 1950s]).

Chapter 1: Life with the Gerards

1 Bernice Gerard, *Converted in the Country: The Life Story of Bernice Gerard* (Jacksonville, FL: McColl-Gerard Publications, 1956), 16.

2 Bernice Gerard, *Converted in the Country*, 17.

3 Bernice Gerard was called "Peggy" until she started to use the name Bernice at the age of thirteen. She revealed that she had never liked the nickname because schoolmates teased her by changing it to "Piggy." Her first foster family, the Motts, and her social worker encouraged her to begin using her birth name, Bernice, and "thus get set to enjoy an altogether new life." Bernice Gerard, *Bernice Gerard: Today and for Life* (Vancouver: Sunday Line Communications, 1988), 45.

4 Veronica Strong-Boag, *Fostering Nation? Canada Confronts Its History of Childhood Disadvantage* (Waterloo, ON: Wilfrid Laurier University Press, 2011), 6.

Notes to pages 25–30

5 Emma Uprichard, "Children as 'Being and Becomings': Children, Childhood and Temporality," *Children & Society* 22 (2008): 311. See also Allison James and Adrian L. James, *Constructing Childhood: Theory, Policy and Social Practice* (London: Red Globe Press, 2004); Allison James and Alan Prout, eds., *Constructing and Reconstructing Childhood: Contemporary Issues in the Sociological Study of Childhood*, 2nd ed. (London: Routledge, 1997). My thanks to Dr. Nicole Yantzi for introducing me to these sources.

6 Mona Gleason, Tamara Myers, Leslie Paris, and Veronica Strong-Boag, eds., *Lost Kids: Vulnerable Children and Youth in Twentieth-Century Canada and the United States* (Vancouver: UBC Press, 2010).

7 Tarah Brookfield, "History of Adoption and Fostering in Canada," *Oxford Bibliographies*, last edited July 25, 2023, https://www.oxfordbibliographies.com/display/document/obo-9780199791231/obo-9780199791231-0157.xml.

8 Bernice Gerard, *Converted in the Country*, 9.

9 The obituary for Howard Gerald Gerard, who died in 1968, mentions two brothers (Joseph and Harold) and one sister, Bernice Gerard. *Vancouver Sun*, August 20, 1968, 27.

10 Bernice Gerard, *Bernice Gerard*, 9.

11 Bernice Gerard, *Bernice Gerard*, 13.

12 Bernice Gerard, *Converted in the Country*, 16–17.

13 See Veronica Strong-Boag, "Interrupted Relations: The Adoption of Children in Twentieth-Century British Columbia," *BC Studies* 144 (Winter 2004/2005): 5–30; Veronica Strong-Boag, *Finding Families, Finding Ourselves: English Canada Encounters Adoption from the Nineteenth Century to the 1990s* (Don Mills, ON: Oxford University Press, 2006); and Veronica Strong-Boag, *Fostering Nation? Canada Confronts Its History of Childhood Disadvantage* (Waterloo, ON: Wilfrid Laurier University Press, 2011).

14 Bernice Gerard, *Bernice Gerard*, 24.

15 Terry Glavin, *Amongst God's Own: The Enduring Legacy of St. Mary's Mission* (Vancouver: New Star Books, 2002). This book, based on oral history accounts from former students, adopts a largely positive tone but does recognize that many students suffered unspeakable abuses there.

16 Bernice Gerard, *Bernice Gerard*, 27.

17 Bernice Gerard, *Bernice Gerard*, 26.

18 *Vancouver Sun*, September 14, 1977, 5. The cultural centre was controversial because it was proposed to be built in a single-family area, and some local residents opposed it.

19 Bernice Gerard, *Converted in the Country*, 17.

20 Bernice Gerard, *Converted in the Country*, 18.

21 Bernice Gerard, *Bernice Gerard*, 10–11. Beyond describing her Stó:lō/Métis siblings, this is one of the only times that Gerard mentioned ethnicity: the girls who died in the river were Japanese Canadians.

22 Gerard, *Bernice Gerard*, 22.

23 Bernice Gerard, *Converted in the Country*, 16–17.

24 Bernice Gerard, *Bernice Gerard*, 63.

25 Bernice Gerard, *Converted in the Country*, 21–22.

26 Bernice Gerard, *Converted in the Country*, 17.

27 Bernice Gerard, *Bernice Gerard*, 21–22.

28 Bernice Gerard, *Bernice Gerard*, 21.

29 Bernice Gerard, *Bernice Gerard*, 21.
30 Bernice Gerard, *Bernice Gerard*, 64.
31 Bernice Gerard, *Converted in Country*, 26.
32 Bernice Gerard, *Converted in Country*, 29.
33 Bernice Gerard, *Converted in Country*, 28–29.
34 Bernice Gerard, *Converted in Country*, 30–31.
35 Bernice Gerard, *Converted in Country*, 32.
36 Bernice Gerard, *Converted in Country*, 32
37 Bernice Gerard, *Converted in Country*, 36.
38 Bernice Gerard, *Converted in Country*, 37.
39 Bernice Gerard, *Converted in Country*, 37.
40 Bernice Gerard, *Converted in Country*, 37.
41 Bernice Gerard, *Converted in Country*, 40.
42 Bernice Gerard, *Bernice Gerard*, 39.
43 For more on the Two by Twos, see Kevin N. Daniel, *Reinventing the Truth: Historical Claims of One of the World's Largest Nameless Sects* (Sisters, OR: Research and Information Services, 1993); G. Irvine Grey, "Two by Two: The Shape of a Shapeless Movement" (unpublished thesis, Queen's University Belfast, Northern Ireland, 2012); James R. Lewis, "Two by Twos," in *The Encyclopedia of Cults, Sects, and New Religions.* (Amherst, NY: Prometheus Books, 1998); J. Gordon Melton, "The Two-By-Twos," *Melton's Encyclopedia of American Religions*, 8th ed. (Detroit: Gale, 2009).
44 Bernice Gerard, *Converted in the Country*, 40.
45 Bernice Gerard, *Converted in the Country*, 40.
46 Bernice Gerard, *Converted in the Country*, 43. Children's spirituality can be manipulated, but this should not lead to the conclusion that childhood faith and ministry is not genuine. The phenomenon of child evangelists is explored in Lanette D. Ruff and Thomas A. Robinson, *Out of the Mouths of Babes: Girl Evangelists in the Flapper Era* (London: Oxford University Press, 2011); and Thomas A. Robinson, *Preacher Girl: Uldine Uttley and the Industry of Revival* (Waco, TX: Baylor University Press, 2016).
47 Bernice Gerard, *Converted in the Country*, 40–41.
48 Bernice Gerard, *Converted in the Country*, 43.
49 Bernice Gerard, *Converted in the Country*, 44.
50 Bernice Gerard, *Converted in the Country*, 45.
51 Bernice Gerard, *Bernice Gerard*, 39–40.
52 Bernice Gerard, *Bernice Gerard*, 63.

Chapter 2: Delivered by Strong Women

1 Bernice Gerard, *Converted in the Country: The Life Story of Bernice Gerard* (Jacksonville, FL: McColl-Gerard Publications, 1956), 45.
2 See Mary Liston, "Evolving Capacities: The British Columbia Representative for Children and Youth as a Hybrid Model of Oversight," in *The Nature of Inquisitorial Processes in Administrative Regimes*, ed. Laverne Jacobs and Sasha Baglay, 4–12 (Aldershot, UK: Ashgate Publishing, 2013), https://ssrn.com/abstract=2047754; and Anne Margaret Angus, *Children's Aid Society of Vancouver, B.C., 1901–1951* (Vancouver: Vancouver Children's Aid, 1951); For accounts by two of the social workers responsible for Gerard's case, Winifred

Urquhart and Nancy Lott, see Jean Bennett, "Development of Social Services in the Okanagan, 1930–1980," in *Forty-Fifth Annual Report of the Okanagan Historical Society* (Okanagan Historical Society, 1981), 20–25, doi:http://dx.doi.org/10.14288/1.0132223.

3 Anne Margaret Angus, *Children's Aid Society of Vancouver*; Marilyn Callahan and Christopher Walmsley, "Rethinking Child Welfare Reform in British Columbia, 1900–1960," in *People, Politics, and Child Welfare in British Columbia*, ed. Leslie T. Foster and Brian Wharf, 10–33 (Vancouver: UBC Press, 2007).

4 Charlotte Whitton, quoted in Anne Margaret Angus, *Children's Aid Society of Vancouver*, 28.

5 Isobel Harvey, "Dickens and De Morgan" (master's thesis, University of British Columbia, 1919), https://open.library.ubc.ca/soa/cIRcle/collections/ubctheses/831/items/1.0088712.

6 "Well-Known City Business Man Dies: William H. Harvey, Long Identified with Vancouver Creosoting Industry," *The Province*, February 10, 1933, 22.

7 "Miss Isobel Harvey on Eugenics Board," *The Vancouver Sun*, March 8, 1937. Her replacement was announced seven years later in "City Woman Appointed to Eugenics Board," *The Province*, May 17, 1944.

8 "Women of the Year," *Vancouver Sun*, December 28, 1940, 10; Doris Milligan, "Women's War Work: Busiest Woman [Miss Isobel Harvey]," *Vancouver Sun*, August 27, 1940; "B.C. Ready to Receive Children: Welfare Workers Active," *The Province*, August 19, 1940, 20; "Registration Opens for Refugee Homes," *The Province*, June 25, 1940; "N. Shore Asks 362 Children," *Vancouver Sun*, June 29, 1940.

9 "Isobel Harvey, Social Work Leader, Dies," *Vancouver Sun*, September 12, 1951, 44.

10 Isobel Harvey, "A Historic Review of the Social Services of the Government of British Columbia," prepared for Annual *Report of the Social Welfare Branch, 1947–48*, 8. For more on the child as citizen of nation, see Allison James and Alan Prout, eds., *Constructing and Reconstructing Childhood: Contemporary Issues in the Sociological Study of Childhood*, 2nd ed. (London: Routledge, 1997), 47; Cynthia Comacchio, *Nations Are Built of Babies: Saving Ontario's Mothers and Children, 1900–1940* (Montreal/Kingston: McGill-Queen's University Press, 1993).

11 Winifred Urquhart, quoted in Jean Bennett, "Development of Social Services in the Okanagan, 1930–1980," 21.

12 Marilyn Callahan and Christopher Walmsley, "Rethinking Child Welfare Reform in British Columbia, 1900–1960," 20–21.

13 Marilyn Callahan and Christopher Walmsley, "Rethinking Child Welfare Reform in British Columbia, 1900–1960," 23.

14 Bernice Gerard, *Converted in the Country*, 48.

15 Rose Fine-Meyer and Willard Brehaut, "Secondary Education," in *The Canadian Encyclopedia*, published February 15, 2012; last edited December 16, 2013, https://www.thecanadianencyclopedia.ca/en/article/secondary-education.

16 Bernice Gerard, *Converted in the Country*, 45.

17 Diane Purvey, "Alexandra Orphanage and Families in Crisis in Vancouver, 1892–1938," in *Dimensions of Childhood: Essays on the History of Children and Youth in Canada*, ed. Russell Smandych, Gordon Dodds, and Alvin Esau, 107–33 (Winnipeg, MN: Legal Research Institute, 1991).

18 Bernice Gerard, *Bernice Gerard*, 40.

19 Bernice Gerard, *Bernice Gerard*, 41.

20 Diane Purvey, "Alexandria Orphanage," 133.

21 Bernice Gerard, *Bernice Gerard*, 41.

22 Bernice Gerard, *Bernice Gerard*, 41.

23 Bernice Gerard, *Bernice Gerard*, 41–42.

24 Veronica Strong-Boag, *Fostering Nation? Canada Confronts Its History of Childhood Disadvantage* (Waterloo, ON: Wilfrid Laurier University Press, 2011), 83–84.

25 Winifred Urquhart, quoted in Bennett, "Development of Social Services in the Okanagan," 21.

26 Veronica Strong-Boag, *Fostering Nation? Canada Confronts Its History of Childhood Disadvantage*, 84.

27 Bernice Gerard, *Converted in the Country*, 50.

28 Bernice Gerard, *Converted in the Country*, 50.

29 Bernice Gerard, *Converted in the Country*, 50.

30 Bernice Gerard, *Converted in the Country*, 51.

31 Bernice Gerard, *Converted in the Country*, 51.

32 Bernice Gerard, *Converted in the Country*, 57.

33 Bernice Gerard, *Converted in the Country*, 56.

34 Bernice Gerard, *Converted in the Country*, 54.

35 Bernice Gerard, *Bernice Gerard*, 60.

36 Bernice Gerard, *Bernice Gerard*, 60.

37 Bernice Gerard, *Bernice Gerard*, 61.

38 Bernice Gerard, *Bernice Gerard*, 61.

39 Bernice Gerard, *Bernice Gerard*, 62.

40 Bernice Gerard, *Converted in the Country*, 55.

41 Bernice Gerard, *Bernice Gerard*, 48.

42 Bernice Gerard, *Bernice Gerard*, 48.

43 See Martin Mittelstadt, "'Canada's First Martyr': The Suspicious Death of Winnipeg's WWI Pentecostal Conscientious Objector David Wells," *Manitoba History: The Journal of the Manitoba Historical Society* 87 (Fall 2018), 12–18; and Linda M. Ambrose, "Principal Purdie Objects: Canadian Pentecostal Students and Conscription during World War Two," in *Worth Fighting For: Canada's Tradition of War Resistance from 1812 to the War on Terror*, ed. Lara Campbell, Michael Dawson, and Catherine Gidney (Toronto: Between the Lines, 2015), 106–17.

44 Michael Wilkinson and Linda M. Ambrose, *After the Revival: Pentecostalism and the Making of a Canadian Church* (Montreal/Kingston: McGill-Queen's University Press, 2020), 13.

45 Michael Wilkinson and Linda M. Ambrose, *After the Revival*. The 2011 Canadian Census reported 478,705 Pentecostals. In 2020, Pentecostal/Charismatics made up one-quarter of all Christians and this is expected to grow to almost 30 percent by 2050. Todd M. Johnson, "Counting Pentecostals Worldwide," in Michael Wilkinson, ed., *Brill's Encyclopedia of Global Pentecostalism* (Leiden, NL: Brill, 2021), xxii.

46 Bernice Gerard, *Bernice Gerard*, 48.

47 Bernice Gerard, *Bernice Gerard*, 48.

48 Bernice Gerard, *Bernice Gerard*, 51.

49 Bernice Gerard, *Bernice Gerard*, 51.

50 Bernice Gerard, *Bernice Gerard*, 53.

51 Bernice Gerard, *Bernice Gerard*, 56.

52 Bernice Gerard, *Converted in Country*, 59.

Notes to pages 51–59 251

53 Bernice Gerard, *Converted in Country*, 60.
54 Frances Layden, quoted in Bernice Gerard, *Converted in Country*, 61.
55 Bernice Gerard, *Converted in Country*, 61.
56 Bernice Gerard, *Converted in Country*, 59.

CHAPTER 3: FIGHTING FOR HER FAITH

1 Bernice Gerard, *Converted in the Country: The Life Story of Bernice Gerard* (Jacksonville, FL: McColl-Gerard Publications, 1956), 62.
2 Bernice Gerard, *Bernice Gerard: Today and for Life* (Vancouver: Sunday Line Communications, 1988), 65.
3 Bernice Gerard, *Bernice Gerard*, 68; and Gerard, *Converted in the Country*, 66–69.
4 Bernice Gerard, *Converted in the Country*, 73–74; Bernice Gerard, *Bernice Gerard*, 72–73.
5 Bernice Gerard, *Bernice Gerard*, 78.
6 Bernice Gerard, *Bernice Gerard*, 79.
7 Muriel Hudson, quoted in Bernice Gerard, *Bernice Gerard*, 79.
8 Bernice Gerard, *Converted in the Country*, 81.
9 See, for example, John R. Rice, *Bobbed Hair, Bossy Wives, and Women Preachers* (Murfreesboro, TN: Sword of the Lord, 1941). While Rice was a fundamentalist who did not share Pentecostalism's views about the Holy Spirit or about women in ministry, the dress codes were commonly shared among conservative Christians with Holiness roots despite their other doctrinal differences. See also Ananís Rentas Vega, "(Un)spoken Codes: Is the New Generation Breaking the Pentecostal Dress Code?" paper 7, major papers by Master of Science students, University of Rhode Island, accessed September 2, 2020, https://digitalcommons.uri.edu/tmd_major_papers/7.
10 Religious groups use practices within their subcultures to establish and reinforce boundaries about who belongs and who does not. See Penny Edgell, "A Cultural Sociology of Religion: New Directions," *Annual Review of Sociology* 38 (2012): 247–65; Michael Wilkinson and Linda M. Ambrose, *After the Revival: Pentecostalism and the Making of a Canadian Church* (Montreal/Kingston: McGill-Queen's University Press, 2020).
11 Bernice Gerard, *Converted in the Country*, 82. The 1927 novel *Elmer Gantry*, by Sinclair Lewis (and the 1960 movie with the same title) is about a con man and a female evangelist who sell religion to small-town America. See Wheeler Dixon, "Cinematic Adaptations of the Works of Sinclair Lewis," in *Sinclair Lewis at 100: Papers Presented at a Centennial Conference*, ed. Michael Connaughton (St. Cloud: St. Cloud State University, 1985), 191–200.
12 Muriel Hudson, quoted in Bernice Gerard, *Converted in the Country*, 82.
13 Bernice Gerard, *Converted in the Country*, 74.
14 Bernice Gerard, *Converted in the Country*, 74; Bernice Gerard, *Bernice Gerard*, 73.
15 Bernice Gerard, *Bernice Gerard*, 73.
16 Bernice Gerard, *Bernice Gerard*, 73.
17 Bernice Gerard, *Bernice Gerard*, 73.
18 Bernice Gerard, *Bernice Gerard*, 71.
19 Bernice Gerard, *Bernice Gerard*, 69.
20 Bernice Gerard, "What the Pentecostal Calling Is: How We Ourselves Perceived It, and in What Ways Time and Experience Have Confirmed Some of Our Unique Insights to be Both Good and Necessary," sermon notes, Summit Pacific College, Bernice Gerard

Collection (hereafter SPC BGC). Gerard preached this sermon on several occasions, including at the Ottawa PAOC General Conference, Clear Lake, Manitoba, n.d.; the WMC [Women's Missionary Council of PAOC] Conference, n.d. [1976?]; and as a radio broadcast on KARI [Christian radio station] Blaine, Washington], September 1976.

21 Bernice Gerard, *Converted in the Country*, 70.

22 Bernice Gerard, *Bernice Gerard*, 74.

23 Bernice Gerard, *Converted in the Country*, 73.

24 Bernice Gerard, *Converted in the Country*, 73.

25 Bernice Gerard, *Bernice Gerard*, 80.

26 Penny Edgell, "A Cultural Sociology of Religion"; Michael Wilkinson and Linda M. Ambrose, *After the Revival*.

27 Bernice Gerard, *Converted in the Country*, 77.

28 Bernice Gerard, *Converted in the Country*, 79.

29 Bernice Gerard, *Converted in the Country*, 83.

30 W.H. Morrow, principal, Lord Byng Secondary School, To Whom It May Concern, August 27, 1942, letter, SPC BGC, Bernice Gerard Nielson Family Scrapbook.

31 Bernice Gerard, *Converted in the Country*, 85.

32 Isobel Harvey, quoted in Bernice Gerard, *Converted in the Country*, 85–86.

33 Isobel Harvey, quote in Bernice Gerard, *Converted in the Country*, 86.

34 Isobel Harvey, quoted in Bernice Gerard, *Converted in the Country*, 87.

35 Bernice Gerard, *Converted in the Country*, 87.

36 Bernice Gerard, *Converted in the Country*, 87.

37 Muriel Hudson, quoted in Bernice Gerard, *Converted in the Country*, 88.

38 Bernice Gerard, *Converted in the Country*, 88.

39 Bernice Gerard, *Bernice Gerard*, 42.

40 Gerard graduated from Lord Byng Secondary School in June 1941. In August 1941, W.H. Morrow, the principal at Lord Byng, wrote a letter of recommendation for Gerard saying that she had attended that school for two and a half years and had completed University Entrance and Senior Matriculation. Her Normal School diploma lists June 11, 1943 as the date of graduation. That places the conversation when Harvey washed her hands of Gerard sometime in the late winter or early spring of 1943, meaning she was nineteen years old, turning twenty in late December 1943. SPC BGC, Bernice Gerard Nielson Family Scrapbook.

Chapter 4: Finding Family

1 Bernice Gerard, *Converted in the Country: The Life Story of Bernice Gerard* (Jacksonville, FL: McColl-Gerard Publications, 1956), 91.

2 Bernice Gerard, *Bernice Gerard: Today and for Life* (Vancouver: Sunday Line Communications, 1988), 101.

3 Allyson Kenning, "Remembering the Old MacLean School, Part One," *Rossland Telegraph*, January 27, 2011, https://rosslandtelegraph.com/news/remembering-old-maclean-school-part-one-9413#.X2DlxsZ7lsM, and "Remembering Old MacLean School, Part 2," *Rossland Telegraph*, February 3, 2011, https://rosslandtelegraph.com/news/remembering-old-maclean-school-part-2-9554#.X2DnOMZ7lsM.

4 Several photographs of Gerard at the MacLean Elementary School in Rossland with fellow staff members and with her class are included in her personal archives at Summit Pacific

Notes to pages 68–72 253

College, Bernice Gerard Collection (hereafter SPC BGC), Bernice Gerard Nielson Family Scrapbook.

5 Jeremy Mouat, *Roaring Days: Rossland's Mines and the History of British Columbia* (Vancouver: UBC Press, 2011); Jean Barman, *The West beyond the West: A History of British Columbia*, rev. ed. (Toronto: University of Toronto Press, 1996), 123–25, 189.

6 David Reed, *"In Jesus' Name": The History and Beliefs of Oneness Pentecostals* (Blandford Forum, UK: Deo Publishing, 2008).

7 "Worker's License," January 1, 1935, SPC BGC, Velma Mae McColl Scrapbook. From 1935 to 1944 the McColl sisters held worker's licences issued by the Apostolic Church of Pentecost and signed by Frank Small, the moderator of the denomination, and by Robert Clark, the clerk.

8 On the question of women in the Apostolic tradition performing weddings and baptisms, see Patricia P. Pickard, *The Davis Sisters: Their Influences and Their Impact* (Bangor, ME: Patricia P. Pickard, 2009), 112.

9 Kevin Kee, *Revivalists: Marketing the Gospel in English Canada, 1884–1957* (Montreal/ Kingston: McGill-Queen's University Press, 2006).

10 "Don't Fail to Hear the Girl Evangelists," undated press clipping, Rouleau, Saskatchewan, SPC BGC, Velma Mae McColl Scrapbook. Girls, teens, and young adult women who performed as itinerant preachers were commonly referred to as "girl evangelists." See Lanette D. Ruff and Thomas A. Robinson, *Out of the Mouths of Babes: Girl Evangelists in the Flapper Era* (London: Oxford University Press, 2011).

11 "Revival Services Continue!," undated press clipping, Rouleau, Saskatchewan, SPC BGC, Velma Mae McColl Scrapbook.

12 "Rossland, B.C., April 1940," various press clippings, SPC BGC, Velma Mae McColl Scrapbook; "McColl Trio Says 'Goodbye' in Rossland, B.C.," SPC BGC, Velma Mae McColl Scrapbook; and "400 Attend M'Coll [*sic*] Girls Last Service" n.d. [1945], press clippings, SPC BGC, Velma Mae McColl Scrapbook.

13 Bernice Gerard, *Converted in the Country*, 91–92.

14 Bernice Gerard, *Converted in the Country*, 93.

15 Bernice Gerard, *Converted in the Country*, 93.

16 Principal Morrow emphasized Gerard's outstanding participation in this school club when he wrote a letter of recommendation for her to receive funding for Normal School, saying, "She has entered fully into the work of the school in every possible way, particularly in the work of the Public Speaking Club." W.H. Morrow, principal, Lord Byng Secondary School, To Whom It May Concern, August 27, 1942, letter, SPC BGC, Bernice Gerard Nielson Family Scrapbook.

17 "McColl Trio Says 'Goodbye in Rossland, B.C.," n.d. [1945], press clipping, SPC BGC, Velma Mae McColl Scrapbook.

18 For more on radio as a medium for Christian ministry, see Spencer Miller Jr., "Radio and Religion," *American Academy of Political and Social Science* 177 (1935): 135–40; William M. Clements, "The Rhetoric of the Radio Ministry," *Journal of American Folklore* 87, 346 (1974): 318–27; David L. Clark, "'Miracles for a Dime': From Chautauqua Tent to Radio Station with Sister Aimee," *California History* 57, 4 (Winter 1978/1979): 354–63; Michael Stamm, "Broadcasting Mainline Protestantism: The Chicago Sunday Evening Club and the Evolution of Audience Expectations from Radio to Television," *Religion and American Culture: A Journal of Interpretation* 22, 2 (2012): 233–64; Tona J. Hangen, *Redeeming the*

Dial: Radio, Religion, and Popular Culture in America (Chapel Hill: The University of North Carolina Press, 2002).

19 Patricia P. Pickard, *The Davis Sisters: Their Influences and Their Impact* (Bangor, ME: Patricia P. Pickard, 2009). Susie Davis died in 1962 and Carro Davis died in 1976.

20 Bernice Gerard, *Bernice Gerard*, 93.

21 Bernice Gerard, *Bernice Gerard*, 93.

22 Bernice Gerard, *Bernice Gerard*, 94.

23 Bernice Gerard, *Bernice Gerard*, 94.

24 The spiritual practice of declaring other people's futures was common among Pentecostals, but part of the so-called Latter Rain Controversy that rocked Canadian Pentecostals in Western Canada in the later 1940s involved individuals who put undue emphasis on their ability to dictate God's plan for other people. The controversy led to a multitude of incidents that saw Pentecostals of various persuasions drawing boundaries and establishing orthodoxy on both sides of the issue. The phenomenon of certain individuals taking it upon themselves to pronounce the details of others' callings, and even going so far as to dictate God's will in the choice of marriage partners, caused alarm among more cautious Pentecostals who worried about self-promotion and abuse that might accompany individuals who claimed to have this gift. At issue were questions of authority, whether that power rested with individuals or with denominational leaders. See Michael Wilkinson and Linda M. Ambrose, *After the Revival: Pentecostalism and the Making of a Canadian Church* (Montreal/Kingston: McGill-Queen's Unversity Press, 2020), 78–84.

25 Bernice Gerard, *Bernice Gerard*, 94.

26 Bernice Gerard, *Converted in the Country*, 97–98.

27 Bernice Gerard, *Bernice Gerard*, 208. The third chapter in that autobiography was entitled "The Growing Up of Nobody's Child," 19–28.

28 Bernice Gerard, *Converted in the Country*, 93–94.

29 Bernice Gerard, *Bernice Gerard*, 92.

30 Bernice Gerard, *Bernice Gerard*, 92.

31 Bernice Gerard, *Converted in the Country*, 96.

32 Bernice Gerard, *Bernice Gerard*, 206.

33 Bernice Gerard, *Bernice Gerard*, 206.

34 Bernice Gerard, *Bernice Gerard*, 207.

35 Bernice Gerard, *Bernice Gerard*, 205. The empathy that Gerard felt for her birth mother is revealed by her choice of words such as "my dear little mother" and "forty lonely institutionalized years." Ada Nielson's experience as a patient, spanning several decades of the twentieth century, largely predated the move toward more empathetic and political considerations of how insanity was regarded in Canada. For example, as a recent book in the field of "mad studies" explains, "In 1981, Toronto activist-survivor Mel Starkman wrote: 'An important new movement is sweeping through the Western world ... The "mad," the oppressed, the ex-inmates of society's asylums are coming together and speaking for themselves.'" Brenda A. LeFrancois, Robert Menzies, and Geoffrey Reaume, eds., *Mad Matters: A Critical Reader in Canadian Mad Studies* (Toronto: Canadian Scholars' Press, 2013), 2. Scholars tracing the evolving history of patient experiences in asylums, point to the scholarship of Phyllis Chesler, to highlight her assertions that, "women were held to different and higher standards of reason and normalcy than were men, that the psychiatrization process was profoundly gender-biased in its premises and effects, and that

Notes to pages 77–82

the very constitution of sanity and 'mental illness' in late 20th-century society was anchored in the bedrock of male normativity."Brenda A. LeFrancois, Robert Menzies, and Geoffrey Reaume, eds., *Mad Matters*, 6, describing Phyllis Chesler, *Women and Madness* (Garden City, NY: Doubleday, 1972). Throughout the 1970s, the historiography of madness continued this concentration on women's experiences, offering a "women-focused interpretation of the malestream psychiatric system through the eyes of those who had encountered, and been damaged by it." Brenda A. LeFrancois, Robert Menzies, and Geoffrey Reaume, eds., *Mad Matters*, 6, referencing Dorothy Smith and Sara David, eds., *Women Look at Psychiatry* (Vancouver: Press Gang, 1975).

36 Bernice Gerard, *Bernice Gerard*, 207.

37 Monica Storrs's June 15, 1930, diary entry in *God's Galloping Girl: The Peace River Diaries of Monica Storrs, 1929–1931*, ed. W.L. Morton (Vancouver: UBC Press, 1979), 125.

38 Monica Storrs, quoted in W.L. Morton, ed., *God's Galloping Girl*, 40.

39 W.L. Morton, ed., *God's Galloping Girl*, note 56, states: "This trustee, variously described as a Swede and a Dane by Monica, was R.H.A. Nielson, who came to Fort St. John in 1919. He later moved to Taylor's Flats where he had a store and continued to work as a telegraph agent and linesman. His daughters Joyce and Violet were among Monica's Guides" (292).

40 W.L. Morton, ed., *God's Galloping Girl*, 59.

41 W.L. Morton, ed., *God's Galloping Girl*, 125.

42 C.A. Dawson, *The Settlement of the Peace River Country: A Study of a Pioneer Area*, vol. 6, (Toronto: Macmillan, 1934), 144.

43 C.A. Dawson, *The Settlement of the Peace River Country*, 252.

44 Mary-Ellen Kelm, "'The Only Place Likely to Do Her Any Good': The Admission of Women to British Columbia's Provincial Hospital for the Insane," *BC Studies* 96 (Winter 1992–93): 89.

45 Megan J. Davies, "Snapshots: Three Women and Psychiatry, 1920–1935," *Canadian Woman Studies* 8, 4 (1987): 47–48.

46 Wendy Mitchinson, "Reasons for Committal to a Mid-Nineteenth-Century Ontario Insane Asylum: The Case of Toronto," in *Essays in the History of Canadian Medicine*, ed. Wendy Mitchinson and Janice Dickin McGinnis (Toronto: McClelland and Stewart, 1988), 88–109.

47 Wendy Mitchinson, "Reasons for Committal," 93.

48 Cheryl Krasnick Warsh, *Moments of Unreason: The Practice of Canadian Psychiatry and the Homewood Retreat, 1833–1923* (Montreal/Kingston: McGill-Queen's University Press, 1989), 10.

49 Mary-Ellen Kelm, "'The Only Place Likely to Do Her Any Good,'" 89.

50 Bernice Gerard, *Bernice Gerard*, 206.

51 Bernice Gerard, *Bernice Gerard*, 207.

52 Bernice Gerard, *Bernice Gerard*, 207.

53 Bernice Gerard, *Bernice Gerard*, 207.

54 Bernice Gerard, *Bernice Gerard*, 207.

55 Bernice Gerard, *Bernice Gerard*, 207.

CHAPTER 5: THE MCCOLL-GERARD TRIO AND PROFESSIONAL BELONGING

1 Bernice Gerard, *Converted in the Country: The Life Story of Bernice Gerard* (Jacksonville, FL: McColl-Gerard Publications, 1956), 97.

2   Bernice Gerard, *Converted in the Country*, 97.

3   Jean and Velma McColl, quoted in Bernice Gerard, *Bernice Gerard: Today and for Life* (Vancouver: Sunday Line Communications, 1988), 94.

4   Bernice Gerard, *Bernice Gerard*, 94.

5   Bernice Gerard, *Bernice Gerard*, 94.

6   William K. Kay, *Pentecostalism: A Very Short Introduction* (Oxford: Oxford University Press, 2011), 1.

7   The travel that the McColl-Gerard Trio undertook was not without precedent. One of Aimee Semple McPherson's biographers described her travel as "a gypsy life" and makes the claim that she "may well have been the first woman to drive a car from New York to California without a man to fix flat tires." Daniel Mark Epstein, *Sister Aimee: The Life of Aimee Semple McPherson* (New York: Harcourt Brace, 1993), 126, 146. See also Robert Rutherdale, "Fatherhood, Masculinity, and the Good Life during Canada's Baby Boom, 1945–1965," *Journal of Family History* 24 (July 1999): 351–73; Christopher Dummitt, *The Manly Modern: Masculinity in Postwar Canada* (Vancouver: UBC Press, 2007), see especially chap. 6, "On the Road"; and Margaret Walsh, "Gendering Mobility: Women, Work, and Automobility in the United States," *History: Journal of the Historical Association* 93, 311 (July 2008): 376–95.

8   Kevin Kee, *Revivalists: Marketing the Gospel in English Canada, 1884–1957* (Montreal/Kingston: McGill-Queen's University Press, 2006).

9   Thomas A. Robinson and Lanette D. Ruff, *Out of the Mouths of Babes: Girl Evangelists in the Flapper Age* (Oxford: Oxford University Press, 2012); and Thomas A. Robinson, *Preacher Girl: Uldine Utley and the Industry of Revival* (Waco, TX: Baylor University Press, 2016).

10 Bernice Gerard, *Converted in the Country*, 100.

11 Assorted news clippings, Summit Pacific College, Bernice Gerard Collection (hereafter SPC BGC), Velma Mae McColl Scrapbook.

12 Virginia Lieson Brereton, *From Sin to Salvation: Stories of Women's Conversions, 1800 to the Present* (Bloomington: Indiana University Press, 1991).

13 On Pentecostalism and masculinity, see Elizabeth Brusco, "Gender and Power," in *Studying Global Pentecostalism: Theories and Methods*, ed. Allan Anderson and Michael Bergunder (Berkeley and London: University of California Press, 2010), 74–92; Elizabeth Brusco, *The Reformation of Machismo: Evangelical Conversion and Gender in Colombia* (Austin: University of Texas Press, 1995); Martin Lindhardt, "Men of God: Neo-Pentecostalism and Masculinities in Urban Tanzania," *Religion* 45, 2 (2015): 252–72; and Bernice Martin, "The Pentecostal Gender Paradox: A Cautionary Tale for the Sociology of Religion," in *The Blackwell Companion to Sociology of Religion*, ed. Richard K. Fenn, 52–66 (Oxford: Blackwell Publishing, 2001).

14 Erica Ramirez, "Reinventing Anderson: *Vision of the Disinherited* and the Pentecostal Body," paper presented to the 47th Annual Meeting Society for Pentecostal Studies, Cleveland, Tennessee, March 10, 2018; see also Bobby C. Alexander, "Pentecostal Ritual Reconsidered: Anti-structural Dimensions of Possession," *Journal of Ritual Studies* 3, 1 (1989): 109–16; and Dan Albrecht, *Rites in the Spirit: A Ritual Approach to Pentecostal/Charismatic Spirituality* (Sheffield, UK: Sheffield Academic Press, 1999).

15 Catherine Booth, *Female Ministry; or, Woman's Right to Preach the Gospel* (New York: Salvation Army Supplies Printing and Publishing Department, 1859).

16 See Virginia Lieson Brereton, *From Sin to Salvation*; Susan Ostrov Weisser, "'What Kind of Life Have I Got?' Gender in the Life Story of an 'Ordinary' Woman," in *Getting a Life: Everyday Uses of Autobiography*, ed. Sidonie Smith and Julia Watson, 249–70 (Minneapolis: University of Minnesota Press, 1996); and Sidonie Smith and Julia Watson, eds., *Women, Autobiography, Theory: A Reader* (Madison: University of Wisconsin Press, 1998).

17 Bernice Gerard, *Bernice Gerard*, 95.

18 See Allan Anderson, "Varieties, Taxonomies, and Definitions," in *Study Global Pentecostalism: Theories and Methods*, ed. Allan Anderson et al. (Berkeley: University of California Press, 2010), 13–29; and Allan Anderson, *To the Ends of the Earth: Pentecostalism and the Transformation of World Christianity* (Oxford: Oxford University Press, 2013), 5–9.

19 Michael Wilkinson and Linda M. Ambrose, *After the Revival: Pentecostalism and the Making of a Canadian Church* (Montreal/Kingston: McGill-Queen's University Press, 2020), 85–106.

20 Michael Wilkinson and Linda M. Ambrose, *After the Revival*, 78–84.

21 Bernice Gerard, *Bernice Gerard*, 96.

22 David Reed, *"In Jesus' Name": The History and Beliefs of Oneness Pentecostals* (Blandford Forum, UK: Deo Publishing, 2008).

23 See Thomas William Miller, *Canadian Pentecostals: A History of the Pentecostal Assemblies of Canada* (Mississauga: Full Gospel Publishing House, 1994), 259–65; R.M. Riss, "Latter Rain Movement," in *The New International Dictionary of Pentecostal and Charismatic Movements*, rev. ed. Stanley M. Burgess and Eduard M. van der Maas (Grand Rapids, MI: Zondervan, 2003), 830–33; and Michael Wilkinson and Linda M. Ambrose, *After the Revival*, 78–84.

24 Bernice Gerard, *Bernice Gerard*, 96.

25 Rev. P.S. Jones, quoted in Bernice Gerard, *Bernice Gerard*, 96.

26 Bernice Gerard, *Bernice Gerard*, 96.

27 Bernice Gerard, *Bernice Gerard*, 96. The Pentecostal Holiness Church was another Oneness group among Pentecostals, and accepting their ministry credentials would have confirmed that Gerard and the McColls were not committed trinitarians, an association that could prove problematic as they tried to move in larger Pentecostal circles.

28 Bernice Gerard, *Bernice Gerard*, 96.

29 C.E. Jones, "Gibson, Christine Amelia (1979–1955)," in *The New International Dictionary of Pentecostal and Charismatic Movements*, rev. ed., ed. Stanley M. Burgess and Eduard M. van der Maas (Grand Rapids, MI: Zondervan, 2003), 664.

30 Bernice Gerard, *Bernice Gerard*, 97.

31 Bernice Gerard, *Bernice Gerard*, 97; See Thomas William Miller, *Canadian Pentecostals: A History of the Pentecostal Assemblies of Canada* (Mississauga, ON: Full Gospel Publishing House, 1994), 165. While Miller identifies Bouchard as the founder of the school, Gerard credits Lassègues as "founder of the French Pentecostal Church and Bible School in Montreal."

32 Bernice Gerard, *Bernice Gerard*, 97.

33 J.H. Blair, Superintendent Western Ontario District, Canada, letter to "Christian Ministers," January 23, 1948, SPC BGC, Bernice Gerard Nielson Family Scrapbook.

34 J.H. Blair, letter to "Christian Ministers."

35 Joy E.A. Qualls, *God Forgive Us for Being Women: Rhetoric, Theology, and the Pentecostal Tradition* (Eugene, OR: Pickwick, 2018); Edith L. Blumhofer, *Restoring the Faith: The*

258 *Notes to pages 96–105*

Assemblies of God, Pentecostalism, and American Culture (Urbana: University of Illinois Press, 1993), 164–79; Margaret M. Poloma, *The Assemblies of God at the Crossroads: Charisma and Institutional Dilemmas* (Knoxville: The University of Tennessee Press, 1989), 101–21.

36 "Ordination Certificate, Bernice Margaret Gerard, 1948," SPC BGC, Bernice Gerard Nielson Family Scrapbook. As this document reveals, Canadians were being ordained by the Assemblies of God headquarters in Springfield, Missouri, under a presbytery called the "Pentecostal Assemblies of Canada."

37 Michael Wilkinson and Linda M. Ambrose, *After the Revival*, 12–59.

38 Bernice Gerard, *Bernice Gerard*, 99.

39 Bernice Gerard, *Bernice Gerard*, 99.

40 SPC BGC, McColl-Gerard Trio photo album 1949–52, BX8762 Z8 M121 1949; McColl-Gerard Trio Missionary photo album 1951; Velma Mae McColl Scrapbook; McColl-Gerard Trio photo album,1956–58, BX8762 Z8 M121 1956.

41 Bernice Gerard, *Bernice Gerard*, 99.

42 Bernice Gerard, *Bernice Gerard*, 99.

43 Bernice Gerard, *Bernice Gerard*, 99.

44 Bernice Gerard, *Bernice Gerard*, 104.

45 Bernice Gerard, *Bernice Gerard*, 104.

46 Bernice Gerard, *Bernice Gerard*, 105.

47 SPC BGC, McColl-Gerard Trio Missionary photo album 1951, BX8762 Z8 M121 1951.

48 Bernice Gerard, *Bernice Gerard*, 93–110. The chapter is aptly titled "Taking the Dream on the Road."

49 Allan Anderson, *Spreading Fires: The Missionary Nature of Early Pentecostalism* (Maryknoll, NY: Orbis Books, 2007). See especially "Bias in Pentecostal Historiography," 5–9.

50 C.M. Robeck Jr., "Pentecostal World Conference," in *The New International Dictionary of Pentecostal and Charismatic Movements*, rev. ed., ed. Stanley M. Burgess and Eduard M. van der Maas, 971–74 (Grand Rapids, MI: Zondervan, 2003), 971.

51 R.P. Spittler, "Du Plessis, David Johannes," in *The New International Dictionary of Pentecostal and Charismatic Movements*, rev. ed., ed. Stanley M. Burgess and Eduard M. van der Maas, 589–93 (Grand Rapids, MI: Zondervan, 2003).

52 D.D. Bundy, "Gee, Donald (1891–1966)," in *The New International Dictionary of Pentecostal and Charismatic Movements*, rev. ed., ed. Stanley M. Burgess and Eduard M. van der Maas (Grand Rapids, MI: Zondervan, 2003), 662.

53 Bernice Gerard, *Bernice Gerard*, 107.

54 Bernice Gerard, *Bernice Gerard*, 107.

55 Bernice Gerard, *Bernice Gerard*, 107.

56 Bernice Gerard, *Bernice Gerard*, 107.

57 Bernice Gerard, *Bernice Gerard*, 107.

58 Bernice Gerard, *Bernice Gerard*, 107.

59 Bernice Gerard, *Bernice Gerard*, 107.

60 Joshua Ziefle, *David du Plessis and the Assemblies of God: The Struggle for the Soul of a Movement* (Leiden, NL: Brill, 2012).

61 Michael McClymond, "Roberts, Oral," in *Brill's Encyclopedia of Global Pentecostalism*, ed. Michael Wilkinson, 552–54 (Leiden: Brill, 2021).

62 Bernice Gerard, *Bernice Gerard*, 109.

63 Bernice Gerard, *Bernice Gerard*, 109.

Notes to pages 105–11

64 Bernice Gerard, *Bernice Gerard,* 109.

65 Bernice Gerard, *Bernice Gerard,* 109–10.

66 Bernice M. Gerard, *The Holy Land: Guide to Faith!* (Jacksonville, FL: McColl-Gerard Publications, n.d. [c. 1950s]).

67 Bernice Gerard, *The Holy Land,* 4.

CHAPTER 6: CAMPUS LIFE

1 Bernice Gerard, *Bernice Gerard: Today and for Life* (Vancouver: Sunday Line Communications, 1988), 112.

2 Summit Pacific College, Bernice Gerard Collection (hereafter SPC BGC), McColl-Gerard Trio photo album 1956–58, BX8762 Z8 M121 1956.

3 Bernice Gerard, *Bernice Gerard,* 112–13.

4 Bernice Gerard, *Bernice Gerard,* 112–13.

5 Bernice Gerard, *Bernice Gerard,* 112–13.

6 Bernice Gerard, *Bernice Gerard,* 114.

7 Bernice Gerard, *Bernice Gerard,* 114.

8 Bernice Gerard, *Bernice Gerard,* 114.

9 Antony Ferry, "Oh, Sing It, You Precious Pentecostal People," *Maclean's,* November 3, 1962. Thanks to Caleb Courtney for bringing this article to my attention.

10 Antony Ferry, "Oh, Sing It."

11 Antony Ferry, "Oh, Sing It." For more on PAOC Bible schools, see Michael Wilkinson and Linda M. Ambrose, *After the Revival,* 69–74.

12 Western Pentecostal Bible College is the former name of Summit Pacific College, the PAOC Bible school now located in Abbotsford, BC. While she was a graduate student the Bible college was located in North Vancouver. Bernice Gerard, *Bernice Gerard,* 118.

13 Bernice M. Gerard, "Milton's Orthodoxy and Its Relation to the Form of *Paradise Lost,*" (master's thesis, University of British Columbia, 1967), https://open.library.ubc.ca/cIRcle/collections/ubctheses/831/items/1.0093631.

14 University calendars, 1962–1986, University of British Columbia Archives, https://open.library.ubc.ca/search?collection=ubcpublications&q=ubc%20calendar. A review of these calendars shows that Gerard's name was included in the list of campus chaplains for the first time in the 1963–64 calendar, 62, 553, and continued to be listed every year until the 1985–86 calendar, when her name was replaced by that of Mr. Reid Johnson, B.A., PAOC Chaplain. UBC Calendar 1985–86, 32.

15 The charismatic movement is a broad term that encompasses new religious experiences that began to emerge among North American Christians (both Protestant and Roman Catholic) in the 1960s. See P.D. Hocken, "Charismatic Movement," in *The New International Dictionary of Pentecostal and Charismatic Movements,* rev. ed., ed. Stanley M. Burgess and Eduard M. van der Maas (Grand Rapids, MI: Zondervan, 2003), 477–519; and Donald S. Swenson, "Charismatic Renewal in the Roman Catholic Church," in *Brill's Encyclopedia of Global Pentecostalism,* ed. Michael Wilkinson (Leiden, NL: Brill, 2021), 115–17.

16 On the changing place of religion on Canadian campuses, see Catherine Gidney, *A Long Eclipse: The Liberal Protestant Establishment and the Canadian University, 1920–1970* (Montreal/Kingston: McGill-Queen's Press, 2004). On secularization in Canada more broadly, see Hugh McLeod, *The Religious Crisis of the 1960s* (Oxford: Oxford University

Press, 2007); Brian Clarke and Stuart Macdonald, *Leaving Christianity: Changing Allegiances in Canada since 1945* (Montreal/Kingston: McGill-Queen's University Press, 2017); Mark Noll, "What Happened to Christian Canada?," *Church History* 75, 2 (2006): 245–73; and Gary Miedema, *For Canada's Sake: Public Religion, Centennial Celebrations, and the Re-making of Canada in the 1960s* (Montreal/Kingston: McGill-Queen's University Press, 2005).

17 Paul Bramadat, Patricia O'Connell Killen, and Sarah Wilkins-Laflamme, eds., *Religion at the Edge: Nature, Spirituality, and Secularity in the Pacific Northwest* (Vancouver: UBC Press, 2022).

18 Bernice Gerard, *Bernice Gerard*, 116.

19 Anthony Ferry, "Oh, Sing It."

20 See, for example, a trilogy of films produced by the Christian production company Pure Flix Entertainment: *God's Not Dead* (2014) 113 min.; *God's Not Dead 2* (2016) 120 min.; and *God's Not Dead: A Light in Darkness* (2018) 106 min., Pure Flix Entertainment, Scottsdale, Arizona. For a Pentecostal critique of these films, see Blaine Charette, "Rethinking Cultural Engagement: Reflections on the God's Not Dead Franchise," *Canadian Journal of Pentecostal-Charismatic Christianity* 8 (2017): 59–69.

21 Bernice Gerard, *Bernice Gerard*, 115.

22 Bernice Gerard, *Bernice Gerard*, 115.

23 Bernice Gerard, *Bernice Gerard*, 116.

24 Bernice Gerard, "The Good News of the Bhagavad-Gita," unpublished paper written for Religion 300, University of British Columbia, October, 1960, uncatalogued, SPC BGC.

25 Gerard mentions this struggle saying, that she "settled in as a student, having learned how to handle footnotes and survive in my new world ..." Bernice Gerard, *Bernice Gerard*, 116. Indeed, in the paper she wrote for Religion 300 (see note 23), her footnotes were not done correctly although the comments in the paper do not indicate that she lost marks for this. Her error was that after direct quotes, rather than create a footnote, she used the page number as the superscript number.

26 Swami Prabhavananda and Christopher Isherwood, trans., *The Song of God: Bhagavad-Gita* (New York: Mentor Books, 1951), 129. This book is now in the author's possession, purchased at a used book sale hosted by Summit Pacific College Library in February 2014.

27 Bernice Gerard, "Milton's Orthodoxy and Its Relation to the Form of *Paradise Lost*," 82.

28 Grant Wacker, *Heaven Below: Early Pentecostals and American Culture* (Cambridge, MA: Harvard University Press, 2001), 10.

29 Bernice Gerard, "Milton's Orthodoxy and Its Relation to the Form of *Paradise Lost*," 94.

30 Bernice Gerard, "Milton's Orthodoxy and Its Relation to the Form of *Paradise Lost*," 74, 82.

31 This is a reference to the teaching of Jesus in the gospel of John, chapters 15–17, where he instructs his disciples to remember that although they are *in* the world, they are not *of* the world.

32 Bernice Gerard, "Bringing Christ on Campus," 7, uncatalogued, SPC BGC.

33 "Counselling service for students ..." uncatalogued press clipping, n.d., SPC BGC.

34 Bernice Gerard, *Bernice Gerard*, 117.

35 Paul Bramadat, "Introduction," in *Religion at the Edge,* ed. Paul Bramadat, Patricia O'Connell Killen, and Sarah Wilkins-Laflamme, 3–22.

36 Michiel Horn, "Under the Gaze of George Vancouver: The University of British Columbia and the Provincial Government, 1913–1939," *BC Studies* 83 (Autumn 1989): 29–67. For more on the history of UBC, see William A. Bruneau, *A Matter of Identities: A History of the UBC Faculty Association, 1920–1990* (Vancouver: UBC Faculty Association, 1990);

William A. Bruneau, "Toward a New Collective Biography: The University of British Columbia Professoriate, 1915–1945," *Canadian Journal of Education* 19, 1 (1994): 65–79; Eric Damer and Herbert Rosengarten, *UBC: The First 100 Years* (Vancouver: University of British Columbia, 2009); William C. Gibson, *Wesbrook & His University* (Vancouver: UBC Press, 1973); H.T. Logan, *Tuum Est: A History of the University of British Columbia* (Vancouver: UBC Press, 1958); Wayne Skene, *UBC: A Portrait* (Vancouver: Tribute Books, 2003); Lee Stewart, *"It's Up to You": Women at UBC in the Early Years* (Vancouver: UBC Press, 1990); and George Woodcock and Tim Fitzharris, *The University of British Columbia – A Souvenir* (Toronto: Oxford University Press, 1986).

37 Hugh Johnston, *Radical Campus: Making Simon Fraser University* (Vancouver: Douglas and McIntyre, 2005).

38 For more on student culture in the 1960s, see for example, Sara Burke, "The Berkeley of Sudbury: Finding a Voice, 1960–1972," in *Laurentian University: A History*, ed. Linda M. Ambrose et al. (Montreal/Kingston: McGill-Queen's University Press, 2010), 165.

39 See Bryan Palmer, *Canada's 1960s: The Ironies of Identity in a Rebellious Era* (Toronto: University of Toronto Press, 2009); Lara A. Campbell, Dominque Clement, and Gregory S. Kealey, eds., *Debating Dissent: Canada and the 1960s* (Toronto: University of Toronto Press, 2012); Dimitry Anastakis, ed., *The Sixties: Passion, Politics and Style* (Montreal/Kingston: McGill-Queen's University Press, 2008); and M. Athena Palaeologu, ed., *The Sixties in Canada: A Turbulent and Creative Decade* (Montreal: Black Rose Books, 2009).

40 Christabelle Sethna, "The Evolution of the *Birth Control Handbook*: From Student-Peer Education Manual to Feminist Self-Empowerment, 1968–1975," in *Rethinking Canada: The Promise of Women's History*, 6th ed., ed. Mona Gleason, Tamara Myers, and Adele Perry (Toronto: Oxford University Press, 2011), 387–408.

41 Catherine Gidney, *A Long Eclipse*.

42 Grant Wacker, *America's Pastor: Billy Graham and the Shaping of a Nation* (Cambridge, MA: Harvard University Press, 2014).

43 John G. Stackhouse Jr., "The Protestant Experience in Canada since 1945," in *The Canadian Protestant Experience, 1760–1990*, ed. George A. Rawlyk (Burlington, ON: Welch Publishing, 1990), 218.

44 Technically, this claim about Gerard being the first Pentecostal campus chaplain in Canada is debatable because Memorial University, in St. John's, Newfoundland, has had a Pentecostal presence on its campus under the auspices of the Pentecostal Assemblies of Newfoundland and Labrador since 1961. See Burton Janes, *History of the Pentecostal Assemblies of Newfoundland* (St. John's: Pentecostal Assemblies of Newfoundland, 1996). Nevertheless, Gerard's work as a campus chaplain was certainly a first for the PAOC.

45 Allan M. McGavin, Office of the Chancellor, UBC, to The Rev. Miss Bernice Gerard, May 29, 1972, uncatalogued, SPC BGC.

46 "Guestbook," uncatalogued, SPC BGC. The guest book was presented to Bernice from Jean McColl as a gift and is inscribed "With loving memories of our happy holiday in Stockholm, Sweden, June 19-July 2, 1949, Jean." Gerard used the book, beginning in 1962 and continuing to 1982. When she hosted events, she asked students from UBC and SFU to sign the book listing their name, faculty, and year, Vancouver address, and hometown. In the same book, the last several pages include signatures and greetings from those who attended Gerard's memorial service at Broadway Church, on November 24, 2008.

47 Bernice Gerard, *Bernice Gerard*, 117.

48 Bernice Gerard, *Bernice Gerard*, 117.

49 Bernice Gerard, draft radio transcript, *Sunday Line* Preview, September 15, 1968, SPC BGC.

50 Bernice Gerard, draft radio transcript, September 15, 1968.

51 Bernice Gerard, draft radio transcript, September 15, 1968.

52 Lynne Marks, *Infidels and the Damn Churches: Irreligion and Religion in Settler British Columbia.* (Vancouver: UBC Press, 2017); and Tina Block, *The Secular North-West: Religion and Irreligion in Everyday Postwar Life* (Vancouver: UBC Press, 2017). This trend of decreased involvement with organized religion was not limited to BC, of course. See Hugh McLeod, *The Religious Crisis of the 1960s* (Oxford: Oxford University Press, 2007); Brian Clarke and Stuart Macdonald, *Leaving Christianity*; Mark Noll, "What Happened to Christian Canada?"; and Gary Miedema, *For Canada's Sake: Public Religion, Centennial Celebrations, and the Re-Making of Canada in the 1960s.*

53 Bramadat, "Introduction," in *Religion at the Edge.*

54 Bernice Gerard, draft radio transcript, *Sunday Line* Preview, September 15, 1968, SPC BGC.

55 Bernice Gerard, draft radio transcript, September 15, 1968.

56 Bernice Gerard, "Bringing Christ on Campus," 7, uncatalogued, SPC BGC. A note at the end of this document reveals that Gerard presented this as part of a talk titled "Campus Evangelism" at the Pentecostal Fellowship of North America, Des Moines, Iowa, November 1971.

57 Bernice Gerard, "Bringing Christ on Campus," 1–2.

58 Bernice Gerard, "Bringing Christ on Campus," 2.

59 Michael Wilkinson and Linda M. Ambrose, *After the Revival.*

60 The author's personal (signed) copy of Gerard's autobiography bears that inscription.

61 Eleanor Wachtel, "The University Chaplains: Generalists in an Age of Specialization," *UBC Alumni Chronicle* 34, 3 (Autumn 1979): 8–9.

62 Eleanor Wachtel, "The University Chaplains," 8.

63 Bernice Gerard, "Bringing Christ on Campus," 3.

64 Linda M. Ambrose, "You Preach like a Man: Beyond the Typical Gender Roles of Canadian Pentecostalism," in *The Pentecostal World*, ed. Michael Wilkinson and Jörg Haustein (Abingdon, UK: Routledge, 2023), 253–63.

65 Bernice Gerard, "Bringing Christ on Campus," 2.

66 Luther P. Gerlach and Virginia H. Hine, "Five Factors Crucial to the Growth and Spread of a Modern Religious Movement," *Journal for the Scientific Study of Religion* 7 (1968): 23–40.

67 Luther P. Gerlach and Virginia H. Hine, "Five Factors Crucial to the Growth and Spread of a Modern Religious Movement."

68 Bernice Gerard, "Bringing Christ on Campus," 5–6.

69 Bernice Gerard, "Bringing Christ on Campus," 4.

70 *The Wayfarer*, March 3, 1966, 2.

71 "Wealthiest individuals and families in Canada as of 2022, by total net worth (in billion U.S. dollars)" [graph], *CEOWORLD Magazine*, October 2, 2022. https://www.statista.com/statistics/608877/canada-richest-people/; See also "Phil Gaglardi," Wikipedia, https://en.wikipedia.org/wiki/Phil_Gaglardi, last edited October 4, 2023.

72 Jean Barman, *The West beyond the West: A History of British Columbia*, rev. ed. (Toronto: University of Toronto Press, 1996), 277.

73 "Ministers Come to Talk Religion," *The Wayfarer*, March 3, 1966, 4.

74 Michael Wilkinson and Linda M. Ambrose, *After the Revival*, Table 1.1, 13.

75 G. Bishop, D. Tingey, and G. Thorp, "Wayfarer Not an AMS [Alma Mater Society] Publication?," letter to the editor, *The Ubyssey*, March 8, 1966, 4.

76 G. Bishop, D. Tingey, and G. Thorp, "Wayfarer Not an AMS Publication?"

77 *The Wayfarer*, November 3, 1966, 1.

78 Editor's note, *The Ubyssey*, March 8, 1966, 4.

79 Pentecostal Assemblies of Canada, Mission Canada, "Serve Campus Network," https://www.paoc.org/canada/workers/priorityservecampus.

80 Bernice Gerard, "Bringing Christ on Campus," 2.

81 In charting the future course for the Pentecostal Assemblies of Canada, General Superintendent David Wells emphasizes that campus outreach projects are central to the strategic future direction of that church. See Pentecostal Assemblies of Canada, Serve Campus Network, accessed October 2, 2020, https://paoc.org/serve-campus. See also Natalie Rogge, "Next Generation Ministries," and Ted Seres, "Engaging the Culture," in David Wells, *Picture This! Reflecting on 100 Years of the PAOC* (Mississauga, ON: Pentecostal Assemblies of Canada International Office, 2018).

Chapter 7: On the Radio

1 "Dear Bernice," letter from listener in Victoria, BC, October 21, 1973, Summit Pacific College, Bernice Gerard Collection (hereafter SPC BGC). Note: because of the sensitive nature of some of the correspondence Gerard received from listeners, I have chosen not to reveal names here, although the letters were all signed.

2 "Dear Bernice," October 21, 1973.

3 "Dear Bernice," October 21, 1973.

4 "Dear Bernice," October 21, 1973.

5 Bernice Gerard, *Bernice Gerard: Today and for Life* (Vancouver: Sunday Line Communications, 1988), 163.

6 A short history and chronology of the Sunday Line ministries and of the work of Bernice Gerard and Velma Chapman is on the Sunday Line website: https://www.sundayline.com/about/history.php (accessed November 5, 2020).

7 Michael Stamm, "Broadcasting Mainline Protestantism: The Chicago Sunday Evening Club and the Evolution of Audience Expectations from Radio to Television," *Religion and American Culture: A Journal of Interpretation* 22, 2 (Summer 2012): 235.

8 David L. Clark, "'Miracles for a Dime': From Chautauqua Tent to Radio Station with Sister Aimee," *California History* 57, 4 (1978/79): 355. According to one source, the first example of religious radio broadcasting in the United States is traced to the Rev. Edwin J. Van Etten, rector of Calvary Episcopal Church in Pittsburg, Pennsylvania, when he transmitted the vesper service from his church on January 2, 1921. Spencer Miller, "Radio and Religion," *The Annals of the American Academy of Political and Social Science*, 177 (January 1935): 135–40. McPherson's station name (KFSG) included the initials of the denomination she founded: FSG = "Four Square Gospel" which refers to her fourfold theological moniker, Jesus as "Saviour, Baptizer, Healer, and Coming King."

9 Tona J. Hangen, *Redeeming the Dial: Radio, Religion, and Popular Culture in America* (Chapel Hill: University of North Carolina Press, 2002), 78.

10 Tona J. Hangen, *Redeeming the Dial*, 79.

11 David L. Clark, "'Miracles for a Dime,'" 363.

12 Leah Payne, *Gender and Pentecostal Revivalism: Making A Female Ministry in the Early Twentieth Century* (New York: Palgrave Macmillan, 2015), 70–73. For more on Semple McPherson and radio, see Tona Hangen, "The Live Wire of Los Angeles: Aimee Semple McPherson on Radio," in *Redeeming the Dial*, 57–79.

13 "Revivaltime," *Pentecostal Testimony*, December 1963, 9.

14 "Revivaltime," *Pentecostal Testimony*, December 1963, 9.

15 David Mainse, *100: An Inspiring Journey of a Life Dedicated to the Call of God* (Burlington, ON: Crossroads Christian Communications Inc., 1999); and David Mainse, *100 Huntley Street: The Exciting Success Story from the Host of Canada's Popular Television Program* (Toronto: G.R. Welch, 1979).

16 Bernice Gerard, "Electronic Evangelism and the Local Church," n.d., uncatalogued, SPC BGC.

17 Tona Hangen, *Redeeming the Dial*, 158.

18 Bernice Gerard, speaking notes for *Sunday Line* radio show, August 3, 1969, SPC BGC.

19 Bernice Gerard, sermon notes, Fraserview Assembly, February 9, 1969, SPC BGC. In that sermon, Gerard was referencing the academic article, Luther P. Gerlach and Virginia H. Hine, "Five Factors Crucial to the Growth and Spread of a Modern Religious Movement," *Journal for the Scientific Study of Religion* 7 (1968): 23–40.

20 Bernice Gerard, untitled radio transcript, November 9, 1972, SPC BGC.

21 Bernice Gerard, untitled radio transcript, November 9, 1972.

22 Bernice Gerard, untitled radio transcript, November 9, 1972.

23 Bernice Gerard, untitled radio transcript, November 9, 1972.

24 Bernice Gerard, *Bernice Gerard*, 163.

25 Bernice Gerard, untitled radio transcript, February 2, 1969, SPC BGC.

26 Michael Stamm, "Broadcasting Mainline Protestantism," 244.

27 Bernice Gerard, *Bernice Gerard*, 127.

28 "Home Cures 80 Per Cent of Addicts," *The Wayfarer*, March 3, 1966, 1.

29 Bernice Gerard, *Bernice Gerard*, 122.

30 Bernice Gerard, *Bernice Gerard*, 122.

31 For a brief biography, see "John Gimenez," Wikipedia, last edited May 30, 2020, https://en.wikipedia.org/wiki/John_Gimenez; a brief history is also provided at "About Us," Rock Church, accessed November 23, 2020, https://www.rockchurch.org/about.

32 "Pentecostal Chaplain Learned Students' Jargon," *Windsor Star*, August 26, 1968.

33 "Pentecostal Chaplain Learned Students' Jargon," *Windsor Star*, August 26, 1968.

34 "Ex-hippies Speak of New Life-Style," *Sunday Line* radio transcript, Radio CJOR, December 8, 1968, SPC BGC.

35 Bernice Gerard, "Bringing Christ on Campus," 1971, 4, SPC BGC.

36 Bruce Douville, "'And We've Got to Get Ourselves Back to the Garden': The Jesus People Movement in Toronto," *Historical Papers 2006: Canadian Society of Church History* (2006): 5–24.

37 "Ex-hippies Speak of New Life-Style," December 8, 1968.

38 "Ex-hippies Speak of New Life-Style," December 8, 1968.

39 "Ex-hippies Speak of New Life-Style," December 8, 1968.

40 "Ex-hippies Speak of New Life-Style," December 8, 1968.

41 "Ex-hippies Speak of New Life-Style," December 8, 1968.

42 "Ex-hippies Speak of New Life-Style," December 8, 1968.

43 "Ex-hippies Speak of New Life-Style," December 8, 1968.
44 "Ex-hippies Speak of New Life-Style," December 8, 1968.
45 "Ex-hippies Speak of New Life-Style," December 8, 1968.
46 "Ex-hippies Speak of New Life-Style," December 8, 1968.
47 Michael Stamm, "Broadcasting Mainline Protestantism," 249.
48 Michael Stamm, "Broadcasting Mainline Protestantism," 251.
49 Listener correspondence, quoted in Stamm, "Broadcasting Mainline Protestantism," 242.
50 Tona Hangen, *Redeeming the Dial*, 6.
51 Tona Hangen, *Redeeming the Dial*, 5.
52 "Dear Bernice," letter from a listener, December 1, 1979, SPC BGC. This writer supplied Gerard with their personal telephone number, probably hoping for a private telephone counselling conversation.
53 "Dear Bernice," letter from a listener, December 1, 1979.
54 "Dear Bernice," letter from a listener, December 1, 1979.
55 "Dear Pastor Bernice," letter from listener, October 11, 1977, SPC BGC. The signature on this letter makes it clear that it is the same person who wrote the December 13, 1973 letter.
56 "Dear Pastor Gerard," letter from listener, December 13, 1973, SPC BGC.
57 "Dear Pastor Bernice," letter from listener, October 11, 1977.
58 "Dear Pastor Bernice," letter from listener, October 11, 1977.
59 "Dear Pastor Bernice," letter from listener, October 11, 1977.
60 "Dear Pastor Bernice," letter from a listener, October 11, 1977.
61 "Dear Bernice," letter from listener, August [n.d.], SPC BGC.
62 "Dear Bernice," letter from listener, August [n.d.].
63 "Dear Bernice," letter from listener, August [n.d.].
64 "Dear Bernice," letter from listener, August [n.d.].
65 "Dear Miss Gerrard [*sic*]," letter from listener, December 12, 1977, SPC BGC.
66 "Dear Miss Gerrard," letter from listener, December 12, 1977.
67 "Dear Miss Gerrard," letter from listener, December 12, 1977.
68 "Miss Gerrad [*sic*]," letter from listener, November 27, 1978, SPC BGC.
69 "Miss Gerrad," letter from listener, November 27, 1978.
70 "Miss Gerrad," letter from listener, November 27, 1978.
71 "Sailors Describe Events Prior to Woman's Death," unidentified newspaper clipping, December 13, 1978, SPC BGC.
72 "Dear Bernice," letter from listener, July 10, 1974, SPC BGC.
73 "Dear Bernice," letter from listener, July 10, 1974.
74 "Dear Bernice," letter from logging camp worker, n.d. [April 1979], SPC BGC.
75 "Dear Bernice," letter from logging camp worker, n.d. [April 1979].
76 "Dear 'S,'" letter from Bernice Gerard to logging camp worker, April 19, 1979, SPC, BGC.
77 "Dear 'S,'" letter from Bernice Gerard to logging camp worker, April 19, 1979.
78 "Dear 'S,'" letter from Bernice Gerard to logging camp worker, April 19, 1979.
79 "Dear 'S,'" letter from Bernice Gerard to logging camp worker, April 19, 1979.
80 "Dear Bernice," letter from Vancouver listener, undated, SPC BGC.
81 "Dear Bernice," letter from listener, January 19, 1977, SPC BGC.
82 "Dear Bernice," letter from listener, January 19, 1977.
83 "Dear Bernice," letter from listener, January 19, 1977.

266   *Notes to pages 154–66*

84 "Dear Bernice," letter from listener, January 19, 1977.
85 "Dear Bernice," letter from listener, January 19, 1977.
86 "Dear Pastor Bernice," letter from listener, November 2, 1973, SPC BGC.
87 "Dear Pastor Bernice," letter from listener, November 2, 1973.
88 "Dear Pastor Bernice," letter from listener, November 2, 1973.

CHAPTER 8: CHALLENGING PATRIARCHAL AUTHORITIES

1 Bernice Gerard, *Bernice Gerard: Today and for Life* (Vancouver: Sunday Line Communications, 1988), 125.
2 Bernice Gerard, *Bernice Gerard*, 125.
3 Bernice Gerard, *Bernice Gerard*, 125.
4 Bernice Gerard, *Bernice Gerard*, 125.
5 Bernice Gerard, *Bernice Gerard*, 125.
6 Bernice Gerard, *Bernice Gerard*, 124–41.
7 P.D. Hocken, "Charismatic Movement," in *The New International Dictionary of Pentecostal and Charismatic Movements*, rev. ed., ed. Stanley M. Burgess and Eduard M. van der Maas (Grand Rapids, MI: Zondervan, 2003), 477.
8 P.D. Hocken, "Charismatic Movement," 514.
9 David Mainse, *100 Huntley Street: The Exciting Success Story from the Host of Canada's Popular Television Program* (Toronto: G.R. Welch, 1979), 147–48. For the reactions of classical Pentecostals to Mainse and his ecumenism, see Ewen H. Butler, *Canadian Winds of the Spirit: Holiness, Pentecostal, and Charismatic Currents* (Lexington, KY: Emeth Press, 2018), 97–124.
10 Ewen H. Butler, *Canadian Winds of the Spirit*, 218–19.
11 Bernice Gerard, quoted in "Pentecostal Chaplain Learned Students' Jargon," *Windsor Star* August 26, 1968.
12 James M. MacKnight to Pastor Justus T. du Plessis, September 24, 1987, uncatalogued, Summit Pacific College, Bernice Gerard Collection (hereafter SPC BGC).
13 Bernice Gerard to Rev. Ray Bringham, May 4, 1971, SPC BGC.
14 Bernice Gerard to Rev. Ray Bringham, May 4, 1971.
15 Bernice Gerard, *Bernice Gerard*, 131.
16 Bernice Gerard, *Bernice Gerard*, 131.
17 Bernice Gerard, *Bernice Gerard*, 131.
18 Bernice Gerard, *Bernice Gerard*, 131.
19 Bernice Gerard, *Bernice Gerard*, 132.
20 Bernice Gerard, *Bernice Gerard*, 132.
21 Bernice Gerard, *Bernice Gerard*, 132.
22 Bernice Gerard, *Bernice Gerard*, 132.
23 Bernice Gerard, *Bernice Gerard*, 139–40.
24 P.D. Hocken, "Ranaghan, Kevin Mathers (1940–), and Dorothy (1942–)," in *The New International Dictionary of Pentecostal and Charismatic Movements*, ed. Stanley M. Burgess and Eduard M. van der Maas, 1018.
25 F.M. Reynolds, "Wilkerson, David Ray," in *The New International Dictionary of Pentecostal and Charismatic Movements*, ed. Stanley M. Burgess and Eduard M. van der Maas, 1195–96.

26 R.P. Spittler, "Du Plessis, David Johannes," in *The New International Dictionary of Pentecostal and Charismatic Movements*, ed. Stanley M. Burgess and Eduard M. van der Maas, 589–93.

27 Joshua R. Ziefle, *David du Plessis and the Assemblies of God* (Leiden, NL: Brill, 2013). See especially 57–101. The Assemblies of God would eventually evolve in its views on the charismatic movement, and they took steps to reinstate du Plessis after he applied to have his ministerial credentials restored in 1980. Ziefle, 169–70.

28 Bernice Gerard, *Bernice Gerard*, 135.

29 Bernice Gerard, *Bernice Gerard*, 135.

30 Margaret English de Alminana and Lois E. Olena, eds., *Women in Pentecostal and Charismatic Ministry: Informing a Dialogue on Gender, Church, and Ministry* (Leiden, NL: Brill, 2017).

31 Michael Wilkinson and Linda M. Ambrose, *After the Revival: Pentecostalism and the Making of a Canadian Church* (Montreal/Kingston: McGill-Queen's University Press, 2020), 86–96.

32 "Influenced by Modern-Day Feminism," *Pentecostal Testimony*, April 1985, 43.

33 Allison E. Murray, "Building Biblical Manhood and Womanhood: White American Evangelical Complementarian Theology, 1970–2010" (PhD diss., University of Toronto, 2021); see also Linda M. Ambrose, "A Messy Mix: Religion, Feminism, and Pentecostals," *Gender & History* 34, 2 (2022): 369–83.

34 "Jesus Called Only Men," *Pentecostal Testimony*, April 1985, 44.

35 "Worldly Cover," *Pentecostal Testimony*, May 1985, 9. The letter was referencing the cover of the December 1984 issue of *Pentecostal Testimony*.

36 Bernice Gerard, *Bernice Gerard*, 144. The following paragraphs on Gerard's feminism were previously published in Linda M. Ambrose, "Canadian Pentecostal Women in Ministry: The Case of Bernice Gerard and Feminist Ideologies," in *Women in Pentecostal and Charismatic Ministry: Informing a Dialogue on Gender, Church, and Ministry*, ed. Margaret English de Alminana and Lois E. Olena, 229–46 (Leiden, NL: Brill, 2017).

37 Bernice Gerard, quoted in Colleen Slater-Smith, "Women's Lib ... Pentecostal Style," *The Leader-Post*, [Regina], August 24, 1974.

38 Bernice Gerard, quoted in Slater-Smith, "Women's Lib ... Pentecostal Style."

39 Bernice Gerard, quoted in Slater-Smith, "Women's Lib ... Pentecostal Style."

40 Slater-Smith, "Women's Lib ... Pentecostal Style."

41 Bernice Gerard, quoted in Slater-Smith, "Women's Lib ... Pentecostal Style."

42 General Conference Minutes, Pentecostal Assemblies of Canada, August 1974, 5–6, Pentecostal Assemblies of Canada Archives (hereafter PAOCA).

43 Homer Cantelon, *Shamgar: The Memories and Musings of Homer Cantelon* (Toronto: Harmony Printing, 1994).

44 General Conference Minutes, Pentecostal Assemblies of Canada, August 1976, 4, PAOCA.

45 General Conference Minutes, Pentecostal Assemblies of Canada, August 1976, 4.

46 For an example of the ongoing debates among evangelicals about women in the church, see Beth Allison Barr, *The Making of Biblical Womanhood: How the Subjugation of Women Became Gospel Truth* (Ada, MI: Brazos Press, 2021).

47 General Conference Minutes, Pentecostal Assemblies of Canada, August 1976, 4.

48 General Conference Minutes, Pentecostal Assemblies of Canada, August 1976, 4.

49 General Conference Minutes, Pentecostal Assemblies of Canada, August 1976, 4.

50 General Conference Minutes, Pentecostal Assemblies of Canada, August 1978, 22, PAOCA.

51 While the formal minutes do not give detail about who spoke in favour or against the motion, anecdotes abound.

52 General Conference Minutes, Pentecostal Assemblies of Canada, August 25, 1984, 13, PAOCA.

53 General Conference Minutes, Pentecostal Assemblies of Canada, August 27, 1984, 20, PAOCA. When voting resumed on other matters that afternoon, the roster committee confirmed that the total voting constituency was 458 people. Had they all been present and voting in the morning, 254 ballots would not have represented the required two-thirds majority.

54 General Conference Minutes, Pentecostal Assemblies of Canada, August 25, 1986, 29, PAOCA.

55 Jim Cantelon, interview by Zoom with author, October 22, 2020.

56 David Wells, interview by Zoom with author, September 17, 2020.

57 General Conference Minutes, Pentecostal Assemblies of Canada, 1988, 41–42, PAOCA.

58 General Conference Minutes, Pentecostal Assemblies of Canada, 1988, 41–42.

59 General Conference Minutes, Pentecostal Assemblies of Canada, 1988, 42.

60 In 2023, of 961 lead ministers, 62 were women (6.5 percent). Pentecostal Assemblies of Canada, "2023 Fellowship Statistics (As at 6 Feb 2024)," https://www.paoc.org/docs/default-source/fellowship-services-documents/fellowship-stats-2022-at-25-oct-2023-final.pdf?sfvrsn=b5e7fc6a_9.

61 General Executive members are listed on the PAOC website. By 2024, the number of women increased to six, but the total membership grew to 26. See: https://paoc.org/family/who-we-are/general-executive.

62 The Pentecostal Assemblies of Canada, "PAOC Statement of Affirmation Regarding the Equality of Men and Women in Leadership, June 2018," https://paoc.org/docs/default-source/church-toolbox/position-papers/statements/paoc-statement-of-affirmation-regarding-the-equality-of-women-and-men-in-leadership.pdf.

CHAPTER 9: FEMINISM, FOOTNOTES, AND FAMILY

1 Bernice Gerard, *Bernice Gerard: Today and for Life* (Vancouver: Sunday Line Communications, 1988), 142. Gerard told South Korean megachurch pastor, Dr. Paul Yonggi Cho, that she intended the account of her life in the second biography to be more of a record of her "intellectual and spiritual pilgrimage." Bernice Gerard to Dr. Paul Yonggi Cho, February 29, 1988, uncatalogued, Summit Pacific College, Bernice Gerard Collection (hereafter SPC BGC).

2 Bernice Gerard, *Bernice Gerard*, 144.

3 Bernice Gerard, *Bernice Gerard*, 150–51.

4 Bernice Gerard, *Bernice Gerard*, 147. Part of this chapter was previously published in Linda M. Ambrose, "Canadian Pentecostal Women in Ministry: The Case of Bernice Gerard and Feminist Ideologies" in *Women in Pentecostal and Charismatic Ministry: Informing a Dialogue on Gender, Church, and Ministry*, ed. Margaret English de Alminana and Lois Olena (Leiden, NL: Brill, 2016), 229–46.

5 Pamela Cochran, *Evangelical Feminism: A History* (New York: New York University Press, 2005), 1–2.

6 Pamela Cochran, *Evangelical Feminism*, 2.

7 Letha Scanzoni and Nancy Hardesty, *All We're Meant to Be: A Biblical Approach to Women's Liberation* (Waco, TX: Word Books, 1974).

8 Pamela Cochran, *Evangelical Feminism*, 23.

9 Letha Scanzoni and Nancy Hardesty, *All We're Meant to Be*, 11, quoted in Bernice Gerard, *Bernice Gerard*, 147.

10 For a series of blog entries explaining the 1970s context and the story behind the publication of *All We're Meant to Be*, see Letha Scanzoni, "Part 1. Coauthoring 'All We're Meant to Be' – The Beginning," *Letha's Calling* (blog), January 7, 2011, http://www.lethadawson scanzoni.com/2011/01/part-1-coauthoring-all-were-meant-to-be-the-beginning/.

11 Donald W. Dayton, "*Man as Male and Female*: A Review," *Daughters of Sarah* 1, 6, (September 1975): 5–8; the book being reviewed is Paul K. Jewett, *Man as Male and Female: A Study in Sexual Relationships from a Theological Point of View* (Grand Rapids, MI: Eerdmans, 1975).

12 Letha Scanzoni, "The Feminists and the Bible," *Christianity Today* (February 1973): 10–15.

13 Nellie McClung, quoted in Bernice Gerard, *Bernice Gerard*, 144.

14 Bernice Gerard, *Bernice Gerard*, 145.

15 Bernice Gerard, *Bernice Gerard*, 145.

16 Bernice Gerard, *Bernice Gerard*, 147.

17 Pamela Cochran, *Evangelical Feminism*, 4.

18 Bernice Gerard, *Bernice Gerard*, 155. Bernice admired the work of Charles Trombley, *Who Said Women Can't Teach?* (South Plainfield, NJ: Bridge Publishing, 1985).

19 See Pamela Cochran, "Is the Homosexual My Neighbour? The Crisis in Biblical Feminism," in *Evangelical Feminism*, 77–109.

20 Leonard J. Swidler, "Jesus Was a Feminist," *Catholic World* (January 1971): 177–83. The full text of the article is available at God's Word to Women, under Articles on Equality, http://www.godswordtowomen.org/feminist.htm.

21 Michael McAteer, "Woman Pentecostal May Rock the Boat," *Toronto Star*, August 16, 1980.

22 "Pentecostal Chaplain Learned Students' Jargon," *Windsor Star*, August 26, 1968.

23 "Pentecostal Chaplain Learned Students' Jargon," *Windsor Star*, August 26, 1968.

24 "Pentecostal Chaplain Learned Students' Jargon," *Windsor Star*, August 26, 1968.

25 Bernice Gerard, speaking notes for "Communicate in '68 W.M.C. Windsor August 24, 1968," SPC BGC.

26 Bernice Gerard, speaking notes for "Communicate in '68 W.M.C. Windsor August 24, 1968."

27 Bernice Gerard, speaking notes for "Communicate in '68 W.M.C. Windsor August 24, 1968."

28 Bernice Gerard, speaking notes for "Communicate in '68 W.M.C. Windsor August 24, 1968."

29 Canada, *The Report of the Royal Commission Report on the Status of Women in Canada* (Ottawa: Queen's Printer, 1970).

30 Germaine Greer, *The Female Eunuch* (London: Paladin, 1971). Gerard was drawing specifically from Greer's chapter titled "Security," 239–45.

31 Germaine Greer, *The Female Eunuch*, 241.

32 Germaine Greer, *The Female Eunuch*, 240, quoted in Bernice Gerard, sermon notes, "Diamonds are Forever," February 1972, SPC BGC.

33 Germaine Greer, *The Female Eunuch*, 244.

34 Bernice Gerard, speaking notes for "Communicate in '68."

35 Bernice Gerard, *Bernice Gerard*, 112.

36 Bernice Gerard, *Bernice Gerard*, 112.

37 Bernice Gerard, *Bernice Gerard*, 5.

38 "In Loving Memory Velma May Chapman, March 30, 1915 – May 22, 2007," funeral program, uncatalogued, SPC BGC.

39 See Find a Grave, database and images (https://www.findagrave.com/memorial/218783140/bernice-gerard: accessed April 12, 2024), memorial page for Rev Bernice Gerard (1923–1 Nov 2008), Find a Grave Memorial ID 218783140, citing Ocean View Burial Park, Burnaby, Greater Vancouver Regional District, British Columbia, Canada; Maintained by William Sloos (contributor 49009963).

40 Bernice Gerard, *Bernice Gerard*, 102.

41 "Jean Evelyn Roberts," July 20, 1983, Sermon Notes, Funeral Sermons, SPC BGC.

42 Bernice Gerard, *Bernice Gerard*, 111.

43 Bernice Gerard, *Bernice Gerard*, 111.

44 Bernice Gerard, *Bernice Gerard*, 136. A few pages earlier, Gerard wrote, "The student gathering was at my home, the Chapman residence in Oakridge," 124.

45 Chapman's first wife, Gladys Dawson Chapman, was seventeen years old in 1921, according to the Canadian census, and he was twenty years old.

46 A published report of the Price meetings recounted that following those meetings, Sunday attendance at Broadway Church was between five hundred and seven hundred people. See *Pentecostal Testimony*, June 1923, 5.

47 "In Memoriam, Richard Willcocks Chapman, 1901–1978," Sermon Notes, Funeral Sermons, SPC BGC.

48 "Funeral Service for Richard W. Chapman," June 15, 1978, Sermon Notes, Funeral Sermons, SPC BGC.

49 "Funeral Service for Richard W. Chapman," June 15, 1978.

50 "Vancouver, Fraserview Ground Breaking," *Pentecostal Testimony*, January 1980, 15.

51 The Reverend Bernice Gerard, obituary, *Vancouver Sun*, November 11, 2008, http://www.legacy.com/obituaries/vancouversun/obituary.aspx?pid=120061573.

52 Bernice M. Gerard, *The Holy Land: Guide to Faith!* (Jacksonville, FL: McColl-Gerard Publications, n.d. [c. 1950s]), 4.

53 "Anita Bryant, Speaker at Pacific National Exhibition," advertisement in *Coast News*, August 22, 1968.

54 David Mainse, *100 Huntley Street*, (Toronto: G.R. Welch, 1979), 1–2, 156–58. Mainse held to a consistent antigay position throughout his public ministry and faced opposition because of it, particularly when his own brother-in-law, Ralph Rutledge, a PAOC pastor of the Queensway Cathedral in Toronto, was disciplined by the denomination and stripped of his ordination credentials because of homosexual activity. George C. Hartwell, "Rev Ralph Rutledge Pastor Queensway Scandal," *Heal My Life* (blog), December 6, 2009, https://healmylife.blogspot.com/2009/12/rev-ralph-rutledge-pastor-queensway.html.

55 Bernice Gerard, *Bernice Gerard*, 197.

56 Bernice Gerard, *Bernice Gerard*, 197.

57 Bernice Gerard, *Bernice Gerard*, 197.

58 Bernice Gerard, *Bernice Gerard*, 197.

59 "The name Anita Bryant is synonymous with homophobic vitriol," according to Molly Sprayregen in "Anita Bryant Devoted Her Life to Terrorizing LGBTQ+ People. Now She Has a Bisexual Granddaughter," *them*, July 29, 2021, "https://www.them.us/story/

anita-bryant-lesbian-granddaughter; Carolyn Tien, "Granddaughter of Famed Anti-Gay Activist Announces Engagement to Woman," *Newsweek,* July 28, 2021, updated July 30, 2021, https://www.newsweek.com/granddaughter-famed-anti-gay-activist-announces -engagement-woman-1614006.

60 Cameron Duder, *Awfully Devoted Women: Lesbian Lives in Canada, 1900–65* (Vancouver: UBC Press, 2010), 10.

61 For more on using "a queer eye" to read sources, see Valerie Korinek, "'Don't Let Your Girlfriend Ruin Your Marriage': Lesbian Imagery in *Chatelaine* Magazine, 1950–1969," *Journal of Canadian Studies* 33, 3 (1998): 83–109.

62 In the fall of 2020, I spoke with four individuals who each offered some insight into Bernice and Velma's relationship: Brian Stiller, David Wells, Susan Wells, and Jim Cantelon. Each of these informants was influenced by Bernice Gerard; some of them worked closely with her and all share a deep respect for her personal integrity, her indefatigable ministry, and her legacy.

63 See Linda M. Ambrose, "You Preach like a Man: Beyond the Typical Gender Roles of Canadian Pentecostalism," in *Pentecostal World,* ed. Michael Wilkinson and Jörg Haustein (Abingdon, UK: Routledge, 2023), 253–63.

64 Cameron Duder, *Awfully Devoted Women,* 11.

65 Cameron Duder, *Awfully Devoted Women,* 16.

66 See "Pastoral Reflection on Human Sexuality," February 7, 2017, General Executive Fonds, Pentecostal Assemblies of Canada Archives; and Mark A.C. Jennings, "Impossible Subjects: LGBTIQ Experiences in Australian Pentecostal-Charismatic Churches," *Religions* 9, 53 (2018): doi:10.3390/rel902053.

Chapter 10: Public Engagement

1 "Anti-porn Queen Bernice Gerard & Other New Rightists on City Council," *Georgia Straight* 11, 480 (January 27–February 2, 1977): cover.

2 Bernice Gerard, *Bernice Gerard: Today and For Life* (Vancouver: Sunday Line Communications, 1988), 199–200.

3 In this regard, Gerard's political life stands in contrast to other BC women in politics including the pioneering Canadian suffragist and politician Laura Jamieson whose biographer observed that while she "was intrigued by faith as a guide to individual ethics, religion appeared at most a flirtation to this committed socialist." Veronica Strong-Boag, *The Last Suffragist Standing: The Life and Times of Laura Marshall Jamieson* (Vancouver: UBC Press, 2018), 202. For Gerard, the opposite was true: she was intrigued by politics as a means to express her religious beliefs and reinforce conservative public morality. But elected political office was only a flirtation for this committed Pentecostal.

4 Sam Reimer, *Evangelicals and the Continental Divide: The Conservative Protestant Subculture in Canada and the United States* (Montreal/Kingston: McGill-Queen's University Press, 2003).

5 David Mainse, *Impact Canada 100: Taking the Spiritual and Moral Pulse of Our Nation* (Burlington, ON: Crossroads, 1992); Michael Wilkinson and Linda M. Ambrose, *After the Revival: The Making of a Canadian Church* (Montreal/Kingston: McGill-Queen's University Press, 2020), 118–22.

6 Jean Barman, *The West beyond the West: A History of British Columbia* (Toronto: University of Toronto Press, 1995), 372.

7 Robert A.J. McDonald, *A Long Way to Paradise: A New History of British Columbia Politics* (Vancouver: UBC Press, 2021), 6.

8 Robert A.J. McDonald, *A Long Way to Paradise,* 315.

9 Robert A.J. McDonald, *A Long Way to Paradise,* 6.

10 Robert A.J. McDonald, *A Long Way to Paradise,* 315.

11 Robert A.J. McDonald, *A Long Way to Paradise,* 6.

12 "5,000 Could Come Here: Hand Held Out to Refugees," *Vancouver Sun,* July 13, 1979.

13 Linda Hossie, "Abused Electorate Sent Volrich a Message," *Vancouver Sun,* November 20, 1980.

14 Daniel Francis, *Becoming Vancouver: A History* (Madeira Park, BC: Harbour Publishing, 2021), 192.

15 Linda Hossie, "Abused Electorate Sent Volrich a Message," *Vancouver Sun,* November 20, 1980.

16 Randy Glover, "City Votes to Keep 3 Hangars but Issue Still Not Resolved," *Vancouver Sun,* September 14, 1977.

17 The Vancouver housing complex Gerard established still operates. See the Shiloh Housing Society website, last accessed February 27, 2023, https://shilohhousing.ca.

18 Linda Hossie, "Abused Electorate Sent Volrich a Message," *Vancouver Sun,* November 20, 1980.

19 Daniel Francis, *Becoming Vancouver,* 257.

20 Ros Oberlyn, "Gerard Out to Change Image of the NPA," *Vancouver Sun,* November 19, 1976.

21 Ros Oberlyn, "Gerard Out to Change Image of the NPA," 6.

22 Bernice Gerard, quoted in Ros Oberlyn, "Gerard Out to Change Image of the NPA," 6.

23 Bernice Gerard, quoted in Ros Oberlyn, "Gerard Out to Change Image of the NPA," 6.

24 Bernice Gerard, quoted in Ros Oberlyn, "Gerard Out to Change Image of the NPA," 6.

25 "Vancouver Voters' Reward: Motley Rightists Join City Council," *Georgia Straight,* January 27–February 3, 1977.

26 Daniel Francis, *Becoming Vancouver,* 272; David Ley, "Liberal Ideology and the Post-Industrial City," *Annals of the Association of American Geographers* 70, 2 (1980): 238–58.

27 Bernice Gerard, *Bernice Gerard: Today and for Life* (Vancouver: Sunday Line Communications, 1988), 183.

28 Michael Wilkinson, "Social Concerns, the Religious Right, and the Pentecostal Assemblies of Canada in the 1980s," paper presented at the Annual Meeting, Society for Pentecostal Studies, Springfield, Missouri, March 6–8, 2014.

29 "Marguerite Ford, Alderwoman," file 17–32, Vancouver Status of Women fonds, Rare Books & Special Collections and University Archives, University of British Columbia.

30 Mayor Jack Volrich to Chief Constable Winterton, July 11, 1977, File 119: Wreck Beach 1977 & 1978, 48-G-3, City of Vancouver Archives (hereafter COVA).

31 T. Dixon, Acting Chief Constable, Vancouver Police Department to Mr. Mayor J.J. Volrich, July 15, 1977, File 119, Wreck Beach 1977 & 1978, 48-G-3, COVA.

32 T. Dixon, Acting Chief Constable, Vancouver Police Department to Mr. Mayor J.J. Volrich, July 15, 1977.

33 T. Dixon, Acting Chief Constable, Vancouver Police Department to Mr. Mayor J.J. Volrich, July 15, 1977.

34 (Mrs.) D. Mansell to Dear Mr. Volrich, July 16, 1977; Mr. & Mrs. R. Corus, n.d. [August] 1977; Dan Gardener to Mayor Jack Volrich, July 27, 1977; H. Ramsey to Dear Mayor Volrich, July 11, 1977; Hector Ford to Mayor Jack Volrich, July 14, 1977, File 119: Wreck Beach, COVA.

35 (Mrs.) D. Mansell to Dear Mr. Volrich, July 16, 1977, File 119: Wreck Beach, COVA.

36 Mr. & Mrs. K.L. Harding to The Mayor & City Council, September 6, 1977, File 119: Wreck Beach, COVA.

37 Dan Gardener to Mayor Jack Volrich, July 27, 1977, File 119: Wreck Beach, COVA.

38 (Mrs.) D. Mansell, to Dear Mr. Volrich, July 16, 1977, File 119: Wreck Beach, COVA.

39 Mary-Ann Shantz, *What Nudism Exposes: An Unconventional History of Postwar Canada,* (Vancouver: UBC Press, 2022), 15.

40 W.N. Longtin, to Mr. Volrich, Mayor of Vancouver, August 2, 1977, File 119: Wreck Beach, COVA.

41 Elizabeth van der Eeden to Dear Mayor, August 9, 1977, File 119: Wreck Beach, COVA.

42 Emily Sion, to Dear Mayor Volrich, September 9, 1977, File 119: Wreck Beach, COVA.

43 L. Zimmerman to Mayor Jack Volrich, August 4, 1977, File 119: Wreck Beach, COVA.

44 E.M. Handy to Major J. Volrich, August 22, 1977, File: Wreck Beach, COVA.

45 Emily Sion to Dear Mayor Volrich, September 9, 1977.

46 Emily Sion to Dear Mayor Volrich, September 9, 1977.

47 Bernice Gerard, "It's Time to Speak Out," transcript, Evening Speaker, Pentecostal Assemblies of Canada General Conference, Saint John, New Brunswick, Spring 1984, 13, Pentecostal Assemblies of Canada Archives.

48 Bernice Gerard, "It's Time to Speak Out," 13.

49 "Protest – A 1981 Short about a Protest against the Film *Caligula* Being Shown in Vancouver," YouTube, posted by BC History, 8:51, accessed April 6, 2022, https://www.youtube.com/watch?v=drSY72BSaQM.

50 Bernice Gerard, *Bernice Gerard,* 182.

51 Bernice Gerard, *Bernice Gerard,* 198.

52 Michael Wilkinson and Linda M. Ambrose, *After the Revival,* 107–28.

53 Brian Stiller, interview with the author, August 20, 2020.

54 Sam Reimer, *Evangelicals and the Continental Divide,* 136. Sometimes the religious right in Canada has expressed its concerns as protecting religious freedom. For a book from this perspective, see Janet Epp Buckingham, *Fighting over God: A Legal and Political History of Religious Freedom in Canada* (Montreal/Kingston: McGill-Queen's University Press, 2014).

55 Michael Wilkinson and Linda M. Ambrose, *After the Revival,* 112.

56 Brenda Cossman et al., *Bad Attitude(s) on Trial: Pornography, Feminism, and the Butler Decision* (Toronto: University of Toronto Press, 1997).

57 Bernice Gerard, *Bernice Gerard,* 183–84.

58 John Faustman, "Avenging Angel in 'Loose City,'" *Vancouver Courier,* July 25, 1979.

59 Bernice Gerard, *Bernice Gerard,* 184.

60 Len Norris editorial cartoon, *Vancouver Sun,* August 16, 1977, 4.

61 Bernice Gerard, "It's Time to Speak Out," 17.

62 Bernice Gerard, It's Time to Speak Out," 17. For more on the British "Festival of Light" see John Capon, *And There Was Light: The Story of the Nationwide Festival of Light*

(London: Lutterworth, 1972); and Amy C. Whipple "Speaking for Whom? The 1971 Festival of Light and the Search for the 'Silent Majority,'" *Contemporary British History* 24, 3 (2010): 319–39.

63 Bernice Gerard, "It's Time to Speak Out," 19.

64 Bernice Gerard, *Bernice Gerard*, 184.

65 Bernice Gerard, *Bernice Gerard*, 183–84.

66 Bernice Gerard, sermon notes, "Too Much Wilderness, Too Few Prophets," Fraserview Assembly, October 1973, Summit Pacific College, Bernice Gerard Collection.

67 Bernice Gerard, *Bernice Gerard*, 184.

68 Bernice Gerard, "Too Much Wilderness, Too Few Prophets."

69 Bernice Gerard, *Bernice Gerard*, 184.

70 Bernice Gerard, "It's Time to Speak Out."

71 Bernice Gerard, "Too Much Wilderness, Too Few Prophets," 10.

72 Bernice Gerard, *Bernice Gerard*, 186.

73 Bernice Gerard, "It's Time to Speak Out," 14.

74 Bernice Gerard, *Bernice Gerard*, 185.

75 Bernice Gerard, *Bernice Gerard*, 185.

76 S.M. Burgess, "Neocharismatics," *The New International Dictionary of Pentecostal and Charismatic Movements*, rev. ed., ed. Stanley M. Burgess and Eduard M. van der Maas (Grand Rapids, MI: Zondervan, 2003), 928.

77 Bernice Gerard, "It's Time to Speak Out," 20–25. For more on John Wimber, see Michael Wilkinson and Peter Althouse, *Catch the Fire: Soaking Prayer and Charismatic Renewal* (Dekalb: Northern Illinois University Press, 2014), 29–33; and C.P. Wagner, "Wimber, John (1934–98)," in *The New International Dictionary of Pentecostal and Charismatic Movements*, rev. ed., ed. Stanley M. Burgess and Eduard M. van der Maas (Grand Rapids, MI: Zondervan, 2003), 1199–200.

78 Anonymous, in conversation with the author, fall 2020.

79 See for example, "Protest – A 1981 Short about a Protest against the Film *Caligula* Being Shown in Vancouver," 8min, 51 seconds, YouTube, last accessed December 10, 2020, https://www.youtube.com/watch?v=drSY72BSaQM.

80 Bernice Gerard, *Bernice Gerard*, 220.

81 Bernice Gerard, *Bernice Gerard*, 222–23.

82 Bernice Gerard, "It's Time to Speak Out," 20.

83 Becki L. Ross, *Burlesque West: Showgirls, Sex, and Sin in Postwar Vancouver* (Toronto: University of Toronto Press, 2009), 220.

84 Becki L. Ross, *Burlesque West*, 219.

85 Becki L. Ross, *Burlesque West*, 220.

86 Becki L. Ross, *Burlesque West*, 220–21.

87 Bernice Gerard, *Bernice Gerard*, 183.

88 Bernice Gerard, "It's Time to Speak Out," 20.

89 Bernice Gerard, "It's Time to Speak Out," 20.

Conclusion

1 Douglas Todd, "British Columbia's 25 Most Influential Spiritual Leaders," *Vancouver Sun*, April 21, 2000.

2 Alex Strohschein, replied to a post by the author on social media platform X, April 10, 2024, reporting that "the 'G House' at UBC was just demolished a few weeks ago."

3 Reports filed with Revenue Canada reveal that Sunday Line Communications typically disperses more than 50 percent of its revenues to other registered charities and qualified donees, while the remainder of its income finances the operation with a modest compensation for the part-time role of the director, occupancy costs, office supplies, professional and consultant services, and other expenditures. The local, national, and international organizations that have benefited from this generosity include the PAOC; ERDO, an emergency relief agency under the auspices of the PAOC; Watoto Child Care Ministries in Uganda; GCM, a global communication ministry; Metro Kids, a Vancouver group working with inner-city children; Villages of Hope Africa, based in Zambia; Calcutta Mercy, a group working with children and founded by PAOC missionaries Mark and Huldah Buntain; Classrooms for Africa; and The Crossing Church, a PAOC congregation in Surrey, BC. The specific amounts vary from year to year, but the detailed taxation information that Sunday Line Communications Society files annually is available on the website of the Revenue Canada Agency, "Charities and Giving," https://apps.cra-arc.gc.ca/ebci/hacc/srch/pub/dsplyBscSrch.

4 For reports and news from the ministries that Sunday Line supports, see the website section "Our Partner Ministries," last accessed March 9, 2024, https://www.sundayline.com/partners/index.php.

5 Gerard emphasized that her own experiences in foster care with families who gave her constant reminders of her "welfare case" status by withholding the best foods and personal care items made her determined to always be generous and hospitable in her own home later in life. Bernice Gerard, *Bernice Gerard*, 73.

6 See House of Hope website, https://www.hohbethlehem.org/ (last accessed November 19, 2020).

7 Gerard recounted the night that she went to the altar for prayer about her sight. "Before I reached the altar ... I knew that I was healed. That night, without glasses, I could read the small typewritten words of the song book on the music stand across the vibra harp. I was healed, and was glad to share my good news with the hundreds in attendance ... the healing lasted a good twenty years. Though I wear glasses now, my eyes are in good condition; it's my age that makes the difference." Bernice Gerard, *Bernice Gerard*, 98.

8 John A. Anonby, Department of English, Trinity Western University, to Bernice Gerard, March 2, 1988, uncatalogued, Summit Pacific College, Bernice Gerard Collection.

9 John A. Anonby, Department of English, Trinity Western University, to Bernice Gerard, March 2, 1988.

10 Karen Lamb, "Will the Real Subject Please Stand Up? Autobiographical Voices in Biography," *Life Writing* 18, 1 (2021): 29.

11 Karen Lamb, "Will the Real Subject Please Stand Up?", 29.

12 Two such people spring immediately to mind because of their recent publications: Michael Coren, *The Rebel Christ* (Toronto: Dundurn Press, 2021); and Brian D. McLaren, *Faith after Doubt: Why Your Beliefs Stopped Working and What to Do about It* (New York: St. Martin's Essentials, 2021), and Brian D. McLaren, *Do I Stay Christian? A Guide for the Doubters, the Disappointed, and the Disillusioned* (New York: St. Martin's Essentials, 2022).

13 As she always insisted, technically Gerard did not take her famous walk along Wreck Beach itself, but along an adjoining beach just a little farther down the shore.

BIBLIOGRAPHY

PRIMARY SOURCES

Newspapers

Georgia Straight
Pentecostal Testimony
The Province
Toronto Star
Ubyssey
Vancouver Province
Vancouver Sun

Archives

Summit Pacific College (SPC)
Bernice Gerard Collection

Pentecostal Assemblies of Canada Archives (PAOC)
Clergy Files

City of Vancouver Archives (COVA)
Abortion
Wreck Beach

University of British Columbia Archives
University Senate
Vancouver Status of Women

Interviews with the Author

Brian Stiller, August 20, 2020, by Zoom.
David Wells, September 17, 2020, by Zoom.
Susan P. Wells, September 22, 2020, by Zoom.
Jim Cantelon, October 22, 2020, by Zoom.

Gerard's Publications

Gerard, Bernice. *Bernice Gerard: Today and for Life*. Vancouver: Sunday Line Communications, 1988.
—. *Converted in the Country: The Life Story of Bernice Gerard*. Jacksonville, FL: McColl-Gerard Publications, 1956.
Gerard, Bernice M. *The Holy Land: Guide to Faith!* Jacksonville, FL: McColl-Gerard Publications, n.d. [c. 1950s].
—. "Milton's Orthodoxy and Its Relation to the Form of *Paradise Lost*." Master's thesis, University of British Columbia, 1967. https://open.library.ubc.ca/cIRcle/collections/ubctheses/831/items/1.0093631.

SECONDARY SOURCES

Airhart, Phyllis D. *A Church with the Soul of a Nation: Making and Remaking the United Church of Canada*. Montreal/Kingston: McGill-Queen's University Press, 2014.
Albrecht, Dan. *Rites in the Spirit: A Ritual Approach to Pentecostal/Charismatic Spirituality*. Sheffield, UK: Sheffield Academic Press, 1999.
Alexander, Bobby C. "Pentecostal Ritual Reconsidered: Anti-structural Dimensions of Possession." *Journal of Ritual Studies* 3, 1 (1989): 109–16.
Alexander, Estrelda. *Black Fire: One Hundred Years of African American Pentecostalism*. Downers Grove, IL: InterVarsity Press Academic, 2011.
—. *Limited Liberty: The Legacy of Four Pentecostal Women Pioneers*. Cleveland, OH: Pilgrim Press, 2008.
—. *The Women of Azusa Street*. Cleveland, OH: Pilgrim Press, 2005.
—, and Amos Yong, eds. *Philip's Daughters: Women in Pentecostal-Charismatic Leadership*. Eugene, OR: Pickwick Publications, 2009.
Alexander, Kimberly Ervin, and James P. Bowers. *What Women Want: Pentecostal Women Speak for Themselves*. Lanham, MD: Seymour Press, 2013.
Allen, Robert Thomas. *My Childhood and Yours: Happy Memories of Growing Up*. Toronto: Macmillan, 1977.
Allitt, Patrick. *Religion in America since 1945: A History*. New York: Columbia University Press, 2003.
Ambrose, Linda M. "Aimee Semple McPherson: Gender Theory, Worship, and the Arts." *Pneuma: The Journal of the Society for Pentecostal Studies* 39 (2017): 105–22.
—. "Canadian Pentecostal Women in Ministry: The Case of Bernice Gerard and Feminist Ideologies." In *Women in Pentecostal and Charismatic Ministry: Informing a Dialogue on Gender, Church, and Ministry*, edited by Margaret English de Alminana and Lois Olena, 229–46. Leiden, NL: Brill, 2016.

—. "Gender." In *Brill's Encyclopedia of Global Pentecostalism*, edited by Michael Wilkinson, 244–48. Leiden, NL: Brill, 2021.

—. "Gender History in Newfoundland Pentecostalism: Alice Belle Garrigus and Beyond." *PentecoStudies* 15, 2 (2016): 172–99.

—. "A Messy Mix: Religion, Feminism, and Pentecostals." *Gender & History* 34, 2 (2022): 369–83.

—. "Pentecostal Historiography in Canada: The History behind the Histories." *Canadian Journal of Pentecostal-Charismatic Christianity* 10 (2019): 15–36.

—. "Principal Purdie Objects: Canadian Pentecostal Students and Conscription during World War Two." In *Worth Fighting For: Canada's Tradition of War Resistance from 1812 to the War on Terror*, edited by Lara Campbell, Michael Dawson, and Catherine Gidney, 106–17. Toronto: Between the Lines, 2015.

—. "'Shaming the Men into Keeping Up with the Ladies': Constructing Pentecostal Masculinities." In *Sisters, Mothers, Daughters: Pentecostal Perspectives on Violence against Women*, edited by Kimberly Ervin Alexander, Melissa L. Archer, Mark J. Cartledge, and Michael D. Palmer, 69–85. Leiden, NL: Brill, 2022.

—. "You Preach like a Man: Beyond the Typical Gender Roles of Canadian Pentecostalism." In *The Pentecostal World*, edited by Michael Wilkinson and Jörg Haustein, 253–63. Abingdon, UK: Routledge, 2023.

—, Tina Block, and Lynne Marks. "Forum Introduction: Challenging Orthodoxies: Religion, Secularism, and Feminism among English-Canadian Women, 1960s–1990s." *Gender & History* 34, 2 (2022): 317–24.

Anastakis, Dimitry, ed. *The Sixties: Passion, Politics and Style*. Montreal/Kingston: McGill-Queen's University Press, 2008.

Anderson, Allan. *Spreading Fires: The Missionary Nature of Early Pentecostalism*. Maryknoll, NY: Orbis Books, 2007.

—. *To the Ends of the Earth: Pentecostalism and the Transformation of World Christianity*. Oxford: Oxford University Press, 2013.

—, Michael Bergunder, André Droogers, and Cornelius van der Laan, eds. *Studying Global Pentecostalism: Theories and Methods*. Berkeley: University of California Press, 2010.

Andersson, Greger. "To Live the Biblical Narratives: Pentecostal Autobiographies and the Baptism in the Spirit." *PentecoStudies* 13, 1 (2014): 112–27.

Andrews, William L., ed. *Sisters of the Spirit: Three Black Women's Autobiographies of the Nineteenth Century*. Bloomington: Indiana University Press, 1986.

Angus, Anne Margaret. *Children's Aid Society of Vancouver, B.C., 1901–1951*. Vancouver: Vancouver Children's Aid, 1951.

Artman, Amy. *Miracle Lady: Kathryn Kuhlman and the Transformation of Charismatic Christianity*. Grand Rapids, MI: Eerdmans Publishing, 2019.

Atter, Gordon F. *The Third Force*. Caledonia, ON: Acts Books; Peterborough, ON: College Press, 1962.

Avishai, Orit. "'Doing Religion' in a Secular World: Women in Conservative Religions and the Question of Agency." *Gender & Society* 22, 4 (August 2008): 409–33.

—. "Theorizing Gender from Religion Cases: Agency, Feminist Activism, and Masculinity." *Sociology of Religion: A Quarterly Review* 77, 3 (2016): 261–79.

Bahr, Robert. *Least of All Saints: The Story of Aimee Semple McPherson*. Lincoln, NE: Authors Guild/Backinprint.com, 2000.

Bibliography

Barfoot, Charles H., and Gerald T. Sheppard. "Prophetic vs. Priestly Religion: The Changing Role of Women Clergy in Classical Pentecostal Churches." *Review of Religious Research* 22 (1980): 2–17.

Barman, Jean. *The West beyond the West: A History of British Columbia.* Rev. ed. Toronto: University of Toronto Press, 1996.

Barr, Beth Allison. *The Making of Biblical Womanhood: How the Subjugation of Women Became Gospel Truth.* Ada, MI: Brazos Press, 2021.

Bass, Diana Butler. *Christianity after Religion: The End of Church and the Birth of a Spiritual Awakening.* New York: Harper One, 2013.

—. *Freeing Jesus: Rediscovering Jesus as Friend, Teacher, Savior, Lord, Way, and Presence.* New York: HarperOne, 2021.

Bendroth, Margaret Lambeth. *Fundamentalism and Gender: 1875 to the Present.* New York: Yale University Press, 1996.

Bennett, Jean. "Development of Social Services in the Okanagan, 1930–1980." In *Forty-Fifth Annual Report of the Okanagan Historical Society,* 20–25. Okanagan Historical Society, 1981. https://dx.doi.org/10.14288/1.0132223.

Berktay, Fatmagul. *Women and Religion.* Montreal: Black Rose Books, 1998.

Bessey, Sarah. *Jesus Feminist: An Invitation to Revisit the Bible's View of Women.* New York: Howard Books, 2013.

Billingsley, Scott. *It's a New Day: Race and Gender in the Modern Charismatic Movement.* Tuscaloosa: University of Alabama Press, 2009.

Block, Tina. *The Secular North-West: Religion and Irreligion in Everyday Postwar Life.* Vancouver: UBC Press, 2017.

Blumhofer, Edith. *Aimee Semple McPherson: Everybody's Sister.* Grand Rapids, MI: Eerdmans, 1993

Blumhofer, Edith L. *Restoring the Faith: The Assemblies of God, Pentecostalism, and American Culture.* Urbana: University of Illinois Press, 1993.

Booth, Catherine. *Female Ministry; or, Woman's Right to Preach the Gospel.* New York: Salvation Army Supplies Printing and Publishing Department, 1859.

Bracco, Katrysha. "Patriarchy and the Law of Adoption: Beneath the Best Interests of the Child." *Alberta Law Review* 35, 4 (1997): 1035–56.

Bramadat, Paul, Patricia O'Connell Killen, and Sarah Wilkins-Laflamme, eds. *Religion at the Edge: Nature, Spirituality, and Secularity in the Pacific Northwest.* Vancouver: UBC Press, 2022.

Brereton, Virginia Lieson. *From Sin to Salvation: Stories of Women's Conversions, 1800 to the Present.* Bloomington: Indiana University Press, 1991.

—. *Training God's Army: The American Bible School, 1880–1940.* Bloomington: Indiana University Press, 1990.

Brookfield, Tarah. "History of Adoption and Fostering in Canada." *Oxford Bibliographies.* https://www.oxfordbibliographies.com/display/document/obo-9780199791231/obo-9780199791231-0157.xml. Last modified Jul 25, 2023.

Brouwer, Ruth Compton. "Transcending the 'Unacknowledged Quarantine': Putting Religion into English-Canadian Women's History." *Journal of Canadian Studies* 17, 3 (1992): 47–61.

Brown, Candy Gunther. "Pentecostal Power: The Politics of Divine Healing Practices." *PentecoStudies* 13, 1 (2014): 35–57.

Bruneau, William A. *A Matter of Identities: A History of the UBC Faculty Association, 1920–1990*. Vancouver: UBC Faculty Association, 1990.

–. "Toward a New Collective Biography: The University of British Columbia Professoriate, 1915–1945." *Canadian Journal of Education* 19, 1 (1994): 65–79.

Bruno-Jofré, Rosa, Heidi MacDonald, and Elizabeth Smyth. *Vatican II and Beyond: The Changing Mission and Identity of Canadian Women Religious*. Toronto/Kingston: McGill-Queen's University Press, 2017.

Brusco, Elizabeth. "Gender and Power." In *Studying Global Pentecostalism: Theories and Methods*, edited by Allan Anderson and Michael Bergunder, 74–92. Berkeley: University of California Press, 2010.

–. *The Reformation of Machismo: Evangelical Conversion and Gender in Colombia*. Austin: University of Texas Press, 1995.

Buckingham, Janet Epp. *Fighting over God: A Legal and Political History of Religious Freedom in Canada*. Montreal/Kingston: McGill-Queen's University Press, 2014.

Burgess, Stanley M., and Eduard M. van der Maas, eds. *The New International Dictionary of Pentecostal and Charismatic Movements*. Rev. ed. Grand Rapids, MI: Zondervan, 2003.

Burke, Sara. "The Berkeley of Sudbury: Finding a Voice, 1960–1972." In *Laurentian University: A History*, edited Linda M. Ambrose et al., 155–72. Montreal/Kingston: McGill-Queen's University Press, 2010.

Burkinshaw, Robert. "Evangelicalism in British Columbia: Conservatism and Adaptability." *Journal of the Canadian Church Historical Society* 38 (1996): 77–100.

–. *Pilgrims in Lotus Land: Conservative Protestantism in British Columbia, 1917–1981*. Montreal/Kingston: McGill-Queen's University Press, 1995.

Bushnell, Katharine C. *God's Word to Women: The Women's Correspondence Bible Class*. London: Women's Correspondence Bible Class, 1912.

Butler, Anthea. *Women in the Church of God in Christ: Making a Sanctified World*. Chapel Hill, NC: University of North Carolina Press, 2007.

Butler, Ewen H. *Canadian Winds of the Spirit: Holiness, Pentecostal and Charismatic Currents*. Lexington, KY: Emeth Press, 2018.

Cain, Barbara. *Biography and History*. London: Red Globe Press, 2019.

Callahan, Marilyn, and Christopher Walmsley. "Rethinking Child Welfare Reform in British Columbia, 1900–1960." In *People, Politics, and Child Welfare in British Columbia*, edited by Leslie T. Foster and Brian Wharf, 10–33. Vancouver: UBC Press, 2007.

Campbell, Lara A., Dominque Clement, and Gregory S. Kealey, eds. *Debating Dissent: Canada and the 1960s*. Toronto: University of Toronto Press, 2012.

Cantelon, Homer. *Shamgar: The Memories and Musings of Homer Cantelon*. Toronto: Harmony Printing, 1994.

Carpenter, Joel A. *Revive Us Again: The Reawakening of American Fundamentalism*. New York: Oxford University Press, 1997.

Carter, Sarah, and Nanci Langford, eds. *Compelled to Act: Histories of Women's Activism in Western Canada*. Winnipeg: University of Manitoba Press, 2020.

Cartledge, Mark. *Testimony in the Spirit: Rescripting Ordinary Pentecostal Theology*. London: Ashgate, 2010.

Casanova, José. *Public Religions in the Modern World*. Chicago: University of Chicago Press, 1994.

Chapman, Mark D. "Review of *Religion, Globalization and Culture,* by Peter Beyer and Lori Beaman, eds." *Studies in Religion* 39, 2 (2010): 302–4.

Charette, Blaine. "Rethinking Cultural Engagement: Reflections on the God's Not Dead Franchise." *Canadian Journal of Pentecostal-Charismatic Christianity* 8 (2017): 59–69.

Chesler, Phyllis. *Women and Madness.* Garden City, NY: Doubleday, 1972.

Chong, Kelly H. *Deliverance and Submission: Evangelical Women and the Negotiation of Patriarchy in South Korea.* Cambridge, MA: Harvard University Asia Center, 2008.

Christie, Nancy, and Michael Gauvreau. *Christian Churches and Their Peoples, 1840–1965: A Social History of Religion in Canada.* Toronto: University of Toronto Press, 2010.

Clark, David L. "'Miracles for a Dime': From Chautauqua Tent to Radio Station with Sister Aimee." *California History* 57, 4 (Winter 1978/1979): 354–63.

Clarke, Brian, and Stuart Macdonald. *Leaving Christianity: Changing Allegiances in Canada since 1945.* Montreal/Kingston: McGill-Queen's University Press, 2017.

Clements, William M. "The Rhetoric of the Radio Ministry." *Journal of American Folklore* 87, 346 (1974): 318–27.

Cochran, Pamela D.H. *Evangelical Feminism: A History.* New York: New York University Press, 2005.

Collins, Kenneth J. *Power, Politics and the Fragmentation of Evangelicalism: From the Scopes Monkey Trial to the Obama Administration.* Downers Grove, IL: InterVarsity Press Academic, 2012.

Comacchio, Cynthia. *Nations Are Built of Babies: Saving Ontario's Mothers and Children, 1900–1940.* Montreal/Kingston: McGill-Queen's University Press, 1993.

Coren, Michael. *The Rebel Christ.* Toronto: Dundurn Press, 2021.

Cossman, Brenda, Shannon Bell, Lise Gotelle, and Becki L. Ross. *Bad Attitude(s) on Trial: Pornography, Feminism, and the Butler Decision.* Toronto: University of Toronto Press, 1997.

Covell, Katherine, and Robert Brian Howe, eds. *A Question of Commitment: Children's Rights in Canada.* Waterloo, ON: Wilfrid Laurier University Press, 2007.

Crouse, Eric. *Revival in the City: The Impact of American Evangelists in Canada, 1884–1914.* Montreal/Kingston: McGill-Queen's University Press, 2005.

Csinos, David M. *Little Theologians: Children, Culture, and the Making of Theological Meaning.* Montreal/Kingston: McGill-Queen's University Press, 2020.

Cunningham, Loren, and David Joel Hamilton. *Why Not Women? A Fresh Look at Scripture on Women in Missions, Ministry, and Leadership.* Seattle, WA: YWAM Publications, 2000.

Curtis, Heather D. *Fath in the Great Physician: Suffering and Divine Healing in American Culture, 1860–1900.* Baltimore, MD: Johns Hopkins University Press, 2007.

Damer, Eric, and Herbert Rosengarten. *UBC: The First 100 Years.* Vancouver: University of British Columbia, 2009.

Daniel, Kevin N. *Reinventing the Truth: Historical Claims of One of the World's Largest Nameless Sects.* Sisters, OR: Research and Information Services, 1993.

Davies, Megan J. "Snapshots: Three Women and Psychiatry, 1920–1935." *Canadian Woman Studies* 8, 4 (1987): 47–48.

Dawson, C.A. *The Settlement of the Peace River Country: A Study of a Pioneer Area.* Vol. 6. Toronto: Macmillan, 1934.

Dawson, Michael. *Selling Out or Buying In? Debating Consumerism in Vancouver and Victoria, 1945–1985*. Toronto: University of Toronto Press, 2018.

de Alminana, Margaret English, and Lois E. Olena, eds. *Women in Pentecostal and Charismatic Ministry: Informing a Dialogue on Gender, Church, and Ministry*. Leiden, NL: Brill, 2017.

Dixon, Wheeler. "Cinematic Adaptations of the Works of Sinclair Lewis." In *Sinclair Lewis at 100: Papers Presented at a Centennial Conference*, edited by Michael Connaughton, 191–200. St. Cloud, MN: St. Cloud State University, 1985.

Douville, Bruce. "'And We've Got to Get Ourselves Back to the Garden': The Jesus People Movement in Toronto." *Historical Papers 2006: Canadian Society of Church History*. (2006): 5–24.

Duder, Cameron. *Awfully Devoted Women: Lesbian Lives in Canada, 1900–65*. Vancouver: UBC Press, 2010.

Dummitt, Christopher. *The Manly Modern: Masculinity in Postwar Canada*. Vancouver: UBC Press, 2007.

Dyck, Erika, and Karissa Patton. "Activists in the 'Bible Belt': Conservatism, Religion, and Recognizing Reproductive Rights in 1970s Southern Alberta." In *Compelled to Act: Histories of Women's Activism in Western Canada*, edited by Sarah Carter and Nanci Langford, chap. 8. Winnipeg: University of Manitoba Press, 2020.

Edgell, Penny. "A Cultural Sociology of Religion: New Directions." *Annual Review of Sociology* 38 (2012): 247–65.

Elliott, David R. "A 'Feminine' Heartbeat in Evangelicalism and Fundamentalism." *Historical Papers: Canadian Society of Church History* (1992): 79–112.

Epstein, Daniel Mark. *Sister Aimee: The Life of Aimee Semple McPherson*. New York: Harcourt Brace, 1993.

Evans, Rachel Held. *Searching for Sunday: Loving, Leaving, and Finding the Church*. Nashville, TN: Thomas Nelson Books, 2015.

Ferry, Anthony. "Oh, Sing It, You Precious Pentecostal People." *Maclean's*. November 3, 1962.

Fessenden, Tracy. "Disappearances: Race, Religion, and the Progressive Narrative of U.S. Feminism." In *Secularisms*, edited by Janet R. Jakobsen and Ann Peregrini, 139–61. Durham, NC: Duke University Press, 2008.

Fettke, Steven M., and Robby Waddell, eds. *Pentecostals in the Academy: Testimonies of Call*. Cleveland, TN: CPT Press, 2012.

Fine-Meyer, Rose, and Willard Brehaut. "Secondary Education." In *The Canadian Encyclopedia*. Article published February 15, 2012; last edited December 16, 2013. https://www.thecanadianencyclopedia.ca/en/article/secondary-education.

Flatt, Kevin. *After Evangelicalism: The Sixties and the United Church of Canada*. Montreal/Kingston: McGill-Queen's University Press, 2013.

Foster, Leslie T., and Brian Wharf, eds. *People, Politics, and Child Welfare in British Columbia*. Vancouver: UBC Press, 2007.

Francis, Daniel. *Becoming Vancouver: A History*. Madeira Park, BC: Harbour Publishing, 2021.

Frederick, Marla F. *Between Sundays: Black Women and Everyday Struggles of Faith*. Berkeley: University of California Press, 2003.

Froese, Brian. "Preaching Premiers: The Political and Religious Errands of William Aberhart and Ernest Manning." *Historical Papers: Canadian Society of Church History* (2014): 81–98.

Gabriel, Andrew, Adam Stewart, and Kevin Shanahan. "Changing Conceptions of Speaking in Tongues and Spirit Baptism among Canadian Pentecostal Clergy." *Canadian Journal of Pentecostal-Charismatic Christianity* 7 (2016): 1–24.

Gerlach, Luther P., and Virginia H. Hine. "Five Factors Crucial to the Growth and Spread of a Modern Religious Movement." *Journal for the Scientific Study of Religion* 7 (1968): 23–40.

Gibson, William C. *Wesbrook & His University*. Vancouver: UBC Press, 1973.

Gidney, Catherine. *A Long Eclipse: The Liberal Protestant Establishment and the Canadian University, 1920–1970*. Montreal/Kingston: McGill-Queen's University Press, 2004.

Glavin, Terry. *Amongst God's Own: The Enduring Legacy of St. Mary's Mission*. Vancouver: New Star Books, 2002.

Gleason, Mona, Tamara Myers, Leslie Paris, and Veronica Strong-Boag, eds., *Lost Kids: Vulnerable Children and Youth in Twentieth-Century Canada and the United States*. Vancouver: UBC Press, 2010.

Grant, John Webster. "The Church and Canada's Self-Awareness." *Canadian Journal of Theology* 13, 3 (1967): 155–64.

–. *The Church in the Canadian Era*. 2nd ed. Burlington, ON: Welch, 1988.

Grey, G. Irvine. "Two by Two: The Shape of a Shapeless Movement." Unpublished thesis, Queen's University Belfast, Northern Ireland, 2012.

Hall, David D., ed. *Lived Religion in America: Toward a History of Practice*. Princeton, NJ: Princeton University Press, 1997.

Hangen, Tona J. *Redeeming the Dial: Radio, Religion, and Popular Culture in America*. Chapel Hill: University of North Carolina Press, 2002.

Hanscombe, Elizabeth. "Now That I'm Old: Writing, Women, and Ageing." *Life Writing* 16, 1 (2019): 127–38.

Harvey, Isobel. "A Historic Review of the Social Services of the Government of British Columbia." Prepared for Annual *Report of the Social Welfare Branch, 1947–48*.

Hayford, Jack W., and S. David Moore. *The Charismatic Century: The Enduring Impact of the Azuza Street Revival*. New York: Warner Faith, 2006.

Heath, Gordon L. *Doing Church History: A User-Friendly Introduction to Researching the History of Christianity*. Toronto: Clements Publishing, 2008.

Henking, Susan E. "The Personal Is the Theological: Autobiographical Acts in Contemporary Feminist Theology." *Journal of the American Academy of Religion* 59, 3 (Autumn 1991): 511–25.

Hepworth, Philip H. *Foster Care and Adoption in Canada*. Ottawa, ON: Canadian Council on Social Development, 1980.

Horn, Michiel. "Under the Gaze of George Vancouver: The University of British Columbia and the Provincial Government, 1913–1939." *BC Studies* 83 (Autumn 1989): 29–67.

Hutchinson, Mark, and John Wolffe. *A Short History of Global Evangelicalism*. New York: Cambridge University Press, 2012.

Hyatt, Eddie, ed. *Fire on the Earth: Eyewitness Reports from the Azuza Street Revival*. Lake Mary, FL: Creation House, 2006.

James, Allison, and Adrian L. James. *Constructing Childhood: Theory, Policy and Social Practice*. London: Red Globe Press, 2004.

—, and Alan Prout, eds. *Constructing and Reconstructing Childhood: Contemporary Issues in the Sociological Study of Childhood*. 2nd ed. London: Routledge, 1997.

Janes, Burton. *History of the Pentecostal Assemblies of Newfoundland*. St. John's: Pentecostal Assemblies of Newfoundland, 1996.

Janes, Burton K. *The Lady Who Came: The Biography of Alice Belle Garrigus, Newfoundland's First Pentecostal Pioneer*. Vol. 1, *1858–1908*. St. John's, NL: Good Tidings Press, 1982.

—. *The Lady Who Stayed: The Biography of Alice Belle Garrigus, Newfoundland's First Pentecostal Pioneer*. Vol. 2, *1908–1949*. St. John's, NL: Good Tidings Press, 1983.

Jennings, Mark A.C. "Impossible Subjects: LGBTIQ Experiences in Australian Pentecostal-Charismatic Churches." *Religions* 9, 53 (2018): doi:10.3390/rel902053.

Johns, Cheryl Bridges, and Lisa P. Stephenson, eds. *Grieving, Brooding, and Transforming: The Spirit, the Bible, and Gender*. Leiden, NL: Brill, 2021.

Johnson, Emily Suzanne. *This Is Our Message: Women's Leadership in the New Christian Right*. Oxford: Oxford University Press, 2019.

Johnston, Hugh. *Radical Campus: Making Simon Fraser University*. Vancouver: Douglas and McIntyre, 2005.

Johnston, Luke Thomas. "Capturing the Spirit: The Pentecostal Testimony and the Crafting of Denominational Memory, 1920–1992." Master's thesis, Queen's University, Kingston, ON, 2006.

Kay, William K. *Pentecostalism: A Very Short Introduction*. Oxford: Oxford University Press, 2011.

Kee, Kevin. *Revivalists: Marketing the Gospel in English Canada, 1884–1957*. Montreal/Kingston: McGill-Queen's University Press, 2006.

Kelm, Mary-Ellen. "'The Only Place Likely to Do Her Any Good': The Admission of Women to British Columbia's Provincial Hospital for the Insane." *BC Studies* 96 (Winter 1992–93): 66–89.

Kidd, Sue Monk. *The Dance of the Dissident Daughter: A Woman's Journey from Christian Tradition to the Sacred Feminine*. New York: HarperOne, 2016).

King, Paul L. *Anointed Women: The Rich Heritage of Women in Ministry in the Christian and Missionary Alliance*. Tulsa, OK: Word and Spirit, 2009.

Koop, C. Everett, and Francis A. Schaeffer. *Whatever Happened to the Human Race?* Rev. ed. Westchester, IL: Crossway Books, 1983.

Kowalski, Rosemarie Daher. "'Whom Shall I Send and Who Will Go for Us?' The Empowerment of the Holy Spirit for Early Pentecostal Female Missionaries." Unpublished paper presented at the 42nd Annual Society for Pentecostal Studies, Seattle Pacific University, WA, 2013.

Kroeger, Richard Clark, and Catherine Clark Kroeger. *I Suffer Not a Woman: Rethinking I Timothy 2:11–15 in Light of Ancient Evidence*. Grand Rapids, MI: Baker Books, 1992.

Kulbeck, Gloria G. *What God Hath Wrought: A History of the Pentecostal Assemblies of Canada*. Toronto: Pentecostal Assemblies of Canada, 1958.

Kydd, Ronald A.N. *Charismatic Gifts in the Early Church: An Exploration into the Gifts of the Spirit during the First Three Centuries of the Christian Church*. Burlington, ON: Welch Publishing, 1991.

Lamb, Karen. "Will the Real Subject Please Stand Up? Autobiographical Voices in Biography." *Life Writing* 18, 1 (2021): 25–30.

Lawless, Elaine. "Rescripting Their Lives as Narratives: Spiritual Life Stories of Pentecostal Women Preachers." *Journal of Feminist Studies in Religion* 7, 1 (1991): 53–71.

Lee, Shayne, and Phillip Luke Sinitiere. *Holy Mavericks: Evangelical Innovators and the Spiritual Marketplace.* New York: New York University Press, 2009.

LeFrancois, Brenda A., Robert Menzies, and Geoffrey Reaume, eds., *Mad Matters: A Critical Reader in Canadian Mad Studies.* Toronto: Canadian Scholars' Press, 2013.

Lewis, James R. "Two by Twos." In *The Encyclopedia of Cults, Sects and New Religions.* Amherst, NY: Prometheus Books, 1998.

Lewis, Paul W., ed. *All the Gospel to All the World: 100 Years of Assemblies of God Missiology.* Springfield, MO: Assemblies of God Theological Seminary, 2014.

Ley, David. "Liberal Ideology and the Post-Industrial City." *Annals of the Association of American Geographers* 70, 2 (1980): 238–58.

Lindhardt, Martin. "Men of God: Neo-Pentecostalism and Masculinities in Urban Tanzania." *Religion* 45, 2 (2015): 252–72.

Lindsay, D. Michael. *Faith in the Halls of Power: How Evangelicals Joined the American Elite.* New York: Oxford University Press, 2007.

Liston, Mary. "Evolving Capacities: The British Columbia Representative for Children and Youth as a Hybrid Model of Oversight." In *The Nature of Inquisitorial Processes in Administrative Regimes,* edited by Laverne Jacobs and Sasha Baglay, 4–12. Aldershot, UK: Ashgate Publishing, 2013. https://ssrn.com/abstract=2047754.

Llewellyn, Dawn, and Marta Trzebiatowska. "Secular and Religious Feminisms: A Future of Disconnection?" *Feminist Theology* 21, 3 (2013): 244–58.

Logan, H.T. *Tuum Est: A History of the University of British Columbia.* Vancouver: UBC Press, 1958.

Lord, Andy. "Transforming Renewal through a Charismatic-Catholic Encounter: An Experiment in Receptive Ecumenism." *PentecoStudies* 13, 2 (2014): 239–61.

Lyon, David, and Marguerite Van Die, eds. *Rethinking Church, State, and Modernity: Canada between Europe and America.* Toronto: University of Toronto Press, 2000.

Mahmood, Saba. *Politics of Piety: The Islamic Revival and the Feminist Project.* Chicago: University of Chicago Press, 2005.

Mainse, David. *100: An Inspiring Journey of a Life Dedicated to the Call of God.* Burlington, ON: Crossroads Christian Communications, 1999.

–. *100 Huntley Street: The Exciting Success Story from the Host of Canada's Popular Television Program.* Toronto: G.R. Welch, 1979.

Manning, Christel. *God Gave Us the Right: Conservative Catholic, Evangelical Protestant, and Orthodox Jewish Women Grapple with Feminism.* New Brunswick, NJ: Rutgers University Press, 1999.

Marks, Lynne. *Infidels and the Damn Churches: Irreligion and Religion in Settler British Columbia.* Vancouver: UBC Press, 2017.

Marr, Lucille. "The Professionalization of Religious Education in the United Church of Canada: Hierarchy and Gender." *Historical Papers: Canadian Society of Church History* (1990): 1–28.

Marshall, David. *Secularizing the Faith: Canadian Protestant Clergy and the Crisis of Belief.* Toronto: University of Toronto Press, 1992.

–. "What Happened to Methodism in Canada during the First World War." *Historical Papers: Canadian Society of Church History* (2014): 51–69.

Martin, Bernice. "The Pentecostal Gender Paradox: A Cautionary Tale for the Sociology of Religion." In *The Blackwell Companion to Sociology of Religion*, edited by Richard K. Fenn, 52–66. Oxford: Blackwell Publishing, 2001.

Martin, David. *A General Theory of Secularization*. Oxford: Basil Blackwell, 1978.

McClendon, James Wm, Jr. *Biography as Theology: How Life Stories Can Remake Today's Theology*. Eugene, OR: Wipf and Stock, 2002.

McClymond, Michael. "Roberts, Oral." In *Brill's Encyclopedia of Global Pentecostalism*, edited by Michael Wilkinson, 552–54. Leiden, NL: Brill, 2021.

McColl, Jean. *Trinkets and Treasures: Jean McColl's Favorite Poems*. Jacksonville, FL: McColl-Gerard Publications, n.d. [after 1948].

McDannell, Colleen. *Material Christianity: Religious and Popular Culture in America*. New Haven, CT: Yale University Press, 1995.

McDonald, Robert A.J. *A Long Way to Paradise: A New History of British Columbia Politics*. Vancouver: UBC Press, 2021.

McGee, Gary B. *Miracles, Missions and American Pentecostalism*. Maryknoll, NY: Orbis Books, 2010.

–. *People of the Spirit: The Assemblies of God*. Springfield, MO: Gospel Publishing House, 2004.

McGowan, Mark G. "Trial Balloons and Other Adventures with Clio: John Sargent Moir, Catholic-Protestant Relations, and the Writing of Canadian Religious History." *Historical Papers: Canadian Society of Church History* (2013): 99–113.

McGuire, Meredith B. *Lived Religion: Faith and Practice in Everyday Life*. Oxford: Oxford University Press, 2008.

McLaren, Brian D. *Do I Stay Christian? A Guide for the Doubters, the Disappointed, and the Disillusioned*. New York: St. Martin's Essentials, 2022.

–. *Faith after Doubt: Why Your Beliefs Stopped Working and What to Do about It*. New York: St. Martin's Essentials, 2021.

McLeod, Hugh. *The Religious Crisis of the 1960s*. Oxford: Oxford University Press, 2007.

Melton, J. Gordon. "The Two-by-Twos." In *Melton's Encyclopedia of American Religions*. 8th ed. Detroit, MI: Gale, 2009.

Miller, Spencer, Jr. "Radio and Religion." *American Academy of Political and Social Science* 177 (1935): 135–40.

Miller, Thomas William. *Canadian Pentecostals: A History of the Pentecostal Assemblies of Canada*. Mississauga, ON: Full Gospel Publishing House, 1994.

Mitchinson, Wendy. "Reasons for Committal to a Mid-Nineteenth-Century Ontario Insane Asylum: The Case of Toronto." In *Essays in the History of Canadian Medicine*, edited by Wendy Mitchinson and Janice Dickin McGinnis, 88–109. Toronto: McClelland and Stewart, 1988.

Mittelstadt, Martin. "'Canada's First Martyr': The Suspicious Death of Winnipeg's WWI Pentecostal Conscientious Objector David Wells." *Manitoba History: The Journal of the Manitoba Historical Society* 87 (Fall 2018): 12–18.

Morton, W.L., ed. *God's Galloping Girl: The Peace River Diaries of Monica Storrs, 1929–1931*. Vancouver: UBC Press, 1979.

Mouat, Jeremy. *Roaring Days: Rossland's Mines and the History of British Columbia.* Vancouver: UBC Press, 2011.

Murray, Allison. "Creating the Feminist Boogey Woman: Popular Evangelical Authors' Portrayal of Feminist Ideas, 1970–2010." Unpublished paper presented at the American Society of Church History, New York, NY, January 2020.

Murray, Allison E. "Building Biblical Manhood and Womanhood: White American Evangelical Complementarian Theology, 1970–2010." PhD diss. University of Toronto, 2021.

Noll, Mark A. *A History of Christianity in the United States and Canada.* Grand Rapids, MI: William B. Eerdmans, 1992.

–. "What Happened to Christian Canada?" *Church History* 75, 2 (2006): 245–73.

Oberlyn, Ros. "Barely Anybody Around for Gerard's March." *Vancouver Sun,* July 11, 1977.

O'Neill, Margaret, and Michaela Schrage-Früh. "Women and Ageing: Private Meaning, Social Lives." *Life Writing* 16, 1 (2019): 1–8.

Opp, James. *The Lord for the Body: Religion, Medicine, and Protestant Faith Healing in Canada, 1880–1930.* Montreal/Kingston: McGill-Queen's University Press, 2005.

Orsi, Robert. "'Have You Ever Prayed to Saint Jude?' Reflections on Fieldwork in Catholic Chicago." In *Between Heaven and Earth: The Religious Worlds People Make and the Scholars Who Study Them.* Princeton, NJ: Princeton University Press, 2005.

–. *The Madonna of 115th Street: Faith and Community in Italian Harlem, 1880–1950.* New Haven, CT: Yale University Press, 1985.

Ozorak, Elizabeth Weiss. "The Power, but Not the Glory: How Women Empower Themselves through Religion." *Journal for the Scientific Study of Religion* 35, 1 (1996): 17–29.

Palaeologu, M. Athena, ed. *The Sixties in Canada: A Turbulent and Creative Decade.* Montreal: Black Rose Books, 2009.

Palmer, Bryan. *Canada's 1960s: The Ironies of Identity in a Rebellious Era.* Toronto: University of Toronto Press, 2009.

Patrick, Margie. "Political Neoconservatism: A Conundrum for Canadian Evangelicals." *Studies in Religion* 38, 3–4 (2009): 481–506.

Payne, Leah. *Gender and Pentecostal Revivalism: Making a Female Ministry in the Early Twentieth Century.* New York: Palgrave Macmillan, 2015.

Phillips, D.W., R.J. Raphael, D.J. Manning, and J.A. Turnbull, *Adoption Law in Canada: Practice and Procedure.* Scarborough, ON: Carswell, 1995.

Pickard, Patricia P. *The Davis Sisters: Their Influences and Their Impact.* Bangor, ME: Patricia P. Pickard, 2009.

Poloma, Margaret M. *The Assemblies of God at the Crossroads: Charisma and Institutional Dilemmas.* Knoxville: University of Tennessee, 1989.

–, and J. Green. *The Assemblies of God: Godly Love and the Revitalization of American Protestantism.* New York: New York University Press, 2010.

Pope-Levison, Priscilla. "Separate Spheres and Complementarianism in American Christianity: A Century's Perspective." In *Sex, Gender, and Christianity,* edited by Priscilla Pope-Levison and John R. Levison, 58–79. Eugene, OR: Wipf and Stock, 2012.

–. *Turn the Pulpit Loose: Two Centuries of American Women Evangelists.* New York: Palgrave Macmillan, 2004.

–, and John R. Levison, eds. *Sex, Gender, and Christianity.* Eugene, OR: Wipf and Stock, 2012.

Purvey, Diane. "Alexandra Orphanage and Families in Crisis in Vancouver, 1892–1938." In *Dimensions of Childhood: Essays on the History of Children and Youth in Canada*, edited by Russell Smandych, Gordon Dodds, and Alvin Esau, 107–33. Winnipeg, MN: Legal Research Institute, 1991.

Purvis, Sally B. *The Stained Glass Ceiling: Churches and Their Women Pastors*. Louisville, KY: Westminster John Knox Press, 1995.

Putnam, Robert D., and David E. Campbell. *American Grace: How Religion Divides and Unites Us*. New York: Simon and Schuster Paperbacks, 2010.

Qualls, Joy E.A. *God Forgive Us for Being Women: Rhetoric, Theology, and the Pentecostal Tradition*. Eugene, OR: Pickwick, 2018.

Ramirez, Erica. "Reinventing Anderson: *Vision of the Disinherited* and the Pentecostal Body." Paper presented to the 47th Annual Meeting Society for Pentecostal Studies, Cleveland, Tennessee, March 10, 2018.

Reed, David A. *"In Jesus' Name": The History and Beliefs of Oneness Pentecostals*. Blandford Forum, UK: Deo Publishing, 2008.

Reilly, Niamh. "Rethinking the Interplay of Feminism and Secularism in a Neo-secular Age." *Feminist Review* 97, 1 (2011): 5–31.

Reimer, Sam. *Evangelicals and the Continental Divide: The Conservative Protestant Subculture in Canada and the United States*. Montreal/Kingston: McGill-Queen's University Press, 2003.

–, and Michael Wilkinson. *A Culture of Faith: Evangelical Congregations in Canada*. Montreal/Kingston: McGill-Queen's University Press, 2015.

Rennick, Joanne Benham. "Towards an Interfaith Ministry: Religious Adaptation and Accommodation in the Canadian Forces Chaplaincy." *Studies in Religion* 39, 1 (2010): 77–91.

Rentas Vega, Ananís, "(Un)spoken Codes: Is the New Generation Breaking the Pentecostal Dress Code?" Paper 7, Major Papers by Master of Science Students, University of Rhode Island, 2019. https://digitalcommons.uri.edu/tmd_major_papers/7.

Rice, John R. *Bobbed Hair, Bossy Wives, and Women Preachers*. Murfreesboro, TN: Sword of the Lord, 1941.

Rinaldo, Rachel. *Mobilizing Piety: Islam and Feminism in Indonesia*. New York: Oxford University Press, 2013.

–. "Pious and Critical: Muslim Women Activists and the Question of Agency." *Gender & Society* 28 (2014): 824–46.

Riss, R.M. "Latter Rain Movement." In *The New International Dictionary of Pentecostal and Charismatic Movements*, rev. ed., edited by Stanley M. Burgess and Eduard M. van der Maas, 830–33. Grand Rapids, MI: Zondervan, 2003.

Robeck, C.M., Jr. "Pentecostal World Conference." In *The New International Dictionary of Pentecostal and Charismatic Movements*, rev. ed., edited by Stanley M. Burgess and Eduard M. van der Maas, 971–74. Grand Rapids, MI: Zondervan, 2003.

Robeck, Cecil M. Jr. *The Azusa Street Mission and Revival: The Birth of the Global Pentecostal Movement*. Nashville, TN: Nelson Reference & Electronic, 2006.

Robert, Dana L., ed. *Gospel Bearers, Gender Barriers: Missionary Women in the Twentieth Century*. Maryknoll, NY: Orbis Books, 2002.

Robins, R.G. *Pentecostalism in America*. Santa Barbara, CA: Praeger ABC-CLIO, 2010.

Robinson, James. *Pentecostal Origins: Early Pentecostalism in Ireland in the Context of the British Isles*. Milton Keynes, UK: 2005.

Robinson, Thomas A. *Preacher Girl: Uldine Uttley and the Industry of Revival*. Waco, TX: Baylor University Press, 2016.

Rogge, Natalie. "Next Generation Ministries." In *Picture This! Reflecting on 100 Years of the PAOC*, edited by David Wells, 182–95. Mississauga, ON: Pentecostal Assemblies of Canada International Office, 2018.

Rooke, Patricia T., and R.L. Schnell. *Discarding the Asylum: From Child Rescue to the Welfare State in English Canada, 1880–1950*. Lanham, MD: University Press of America, 1983.

Ross, Becki L. *Burlesque West: Showgirls, Sex, and Sin in Postwar Vancouver*. Toronto: University of Toronto Press, 2009.

Rudd, Douglas. *When the Spirit Came upon Them: Highlights from the Early Years of the Pentecostal Movement in Canada*. Mississauga, ON: Pentecostal Assemblies of Canada, 2002.

Ruelas, Abraham. *No Room for Doubt: The Life and Ministry of Bebe Patten*. Laurel, MD: Seymour Press, 2012.

–. *Women and the Landscape of American Higher Education: Wesleyan Holiness and Pentecostal Founders*. Eugene, OR: Pickwick Publications, 2010.

Ruff, Lanette D., and Thomas A. Robinson. *Out of the Mouths of Babes: Girl Evangelists in the Flapper Era*. London: Oxford University Press, 2011.

Rutherdale, Robert. "Fatherhood, Masculinity, and the Good Life during Canada's Baby Boom, 1945–1965." *Journal of Family History* 24 (July 1999): 351–73.

Scanzoni, Letha. "The Feminists and the Bible." *Christianity Today* (February 1973): 10–15.

–. "Part 1. Coauthoring 'All We're Meant to Be' – The Beginning." *Letha's Calling* (blog), January 7, 2011, http://www.lethadawsonscanzoni.com/2011/01/part-1 -coauthoring-all-were-meant-to-be-the-beginning/.

–, and Nancy Hardesty. *All We're Meant to Be: A Biblical Approach to Women's Liberation*. Waco, TX: Word Books, 1974.

Schmidt, Leigh Eric. *Consumer Rites: The Buying and Selling of American Holidays*. Princeton, NJ: Princeton University Press, 1995.

Schuurman, Peter. "Review of *Holy Mavericks: Evangelical Innovators and the Spiritual Marketplace*, by Shayne Lee and Phillip Luke Sinitiere." *Studies in Religion* 39, 3 (2010): 471–73.

Seres, Ted. "Engaging the Culture." In *Picture This! Reflecting on 100 Years of the PAOC*, edited by David Wells, 98–108. Mississauga, ON: Pentecostal Assemblies of Canada International Office, 2018.

Sethna, Christabelle. "The Evolution of the *Birth Control Handbook*: From Student-Peer Education Manual to Feminist Self-Empowerment, 1968–1975." In *Rethinking Canada: The Promise of Women's History*, 6th ed., ed. Mona Gleason, Tamara Myers, and Adele Perry, 387–408. Toronto: Oxford University Press, 2011.

Shantz, Mary-Ann. *What Nudism Exposes: An Unconventional History of Postwar Canada*. Vancouver: UBC Press, 2022.

Skene, Wayne. *UBC: A Portrait*. Vancouver: Tribute Books, 2003.

Skinner, Bob. "Next Generation of Women in Ministry Please Stand Up!" *Pentecostal Testimony*, June 1991, 2.

Slater-Smith, Colleen. "Women's Lib ... Pentecostal Style." *The Leader-Post* [Regina], August 24, 1974.

Smith, Christian. *American Evangelicalism: Embattled and Thriving*. Chicago: University of Chicago Press, 1998.

Smith, Dorothy, and Sara David, eds. *Women Look at Psychiatry*. Vancouver: Press Gang, 1975.

Smith, Sidonie, and Julia Watson, eds. *Getting a Life: Everyday Uses of Autobiography*. Minneapolis: University of Minnesota Press, 1996.

–. *Women, Autobiography, Theory: A Reader*. Madison: University of Wisconsin Press, 1998.

Stackhouse, John G., Jr. "The Protestant Experience in Canada since 1945." In *The Canadian Protestant Experience, 1760–1990*, edited by George A. Rawlyk, 198–252. Burlington, ON: Welch Publishing, 1990.

Stamm, Michael. "Broadcasting Mainline Protestantism: The Chicago Sunday Evening Club and the Evolution of Audience Expectations from Radio to Television." *Religion and American Culture: A Journal of Interpretation* 22, 2 (2012): 233–64.

Stephens, Randall J., and Karl W. Giberson. *The Annointed: Evangelical Truth in a Secular Age*. Cambridge, MA: Belknap Press, 2011.

Stephenson, Lisa P. *Dismantling the Dualisms for American Pentecostal Women in Ministry: A Feminist-Pneumatological Approach*. Leiden, NL: Brill, 2012.

Stewart, Adam. "From Monogenesis to Polygenesis in Pentecostal Origins: A Survey of the Evidence from the Azuza Street, Hebden and Mukti Missions." *PentecoStudies* 13, 2 (2014): 151–72.

–, ed. *Handbook of Pentecostal Christianity*. DeKalb: Northern Illinois University Press, 2012.

–. *The New Canadian Pentecostals*. Waterloo, ON: Wilfrid Laurier University Press, 2015.

Stewart, Lee. *"It's Up to You": Women at UBC in the Early Years*. Vancouver: UBC Press, 1990.

Stiller, Brian C., Todd M. Johnson, Karen Stiller, and Mark Hutchinson, eds. *Evangelicals around the World: A Global Handbook for the 21st Century*. Nashville, TN: Thomas Nelson, 2015.

Strong-Boag, Veronica. *Finding Families, Finding Ourselves: English Canada Encounters Adoption from the Nineteenth Century to the 1990s*. Don Mills, ON: Oxford University Press, 2006.

–. *Fostering Nation? Canada Confronts Its History of Childhood Disadvantage*. Waterloo, ON: Wilfrid Laurier University Press, 2011.

–. "Interrupted Relations: The Adoption of Children in Twentieth-Century British Columbia." *BC Studies* 144 (Winter 2004/2005): 5–30.

Stroud, Marilyn. "Bernice Gerard: A Life Lived in the Power of the Spirit." *Testimony* 90, 3 (March 2009): 8–9.

Sutton, Matthew Avery. *Aimee Semple McPherson and the Resurrection of Christian America*. Cambridge, MA: Harvard University Press, 2007.

Swenson, Donald S. "Charismatic Renewal in the Roman Catholic Church." In *Brill's Encyclopedia of Global Pentecostalism*, edited by Michael Wilkinson, 115–17. Leiden, NL: Brill, 2021.

Swidler, Leonard J. "Jesus was a Feminist." *Catholic World* (January 1971): 177–83.

Taylor, Marion Ann, and Heather E. Weir. *Let Her Speak for Herself: Nineteenth-Century Women Writing on Women in Genesis.* Waco, TX: Baylor University Press, 2006.

Thiessen, Joel. *The Meaning of Sunday: The Practice of Belief in a Secular Age.* Montreal/Kingston: McGill-Queen's University Press, 2015.

–, and Sarah Wilkins-Laflamme. *None of the Above: Nonreligious Identity in the US and Canada.* Regina, SK: University of Regina Press, 2020.

Thorn, Brian T. *From Left to Right: Maternalism and Women's Political Activism in Postwar Canada.* Vancouver: UBC Press, 2016.

Trombley, Charles. *Who Said Women Can't Teach?* South Plainfield, NJ: Bridge Publishing, 1985.

Tucker, Ruth A., and Walter Liefeld. *Daughters of the Church: Women and Ministry from New Testament Times to the Present.* Grand Rapids, MI: Zondervan Academic, 1987.

Uprichard, Emma. "Children as 'Being and Becomings': Children, Childhood and Temporality." *Children & Society* 22 (2008): 303–13.

Van Die, Marguerite. "'We Who Speak ... and Write Books': Writing and Teaching the History of Christianity in a Secular Canada, 1960–2010." *Historical Papers: Canadian Society of Church History* (2010): 95–107.

Wachtel, Eleanor. "The University Chaplains: Generalists in an Age of Specialization." *UBC Alumni Chronicle* 34, 3 (Autumn 1979): 8–9.

Wacker, Grant. *America's Pastor: Billy Graham and the Shaping of a Nation.* Cambridge, MA: Harvard University Press, 2014.

–. *Heaven Below: Early Pentecostals and American Culture.* Cambridge, MA: Harvard University Press, 2001.

Wald, Gayle F. *Shout, Sister, Shout! The Untold Story of Rock-and-Roll Trailblazer Sister Rosetta Tharpe.* Boston: Beacon Press, 2007.

Walsh, Margaret. "Gendering Mobility: Women, Work, and Automobility in the United States." *History: Journal of the Historical Association* 93, 311 (July 2008): 376–95.

Warner, Wayne. *Maria Woodworth-Etter: For Such a Time as This Her Healing and Evangelizing Ministry.* Gainseville, FL: Bridge-Logos, 2004.

Warsh, Cheryl Krasnick. *Moments of Unreason: The Practice of Canadian Psychiatry and the Homewood Retreat, 1833–1923.* Montreal/Kingston: McGill-Queen's University Press, 1989.

Weisser, Susan Ostrov. "'What Kind of Life Have I Got?' Gender in the Life Story of an 'Ordinary' Woman." In *Getting a Life: Everyday Uses of Autobiography,* edited by Sidonie Smith and Julia Watson, 249–70. Minneapolis: University of Minnesota Press, 1996.

Welch, Kristen Dayle. *'Women with the Good News': The Rhetorical Heritage of Pentecostal Holiness Women Preachers.* Cleveland, TN: CPT Press, 2010.

Wells, Susan. "Against All Odds: Bernice Gerard's Rich and Vibrant Life." *Testimony* 90, 3 (March 2009): 11.

Wilkinson, Michael, ed. *Brill's Encyclopedia of Global Pentecostalism.* Leiden, NL: Brill, 2021.

–, ed. *Canadian Pentecostalism: Transition and Transformation.* Montreal/Kingston: McGill-Queen's University Press, 2009.

–. "Social Concerns, the Religious Right, and the Pentecostal Assemblies of Canada in the 1980s." Paper presented at the Annual Meeting, Society for Pentecostal Studies, Springfield, Missouri, March 6–8, 2014.

–. *The Spirit Said Go: Pentecostal Immigrants in Canada.* New York: Peter Lang, 2006.

–, and Peter Althouse. *Winds from the North: Canadian Contributions to the Pentecostal Movement.* Leiden, NL: Brill, 2010.

–, and Linda M. Ambrose. *After the Revival: Pentecostalism and the Making of a Canadian Church.* Montreal/Kingston: McGill-Queen's University Press, 2020.

–, and Linda M. Ambrose, eds. *The Canadian Pentecostal Experience.* Leiden, NL: Brill, forthcoming 2024.

–, and Steven M. Studebaker, eds. *A Liberating Spirit: Pentecostals and Social Action in North America.* Eugene, OR: Wipf and Stock, 2010.

Williams, Carol. "Reproductive Self-Determination and the Persistence of 'Family Values' in Alberta from the 1960s to the 1990s." In *Compelled to Act: Histories of Women's Activism in Western Canada,* edited by Sarah Carter and Nanci Langford, 364–414. Winnipeg: University of Manitoba Press, 2020.

Woodcock, George, and Tim Fitzharris. *The University of British Columbia – A Souvenir.* Toronto: Oxford University Press, 1986.

Woodhead, Linda. "Feminism and the Sociology of Religion: From Gender-Blindness to Gendered Difference." In *The Blackwell Companion to Sociology of Religion,* edited by Richard K. Fenn, 72. Oxford: Blackwell, 2003.

Wuthnow, Robert. *The Restructuring of American Religion: Society and Faith since World War II.* Princeton, NJ: Princeton University Press, 1988.

Young, Pamela Dickey. "Book Note on *Turn the Pulpit Loose: Two Centuries of American Women Evangelists,* by Priscilla Pope-Levison." *Studies in Religion* 39, 1 (2010): 126.

–. "Taking Account of Religion in Canada: The Debates over Gay and Lesbian Marriage." *Studies in Religion* 39, 3 (2010): 333–61.

Ziefle, Joshua. *David du Plessis and the Assemblies of God: The Struggle for the Soul of a Movement.* Leiden, NL: Brill, 2012.

INDEX

Note: "(f)" after a page number indicates a figure.

100 Huntley Street, 161, 162(f)

Abbotsford, BC, 7, 16, 259*n*12
abortion, 120, 153–55, 201, 203, 208–9, 216
addiction, 141, 150–51, 153, 205. *See also* alcohol and alcoholism
After the Revival (Wilkinson and Ambrose), 10, 215
Alberta, 70
Alberta Five, 181
alcohol and alcoholism, 23, 29, 55–56, 88, 150–51, 214, 227–28
Alexandria Orphanage, 42–43, 44
Allen, Robert Thomas, 26
All We're Meant to Be (Scanzoni and Hardesty), 180
Anderson, Allan, 103
Angelus Temple, 9, 90
Anglican faith, 54, 59
antiabortion protests, 12, 13, 130(f), 208–9, 229, 230
Apostolic Church of Pentecost, 69, 253*n*7
Apostolic Mission, 69, 71, 92
Argue, Robert M., 171

Argue sisters, 190
Assemblies of God (AG)
as American organization, 92, 96
on ecumenical approach, 166
networks of, 97, 98, 100, 101(f), 102–3
ordination through, 107, 170(f), 193. *See also* Gerard, Bernice: ordination
Associated Full Gospel Students, 128, 129, 131, 141
atheism, 123
Australia, 218
Avishai, Orit, 13, 14
Awfully Devoted Women (Duder), 197, 198
Azusa Street Revival, 11

baby boomers, 119
Baldwin, Bill, 166
Baldwin, Lorraine, 166
baptism. *See* Spirit baptism
Baptist church, 45
Barman, Jean, 128, 207
BC Catholic, 207
Bennett, W.A.C., 128, 207
Berea Bible Institute, 94

Bernice Gerard (Gerard), 17
Bessey, Sarah, 6
Bible, 97, 64–65, 114, 151, 152, 155, 171–72
Bible college training, 172
Biography and History (Caine), 16
birth control, 120
Birth Control Handbook (McGill University student group), 120
Black Like Me (Griffin), 225–26
Blair, Rev. J.H., 95, 103
Block, Tina, 123
Bolivia, 98
bondage themes, 227
Booth, Catherine, 90, 179
Bouchard, W.L., 94, 95
Braeside Camp, 94–95
Brereton, Virginia Lieson, 87–88
British Columbia, 7, 70, 123, 203–4, 231.
   See also individual places in
British North America Act, 181
Broadway Church, 261n46, 270n46
Bryant, Anita, 196–97, 270n59
Burlesque West (Ross), 227
Bushnell, Katharine C., 179
Butler, Ewen, 162

Caine, Barbara, 16
Caligula (1979), 201, 212, 213(f), 217, 222, 225
Campus Crusade for Christ, 120
Canadian Council on Child Welfare, 39
Canadian Journal of Pentecostal-Charismatic Christianity, 10
Canadian Mining and Smelting Company (Cominco), 71
Cantelon, Homer J., 171
Cantelon, Jim, 271n62
capitalism, 204
Catholicism, 32, 140–41, 159–64, 166–67, 183, 215
Catholic-Pentecostal dialogue meeting, 141, 163, 165
Catholic Thought and Interreligious Dialogue, Temple University, 183
Catholic World, 183
Catrano, Pastor, 58–59

Central America, 98, 100, 101(f)
Chapman, Dick, 108, 188(f), 189, 190–91, 192(f), 193–94, 270n45
Chapman, Gladys Dawson, 193, 270n45
Chapman, Velma McColl. *See* McColl, Velma
charismatic movement, 104–5, 127, 131, 160, 163–67, 176, 239, 259n15
Chesler, Phyllis, 254n35
child protection services, 39–40, 42
child welfare system, 35–40, 59
church and state, separation of, 126, 129
CJOR radio station, 147(f)
Clark, David, 136
Clark, Robert, 253n7
classical Pentecostalism, 68, 97
Cobourg, ON, 94–95
Cochran, Pamela, 180, 182
Committee of Progressive Electors (COPE), 207
Community Service Committee, 214
conservatism, 203, 204–5
Converted in the Country (Gerard), 15, 90
Costa Rica, 101(f)
Criminal Code of Canada, 203, 210
Cross and the Switchblade, The (Wilkerson), 166
Crossroads Christian Communications, 161, 162(f)

Daughters of Sarah (People's Christian Coalition), 181
Davies, Megan J., 78–79
Davis, Carro, 72–73, 190
Davis, Susie, 72–73, 190
Dawson Creek, BC, 77
Denmark, 217
denominational divisions, 126, 137, 160–63. *See also* ecumenical mindset; inter-denominational approaches
Dick Chapman Memorial Hall, 194
divorce, 109, 120, 203
Dixon, Acting Chief Constable, 209–10
Douville, Bruce, 142–43
dress codes, 55, 251n9
drug culture, 143–44, 145

Duder, Cameron, 197, 198–99
Duncans, Helen, 31(f)
du Plessis, David, 103, 104, 166

Eastern religions, 114, 155–56, 158
ecumenical mindset, 97, 160–63, 162(f), 164, 166–67, 183, 216, 236
Edwards, Josephine, 27–28, 205
Edwards, Patrick, 27
"Electronic Evangelism and the Local Church" (Gerard), 138
Elmer Gantry (Lewis), 56
England, 103, 105, 106
Essondale Psychiatric Hospital. *See* Provincial Mental Hospital, Essondale
Eugenics Board, BC, 40
Europe, 104, 105, 107
Evangel Press, 193
Evangel Temple, 48, 52, 84
Evangelical Fellowship of Canada (EFC), 215, 216
Evangelical Feminism (Cochran), 180
evangelical meetings, 70–71, 73
Evangelical Women's Caucus, 180
Evangelicals and the Continental Divide (Reimer), 273*n*54
Evangelism
  in BC politics, 207
  as a business and career, 85–87, 88(f), 90
  electronic media and, 138
  engagement with counterculture, 142–43
  feminism and, 180–83, 196
  as hard work, 99
  lack of activism in, 219
  opportunities for, 123–24
  travelling, 256*n*7
  on university campuses, 120–21, 124, 137–31
  US vs Canada, 216
  women in, 91, 140
Evans, Rachel Held, 6
exotic dancers, 227, 228

Female Eunuch (Greer), 186
Female Ministry (Booth), 179

feminism
  becoming widespread, 172–73
  commitment to, 134
  compatibility with religion, 5–6
  in confronting patriarchy, 167–68
  evangelical, 180–83
  influenced by varieties of, 12–13, 178–80
  momentum of, 171
  on pornography, 216–17, 227
  religion and, 5–6, 13
  secular, 169–70, 186–87
"Feminists and the Bible" (Scanzoni), 181
Ferry, Antony, 112
"Five Factors Crucial to the Growth and Spread of a Modern Religious Movement" (Gerlach and Hine), 126–27
Florida, 92–93
Ford, Marguerite, 208–9
Forsey sisters, 190
Foursquare Pentecostal denomination, 90
Francis, Daniel, 204, 205
Fraser River, 28
Fraserview Assembly, 158, 185, 191, 192–93, 194, 195(f), 219
French Pentecostal Assembly, 94
Fuller Theological Seminary, 223
Full Gospel Assembly of Saint John, 72–73
Full Gospel Business Men's Fellowship, 128

Gaglardi, Bob, 128
Gaglardi, Honourable P.A., 128
Gaglardi, Ken, 128
Gaglardi, Philip, 207
Gaglardi family, 127, 129
gang members, 141
Garrigus, Alice Belle, 9
gay liberation movement, 148–50
Gee, Donald, 103
gender. *See* women in Pentecostalism
gender theory, 18
genocide, 226
Georgia Straight, 201, 202(f), 206, 225
Gerard, Annie, 26, 32, 88
Gerard, Bernice
  activism, 3, 4(f), 181, 201–3, 207–14, 222–24, 226–27, 229

adoption at birth, 24, 30, 75

adoptive family, rescue from, 35–38, 39(f), 49, 89, 94, 225

alderman role, 5, 201, 203, 206, 207, 214, 227–28

appearance, 55

authority, 96–97

autobiography, 15–16, 17, 53, 56, 179–80, 189, 233–34

baritone voice, 8, 72, 87, 190, 198, 231

beliefs, standing up for, 41

belonging, sense of, 32–33, 43–44, 51, 59, 60, 67–68, 73–74, 76, 83, 106–7, 165, 236, 251n10

birth family, 26, 74–77, 80–81, 254n35

born-again experiences, 89, 111

campus ministry, 137, 232. *See also* Gerard, Bernice: chaplaincy

caricatures of, 217, 221, 228, 231, 240

chaplaincy, 110–11, 117, 118(f), 119, 120–27, 131, 161, 259n14

charities, 232, 275n3

childhood, background, 25, 26, 27(f), 28–29, 32–33, 46–47, 235–36, 248n46

commemoration and legacy, 232–33

communication of the gospel, 115, 116, 132, 142, 157

compassion and empathy, 4–5, 80, 81, 97, 102, 138, 147–50, 156–57, 204, 225, 226, 254n35

conversion experiences, 16, 18–20, 25, 32–35, 87, 88–89, 193, 236

conviction, 3, 14, 59–60, 213–15, 221, 229

credibility, 93

death, 189, 194, 200, 234, 261n46

domestic work, 57, 58

education, 37, 42, 54, 56, 61, 62(f), 63, 65, 71, 78–79, 109–10, 112–16, 119, 132, 252n40, 253n16, 260n25

emotions experienced, 46–47, 58, 59–60, 80, 81, 125, 213, 224, 225, 229, 230

family reunion, 76

foster care, time at, 37, 41–46, 54, 56–59

health, 46, 52–53, 275n7

housing changes, 53, 58, 60

income, 71, 91, 93

influence, 3, 231, 233, 235

intellect, 20, 134, 139, 142, 157, 175, 178–80, 234

international work, 217–19, 232–33

intimacy, 139, 147, 156, 157, 197–98

labels, 198

maturity, 81

ministry, early career in, 69–70, 72, 73–74, 82–83. *See also* Gerard, Bernice: campus ministry

moral stances, 54, 55, 59, 61, 143–44, 203, 205, 212–13, 215, 216, 218(f), 221–22, 224, 225, 227

musical talent and singing, 72, 74(f), 82, 83, 87, 190, 200. *See also* McColl-Gerard Trio

open-mindedness, 97, 110–12, 116, 132, 142, 146–48, 155–56, 165–66, 183

ordination, 96, 97, 107, 109, 118, 160, 170(f), 258n36

orphanage, time at, 42–23

paradoxical thoughts, 13–14, 19

partnership with Velma, 187–98, 195(f), 200, 232, 271n62. *See also under* McColl, Velma

"Peggy nickname," 246n3

politics, 119, 120, 201–7, 208, 214, 215, 271n3

popularity of, 221

public engagement, 38, 216, 219, 221, 224, 229

public speaking skills, 9(f), 71, 198

prayer, importance of, 60–61, 275n7

radio ministry, 4–5, 72, 134–37, 139, 141–55, 156–57, 159, 211, 242n4, 263n8

refugee work, 215

religious identity, 50, 54–55, 56, 59, 65

resilience, 5, 25, 35–36, 58, 65

self-portrait, 15(f)

sermon notes, 219

sexual expression, 119–20, 148–50, 196–97, 198, 199, 227

sexual orientation, 148–50, 183, 196, 198, 203

sexual violence and abuse, 29–32, 34–36, 211, 212, 213(f), 216, 224–25, 230, 232

silent protests, 4(f), 6–7, 209–10, 213–14, 216, 224, 240–41
socialization, 54–55, 56, 58, 60
spiritual gifting and gifts, 73, 92, 160, 222–24, 229
storytelling, 71–72, 87, 88–89
summer camps, 94–95
teaching, 59, 61–62, 67–68, 69(f), 72–73, 106–7
teenage years, 33–38, 39(f), 41, 42, 47(f), 65, 165
tomboy, identifying as, 28, 85, 198
trauma and abuse, 15, 24–26, 29–32, 30, 31(f), 34–36, 56, 88–89, 224–25, 227
travel, 15(f), 72–73, 84, 85, 93–94, 98–99, 100(f), 101(f), 103–4, 106–7, 256n7
worldliness, 54–55, 60, 168
worldview expansion, 111–12
young adulthood, 38
Gerard, Howard Gerald, 247n9
Gerard, Leo, 24–26, 29, 30, 32, 34–35, 56
Gerard-Chapman Benevolence Kitchen, 233
Gerard House, 232
Gerlach, Luther P., 127
Gibson, Christine Amelia, 94
Gidney, Catherine, 120
Gimenez, John, 141
Girl Evangelists, 70–71
Girl Guides, 78
God's Word to Women (Bushnell), 179
gold mining, 68–69, 71
gospel work, marketing efforts for, 85–87, 88(f), 90
Graham, Billy, 120
Great Britain. See United Kingdom
Great Commission, 220
Great Depression, 44
Greer, Germaine, 12, 169, 186

Haist, Coralee, 193
Hamilton, ON, 95, 173
Hangen, Tona J., 136, 146–47
Hardesty, Nancy, 180, 183, 196
Harvey, Isobel
  background on, 40

under care of, 57
concern about religiosity, 44, 45, 58–59
final rejection of, 64
Gerard's perceptions of, 53–54
opinion on preaching, 63
visit from, 75
Hawkins, Abbot Father Columban, 165
Henking, Susan E., 17
heteronormativity, 187–88, 189, 199
heterosexuality, 189, 190
Hine, Virginia H., 127
hippies, 141–46, 205
Hocken, Peter D., 160
Holiness movement, 33
Holocaust, 226
Holy Land, 19, 194, 226
Holy Land (Gerard), 105–6
holy rollers, 125
Holy Spirit, 220, 222, 223
homelessness, 204
homophobia, 188, 196, 199
homosexuality, 120, 148–50, 183, 196–97, 203
House of Hope, 233
housing, affordable, 205
Hudson, Clem, 54
Hudson, Muriel, 54, 56, 58, 61, 64
Hudson family, 54–59, 61
Humanist League, 123

Indecent Act, 210
Indigenous cultural centres, 202(f), 205
Indigenous knowledge, 27–28
inmates, 150–51
interdenominational approaches, 137–38, 156, 159–64, 183, 216
International Roman Catholic/Pentecostal Dialogue, 163
Inter-Varsity Christian Fellowship, 120
irreligion, 123
Israel, 18–19, 105–6, 194, 219–20, 226, 234(f)

Jackson, Alan, 118
Jamieson, Laura, 271n3
Jericho Beach neighbourhood, 54

Jerusalem, 105, 226
Jesus, 12, 33–34, 45, 46, 64, 134–35, 182–84
Jesus Movement, 142–43
"Jesus Was a Feminist" (Swidler), 183
Jewish people, 226
Journal for the Scientific Study of Religion, 126–27

Kay, William, 85
Kechnie, Margaret, xi, 22, 23, 235
Kee, Kevin, 86
Kelowna, BC, 46, 47, 49, 51
KFSG radio station, 136
Kitsilano Junior High School, 44
Klein, Bonnie Sherr, 227

LaPierre, Laurier, 215
Lassègues, Rev. E.L., 94
Latter Rain issue, 92–93
Layden, Frances, 33, 35, 45, 49, 50–51
Leader-Post, The, 171
lesbians, 148–50, 183, 196, 197, 198–99
LGBTQ+ activists, 196
liberalism, 119, 120, 202, 203, 204
Liberal Party of Canada, 203
Lindahl, Evelyn, 46, 47–48
Lindahl, John, 46
Lindahl family, 46–47, 51, 52
liquor licenses, municipal, 227–28
London, UK, 105
Long Eclipse (Gidney), 120
Long Way to Paradise (McDonald), 204
Lord Byng Secondary School, 54, 56, 62–63, 65, 71, 252n40, 253n16
Lott, Nancy, 44
LSD, 144, 145, 149

MacDougall, Father Bob, 161
MacGregor, Dr. Malcolm, 109
MacKnight, Rev. James M., 163, 174–75
MacLean Elementary School, 68, 69(f), 252n4
Maclean's magazine, 110, 112
Mainse, David, 7, 137, 161–62, 162(f), 196
mainstream society, 54–55
Manary, Clara, 33

mansplaining, 237. *See also* patriarchy
marijuana, 144, 145
Marks, Lynne, 123
marriage, 107–9, 187, 188(f), 189, 190–91, 197
marriage equality, 199
materialism, 119, 143, 205
McAlister, W.E., 110
McClung, Nellie, 179, 181
McColl, Jean, 67–68, 83, 86(f), 108, 178(f), 189–90, 261n46
McColl, Velma
  accepting marriage proposal, 108, 190–91
  as co-pastor, 158, 187, 192–93, 195(f), 223
  femininity of, 198
  Gerard's first meeting with, 67–68
  helping produce radio shows, 191
  at home, 192(f)
  in Israel, 234(f)
  leading Fraserview Assembly with Gerard, 158
  obituary, 189
  partnership with Gerard, 187–90, 188(f). *See also under* Gerard, Bernice
  travelling as an evangelist, 74(f), 83, 86(f), 101(f), 178(f). *See also entry below*
McColl-Gerard Trio
  context of, 190
  disbanding in 1958, 108
  endorsements for, 95
  fame of, 99, 104
  formation of, 72
  with Frederick Reidenbach, 178(f)
  helping to spread Assemblies of God, 102–3
  income of, 90–91
  in Latin America, 102(f)
  leaving Rossland, 83
  in Montreal, 94
  Pentecostal gospel message of, 85
  portrait of, 70(f), 74(f)
  poster for, 88(f)
  program of, 87
  revival meetings of, 86(f)

McDonald, Bob, 203, 204, 206, 207
McGill University, 120
McPherson, Aimee Semple, 9, 73, 90, 136, 256n7
Memorial University, 261n44
mental health institutions, 56, 76, 78–79, 80, 81, 254n35
Mexico, 98, 98(f), 102, 102(f)
Miami, FL, 84, 91, 92
Middle East, 105
Milton, John, 110, 114–16
"Milton's Orthodoxy and Its Relation to the Form of *Paradise Lost*" (Gerard), 114–15
Mission, BC, 27
Mitchinson, Wendy, 79
Montreal, QC, 94
Morgentaler, Dr. Henry, 208
Mothers' Allowance Branch, 40
Mott, Emily, 44, 45–46
Mott, John, 44, 45–46
municipal liquor licenses, 227–28
Murphy, Emily, 179, 181
Murray, Allison, 168
My Childhood and Yours (Allen), 26

National Committee on Moral Standards, 215
National Home Missions Department, 171
Neese, Rev. Charles, 84, 93
networks, church, 82, 94, 96–98, 101, 103, 165, 237
New Brunswick, 72–73, 168, 173, 175
New Democratic Party, 128, 203, 204, 205
Newfoundland, 9
New Order of the Latter Rain controversy, 92–93
Nielson, Ada, 76, 78, 79, 254n35
Nielson, Fred, 76, 77
Nielson, Joyce, 75–76
Nielson, Violet, 76
Nielson family, 76–77, 78
Non-Partisan Association (NPA), 204–5, 206
nudity, public, 3, 4(f), 209–12, 214, 216, 240–41. *See also* Wreck Beach

Oh! Calcutta!, 212, 225
Okanagan Valley, BC, 44
Oneness Pentecostalism, 69, 257n27
orphanages, 42–43, 102, 102(f)
Orpheum Theatre, 196
orthodoxy, 114–16
Ottawa, ON, 130(f)
Overseas Missions Department, 171
Ozorak, Elizabeth Weiss, 13

Pacific Spirit Regional Park, 209
Paradise Lost (Milton), 110, 114–16
Paris, France, 103
Paris, ON, 94–95
Parkinson, Marion, 171
Parkinson's disease, 234
patriarchy, 167–68, 170–76, 177, 186–88, 200, 236–37, 238
Payne, Leah, 136
Peace River District, BC, 77, 78, 80
Pentecost (periodical), 103
Pentecostal Assemblies of Canada (PAOC)
author's connection to, 237
Bible schools, 110
complicated relationship with, 158, 160–63
donations from Sunday Line to, 233
endorsing Bernice and Velma as co-pastors, 192–93
General Conference, 168, 171, 173, 175, 176, 181, 184–85, 199, 217, 239(f)
magazine of, 136
male ministers in, 175
McColl sisters' relationship to, 92
networking with, 95, 96
new church in Vancouver South, 191
ordination of women in, 8, 168, 170–76, 268n51, 268n53
outreach projects of, 263n81
on public campuses, 131
rise of, 10, 48
Social Concerns Committee, 215
Susan Wells involved in, 6
university chaplain, 120–22, 126
Pentecostal Assemblies of Newfoundland and Labrador, 261n44

Pentecostal Fellowship of North America, 117

Pentecostal Holiness Church, 93, 257n27

Pentecostalism
attitudes on education in, 110, 116, 124–25, 131
benefits from, 60
on campus, 121, 124
cementing identity in, 83
classical, 68
cross-border collaboration in, 10–11, 84, 96
cross-border differences in, 216
Dick Chapman's involvement in, 193
divisions in, 84, 91–92, 97
evangelical meetings, 70–71
Gerard's conversion story, 87
Gerard's place in, 8
global network of, 68
growing popularity of, 103, 127, 129
homophobia in, 199
identifying with, 37–38, 51, 231
Lindahl family in, 48, 49
moral and dress codes of, 55
Oneness, 69
perceived negative influence of, 53
as percentage of Christianity, 250n45
pragmatism in, 115
radio ministry in, 136–37
rituals of, 50
youth activities, 58, 59

Pentecostalism (Kay), 85

Pentecostal Testimony, 8, 136, 168, 194

Pentecostal World Conference, 103, 104, 105, 107, 166, 190

People's Christian Coalition, 181

Pitt, Rev. John, 128

Point Grey neighbourhood, 58, 201, 209

political cartoons and satire, 201, 202(f), 206, 211, 217, 218(f), 228, 231

politics
in BC, 7, 128, 203–4, 229. *See also under* Gerard, Bernice
evangelicals concerned about involvement in, 219
on university campuses, 119, 120

Pope, 140

pornography, 201, 202(f), 210, 213, 213(f), 216–18, 222, 227

poverty, 205, 206

premarital sex, 119, 148, 153–54

Price, Charles, 193

prophets, 220–22, 229, 232

Protestantism, liberal, 119, 120, 142–43, 161

Provincial Mental Hospital, Essondale, 56, 76, 78–79, 81

Provincial Normal School, 63, 64, 65–66, 253n16

Purvey, Diane, 43

Quebec, 94

racism, 225–26

Ramirez, Erica, 89

Ranaghan, Dorothy, 166

Ranaghan, Kevin, 140–41, 166

Rathjen, John, 128

Redeeming the Dial (Hangen), 136

Regina, SK, 69, 71, 92, 171, 189

Reidenbach, Frederick, 86(f), 178(f)

Reimer, Sam, 216, 273n54

reincarnation, 156

religion
in author's life, 236, 237–38
compatibility with feminism, 5–6
determined to be extremism, 53
entrepreneurship and, 85–87
exposure to other ideas in, 110–11
fanaticism, 56
fundamentalism, 123
Harvey's perceptions of, 63–64
irreligion, 123
people leaving, 239
religious experiences, 145
sociology of, 18
on university campuses, 121–29

religious right, 7, 202, 203, 229, 273n54

revivalist messages, 89, 137

revival meetings, 86(f), 193

Revivaltime, 137

Rhode Island, 94

Riverview Hospital. *See* Provincial Mental Hospital, Essondale
Roberts, Oral, 105
Rock Church, 141
Rock Satellite Network, 141
Roman Catholic Indian Mission School, 27
Roman Catholic-Pentecostal Conference, 164, 165. *See also* charismatic movement
Roman culture, 183
Ross, Becki, 227
Rossland, BC, 66, 67, 68–69, 69(f), 71, 83, 252*n*4
Rowan, Professor, 109, 112–13
Royal Commission on the Status of Women in Canada, 185

Saint John, New Brunswick, 72, 173
Salvation Army movement, 90
same-sex attraction, 148–49. *See also* homosexuality
same-sex leadership couples, 187–88, 199
same-sex relationships, 197, 198
Saskatchewan, 69, 70, 92
Scanzoni, Letha, 180, 181
Scranton, PA, 178(f)
secular feminism, 13, 169, 184–85, 186
secularism, 112, 118–19, 120, 123, 179, 186
Senate Committee on Religion on Campus, 121
Sexual Sterilization Act, 40
sex workers, 225, 230
Shantz, Mary-Ann, 210–11
Shiloh Project, 205
silent protest march, 4(f), 6–7, 209–10, 213–14, 216, 224, 240–41
Simon Fraser University (SFU), 16, 117, 118–19, 118(f), 122, 144, 178–79
Singing Addicts, 141
Sixth Avenue Pentecostal Tabernacle, 193
Smallwood, Joey, 9
Social Concerns Committee (PAOC), 215
social conservatives, 202
Social Credit Party, 128, 129, 203, 204, 205, 207
social justice, 204

social workers, 39–40, 41, 49, 75
Song of God (Krishna), 113–14
South Africa, 103
South America, 98, 100
Southern Methodist Church, 159
speaking in tongues, 49–50
Spirit baptism, 50, 111, 125, 131–33, 146, 162, 223
Stackhouse, John, 120
Stamm, Michael, 136
Starkman, Mel, 254*n*35
Stiller, Brian, 7, 216, 235, 271*n*62
St. Mary's Indian Residential School, 27
Stó:lō people, 26, 27, 28, 88, 205
Storrs, Monica, 77, 78
Strong-Boag, Veronica, 44
Student Christian Movement, 120
student newspapers, 127–30
Summerland, BC, 44
Summit Pacific College, 16, 259*n*12
Sunday Line, 136, 148, 150, 194, 232, 233, 263*n*6
Sunday Line Communications Society, 232–33, 275*n*3
Swidler, Leonard J., 183–84

Teen Challenge, 141, 166
Temple University, 183
The Electors Action Movement (TEAM), 207
Todd, Douglas, 3, 231, 235
"Too Much Wilderness, Too Few Prophets" (Gerard), 219–20
Toronto, ON, 107
Toronto Star, 184
Trail, BC, 67, 69, 69(f), 72
Trappist Monastery, 165
"Trees for Israel" campaign, 194–95
Trombley, Charles, 182
Trudeau, Pierre, 120
Two by Twos, 33–34, 36, 45, 47, 49
Tyson, Tommy, 159

Ubyssey, 127, 129–30, 141
United Church, 10, 59, 238
United Kingdom, 103, 104, 105, 217, 218

Index

United Methodist Church, 159
United States, 11, 35, 84, 93, 94, 96–97, 103, 203
universities (*See also* individual universities)
  background on, 118–21
  governance in, 119
  evangelism at, 124
  Pentecostalism at, 131–32
  religion at, 121–30
University of British Columbia
  archives, 16
  chaplaincy at, 117–18, 118(f), 125–26
  enrolment in, 109
  experience as a student at, 110–13
  Gerard House at, 232
  impact of time at, 178–79
  Isobel Harvey a graduate of, 40
University of Minnesota, 127
University of Notre Dame, 164, 165, 166
University of Victoria, 119
Urquhart, Wini, 49, 80

Vancouver, BC
  Chapmans living in, 108
  Downtown East Side, 205
  as Gerard's radio ministry scope, 137, 138
  Gerard's high school years in, 65
  Gerard living in during childhood, 52–53, 54, 58
  perceptions of Gerard in, 3, 4, 6–7
  social context of, 119–20
Vancouver Children's Aid Society, 39, 53
Vancouver City Archives, 16
Vancouver City Council, 203. *See also* alderman role
Vancouver Court House, 65
Vancouver General Hospital, 201, 209
Vancouver Normal School, 61–62
Vancouver Police Department, 209–10
Vancouver Refugee Committee, 215
Vancouver South neighbourhood, 191
Vancouver Status of Women Committee, 201, 208
Vancouver Sun, 3, 138, 204, 211–12, 217, 218(f), 231, 235

Venture into Faith (Roberts), 105
Vietnam War, 119
Vineyard movement, 224
Volrich, Mayor Jack, 204–5, 209, 210, 215

Wachtel, Eleanor, 125–26, 232
Wacker, Grant, 115
Walk for Life event, 130(f)
Ward, C.M., 136–37
Washington State, 136
Wayfarer, 127–29, 130
welfare state, 38, 41, 59
Wells, David, 7, 175, 235, 263n81, 271n62
Wells, Susan, 6, 271n62
West Beyond the West, The (Barman), 207
West Coast region, 123
Western Pentecostal Bible College, 110, 259n12
What Nudism Exposes (Shantz), 210–11
Whitton, Charlotte, 39–40
Who Said Women Can't Teach? (Trombley), 182
Wilkerson, David, 141, 166
Wilkinson, Michael, 10, 215
Wimber, John, 223, 224
Windsor, ON, 184–85
Windsor Star, 184
women, exploitation of, 227, 228, 230
women in Pentecostalism
  apologies issued to, 175
  author's experiences in, 236–37
  backlash against, 172–73
  in campus ministry, 118–19
  challenges of, 160
  critiques of business approaches to ministry, 126
  discrimination against, 169–70
  expected roles in, 69–70
  feminism and, 181–82
  gender norms in, 91
  Gerard's experience, 8–10, 17–18, 177–78
  "girl evangelists," 253n10
  history of, 11, 168, 181–82
  leadership roles of, 95–96, 174, 176, 187

limits on, 167
ordination in, 168–76, 268n51, 268n53
preaching and, 90
in radio broadcasting, 134–39, 156, 157
ritual and, 89
same-sex leadership couples, 199
scholarship on, 184–85
travel and, 85, 86, 190
views shaped by academia, 178–79
women in society, 185–86
Women's Ministries. *See* Women's
    Missionary Council
Women's Missionary Council, 171

women's movement, second-wave, 169,
    179. *See also* feminism
women's rights, 181–82
Worker's Licence, 69–70, 253n7
World Ministries, 232
Wreck Beach, 4(f), 209, 210, 240–41,
    275n13. *See also* nudity, public

Yad Vashem, 226
Yorkville, Toronto, ON, 142–43

Zion Bible Institute, 94
Zurich, Switzerland, 103

Set in Caslon and Fournier by Artegraphica Design Co.
Copyeditor: Robin So
Proofreader: Alison Strobel
Indexer: Emily LeGrand
Cover designer: George Kirkpatrick

Printed and bound by CPI Group (UK) Ltd, Croydon, CR0 4YY
05/01/2025
14620672-0003